Applied Linguistics

Introducing Linguistics

This outstanding series is an indispensable resource for students and teachers – a concise and engaging introduction to the central subjects of contemporary linguistics. Presupposing no prior knowledge on the part of the reader, each volume sets out the fundamental skills and knowledge of the field, and so provides the ideal educational platform for further study in linguistics.

1. Andrew Spencer   *Phonology*
2. John I. Saeed   *Semantics*, Third Edition
3. Barbara Johnstone   *Discourse Analysis*, Second Edition
4. Andrew Carnie   *Syntax*, Third Edition
5. Anne Baker and Kees Hengeveld   *Linguistics*
6. Li Wei, editor   *Applied Linguistics*

Applied Linguistics

Edited by

Li Wei

WILEY Blackwell

This edition first published 2014
© 2014 John Wiley & Sons, Ltd

Registered Office
John Wiley & Sons, Ltd, The Atrium, Southern Gate, Chichester, West Sussex, PO19 8SQ, UK

Editorial Offices
350 Main Street, Malden, MA 02148–5020, USA
9600 Garsington Road, Oxford, OX4 2DQ, UK
The Atrium, Southern Gate, Chichester, West Sussex, PO19 8SQ, UK

For details of our global editorial offices, for customer services, and for information about how to apply
for permission to reuse the copyright material in this book please see our website at
www.wiley.com/wiley-blackwell.

The right of Li Wei to be identified as the author of the editorial material in this work has been asserted
in accordance with the UK Copyright, Designs and Patents Act 1988.

Library of Congress Cataloging-in-Publication Data

Applied linguistics / Edited by Li Wei.
    pages   cm.
  Includes bibliographical references and index.
  ISBN 978-1-4051-9359-7 (cloth) – ISBN 978-1-4051-9358-0 (pbk.)
1. Applied linguistics.   I. Li, Wei
  P129.A665 2014
  418–dc23
                                                2013021026
A catalogue record for this book is available from the British Library.

Cover image: Wu Guanzhong, *The Easterly Breeze Blows Open the Wisteria* (detail), 2009, ink and colour on
paper. Hong Kong Museum of Art Collection
Cover design by Nicki Averill Design.

Set in 9.5/11.5pt Palatino SPi Publisher Services, Pondicherry, India
Printed in Malaysia by Ho Printing (M) Sdn Bhd

1   2014

Contents

Notes on Contributors

Editor

Li Wei is Chair of Applied Linguistics at Birkbeck College, University of London, UK, where he is also Pro-Vice-Master and Director of the Birkbeck Graduate Research School. His research interests are primarily in bilingualism and multilingualism. He is the Principal Editor of the *International Journal of Bilingualism*. Among his many publications is the award-winning *Blackwell Guide to Research Methods in Bilingualism and Multilingualism* (co-edited by Melissa Moyer). He is Chair of the University Council of General and Applied Linguistics (UCGAL), UK and an Academician of the Academy of Social Sciences, UK.

Contributors

Jean-Marc Dewaele is Professor of Applied Linguistics and Multilingualism at Birkbeck College, University of London, UK. His research interests cover a wide range including multilingualism, multiculturalism, and psycholinguistic, sociolinguistic, pragmatic and psychological aspects of second/foreign language acquisition and production. He is specifically interested in individual differences in foreign language acquisition and multilingualism. He has published numerous books and articles, including the monograph *Emotions in Multilingual Languages*. He is a former President of the European Second Language Association (EUROSLA) and is currently Editor of the *International Journal of Bilingual Education and Bilingualism*.

Malcolm Edwards is Senior Lecturer in Applied Linguistics at Birkbeck College, University of London, UK. His research interests cover descriptive and theoretical syntax as well as Discourse Analysis and translation studies. He has published on the syntax of spoken Egyptian Arabic, grammatical issues in the analysis of code-switching, and semantic and pragmatic issues in film translation.

Penelope Gardner-Chloros is Professor of Sociolinguistics and Language Contact at Birkbeck College, University of London, UK. Her research interests include code-switching, pronouns of address, minority languages in Europe and bilingual arts and artists. She is author of *Language Selection and Switching in Strasbourg* and *Code-Switching*. She is currently carrying out a large comparative study of the influence of multilingualism on Parisian French and London English.

Marjorie Lorch is Professor of Neurolinguistics at Birkbeck College, University of London, UK. Her main research interest is in understanding how language is organized in the brain through the investigation of neurogenic language and communication disorders, with a specific interest in cross-linguistic comparisons and bilingual speakers. In addition, she carries out theoretical work in neurolinguistics from a historical perspective, focusing on the nineteenth-century history of ideas about language and communication.

Lisa J. McEntee-Atalianis is Lecturer in Applied Linguistics and Communication at Birkbeck College, University of London, UK. Her research interests include language and identity, Deaf Studies and psycholinguistics. She has published on agrammatism, sign language, language attitude and ethnolinguistic vitality, and is currently researching the globalization of English and its impact on issues of language planning, policy and practice at an organizational level.

María Elena Placencia is Reader in Spanish Linguistics at Birkbeck College, University of London, UK. She is co-founder of the International Association for the Study of Spanish in Society (SIS). Her main research interests lie in socio- and variational pragmatics, Discourse Analysis and Intercultural Communication. She has published extensively on (im)politeness in familial and institutional contexts, cultural styles of rapport management, forms and functions of small talk, the language of service encounters, address forms and discursive racism in interethnic communication, as well as Spanish as a foreign language.

Zhu Hua is Professor of Applied Linguistics and Communication at Birkbeck College, University of London, UK. Her research interests span across Intercultural Communication and child language development. She is author of *Exploring Intercultural Communication: Language in Action* and *Phonological Development in Specific Contexts,* and editor of *The Language and Intercultural Communication Reader* and *Phonological Development and Disorders* (with Barbara Dodd).

Acknowledgements

This book has truly been a long time coming! It started as a team project, with a genuine belief that a multi-voiced volume would be more appropriate for an introductory text on a field as diverse as Applied Linguistics than a single-authored one. We still believe it, although we are not 100 % sure if the end result is discord or harmony. We certainly have tried our best to achieve an acceptable level of consistency in the text, but individuality definitely shines through.

The assignment of the chapters was not based entirely on the author's proven expertise. Indeed, some of us are writing for the first time on the assigned topics. The nature of the introductory textbook means that we have to draw on a huge amount of work done by colleagues in the field other than ourselves. We have tried to acknowledge this fact through the references, but it is inevitable that not every single source of information is completely acknowledged. We hereby ask for your understanding and forgiveness.

We are most grateful to Danielle Descoteaux for her faith in us in commissioning this volume, and to Julia Kirk for her patience and support throughout the project. Too many people have been involved in various aspects of the project to be named here. Our students over the last three years have used draft versions of parts of the text, probably without fully realizing it. Colleagues from other institutions have contributed to the volume by discussing various issues with us and providing crucial information and references.

Contributors to the volume are all members of the Applied Linguistics team at Birkbeck College, University of London. Three people spent a considerable amount of time helping the editor with copy-editing, checking references, formatting and proofreading the drafts. They are Rosemary Wilson, Jennifer Watson and Brigid O'Connor. The project could not have been completed without their help.

The diagrams in Chapter 1 were drawn by Steve Stamp, who also helped with other technical issues. Part of the text in Chapter 1, Section 1.2 is taken from the introduction written by Vivian Cook and Li Wei in their edited volume *Contemporary Applied Linguistics* (2009), and part of Section 1.3 taken from the chapter Doing Applied Linguistics, in Li Wei's *The Routledge Applied Linguistics Reader* (2011: 497–514), co-authored with Zhu Hua. The contributions of Vivian Cook and Zhu Hua are gratefully acknowledged.

The Resources List is based on the list in Li Wei's *The Routledge Applied Linguistics Reader* (2011: 515–526), updated by Zhu Hua.

Copyright permission for the two figures in Chapter 4 is as follows:

The Cookie Theft picture, from Goodglass, Harold and Edith Kaplan. 1983. *The Assessment of Aphasia and Related Disorders*. Philadelphia: Lea & Febiger. Permission granted by Pro-Ed, Inc., Texas.

Examples of paraphasias in deaf left-hemisphere damaged (LHD) signers, from Hickok,
    Gregory, Ursula Bellugi and Edward Klima. 1998. The neural organization of language:
    Evidence from sign language aphasia. *Trends in Cognitive Sciences* 2 (4), 129–136.
    Permission granted by Elsevier.

Permission to reproduce the image in Chapter 8, 'Sri Lankan Brit shows true grit' by
Carole Malone, *News of the World*, 22 March 2009, granted by The Newspaper Marketing
Agency, www.nmauk.co.uk.

chapter 1

Introducing Applied Linguistics

Li Wei

Chapter Outline

1.1 What is Language and What is Linguistics?
1.2 Applied Linguistics as a Problem-solving Approach
1.3 Doing Applied Linguistics: Methodological Considerations
1.4 Structure and Content of this Volume

Learning Outcomes

After reading this chapter, you should

- have an understanding of the different approaches to language;
- be able to appreciate the connections between different branches of linguistics;
- be able to appreciate the scope of Applied Linguistics as a problem-solving approach to language;
- have an understanding of the process of doing Applied Linguistics research;
- have an understanding of the different research designs.

Applied Linguistics, First Edition. Edited by Li Wei.
© 2014 John Wiley & Sons, Ltd. Published 2014 by John Wiley & Sons, Ltd.

Key Terms

- Applied Linguistics
- Bilingualism
- Language
- Linguistics

- Methodology
- Research design
- Sociolinguistics

If you describe yourself as a linguist to other people outside the discipline, chances are that they will ask you, 'How many languages do you speak?' But if you describe yourself as an Applied Linguist, they may well go silent completely, wondering what they should say to you next. If you are lucky, you might get asked, 'Is that how to teach languages?' or 'Is that translation?' These questions are not entirely unreasonable, as Applied Linguistics can mean different things to different people, even among those who would describe themselves as Applied Linguists.

The International Association of Applied Linguistics (AILA) proclaims:

> Applied Linguistics is an interdisciplinary field of research and practice dealing with practical problems of language and communication that can be identified, analysed or solved by applying available theories, methods or results of Linguistics or by developing new theoretical and methodological frameworks in linguistics to work on these problems

The AILA definition is both broad in including, potentially, many different areas such as child language acquisition, language and communication disorders, multilingualism, language testing, communication in the workplace, and so on, and narrow in relating Applied Linguistics to linguistics proper. The latter has caused a perpetual controversy, not least because linguistics has also been conceptualized in many different ways to produce a unified theory. In this introductory chapter, we begin with a discussion of what linguistics is, focusing, in particular, on the differences as well as the similarities between the different approaches to language. The main objective is to highlight the connections between the various branches and sub-branches of linguistics, as Applied Linguists may apply one specific approach or a combination of several different ones to the problems that they wish to solve. We then go on to describe Applied Linguistics as a problem-solving approach, outlining its key elements and characteristics. A substantial part of the chapter, Section 1.3, is on the methodological considerations in doing Applied Linguistics, covering all the main stages of doing a research project. The last section outlines the structure and content of the book.

1.1   What is Language and What is Linguistics?

All linguistics work, whatever specific perspective one may adopt, should ultimately have something to say about the question, 'What is this thing called language?' (Nunan, 2013). Ron Macaulay (2011) presents 'Seven Ways of Looking at Language':

- language as meaning
- language as sound
- language as form
- language as communication
- language as identity
- language as history
- language as symbol.

These can be summarized in three rather different conceptualizations of language:

- as a particular representational system based on the biologically rooted language faculty;
- as complex and historically evolved patterns of structures;
- as a social practice and a culturally loaded value system.

The different conceptualizations of language lead to very different methodological perspectives which together constitute the field of linguistics today. The following is a list of some of the commonly occurring terms for different branches of linguistics:

- theoretical linguistics
- formal linguistics
- descriptive linguistics
- historical linguistics
- sociolinguistics
- psycholinguistics
- neurolinguistics
- clinical linguistics
- cognitive linguistics
- forensic linguistics
- educational linguistics
- computational linguistics
- corpus linguistics
- geolinguistics.

To these we can add sub-branches:

- phonetics
- phonology
- morphology
- syntax
- semantics
- pragmatics
- dialectology
- Discourse Analysis
- Critical Discourse Analysis
- stylistics
- genre analysis
- second language acquisition
- language pathology.

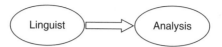

Figure 1.1   Approach to Linguistics 1.

Figure 1.2   Approach to Linguistics 2.

Indeed, the list can go on. It may be useful to look at the differences, but also similarities, between these different kinds of linguistics in terms of the relationship between the linguist who does the studying of language and the evidence he or she uses for the study, paying particular attention to how the evidence is gathered and used in the analysis.

In the first schematized approach (Figure 1.1), the linguist arrives at an analysis of the language being studied using his or her own intuition or intimate knowledge of it. The linguist may test the intuition and intimate knowledge on other speakers who are deemed to have similarly intimate knowledge of the target language. But other than that, no separately collected linguistic data would be used as evidence for the analysis the linguist undertakes. The focus of the analysis tends to be on general rules and principles. This approach characterizes much of formal and descriptive linguistics.

The second schematized approach (Figure 1.2) differs from the first in that it involves a separately collected body of data, rather than the linguist's own knowledge and intuition, for the analysis. The focus of the analysis may still be the general rules and principles, or specific patterns and features, but they are derived from the database. This characterizes corpus linguistics approaches, which have in turn been applied to various contexts including, for example, writing grammar books, compiling dictionaries, designing language tests and teaching material, doing genre analysis, contrastive analysis and comparative analysis. Sometimes, this approach can also be used to show that the linguist's own intuitions about a particular language may be 'wrong' in the sense that the majority of its users use it differently from the linguist's own intuition about the usage.

There are three other approaches, which are schematized in Figure 1.3, Figure 1.4 and Figure 1.5. Like the second approach, a separately collected database is used for the analysis in each of these. But here, particular attention is paid to the language users, who are carefully selected to provide the data in specific contexts. And the analytic focus is on the relationship between the language users and the linguistic evidence they provide. In the third approach, which characterizes that of pragmatics and Discourse Analysis, for instance, the focus is on how the language user produces context-dependent linguistic patterns. In the fourth approach, on the other hand, the focus is on the language users' internal state, personal characteristics and the cognitive process when producing the language data. For example, how does age impact on the language user's ability to discriminate sound differences in different languages; how does anxiety affect the retrieval of certain lexical items; or what level of cognitive control is needed when a bilingual language user changes from one language to another in the middle of an utterance as opposed

Figure 1.3 Approach to Linguistics 3.

Figure 1.4 Approach to Linguistics 4.

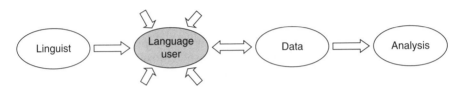

Figure 1.5 Approach to Linguistics 5.

to switching with different interlocutors. Such an approach is typical of psycholinguistic and clinical linguistic studies. The last schematized approach is characteristic of that of sociolinguistics, which focuses more on the influence of external factors on the language user – for example, audience, setting, topic and how the language user uses language strategically in response to the external factors.

The schematization of the various approaches helps to highlight the commonalities as well as differences between the various branches and sub-branches of linguistics. Applied Linguists may apply one specific approach from these to the problems they wish to solve, or be eclectic and use a combination of approaches. Moreover, Applied Linguists have applied theories and models from other disciplines beyond linguistics. Indeed, contemporary Applied Linguists feel free to draw on almost any field of human knowledge, and use ideas from philosophy, education, sociology, feminism, Marxism and media studies, to name a random few. They have, for example, explored psychological models such as declarative/procedural memory and emergentism, mathematical models such as dynamic systems theory or chaos theory, early Soviet theories of child development such as those of Vygotsky, French thinkers such as Foucault and Bourdieu, and so on. Ben Rampton (1997: 14) described Applied Linguistics as 'an open field of interest in language', while David Block (2009) called it 'an amalgam of research interests'.

—— 1.2 Applied Linguistics as a Problem-solving Approach

While most Applied Linguists seem happy with the idea that their discipline is concerned, as AILA proclaims, with 'practical problems of language and communication', the term 'problem' does raise issues of its own. In one sense it means a research question posed in a particular discipline; in another sense it is something that has gone wrong which can be solved. Some 30 years ago, when Hugo Baetens Beardsmore, a Belgian scholar in the field of bilingualism and language contact, asked his university in Brussels to allow him to teach a course on bilingualism, he was told that he could only do so if the course was called 'The Problem of Bilingualism'. Talking about the problem of bilingualism is ambiguous between defining it as a research area and claiming that it is in some way defective. Calling areas or topics problems fosters the attitude that there is something wrong with them. Bilingualism is no more intrinsically a problem to be solved than is monolingualism. Applied Linguists have to be clear that they are solving problems within an area of language use, not regarding the area itself as a problem except in the research question sense. Language teaching, for example, is not itself a problem to be solved; it may nevertheless raise problems that Applied Linguists can resolve.

So what problems does Applied Linguistics solve? If you are worried about your child's speech, you are more likely to go to a speech therapist than to an Applied Linguist. If your country is torn by civil war between people who use two scripts, you ask for a United Nations Peacekeeping Force. If you are drafting a new law, you go to a constitutional lawyer or a civil servant. The problem-solving successes of Applied Linguistics have included devising orthographies for languages that have no written form and inventing simplified languages for mariners; Applied Linguists have played a part in EU projects on translation and on linguistic diversity. Most successes have, however, had to do with language teaching, such as the syllabuses and methods that swept the world from the 1970s onwards, particularly associated with the Council of Europe.

At a general level we can draw three implications from this:

1. *The Applied Linguist is a Jack of all trades.* Real-world language problems can seldom be resolved by looking at a single aspect of language. Since Applied Linguistics is interdisciplinary, the Applied Linguist is expected to know a little about many areas, not only of language, but also of philosophy, sociology, computer programming, experimental design, and many more. In a sense, Applied Linguists are not only Jacks of all trades but also master of none as they do not require the in-depth knowledge of the specialist so much as the ability to filter out ideas relevant to their concerns. An Applied Linguist who only does syntax or Discourse Analysis is an applied syntactician or an applied discourse analyst, not a member of the multidisciplinary Applied Linguistics profession. In other words, multidisciplinarity applies not just to the discipline as a whole but also to the individual practitioner.

2. *The Applied Linguist is a go-between, not an enforcer, a servant, not a master.* The problems that Applied Linguistics can deal with are complex and multi-faceted. As consultants to other people, Applied Linguists can contribute their own interpretation and advice. But that is all. The client has to weigh in the balance all the other factors and decide on the solution. Rather than saying, 'You should follow this way of language teaching', the Applied Linguist's advice is, 'You could try this way of language teaching and see whether it works for you'. Alternatively, the Applied Linguist should be responding to problems put forward by language teachers, not predetermining what the problems are; the Applied Linguist is there to serve teachers' needs – a garage mechanic interpreting the customer's vague idea of what is wrong with their car and putting it right, rather than a car designer.

3. *Sheer description of any area of language is not Applied Linguistics as such but descriptive linguistics.* Some areas concerned with the description of language are regarded as Applied Linguistics, others are not. Make a corpus analysis of an area or carry out a Conversation Analysis and you're doing Applied Linguistics; describe children's language or vocabulary and it is first language acquisition; make a description of grammar and you are doing syntax. Overall, making a description is not in itself solving a problem, even if it may contribute to the solution.

Outside language teaching, Applied Linguists have taken important roles behind the scenes as advisors to diverse governmental and inter-governmental bodies – for example, John Trim's work on the Common European Framework of Reference for languages. But on the whole, they have had little impact on public debate or decision-making for most language problems, the honourable exceptions being David Crystal and Deborah Cameron, who may not even consider themselves primarily as Applied Linguists. Problems are not solved by talking about them at Applied Linguistics conferences; the solutions have to be taken out into the world to the language users. Take the political correctness issue of avoiding certain terms for reasons of sexism, racism and so on. This is based on one interpretation of the relationship between language and thinking: not having a word means you can't have the concept, as George Orwell suggested with Newspeak. Yet Applied Linguists have been reluctant to contribute their expertise to this debate, despite the extensive research into linguistic relativity of the past decade. Public discussion of language issues is as ill-informed about language as it was 50 years ago at the dawn of Applied Linguistics.

A recent theatre piece, *Lipsynch*, by the Canadian director Robert Le Page, was crucially concerned with language. The dialogue took place in three languages with the aid of subtitling running along the front of the stage; it took for granted the multilingualism of the modern world. The heroine was attempting to recover the voice of her father who had died when she was young. All she had was a silent home movie. So she engaged a lip-reader to find out the words, then a lipsynch actor to read them in alternative voices till she recognized her father's. This didn't work until she herself uttered her father's words. In another scene an elderly aphasic patient delivered a monologue; judging by audience reaction this was the first time that most of them had encountered this kind of discourse. At a dinner party, film actors and agents attempted to converse simultaneously in three languages, to comic effect. *Lipsynch* movingly showed the importance of language to people's lives and the language problems they encountered.

As this reminds us, language is at the core of human activity. Applied Linguistics needs to take itself seriously as a central discipline in the language sciences, dealing with real problems. Applied Linguistics has the potential to make a difference. It seems important, therefore, to reassert the focus on language in Applied Linguistics. The unique selling point of Applied Linguistics that distinguishes it from the many domains and sub-domains of sociology, economics, politics, law, management and neuroscience is language. At its core it needs a coherent theory of language – whether this comes from a particular branch of linguistics or from some other discipline – a set of rigorous descriptive tools to handle language, and a body of research relevant to language practice.

Case Study 1.1: The Black English Trial in Ann Arbor (Labov, 1982)

The question of whether linguists could contribute to the debate about the educational failure of black children in the United States was sharply brought into focus by a case which arose in Ann Arbor, Michigan, in 1977. This has to be seen against a backdrop where psychologists had written that the language of black children did not provide the means for logical thought, that they spoke a 'restricted code' which did not allow them to access abstract discussion. In the 1960s, educational psychologists had assumed that any differences between black and white children were marks of black inferiority, which could be eliminated by compensatory education. However, if linguists were to intervene in this debate, it was first essential that they should agree among themselves about the linguistic facts. Labov shows in this article that it was through a happy conjunction of developments in the academic world that a consensus was reached just at the time when evidence was required in this case, and the linguists' testimony was therefore clear and relevant.

The Martin Luther King Elementary School in Ann Arbor had a racial balance of 80% white, 13% black and 7% Asian and Latino children. A minority of the black children, who came from a low-income housing estate which was situated within the catchment area of the school, were doing very badly. Their parents were not satisfied with the school's interpretation of these poor results, which was to brand the children as learning disabled, emotionally disturbed or having behaviour problems. They got in touch with a legal advisory service and then with a public-interest law firm on behalf of 15 of the children and brought a case against the school, the School District and the Michigan Board of Education for failing to diagnose the relevant cultural, social and economic factors which would have allowed them to help solve the problems. They claimed the children had been branded as learning disabled, mentally handicapped and even hard of hearing on the basis of tests which were inappropriate for them. For example the Wepman test included various oppositions which were non-existent in Black English Vernacular (BEV): *pin* vs. *pen*, *sheaf* vs. *sheath*, *clothe* vs. *clove*, and so on. This is despite the fact that this had been known, along with the problem of misreporting the hearing abilities of normal black children, for 12 years.

The judge threw out the motions, which claimed special services should be provided to overcome poor academic performance based on cultural, social or economic background, as no law secured any such right. However, he retained the action on the basis of a failure of the defendants to take appropriate action to overcome *linguistic* barriers (Title 20 of the US Code, Section 1703 (f)). The judge held that it was not necessary for the language barrier to be the fact of having a different mother tongue, and that such a barrier could result from the use of 'some type of non-standard English'. He therefore refused to pursue matters relating to the plaintiffs' cultural characteristics and asked for more evidence to be produced to show the nature of the linguistic barriers that the children faced. The important thing is that the lawyers, and all those involved, who had originally thought of the case in terms of social, political and economic issues, found themselves involved in the linguistic issue and the 'King School case' became the 'Black English case'. Prima facie, the children's English was characteristic of Black English Vernacular, as described in several northern US cities, with features including the zero form of the possessive ('*My Momma name is Annie*'), habitual *be* ('*When it be raining, I be taking it to school*'), absence of 3rd person singular *s* ('*It don't sound like me, do it?'*), and so forth. A team of linguists including William Labov was therefore assembled to give evidence on the fact that the children spoke a distinct dialect of English used by about 20 million people in the US. An important part of the argument was that the language differences involved were the result of racial segregation, and it was therefore preferable to be able to show that BEV had Creole origins. This had been denied by certain white dialectologists who claimed that black people's speech was the same as that of white people from the same localities and social class, although they of course agreed that vernacular dialects were as logically consistent as standard ones. Some black scholars also rejected the hypothesis of Creole origins, fearing that the argument that 'Black English' was a separate dialect would lead to arguments for separate development and education and thereby prevent black children from reaching the top.

Labov then digresses briefly from the case to enunciate various principles which he believes scientists should follow in relation to social action. These include, among others,

- *a principle of error correction*: scientists should bring to the public's attention any aspect of their data with important consequences for social practices or widespread ideas;
- *a principle of obligation*: investigators should make knowledge of their data available to the community they have obtained it from, when the community needs it; this can be rephrased more actively to the effect that the knowledge based on the data obtained should be used for the community's benefit.

In order to fulfil these obligations it was essential for the linguists to present a united front at the trial, which seemed unlikely given the sort of disagreements outlined above. But in 1979, fortuitously, a consensus was finally reached by linguists on some of these contentious issues. Black linguists such as Beryl Bailey were able to demonstrate a consistent pattern for various linguistic features, notably copula deletion in BEV (*'He tired out'*), other dialects of English showing a different pattern of contraction and deletion. There were also phonological differences and aspectual differences involving *be*. For example, the sentence *'I'll be done killed that motherfucker if he tries to lay a hand on my kid again'*, uttered by an enraged black father, cannot be translated by the future perfect *'I will have killed...'*, which would suggest that the speaker will have killed the victim *before* he lays a hand on the kid, nor by any other one-to-one translation into another English dialect. The sense of the BEV future perfective is merely that the action will be completed without relating it to the state or event that follows. The linguists working on BEV at this time were also able to show the remarkable geographic unity of BEV across different parts of the US. The argument that whites of a similar social position shared the same dialect was shown to be flawed, despite the adoption by those whites of certain features from BEV.

When it came to the defence's turn to present their evidence, after several weeks of testimony by the plaintiffs, they did not call any witnesses and merely told the press that the plaintiffs' case was so weak that no defence was needed. The judge found for the plaintiffs and asked Ann Arbor School Board to submit a plan within 30 days defining the steps they would take to identify BEV-speaking pupils and to use that knowledge to teach them to read Standard English. The decision was not appealed, and the plan submitted by the School Board included in-service training for teachers to identify BEV and strategies for helping children to switch to Standard English as required.

Labov adds that despite the remarkable consensus reached by the linguists, which allowed the case to be won, the national press managed to misreport the outcome and to cause indignation that the judge had supposedly told teachers they should learn BEV in order to teach it to the children.

Labov's conclusion highlights the difficulty of reconciling the 'objectivity' and the 'commitment' of the article's title. He points out what a rarity it is for such agreement to be reached by academics such that it can be put to the cause of a clear, socially relevant policy. Another lesson is the importance of the involvement of members of the community itself, in this case of black linguists, as true progress, he claims, only occurs when people take charge of their own affairs.

In citing this case, we are illustrating the kind of 'applied' work linguists can do beyond academia. It is unlikely that Labov would describe himself as an Applied Linguist – he is best known as a sociolinguist, though his official title simply has linguistics in it – and he uses a very specific kind of sociolinguistic method which he has developed, namely variationist sociolinguistics, in his analysis, represented in the schematized approach in Figure 1.5 above. Nevertheless, the concern for practical social issues that Labov shows in this particular case is shared by all Applied Linguists.

Questions for discussion

- What are the main issues and principles behind the Ann Arbor trial described above?
- To what extent was the school's categorization of the black children based on understandable mistakes and to what extent on other factors?
- Is it right that linguistic differences should be given the type of protection that was guaranteed by Title 20 of the US Code when being subject to social disadvantage is not considered in the same way? Why?
- Could a similar case have arisen in a school where the *majority* of pupils were black?
- The case was brought on the assumption that speaking BEV was tantamount to speaking another language. In what way were the measures proposed to help the black children similar to or different from those that could be applied to pupils of a different mother tongue – for example, Spanish?
- Do you agree with Labov that the involvement of black linguists was crucial here?
- How different does a dialect have to be from the standard, in your view, for its speakers to qualify for special treatment in this way?
- Is it realistic to insist on the sort of principles that Labov outlines for linguistic fieldworkers?
- The measures adopted by the school aim at making it easier for speakers of BEV to switch to Standard English at school. Is this the right educational objective to aim for? Can you see any alternatives?

(Summarized by Penelope Gardner-Chloros.)

This is not to say that the language element has to dominate or that a particular linguistics theory or model has to feature, but it does not count as Applied Linguistics

1. *if there is no language element*. Many of the concerns Applied Linguists have are, equally, concerns of sociologists, neuroscientists and other professional researchers. Crucially, however, Applied Linguists focus on the role of language in the broad issues of sociological or neurological concern. Why call it Applied Linguistics if it has no language connection?
2. *if the language elements are handled without any theory of language*. The theory of language does not need to come from linguistics but might be from philosophy, history, social theory or literary theory. Yet Applied Linguistics cannot treat language as if there were no traditions of language study whatsoever. Nor can the language elements be based solely on folk ideas from the school tradition of grammar or the practical EFL teaching tradition, which would be rather like basing physics on folk beliefs or alchemy. Indeed, one of the responsibilities of the Applied Linguist should be to challenge both the folk notions of language and grammar and the theoretical linguists' models of how language works.
3. *if the research base is neither directly concerned with language issues nor related to them in a demonstrable way*. That is to say, a theory from other disciplines cannot be applied without a clear chain showing how and why it is relevant. An idea from mathematical theory, computer simulation or neural networks needs to show its credentials by providing practical solutions to real-life language problems (e.g. how bilingual speakers with aphasia process sentences), not imposing itself by fiat, by analogy, or by sheer computer modelling. This is an area where there is huge potential for further development, as more and more Applied Linguists become attracted by theories and ideas from other disciplines.

STUDY ACTIVITY 1.1

1. Pick a recent newspaper or magazine and find one article that talks about a language or about a language-related problem. What is the problem? To whom is it a problem? How can descriptive linguistics help? To what extent is the problem also related to historical, political, cultural and policy issues?
2. Reflecting on your own language learning or teaching experience, how much did linguistics help you? Were there any issues for which you had to go to other disciplines, such as psychology, sociology or cultural studies, to find possible solutions or ideas and inspirations? What are these disciplines?
3. Keep a diary for a week and see how many events you have experienced that are related to language and communication issues. What are the issues? Are there practical solutions to any of them? What research questions can be formulated about the issues for further investigation?

Careers for Applied Linguists

While specific employers seek individuals with specific skills for specific jobs, all employers want those with the ability to express themselves clearly, to solve novel problems and to present their solutions in a clear and accessible form. These skills are central to the study of Applied Linguistics. Applied Linguistics training prepares students well for employment in government agencies, non-profit organizations, educational institutions and businesses. In a globalizing world today there is a growing demand for people equipped to analyse language and language practice.

Graduates with a background in Applied Linguistics also gain an enhanced understanding of how people learn first, second and foreign languages and of how language is used in the community. This knowledge will be relevant to those who are interested in preparing for careers as language teachers, language education and assessment experts, speech pathologists, interpreters and translators, and a variety of jobs in industry where language and communication are issues of concern.

The following list of job titles comes from various databases of recent graduates who did an Applied Linguistics degree or had Applied Linguistics as a major in their degree. There are, of course, many other professions that are concerned with language and communication that Applied Linguistic graduates can enter.

Advertising Executive
Administrative Assistant
Bilingual Assistant
Campaign Coordinator
Careers Advisor
Communication Advisor
Community Project Manager
Customer Relations Manager
Data Analyst
Dialect Coach
Document Processing Specialist
Documentation Training Manager
Editor
Educational Consultant
Electronic Lexicographer
Event Manager
Fund Raiser
Grants Manager
Human Resources Administrator
Lab Manager
Marketing Consultant
News Reporter
Policy Analyst
Publisher
Research Associate

Resources Manager
Student Advisor
Teacher of English as a Foreign Language
Teaching Assistant
Technical Copy Editor
Technical Writer
Test Designer
Training and Development Manager
Translator/Interpreter
Volunteer Services Coordinator
Web Developer
Youth Project Manager

1.3   Doing Applied Linguistics: Methodological Considerations

If the Applied Linguist is a Jack of all trades, or a go-between across different disciplines and approaches, does Applied Linguistics have a coherent methodology? Does it need one? How would an Applied Linguistics methodology be different from that of, say, formal linguistics, or sociolinguistics and psycholinguistics? To try to answer questions such as these, which often exercise those new to the field, let us, first of all, remind ourselves of the distinction between method and methodology. There is quite a lot of confusion about the meanings of these two terms. *Methods* refer to specific techniques of collecting and analysing data. For example, a survey questionnaire is a method, and ethnographic fieldwork is another. Sometimes people use 'methods' to refer to tools or instruments, for instance, computer software for analysing data, or multiple choice questions (MCQs). Students are often very concerned about choosing the right method for their research project, and they want to learn how to do it, be it doing an interview or using a data bank. But the method chosen for a particular research project depends on the methodology, which is the underlying logic of methods. More precisely, *methodology* is the principle or principles that determine how specific methods or tools are deployed and interpreted. In one sense, Applied Linguistics is a methodology in itself, because it is concerned with real-world problems in which language plays a central role. Such a problem-solving approach distinguishes Applied Linguistics from other methodologies where the main concern may be hypothesis testing or theorization. In the meantime, Applied Linguists can employ a wide range of methods in collecting and analysing data, many of which are commonly used by sociolinguists, psycholinguists, clinical linguists, educational linguists and others.

There are various ways of characterizing different research methodologies. People often think of research methodology in terms of a quantitative versus qualitative dichotomy. In general terms, *quantitative methodology* aims to uncover facts and truths in an objective way by delineating patterns or structures, whereas *qualitative methodology* attempts to interpret meanings of and relationships between objects in context. For instance, a language class could be regarded as an object for investigation. A quantitative

Table 1.1 Four worldviews used in research

Postpositivism	Constructivism	Advocacy and Participatory	Pragmatism
Determination	Understanding	Political	Consequences of
Reductionism	Multiple participant	Empowerment and	actions
Empirical observation	meanings	issue oriented	Problem centred
and measurement	Social and historical	Collaborative	Pluralistic
Theory verification	construction	Change oriented	Real-world practice
	Theory generation		oriented

approach might focus on how the class is structured, what the key components of the class are, and what role each component plays in the structuring of the class in terms of frequency and regularity. A qualitative perspective, on the other hand, would be most likely to ask what the definition of a class is in comparison with some other event, how the different components of a class (e.g. participants, topic, setting) are related to each other, and why a particular language class takes place in the way it does. Quantitative methodology is used a great deal in science disciplines, while qualitative methodology is more common in the humanities and arts. The social sciences often use both: there are social scientists who are more interested in the 'what' and 'how' questions and adopt a quantitative perspective, while others are more concerned with the 'how' and 'why' questions and lean towards a qualitative methodology. Applied Linguistics as a problem-solving approach does, on the surface, seem to lean towards the qualitative perspective, although there are also plenty of Applied Linguists who are interested in facts and figures and therefore adopt a quantitative methodology.

Perhaps a better way to understand the differences in the various methodologies is to look at the objectives of the research. Creswell (2003: 6) proposed the classifications listed in Table 1.1, which he terms 'worldviews in research'. Such a classification helps us to think of research methodologies in more practical ways and avoids the quantitative versus qualitative dichotomy and the potential confusions between methodology and methods. One can use specific quantitative or qualitative methods and techniques, or a combination of the two, within each of these methodological perspectives.

Whatever methodology you choose to adopt, there are certain steps you need to take in conducting a research project. These typically include

1. defining the research question or questions;
2. collecting evidence;
3. analysing and presenting findings.

1.3.1 Defining the Research Question

Defining the research question is a crucial first step. The question has to be researchable, which means that

1. there are potentially different answers to it;
2. there is evidence available for you with which to answer the question.

The most common ways of finding research questions are through personal experience or reading other people's work. These two ways also often go hand in hand with each other. Many Applied Linguists come into the field because of professional and personal interests. Some may have taught languages in different parts of the world, to different groups of learners, at different levels, and they are interested in researching questions that are directly related to their work experience. Others may themselves be multilingual, have raised children in diverse linguistic and cultural environments, worked in a particular institution, for example multinational corporates, the media, translation and interpreting services, and would like to gain knowledge and understanding of the key issues in these domains. Most of the people entering Applied Linguistics with professional or personal interests tend to have a better idea of the broad area or topic they want to research into than of a specific, researchable question. For example, they may say that they are interested in researching heritage language schools, or intergenerational communication in multilingual families, or attitudes towards certain languages in a particular community. To make the journey from such broad areas of interests to specific research(able) questions is not always an easy or straightforward process. This is where critical reading of the literature comes in.

A good literature review serves two closely related purposes:

1. to make the reader understand why you are doing what you are doing in the way you are doing it; and
2. to prepare your own argument.

It should cover the following questions:

- What has been done on the topic or area of interest? Are you interested in exactly the same topic or area, or in something that is similar but different?
- What are the questions asked by the other researchers? Can you ask the questions in a different way? Do you have other questions to ask?
- From what methodological perspective did they ask the questions: postpositivism, constructivism, advocacy and participatory, or pragmatism? What methodology would you use?
- What methods and data did they use in answering the questions? Can you improve on the research design and method? Is there other evidence that you can provide to address the questions?
- How did the researchers interpret their results and what argument did they put forward on the basis of their data analysis? Do you agree with their analysis? Are there other ways of interpreting the data?

In other words, a good, critical review should show that not only have you read extensively the existing work in the field but you have also understood the methodology and arguments, by pointing out the strengths and weaknesses, by comparing the results of different studies and by evaluating them with reference to your own interests. Once you have answered the above questions, you are likely to have a research question or even a set of questions for your own project.

1.3.2   Research Design

It is often said that a research project only really begins when one starts to collect evidence or data. Many students are anxious about the amount of data they collect and whether the data they have collected is 'good enough'. To ensure that the data you have is of sufficient quantity and quality, you need to consider carefully a number of design issues. The first and foremost is: 'given this research question (or theory), what type of evidence is needed to answer the question (or test the theory) *in a convincing way?*' (de Vaus, 2001: 9, original emphasis). Using an analogy, de Vaus compares the role and purpose of research design in a project to knowing what sort of building one is planning (such as an office building, a factory for manufacturing machinery, a school, etc.). You can normally get a sense of what kind of evidence or data is appropriate for the research question by reviewing existing studies – what evidence did other researchers use to support their arguments? More specifically, you can ask the following questions:

1. Is the primary aim of the study to compare two or more individuals, situations, behaviours, or to focus on just one? (etic vs. emic)
2. Is the data collected and analysed in numerical form or not? (quantitative vs. qualitative)
3. Is the data collected under controlled conditions or not? (experimental vs. non-experimental)
4. Is the study conducted over a period of time or at one point in time? (longitudinal vs. non-longitudinal)
5. Does the study involve one single participant, a small group of participants or a large number of participants? (case study vs. group study)

The terms in brackets after each of the above questions are different types of research design. An *etic* study is often known as a comparative study, which involves comparing one individual, or situation, or behaviour, with another. An *emic* study, on the other hand, is one in which researchers try to explore and discover patterns and meanings *in situ*. The use of numerical data lies behind the difference between *quantitative* and *qualitative* research design. A quantitative study is essentially about explaining phenomena and identifying trends and patterns by collecting and analysing data numerically, while a qualitative design is an umbrella term that covers a variety of methods which focus on the meaning of the phenomenon being investigated and do not involve numerical data. *Experimental* studies collect data under controlled conditions. The purpose of the 'control' is to keep everything, except for the variables under investigation, as similar or comparable as possible so that the experimental results can be reliably attributed to the changes in variables. In a *non-experimental* design, researchers do not manipulate the conditions. This design is suitable for research questions that aim to explore the phenomena in a more natural manner, such as spontaneous interaction, to find out opinions, attitudes or facts or to assess current conditions or practice. *Longitudinal* design refers to studies in which data are collected from a small number of subjects over a period of time, and is suitable for answering research questions that aim to explore changes and development over time or to evaluate the effectiveness of a training programme or the impact of an experience. *Cross-sectional* design, on the other hand, refers to the type of studies in which data is collected at one point in time from a large number of subjects grouped together according either to age or to other variables such as length of stay in a new country. It can be used to explore the relationship between various variables, for example, the correlation between the degree of appropriateness in use of the speech act by an English-as-a-foreign-language learner and the length of stay in an English-speaking country; or to describe the developmental pattern of a particular feature or skill such as the development of Intercultural

Communicative Competence. *Case study* design is an in-depth investigation of, usually, a single subject. It can be used to describe the linguistic or communicative behaviour of an individual member of a group, to refute a claim by providing counter-evidence, or alternatively to show what is possible as positive evidence. *Group study* involves a group of individuals instead of one subject. Single case study and group study are very often combined with longitudinal and cross-sectional designs. For example, a case study can be conducted longitudinally, and a group study can be done cross-sectionally.

There are two further types of research that are increasingly popular in Applied Linguistics, namely, *action research* and *critical research*. Action research belongs to the pragmatist and the advocacy and participatory methodological perspectives in Creswell's framework. It is a reflective process of problem solving. Some people think of action research as case studies. It is true that most often action research is done on a case-by-case basis. But the key to action research is that it is aimed at improving the way the individuals involved in the research process address issues and solve problems. Action research can also be undertaken by larger organizations or institutions, assisted or guided by researchers, with the aim of improving their strategies, practices, and knowledge of the environments within which they practise. Kurt Lewin, who is believed to have coined the term *action research*, described it as 'a comparative research on the conditions and effects of various forms of social action and research leading to social action' that uses 'a spiral of steps, each of which is composed of a circle of planning, action, and fact-finding about the result of the action' (1946). Action research has been particularly popular among language teaching professionals who wish to improve their own as well as their organization's professional practice through the reflective research process.

Critical research cuts across the constructivist, the advocacy and participatory as well as the pragmatist methodological perspectives. Critical research has two rather different origins and histories, one originating in literary criticism and the other in sociology. This has led to the rather literal use of 'critical theory' as an umbrella term to describe theoretical critique. Starting in the 1960s, literary scholars, reacting against the literary criticism in the previous decades which tried to analyse literary texts purely internally, began to incorporate into their analyses and interpretations of literary works semiotic, linguistic and interpretive theory, structuralism, post-structuralism, deconstruction, psychoanalysis, phenomenology and hermeneutics, as well as feminist theory, critical social theory and various forms of neo-Marxist theory. With the expansion of the mass media and popular culture in the 1960s and 70s, social and cultural criticism and literary criticism began to be intertwined in the analysis of popular cultural phenomena, giving rise to the field of Cultural Studies. Critical research in the sociological context, on the other hand, arose from a trajectory extending from the non-positivist sociology of Weber, the neo-Marxist theory of Lukács, to the so-called Frankfurt School of social theorists, most notably Horkheimer and Habermas. It is underpinned by a social theory that is oriented toward critiquing and changing society in its totality, in contrast to traditional theories oriented only to understanding or explaining it. It was intended to be a radical, emancipatory form of social research and concerned itself with 'forms of authority and injustice that accompanied the evolution of industrial and corporate capitalism as a political-economic system' (Lindlof and Taylor, 2002: 52). A newer, postmodern version of the critical social theory focuses on what has been called the 'crisis of representation' and rejects the idea that a researcher's work is considered an 'objective depiction of a stable other'; instead, it tries to politicize social problems 'by situating them in historical and cultural contexts, to implicate themselves in the process of collecting and analyzing data, and to relativize their findings' (Lindlof and Taylor, 2002: 53). Meaning itself is seen as unstable because of the rapid transformation in social structures and as a result the focus of the research is centred on local manifestations rather than broad generalizations.

Critical research has been particularly appealing to some Applied Linguists because of the shared interests in language, symbolism, text and meaning. In the 1970s and 1980s, Jürgen Habermas redefined critical social theory as a theory of communication, that is, communicative competence and communicative rationality on the one hand, distorted communication on the other. Applied Linguists who adopt the critical research perspective have focused on the processes of synthesis, production or construction by which the phenomena and objects of human communication, culture and political consciousness come about. This is reflected in much of the discussion on language ecology, language rights and linguistic imperialism, as well as on gender and ethnicity in language learning and language use (e.g. Pennycook, 2001; Sealey and Carter, 2004). Sociolinguistics, once focused on linguistic variation and change in relation to societal structures and speaker identities, has also taken a critical turn in the last two decades, leading to further blurring of boundaries with Applied Linguistics and other adjacent approaches such as Critical Discourse Analysis. Nowadays, it is common to find in sociolinguistics journals studies that are concerned with topics such as linguistic ideology, media representation of minority language users or equality and discrimination in workplace communication.

1.3.3 Data Collection

The data that Applied Linguists are interested in can be broadly identified in two categories: interactional and non-interactional data. As has been discussed in Section 1.2, Applied Linguistics research should have language as its main object. This does not mean, however, that it has to be language in interaction; it could be language attitude, language awareness, motivations and strategies for language learning, language policy, language assessment, and so on. In fact, interactional data only constitutes the database for a small proportion of Applied Linguistics.

Interactional data consist of a continuum with elicited conversation and naturally occurring conversation at each end, according to the degree of naturalness. Conversation can be elicited through a range of methods and techniques such as discourse completion tasks, recall protocols, or role play. The key issue for the interaction obtained through elicitation is its comparability to naturally occurring interaction. For naturally occurring conversation, the key issue is how to capture it (using observation sheet vs. audio-visual recording, for example) and how to strike the balance between details and analytical approach (Interactional or Conversation Analysis). In addition to elicited and recorded conversation, conversation data are also available in a number of other sources such as data banks, the Internet and other mass and social media.

The so-called *non-interactional data* are data about language practices rather than samples of language practices themselves. Surveys, questionnaires, interviews, self-reports, standard assessments and laboratory experiments can all be used to collect non-interactional data. They are often used to collect large amounts of information from sizeable populations. With the exception of self-reports, the researcher normally has an expectation of what the responses (i.e. data, findings) will be. They are therefore more often used to test hypotheses or verify existing findings and claims. Some Applied Linguists are also interested in critical analysis of public discourse or media language.

Ethnography is sometimes used as a data collection technique when the researcher is particularly interested in exploring the meaning of a phenomenon. Ethnography is in fact more of a methodology than a method; it is a holistic approach to social phenomena and social practices, including linguistic practices, with specific references to both historical and present contexts. Ethnography requires rich data, often collected through a combination of different means including recordings, interviews and questionnaires. But the key data collection method for ethnography is *in situ* observation. Observation enables the investigator to describe events, actions, behaviours, language use, and so on, in detail and to interpret what has happened in context. During observation, researchers make field notes of what they see in as much detail as possible. There are different types of observations, depending on the researcher's role and visibility in the event under study. Researchers can either actively take part in observation and have maximum contact with the people being studied or remain as unobtrusive as possible. The main advantages of ethnographic observation are that it allows the researcher to uncover information previously unknown, to gain an in-depth description, and to capture a series of events and processes over time. The challenges are several: researchers may have biases in selecting what to note down; it is difficult to differentiate describing from interpreting what has happened; documenting an event while observing and participating in activities can be a demanding task.

There is a huge amount of published literature on specific techniques and tools for collecting data. Some of the key references and useful guides are given at the end of the chapter, and in the Resources List at the end of this book.

1.3.4 *Analysing and Presentation Findings*

Data analysis follows closely from research design. It is advisable to consider how you intend to analyse and present the findings during the design stage of the research process, before you start collecting data.

Quantitative data are most often analysed through statistics and presented in various figures, tables, graphs and diagrams. There are ample guide books for students on how to do quantitative and statistical data analysis. Qualitative data, on the other hand, are usually presented in discursive accounts, with quotations and samples of actual data. For both quantitative and qualitative data analysis, accuracy and accountability are paramount. We are talking about accountability to the participants, to the situation that has been investigated, to the researcher himself or herself, as well as to the wider audience. The researcher should be truthful and honest not only in describing what they have observed but also in explaining what their ideological stance may be, what they expected to find, and how their identity and relationship with the people they studied impacted on the findings.

If you have collected interactional data, transcription is the key first step towards analysis. There are different techniques of transcribing language in interaction; for example, Conversation Analysis (CA) specifies a set of conventions for sequential analysis. There are also computer software and other new technologies to assist you in transcribing interactional data, including nonverbal communication and multimodality data. However, most people do not follow a specific set of transcription conventions tightly. And most people do not transcribe everything that has been recorded. It could be argued that one cannot transcribe everything after the event has taken place anyway. There are, therefore, certain decisions one has to make in transcribing interactional data: what is to be transcribed and what is to be left out; what gets highlighted or emphasized and how; what should be done to ambiguous elements, for example, when it is not clear who the speaker was, or what was being referred to. As Ochs (1979) remarked over 30 years ago, such decisions in transcription are also theoretical decisions that would affect the way data is interpreted.

1.3.5   Ethical Considerations

As Applied Linguistics research often involves human subjects, ethical considerations are crucial. These include

- Justification: the proposed research will achieve worthwhile objectives and the time and resources needed for the research are justifiable. Participants' welfare and public responsibility are paramount. Where the project may potentially put the participants at risk, either physically or psychologically, care must be taken to ensure that the benefits of the project outweigh the risks. Appropriate support mechanisms need to be provided to minimize any potential risk. Where there is a possible conflict of interest (e.g. the work is to be carried out in the same organization or sponsored by an organization), again a case must be made.
- Access to participant(s): this includes issues of participants' privacy, the need to reduce invasiveness of the presence of researchers, issues of confidentiality and anonymity, and so on.
- Informed consent: when seeking consent, participants need to be fully informed about the aim and nature of the project and any potential risks. They should be made aware of their rights in the project, such as the right to withdraw at any time, the right to refuse to answer any question, the right to ask any question, and so on. With young and school-age children and vulnerable populations such as patients, consent must be sought from their parents, guardians, carers or schools (if the research is carried out on the school premises or with assistance from the school).

Other ethical concerns relevant to studies in Applied Linguistics include

- Participants' language ability: whether participants' language ability is sufficient for them to understand the informed consent form.
- Cross-cultural differences in ethics: there may be differences in the ethical considerations between the culture in which the research is carried out and the culture from which participants come. This issue is particularly relevant to studies on Study Abroad and intercultural interactions. It is important to anticipate any potential differences and clarify any misunderstandings.

STUDY ACTIVITY 1.2

1. Choose two recently published studies on a topic in Applied Linguistics. Compare the way the researchers ask the questions and design the studies. Is there any difference? How do they justify the questions and the designs?
2. Choose a study that has used a mixed design, for example, longitudinal and cross-sectional, quantitative and qualitative. What is the added value of the mixed design, that is, what are the things that a single design is unable to reveal? Are there any contradictions in the findings by different research designs? If yes, how does the researcher interpret them?
3. Carry out an observational study in an everyday situation. How does your own identity affect the relationship with the people you are observing, your perspective on what you observe and how you interpret what you observe? What ethical issues do you need to consider for the study?

Most educational institutes have an ethics committee which oversees the ethical approval and a set of ethical approval procedures. Students must check the procedure and seek approval before carrying out data collection. In addition, ethical guidelines are provided by some professional bodies or research journals. For example:

- TESOL Quarterly Research Guidelines are available at: www.tesol.org/.
- British Association for Applied Linguistics (BAAL) has a set of recommendations for good practice in Applied Linguistics student projects at: www.baal.org.uk/.
- American Association for Applied Linguistics (AAAL) has passed a range of resolutions that affirm the commitment to promoting diversity, oppose discrimination on the basis of accented speech, support the use of language analysis in relation to questions of national origin in refugee cases, oppose the labelling of English as the national language in the US, and so on: www.aaal.org/.

Wray and Bloomer (2006) also provides useful information on the differences between confidentiality and anonymity and on data protection laws.

1.4 Structure and Content of this Volume

This volume is an attempt to introduce the field of Applied Linguistics as a broad, multidisciplinary approach to language and language-related issues. It aims to provide a comprehensive survey of the theories, methods and key findings within Applied Linguistics, covering a wide range of topics. As such, we decided to have a team-authored text, against the tradition of single-authored introductory textbooks, because we want to highlight the multiple voices that characterize contemporary Applied Linguistics research.

It reflects our conviction in pluralism and our belief that no one person can singularly provide the authoritative account of a field as diverse as Applied Linguistics.

Nevertheless, the volume is tightly structured. It is divided into four main parts, each consisting of three chapters. Part I covers three areas of language development: first language development, second and additional language learning and teaching, and language impairment and loss. Part II is entitled Language in Use and includes chapters on language in interaction, Intercultural Communication, and literacy and multimodality. The three chapters in Part III of the volume are on language in society, covering language diversity and contact, language, identity and power, and language policy and planning. Part IV consists of three chapters on language in public life, including language assessment, language in professional contexts, especially in media, health and law, and translation and interpreting.

All the chapters take a problem-solving approach, introducing the reader to key research questions and guiding them through various ways of tackling these. Each chapter features a number of additional study aids, including chapter outline, learning objectives, key terms, case studies, study activities, study questions and recommended reading. The case studies and the study activities embedded in the chapters are aimed at enabling the user of the textbook to relate everyday language and communication issues to the Applied Linguistics research agenda, and to draw on their own personal experiences in addressing such issues. The study questions at the end of each chapter are aimed at reflecting on what is discussed in the chapter. There is a glossary of the key terms that have occurred in the chapters at the end of the volume, as well as a comprehensive Resources List including key references, handbooks, book series, journals, corpora, professional associations and websites.

Study Questions

1. What are the different conceptualizations of language?
2. How do the different conceptualizations of language affect the way linguists research issues of language?
3. What are the different relationships between the linguist and the linguistic evidence, or data, he/she uses for the analysis?
4. What other disciplines have Applied Linguists drawn on in terms of theory and methods?
5. Why should language be the core element of Applied Linguistics?
6. What are the key methodological perspectives according to Creswell's 'worldview' classification?
7. What are the main advantages and disadvantages of the different research designs – etic vs. emic, quantitative vs. qualitative, experimental vs. non-experimental, longitudinal vs. cross-sectional, single case study vs. group study?
8. What is *action research*? What is *critical research*?
9. How does the identity of the research affect data collection and data analysis?
10. What are the key ethical considerations in Applied Linguistics research?

Recommended Reading

Cook, Guy. 2003. *Applied Linguistics*. Oxford: Oxford University Press. A concise but comprehensive overview of the central issues in Applied Linguistics.

Cook, Vivian J. and Li Wei (eds.). 2009. *Contemporary Applied Linguistics, vol. 1: Language Teaching and Learning; vol. 2: Linguistics for the Real World*. London: Continuum. These consist of 24 introductory chapters, showcasing cutting-edge research in Applied Linguistics. The contributors in the first volume present current research in areas such as multilingualism, language education, teacher–learner relationships and assessment. Chapters in the second volume present an overview of new and interdisciplinary fields such as language and economics, language and the law, language and religion, language and tourism, language and the media, and language and health.

Cooke, Melanie and James Simpson. 2008. *ESL: A Critical Guide*. Oxford: Oxford University Press. This is aimed at English language teachers and teacher-educators who wish to extend their understanding of the issues and debates surrounding English for speakers of other languages (ESOL) in an age of globalization and mass migration.

Davies, Alan. 1999. *An Introduction to Applied Linguistics: From Practice to Theory*. Edinburgh: Edinburgh University Press. This surveys the history and definitions of the field and discusses issues such as Applied Linguistics and language learning and teaching, Applied Linguistics and language use and the professionalizing of Applied Linguistics.

Hunston, Susan and David Oakey. 2009. *Introducing Applied Linguistics: Concepts and Skills*. Abingdon: Routledge. This is a short, introductory text that introduces students to the key concepts faced when studying Applied Linguistics, as well as the study skills needed for academic reading and writing.

Li Wei. 2011. *The Routledge Applied Linguistics Reader*. London: Routledge. This contains 26 selected readings and focuses on the topics and issues to which Applied Linguistics research has made a significant contribution, including, for example, reconceptualizing the native speaker, the language learner and the language in language learning and practice, critical issues in Applied Linguistics and Applied Linguistics in a changing world. It also has an extended introduction to Applied Linguistics, a critical discussion of methodological issues in Applied Linguistics research, as well as study questions, recommended further reading and a comprehensive resource list.

McCarthy, Michael. 2001. *Issues in Applied Linguistics*. Cambridge: Cambridge University Press. This outlines the historical roots of the field and its major developments over the years. It also examines issues such as language modelling and the analysis of discourse.

Pennycook, Alastair. 2001. *Critical Applied Linguistics: A Critical Introduction*. Mahwah, NJ: Lawrence Erlbaum Associates. This discusses an alternative approach to critical questions in language education, literacy, Discourse Analysis and language in the workplace, translation and other language-related domains.

Schmitt, Norbert (ed.). 2010. *An Introduction to Applied Linguistics*, 2nd edn. London: Hodder Education. This provides a comprehensive survey of the key topics in Applied Linguistics. It contains three parts, focusing on the description of language and language use, essential areas of enquiry in Applied Linguistics and language skills and assessment.

Sealey, Alison and Bob Carter. 2004. *Applied Linguistics as Social Science*. London: Continuum. This shows how social theory and Applied Linguistics share common concerns and argues that a social scientific account of Applied Linguistics is needed to explain the interaction between social structures, human agents and language.

Seidlhofer, Barbara (ed.). 2003. *Controversies in Applied Linguistics*. Oxford: Oxford University Press. This reprints the exchanges between some of the leading Applied Linguists on controversial issues, such as the global spread of English, corpus linguistics and language teaching, Critical Discourse Analysis, second language acquisition and the nature of Applied Linguistics.

Two handbooks provide comprehensive and in-depth surveys of the field:

Davies, A. and C. Elder (eds.). 2004. *Handbook of Applied Linguistics*. Oxford: Blackwell.
Kaplan, Robert. 2005. *The Oxford Handbook of Applied Linguistics*. Oxford: Oxford University Press.

Two popular introductory texts on language generally that are mentioned in this chapter are:

Macaulay, Ronald K.S. 2011. *Seven Ways of Looking at Language*. Basingstoke: Palgrave.
Nunan, David. 2013. *What is This Thing Called Language?* 2nd edn. Basingstoke: Palgrave.

Other useful references include:

Davies, Alan. 2005. *A Glossary of Applied Linguistics*. Edinburgh: Edinburgh University Press.
Johnson, Keith and Helen Johnson (eds.). 1999. *Encyclopedic Dictionary of Applied Linguistics*. Oxford: Blackwell.
Richards, Jack and Richard Schmidt (eds.). 2010. *Longman Dictionary of Language Teaching and Applied Linguistics*, 4th edn. Harlow: Longman.
Spolsky, Bernard and Francis M. Hult. 2007. *Handbook of Educational Linguistics*. Oxford: Wiley-Blackwell.

There are literally hundreds of books on research methodology, research design and methods of data collection and analysis. Publishers such as SAGE and Palgrave specialize in books on research methods:

Creswell, John. 2003. *Research Design: Qualitative, Quantitative, and Mixed Methods Approaches*. London: SAGE. This book, which has been referred to in this chapter, provides a useful overview of different methodological perspectives in research design.
Dörnyei, Zoltán. 2007. *Research Methods in Applied Linguistics: Quantitative, Qualitative, and Mixed Methodologies*. Oxford: Oxford University Press. This offers a practical guide to different designs and methods in Applied Linguistics.
Gorard, Stephen. 2013. *Research Design: Creating Robust Approaches for the Social Sciences*. London: SAGE. This offers a fresh look at the nature of research design, and presents a range of standard design models, as well as tips for real-life problems and compromises.
Paltridge, Brian and Aek Phakiti. 2010. *Continuum Companion to Research Methods in Applied Linguistics*. London: Continuum. This is a useful one-volume guide for students. The book includes: qualitative and quantitative methods; research techniques and approaches; ethical considerations; sample studies; a glossary of key terms; and resources for students. It also looks at various topics in Applied Linguistics in depth, including gender and language, language and identity, pragmatics, vocabulary and grammar.
Perry, Fred Lehman. 2005. *Research in Applied Linguistics: Becoming a Discerning Consumer*. Abingdon: Routledge. This is an introduction to the foundations of research methods, with the goal of enabling students and professionals in the field of Applied Linguistics to become not just casual consumers of research who passively read bits and pieces of a research article, but discerning consumers able to use published research effectively for practical purposes in educational settings.

Other introductory texts on research methods in Applied Linguistics include:

Brown, James Dean and Theodore Rodgers. 2003. *Doing Second Language Research*. Oxford: Oxford University Press.
Larsen-Freeman, Diane and Michael Long. 1991. *An Introduction to Second Language Acquisition Research*. London: Longman.

Mackey, Alison and Susan Gass. 2005. *Second Language Research: Methodology and Design*. Abingdon: Routledge.

Nunan, David. 1992. *Research Methods in Language Learning*. Cambridge: Cambridge University Press.

Practical guides to specific methods include:

Burns, Anne. 2009. *Doing Action Research in English Language Teaching*. Abingdon: Routledge.

Dörnyei, Zoltán. 2002. *Questionnaires in Second Language Research: Construction, Administration and Processing*. Hove: Psychology Press.

Duff, Patricia. 2008. *Case Study Research in Applied Linguistics*. Mahwah, NJ: Lawrence Erlbaum Associates.

Guides on quantitative and statistical methods in Applied Linguistics include:

Baayen, R. Harald. 2008. *Analyzing Linguistic Data: A Practical Introduction to Statistics using R*. Cambridge: Cambridge University Press.

Bitchener, John. 2009. *Writing an Applied Linguistics Thesis or Dissertation: A Guide to Presenting Empirical Research*. Basingstoke: Palgrave. This introduces first-time thesis writers to the process of writing up empirical research.

Hatch, Evelyn and Anne Lazaraton. 1991. *The Research Manual: Design and Statistics for Applied Linguistics*. Boston: Heinle & Heinle.

Larson-Hall, Jenifer. 2009. *A Guide to Doing Statistics in Second Language Research Using SPSS*. Abingdon: Routledge.

Li Wei and Melissa Moyer (eds.). 2008. *The Blackwell Guide to Research Methods in Bilingualism and Multilingualism*. Oxford: Wiley-Blackwell. This has comprehensive coverage of research designs and methods ranging from sampling, recording and transcription to laboratory experiments and brain imaging techniques. The examples are drawn from studies of bilingualism and multilingualism.

Wray, Alison and Aileen Bloomer. 2006. *Projects in Linguistics: A Practical Guide to Researching Language*, 2nd edn. London: Hodder Arnold. This provides advice on research projects in different areas of linguistics and useful information on the differences between confidentiality and anonymity and on data protection laws.

Wiley-Blackwell publishes a book series on Research Methods in Language and Linguistics. Already published are volumes on second language acquisition, child language, clinical linguistics and phonetics, and sociolinguistics.

part I

Language in Development

First Language Acquisition

Zhu Hua

Learning Outcomes

After reading this chapter, you should be able to

- outline the stages or milestones of first language acquisition in monolingual children;
- explain the 'logical' problem and unique features of first language acquisition;

Applied Linguistics, First Edition. Edited by Li Wei.
© 2014 John Wiley & Sons, Ltd. Published 2014 by John Wiley & Sons, Ltd.

- outline the characteristics of child-directed speech;
- understand the nature–nurture debate and the interaction between innateness and input;
- explain the special features of bilingual and multilingual first language acquisition (BAMFLA);
- understand the role of cross-linguistic and multilingual studies in child language studies, in particular their contribution to the identification of language-specific patterns and developmental universals;
- define what language socialization is and explain how it helps us understand social, cultural and pragmatic development in first language acquisition.

Key Terms

- Bilingual and multilingual first language acquisition
- Child-directed speech
- Competence
- Developmental stages/milestones
- Developmental universals
- Early second language learning
- Language Acquisition Device

- Language faculty
- Language socialization
- Language-specific patterns
- Language transfer
- The logical or projection problem of language acquisition
- Performance
- Universal Grammar

2.1   Introduction

- Dominic is a four-year-old boy, who was born and grew up in Bonn. His parents are monolingual German speakers. He has two brothers. All three boys speak only German.
- Mia is a two-year-old girl living with her English-speaking parents in California. She was adopted at the age of 19 months from an orphanage in China.
- Diego is a two-year-old boy born in Paraguay. His father, a Paraguayan, speaks Spanish and Guarani, two official languages of Paraguay. His mother, originally from Taiwan, is a native speaker of Mandarin and Taiwanese and a fluent second language speaker of Spanish. Diego also spends a lot of time with his maternal grandmother, who is a native speaker of Mandarin and Taiwanese but, unlike Diego's mother, speaks little Spanish.

Dominic, Mia and Diego differ from each other in the conditions and tasks of language development. Dominic has been exposed to German only. Mia needs to deal with the change in the languages spoken around her and the task of being socialized into a new living environment, in addition to distress, neglect and lack of interaction in her early development as an orphan. Diego, like many other multilingual children, has been exposed to at least three languages from birth. He has the task of developing his understanding and production of the multiple languages spoken around him. This leads to the questions we are going to explore in this chapter: how children, in either a monolingual or a multilingual context, acquire their first language(s) and how language environment impacts on children's acquisition.

2.2 What Are the Facts and Problems of First Language Acquisition?

The need to communicate and socialize drives children to learn to speak the languages spoken around them. In the literature on first language acquisition of monolingual English-speaking children, the terms 'developmental stages' or 'milestones' are very often used to describe progress that children have made in their process of learning to speak. Most of the children will follow the sequence of developmental stages or milestones and make the transition from one stage to the next gradually, despite individual variations regarding timing, speed and manner of transition. Lust (2006) provides a detailed summary of various developmental milestones both in perception and production, and in different domains of language such as phonology, syntax and semantics.

1. Pre-speech and babbling: *'goo-goo-gaa-gaa'*
   As early as three months, infants begin to produce cooing and vocalizations, which turn into babbling at around six months. These vocalizations are often characterized by reduplications, that is, repetitions of a syllable. They are not the exact match to the target language; some vocalizations do not exist in the target language while some sounds in the target language are missing from vocalizations. Although it is difficult to pinpoint the time when an infant's behaviour can be reliably described as being intentionally communicative, evidence shows that the potential for developing communicative ability is present at this stage. For example, infants soon learn that they can use sounds and gestures to attract attention, and to send out affective signals of being content, agitated, uncomfortable, and so on.
2. First words: 'ma-ma' for 'mum', 'lu_' for 'look'
   Some children can produce first words as early as nine months. Deaf children whose parents use sign language begin their first word/gesture around the same time. Children's first words are very often restricted to simple syllable structures such as CV, V, or CVC (C: consonant; V: vowel). They tend to be names of objects and significant people such as dog, car, daddy, mummy, or related to social activities or routines such as hi, bye, nite-nite, and so on. These first words are often over-extended in meaning (for example, 'car' can be used to refer to any moving object) or perform a range of functions such as request or exclamation (for example, 'get me the car', 'I like the car!').
3. First sentences/combining words: 'daddy car', 'dog gone'
   Once children have about 50 words in their spoken vocabulary, they begin to combine them into utterances of two or several words to describe a variety of meanings such as ownership (daddy car), events (ball fall), location (key box), action (eat bickie), and so on. These utterances usually lack grammatical structure or relevant morphological inflections compared with the target languages.

4. Complex sentences and increased vocabulary size: 'please may I have some more?'
   By the age of four, most children have experienced a rapid expansion in the size of their vocabulary, complexity of sentences (not only in length, but also with various forms of embedding and transformations) and accuracy and range of morphemes (e.g. plurals, past tense). They continue to fine-tune their pragmatic skills, in particular, politeness routines, and learn to perform a range of speech acts appropriately. Overgeneralizations often occur in children's speech towards the end of the First sentences stage and at the beginning of the Complex sentences stage. For example, with morphological inflections, once children learn to use 'ed' to indicate past tense such as 'walked' for 'walk', 'opened' for 'open', they may produce forms such as 'goed', 'bringed', and so on. Overgeneralization is resistant to correction.

5. Conversational skills
   From four years on, children rapidly build up their conversations skills. They learn how to initiate conversations, organize their discourse and adjust their conversation styles according to the context, such as to whom and where they are speaking and what they are talking about.

There are many unique features with regard to first language acquisition of all normally developing children. These are

- Speed and ultimate success: children do not produce adult-like utterances from the very beginning, but they master the skills of understanding and production by the age of four or five.
- Individual differences: there are individual differences in the speed and manner of acquisition, but the outcome of first language acquisition is the same.
- Resourcefulness: they can communicate a wide range of meanings and make their intentions known with a 'limited' size of vocabulary by extending word meanings or using a mixture of words, gestures, facial expressions, vocalizations, and so on.

However, underneath the general impression that acquiring a first language is effortless and natural and guaranteed to be successful, children face an essential learning problem, a problem sometimes referred to as 'the projection problem' or 'the logical problem of language acquisition'. They are expected to develop adult-like performance and competence. The input they are exposed to, however, does not offer optimal opportunities. To understand the extent of this problem, let's look at what is to be acquired and what is available.

- What is to be acquired? When children are acquiring a language, they are not only learning how to interpret and put together a string of words appropriately (i.e. performance), but also developing implicit knowledge of what is permissible or not in a language (i.e. competence). It is the latter, that is, knowing what is permissible or not, that allows a native speaker to create new utterances they may not have heard, and to differentiate those new but permissible utterances from those not permissible in a language. For example, in uttering the sentence, 'she were crying', a native speaker makes a performance error, but he or she would know that the sentence is ungrammatical.

STUDY ACTIVITY 2.1

Read the following exchange between the child and his father. What does it tell you about the child's speech?

CHILD: There is a fiss in there.
FATHER: You mean there's a fish in there.
CHILD: Yes, there's a fiss.
FATHER: There is a fiss in there?
CHILD: No, there's a FISS in there.

(Smith, 1973)

- What is available? In order for children to acquire competence, they need to experience what occurs in a language (*positive evidence*) and to find out what does not (*negative evidence*). However, neither positive nor negative evidence appears to be directly and readily available to them. Although children are exposed to the correct form of the target language regularly, exposure itself is not enough. They need to work out how to extract sounds and word units from continuous speech or *bootstrap* into the language system. In addition, adults would never be able to introduce every possible lexical item or sentence. There is also a lack of negative evidence in the input in the sense that parents do not always correct children's utterances unless the meaning of an utterance is compromised (more discussion on the nature of input can be found in the following section).

The logical problem prompts many linguists and psycholinguists to believe that children have an innate knowledge of universal grammar, a view advocated by Noam Chomsky and his followers (e.g. Chomsky, 1965; Radford, 1996; Clahsen, Eisenbeiß and Penke, 1996; Hyams, 1996; Wexler, 1994; Rizzi, 1993/1994) and referred to as the generative paradigm to differentiate it from the then prevalent behaviourist approach to language acquisition (e.g. Skinner, 1957). The main arguments in the generative paradigm are as follows:

- There is a specific faculty of the mind that is responsible for the acquisition and use of language. Referred to as the language faculty by Chomsky (1965), it is assumed to be *innate* and biologically determined.
- The generative paradigm explains the language faculty through the so-called Universal Grammar (UG), which contains a set of universal principles that underlie the structure of all human languages and a finite set of parameters to account for cross-linguistic variations. In essence, UG restricts the set of grammars that are compatible with the input and, meanwhile, provides children with a template which helps them to generalize about the target grammar. Over-generalization errors frequently found in children's speech are evidence for children's attempt to form abstract representation and build hypotheses.
- Input is necessary, but not sufficient, for language development.

The generative paradigm has been influential and several theories and models are now available to account for the mechanisms that facilitate the transition from UG to the target grammar of specific languages in first, second and bilingual acquisition. One example of such models is Optimality Theory, which argues that language acquisition takes place through a ranking process whereby output candidates are evaluated against a set of ordered constraints, such as markedness (also known as well-formedness) and faithfulness constraints. Since highly ranked constraints have priority over constraints of lower ranks, output candidates would be checked against higher ranked constraints first before being passed along to the next constraint in the hierarchy (for a review, see McCarthy, 2001; Eisenbeiß, 2009). Another example is the so-called bootstrapping account, which focuses on how children 'bootstrap' or break into the system of the target language to start off the process of acquisition. It is hypothesized that bootstrapping mechanisms serve as filters between input and learning and help children to attend to specific input cues in linguistically relevant structural units and properties (Pinker, 1984, 1987; Höhle, 2009 for a review).

In the last 20 years, several competing models and theories have emerged as alternative accounts of the mechanisms and processes of first language acquisition. One is the statistical learning model, which regards language acquisition as a process of detecting regularities at various levels of the linguistic structure and building categories out of the regularities, through general cognitive abilities, not language-specific mechanisms (Thiessen, 2009, for a review). Another model is the connectionist approach, which explains learning in terms of the strength of interconnection between neurons in neural networks as the result of exposure to a stimulus (Westermann, Ruh and Plunkett, 2009, for a review). The third alternative is the usage-based approach developed by Tomasello (2009). Tomasello emphasizes that children construct language structures from actual use and communication through general cognitive abilities such as intention-reading and pattern-finding abilities. Departing from the statistical model and the connectionist approach, the usage-based approach regards communicative function, the need to understand others and make one's intentions understood, as the driving force of language acquisition.

Two key issues seem to be at the centre of the tensions between the generative paradigm and the alternative ones: one is whether there is an innate language-specific capacity with which children are born; the other is what role input plays in the process of language acquisition, which we will turn to in the next section.

───── 2.3   How Do Adults Speak to Children and What Roles Does Input Play in Language Acquisition?

In Chomsky's concept of innateness, he has brought our attention to the problem of 'poverty of stimuli', that is, there is a shortage of both positive and negative evidence in the speech to which children are exposed. However, subsequent studies on child-directed speech (CDS, speech directed to young children by caregivers such as mothers, fathers or older siblings, also known as 'motherese' or 'baby talk') have revealed that CDS has many unique features of its own. It differs from normal speech in a variety of dimensions.

Case Study 2.1

The following description of the main characteristics of CDS is adapted from Harris (1990: 200–201, summarized in Matychuk, 2005: 332).

1. Compared with adult-directed speech, CDS is simpler in syntax, vocabulary and phonology, slower in speed, exaggerated in prosody and in general geared to greater communicative clarity, among other things.
2. It deals with the child's interests: actions, objects, people and events which are present here and now.
3. It is semantically related to the child's language (i.e. semantically contingent) so that the child will recognize the connection between her own communicative intentions and the language structures presented by the adult. This can be done by:
   a. repetition of the child's utterance in a conventional way
      Example:
      CHILD: buh
      ADULT: butter
   b. expansion of the child's utterance
      Example:
      CHILD: play bath
      ADULT: You want to play with your toys in the bath.
   c. recasting the child's utterance to illustrate an alternative grammatical structure
      Example:
      CHILD: 'You can't get in.'
      ADULT: 'No I can't get in, can I?'
4. It is filled with phatic responses such as 'yes', 'oh', 'mmmm' and 'I see' to indicate the adult is listening and attending to what the child is saying.
5. It does not simply use questions to get children to speak, but rather uses meaningful contributions from the adult to talk about the conversation context.
6. Whenever possible, it uses naturally occurring conversational slots so that the adult's language fits in with other activities and the child's increasing ability to participate in verbal and nonverbal interactions.

At the heart of CDS is negotiation between caregivers and children. Children do not always respond with complete or near-complete linguistic units. However, adults adjust or fine-tune their speech based on a child's responses. But how do adults fine-tune CDS? We now know that fine-tuning CDS is a complex matter. It is very often the result of interaction between individual factors such as the child's age, language ability (normally or atypically developing) and macro factors such as social and cultural norms (Snow, 1995; Lust, 2006).

First of all, adults adjust CDS to the child's age and language ability. Evidence suggests that fine-tuning changes with the child's age, and in particular, the child's language ability, to accommodate the fact that the child has a limited resource of communication at various stages of development. Prosodic fine-tuning such as high pitch and exaggerated intonation is most evident at the pre-linguistic stage when infants begin to respond to stimuli, but gradually disappears by age five, if not earlier. Phonetic and phonological

---

STUDY ACTIVITY 2.2

Read the following transcripts. What do they tell us about child-directed speech?

1.
SARAH: There's the animal farmhouse.
MOTHER: No, that's a lighthouse.

2.
EVE: Mama isn't boy, he a girl.
MOTHER: That's right.

(Source: both from Lust, 2006: 29)

---

fine-tuning, such as reduplication, enhanced clarity of vowels, and full production of often-reduced consonants, are most frequent at first word stage. In syntax, Mean Length of Utterances and the number of different word types in CDS tend to correlate with those of the child. In addition, adults tend to add the missing item for the child and the more 'telegraphic' the child speech, the more likely the parent is to fill in the missing item(s).

Fine-tuning CDS is also evident in the speech of adults interacting with children in atypically developing circumstances. Despite discrepancies in the nature and severity of atypical conditions, children with hearing impairments, visual disabilities, Down syndrome, specific language impairments and learning difficulties are very often presented with CDS which is more directive and less semantically contingent than speech to normally developing children. For example, studies have shown that there is a less frequent use of recasts, that is, responses to children's utterances that include not only most of the content words in the children's speech but also added elements, in CDS to children with Specific Language Impairment. These adjustments may arise out of parents' compensation for poor comprehensibility or the low responsiveness very often experienced in the interaction of children with atypically developing conditions.

CDS is essentially a form of socialization and therefore subject to sociocultural factors that may impact on what constitutes CDS and the way it is fine-tuned. For example, in the Qu'che Mayan culture, high pitch is very often used to persons of high status and, therefore, mothers in that culture rarely use high pitch when they speak to their babies. There is more discussion on socialization in the following section.

2.3.1   A Trigger/Catapult or a Source of Opportunities for Incremental Learning?

Clearly input is necessary to children's language acquisition. Yet, what we are less certain about is how exactly CDS and other input, such as peer-to-peer interaction, facilitate language acquisition. There are two different views on this (Snow, 1995). One is to compare input as a trigger or catapult, something that launches the child into the language system. The other is to see input as a source of opportunities for incremental learning. While both suggest that input plays an important role in language acquisition, neither of them can completely account for the observed and identified impact of CDS and other input on language development, both in normally and atypically developing monolingual/ bilingual children.

Firstly, *individual differences in CDS can account for variations in the child's development to some extent, but no firm cause-and-effect relationship has been established so far*. For example, some research evidence suggests that the preference of referential children for common nouns or general nominals may be related to their mothers' tendency to name objects. However, research findings on this remain tentative.

Secondly, *other types of input, which differ from CDS in features, help with children's development too*. While children generally benefit from the greater communication clarity underlying CDS, other input by fathers or other less familiar conversation partners such as older siblings can provide children with important opportunities to learn skills needed for communication to less familiar audiences. However, this type of input is generally less finely tuned to the child's development level.

Thirdly, *input is not equivalent to intake*. We know impoverished input is not conducive to language acquisition – for example, hearing children of deaf parents fail to learn language from television and casual encounters with hearing adults. This suggests that input cannot simply be assumed as anything the child is exposed to; it has to be made relevant to children and there has to be a minimal threshold. We also know that simultaneous bilingual children, who are exposed to two languages from birth, can become bilingual speakers (more discussion in the following section on bilingual and multilingual children). These children, in a one parent/one language situation, may have less input in each language compared with monolingual children in their language.

CDS, together with other input, plays an important role in language acquisition, but how it influences language acquisition remains to be further explored. One possible angle of investigation could be looking at the role of CDS in language socialization, which will be further discussed in Section 2.6.

2.4 What Are the Special Features of Bilingual and Multilingual First Language Acquisition (BAMFLA)?

The discussion in the previous two sections is based on monolingual children. However, there are increasing numbers of children who have two or more languages spoken to them from birth. Bilingual and multilingual first language acquisition (BAMFLA) refers to the development of languages in such children. It differs from monolingual first language acquisition, in which children only hear one language from birth. It also differs from early second language learning, in which monolingual children are exposed to a second language after they have already started learning their first language. We will focus on the special features of BAMFLA in relation to monolingual first language acquisition in this section. We will also revisit the discussion on the 'problem' of language acquisition and the role of input in the light of evidence from BAMFLA. Our discussion is based mainly on De Houwer (2009a, b), Li Wei (2000) and Zhu Hua and Li Wei (2005).

STUDY ACTIVITY 2.3

Read the following case study, which is referred to in the introduction to this chapter, and discuss the implication of language environments for language development.

Diego is a two-year-old boy, born in Paraguay. His father, a Paraguayan, speaks Spanish and Guarani, two official languages of Paraguay. His mother, originally from Taiwan, is a native speaker of Mandarin and Taiwanese and a fluent second language speaker of Spanish. Diego has also spent a lot of time with his maternal grandmother from birth. The grandmother is a native speaker of Mandarin and Taiwanese but speaks little Spanish.

Diego's mother speaks to him in Mandarin most of the time, although she sometimes speaks a little Spanish. His father only speaks to him in Spanish, while D's grandmother speaks to him in both Taiwanese and Mandarin. D spends most of the time during the day with his grandmother and mother and his evenings and weekends with his father and mother. He watches Spanish television programmes regularly.

(*Source*: Yang and Zhu Hua, 2010)

In very general terms, BAMFLA is similar to monolingual first language acquisition in many ways: both follow a particular order in overall language development, that is, an initial babbling stage, followed by first words, multi-word stage, and then complex utterances; both follow a similar overall time frame, that is, over five years; and in both cases, there are variations in the ages at which children reach each milestone. Some people are concerned that children exposed to two or more languages might reach milestones later than children exposed to one language only. However, the concern has no research evidence. What appears to be the *late* onset of speech or age of reaching milestones observed in some bilingual and multilingual children is due to normal variation in the speed and manner of acquisition, which is evident in monolingual children too.

Despite these similarities, differences between bilingual and multilingual first language acquisition and monolingual first language acquisition suggest that the former is qualitatively different from the latter. The most noticeable difference is the use of code-switching, that is, the alternation of languages in production, in the speech of bilingual and multilingual children as soon as they can produce two-word utterances. We now know that the existence of code-switching is the norm for bilingual/multilingual children rather than the exception. Similar to adults' code-switching, code-switching in bilingual and multilingual children is highly structured and grammatically constrained, suggesting that bilingual/multilingual children have added capacity to coordinate their two languages on-line in accordance with the grammatical constraints of both languages during switching. There are, however, some features associated with children's code-switching. For example, young children may *appear* to mix languages at different levels, partly because of the developmental nature of their linguistic resources in all the languages they are acquiring. In the following examples, the child, Hannah, mixed the verb 'strap' in German and English morphologically, phonologically and syntactically. In (b), she omitted the German infinitive form '–en' and simplified the consonant cluster by dropping /s/; in (c) and (d), she blended the German prefix 'ein' (meaning 'in') and English verb 'strap'; in (e), she used the English verb phrase 'strap in' but simplified the consonant cluster in 'strap'; and in (f), she deleted the initial consonant in 'strap', but produced an aspirated /t/.

Examples of Code-switching (Tracy, 2000, cited in Gardner-Chloros, 2009: 148–149)

Hannah, aged 2;3, a German-English bilingual, was trying to get some help from her mother to strap a doll into a buggy.

a. die dolly [ənstræpən]
    the dolly strap-in INF
b. die dolly [əntræp]
    the dolly ..trap
c. das eins-[straːp iːn] die puppe
    it in- strap in the dolly
d. die ein-[straːp iːn] die dolly
    it in strap in the dolly
e. die mama helf mir [tap] it [iːn]
    (the) mummy help me strap it in
f. mama (=voc.) [tʰap it [iːn] die dolly
    mummy [=voc.] strap it in the dolly

Another feature of language acquisition unique to BAMFLA is the difference between the languages used in terms of outcome and input. The languages a bilingual or multilingual child is acquiring do not always develop in the same way or at the same speed. The bilingual or multilingual child may not necessarily speak both or all the languages equally well: there may be variations in the level of comprehension and/or production, probably owing to an imbalance in language input and the resulting imbalance in language dominance. It is very often the case that the developing bilingual or multilingual child has more input in one language than the other. The more input in a particular language, either at the macro-community level (e.g. living in a community with a clearly dominant language) or at the micro-interactional level (e.g. conversational exchanges with parents and other caregivers), the faster the language concerned develops. However, we now know that the quantity of input is not the sole determining factor in children's language development – the quality of input is equally or more important.

What is worth pointing out is that, in BAMFLA, the bilingual or multilingual child is not two or three monolinguals in one. Apart from code-switching, research evidence shows that the languages being acquired also interact or interfere with each other. The interdependence between the developing languages can take the form of *transfer* (one feature of one language occurs in the other and results in atypical error patterns), *acceleration* and *delay* (one feature from one language is acquired earlier or later than expected because of the influence of another language). Such interaction or interference occurs probably because of the existence of the interlanguage structural ambiguity in the input (termed 'vulnerable domains'), or the degree of relatedness of the languages being developed. However, it is unclear whether and how the degree of typological similarity facilitates or impedes the development of the languages concerned.

Bilingual and multilingual first language acquisition is a highly complex and dynamic process. BAMFLA demonstrates children's extraordinary capacity in language development; successful bilingual or multilingual children can speak two or more languages just as well as monolinguals, despite relatively limited access to input in each language compared with monolingual children. Similarities observed between monolingual and bilingual/multilingual children in the manner of acquisition, and between different languages acquired by bilingual/multilingual children, indicate that language development is constrained by a set of universals that operates in interaction with a variety of linguistic, environmental, social, cultural, political, economic and historical factors.

—————— 2.5 What do Cross-linguistic Studies Tell Us about First Language Acquisition?

Despite their noticeable omission from the *Handbook of Child Language* edited by Fletcher and MacWhinney (1995), cross-linguistic studies have been on the increase in the past 20 years. Cross-linguistic studies not only explore and suggest new and neglected areas for investigation, but also evaluate and challenge claims about language acquisition. As discussed in the earlier section, both innateness and input are essential for language development. However, it is unclear to what extent and how these two factors interact with each other in language acquisition. Cross-linguistic studies offer special opportunities to compare patterns of language development across children acquiring different languages and to identify patterns that are common across languages (termed 'developmental universals') and language-specific patterns (termed 'particulars'). By doing so, cross-linguistic studies can help us understand which properties of language development are determined by the structure of the language to which the child is exposed and which properties of language development are universal. In what follows, we look at a few claims about 'developmental universals' that have been either corroborated or rejected through cross-linguistic studies.

In phonological development, the first general claim of developmental universals was proposed by Jakobson (1968[1941]). He suggested that whether a sound would be acquired early could be explained in terms of the distribution of the sounds among the world's languages. Therefore, nasals, front consonants and stops, which are found in virtually all languages, would be acquired early. His claim was subsequently challenged by counterexamples on two fronts: individual variations within one language and language variations in the acquisition of the same sounds.

In lexicon development, the previous claim of a universal *noun bias* (i.e. nouns were acquired first, followed by relational and expressive words and later by verbs) in children's early lexical development, based on studies of English- and Italian-speaking children, has been challenged by studies of French, Mandarin, Korean and Tzeltal (Kauschke and

Case Study 2.2

Zhu Hua and Dodd (2006) observed similarities and differences in phonological development in 11 languages including English, German, Putonghua, Cantonese, Maltese, Telugu, Colloquial Egyptian Arabic, Turkish, Spanish, Mirpuri/Punjabi/Urdu and Welsh. Some general conclusions are:

1. There are discrepancies in the age of acquisition of sounds common to all the languages studied.
2. Unaspirated phonemes tend to be acquired earlier than their aspirated pairs, suggesting that unmarked sounds precede marked sounds in acquisition.
3. Regardless of their language backgrounds, there are common error patterns among children – for example, the tendency to replace marked sounds with unmarked sounds, replacing fricatives with stops (stopping) and moving the place of articulation to a more anterior position (fronting).
4. The language-specific influence is manifested in different acquisition patterns of the same sound, among others. For example, nearly all the languages studied have /r/ in different forms. However, each language differs in its replacement patterns. In English, /r/ tends to be replaced with [w/ʋ]; in Putonghua, it is replaced with [j]; in Maltese and Colloquial Egyptian Arabic, /r/ becomes [l]; in Turkish, it is replaced with [j] or a vowel.

Hofmeister, 2002). The counter evidence suggests that the role played by nouns during early vocabulary development does not seem to be as prominent as had been assumed. Noun preference observed in some languages may be the artefact of methodology; we do not know whether the categorizations of vocabulary in terms of nouns, verbs, descriptive words, and so on, represent children's mental world. Alternatively, it is argued that noun preference may be related to characteristics of the specific language and the influence of the pragmatic focus of CDS in certain languages.

In the acquisition of syntax, the early claim that children may begin with a general word order or a non-linguistic 'cognitive'-based order has been rejected by cross-linguistic studies of various languages such as Finnish, Polish, Turkish and Dutch. These studies have successfully demonstrated that children's first sentences generally follow the basic word order of their languages, whether it is SVO, SOV, VSO (S: subject; V: verb; O: object) or other types. Similarly, the hypothesis which claims that children may universally believe that sentence subjects can be omitted (referred to as 'pro-drop parameter setting') is challenged by a study on Japanese-speaking children who were found to use subjects in early sentences very frequently. It is further challenged by a comparative study of English and Italian children in which children acquiring English (a target language not permitting omission of subjects) were found to provide lexical subjects about twice as often as those acquiring Italian (a target language permitting omission of subjects).

In the acquisition of pragmatics and discourse, cross-linguistic studies have revealed that what is normal in one language can be seen as atypical or deviations from rules in another language. For example, the communicative use of nonverbal behaviours, such as gestures or silence, can carry different meanings in different languages. More discussion can be found in the following section on socialization.

Although English remains the best-researched language with regard to language acquisition, cross-linguistic studies together with bilingual and multilingual studies have been expanding rapidly and have brought us much-needed evidence in our understanding of language development. The following section will bring further dimensions to the discussion of language development: that is, social and cultural dimensions.

2.6   What Is Language Socialization and What Is Its Impact on Language Acquisition and Learning?

Language socialization is the process in which children, adolescents or newer members of communities learn to speak the language in a way appropriate to the community and adapt to the beliefs and norms associated with speaking a/that language. The dual nature of the relationship between language and socialization is well summarized by Ochs and Schieffelin (1995), who state, 'language serves as a means by which to reach the end of socialization and an end of socialization in itself.'

Broadly speaking, language socialization takes place in four different ways:

* *Explicit instruction and learning on what to say and how to say it.* This is an essential part of the process of developing communicative and pragmatic competence. It occurs when parents: urge young children in pre-lingual and early speech development stages to join in games and activities and to take turns in interactions; make efforts to teach children a variety of routines, particularly politeness routines and address terms; and teach children the practice of different speech genres such as narratives, story-telling, negotiating, and so on.
* *Inexplicit instruction and learning on what to say and how to say it.* Parents do not always give direct instructions to children on what to say and how to say it. Instead, they help children to construct and complete utterances (see the previous section on

STUDY ACTIVITY 2.4

Read the following transcript. What are the parents trying to achieve and how?

Jordan: eight years old; Sandra: four years old.
FATHER: Jordan, would you like some more meat?
SANDRA: Meat!
MOTHER: How do you ask, dear?
JORDAN: xxx (inaudible utterance)
SANDRA: Please.

(Source: Blum-Kulka, 1997: 203)

child-directed speech). Parents do not always correct children's speech, but sometimes draw attention to children's language through repetition, extensions and comments, and in doing so they reaffirm the speech practices of the community.

- *Explicit instruction and learning of norms, beliefs and values.* Parents frequently give instructions and comment on what constitutes appropriate behaviours. It is not uncommon to hear people say things such as 'big boys do not cry', 'clever boy', 'you need to share', 'we are a family', and so on. These instructions and comments convey explicit messages about the values and norms of a community.
- *Inexplicit influence.* Language socialization is essentially about making children or newer members of a community aware of, and subsequently conform to, the norms, values and beliefs of a community. Apart from those occasions when attention is drawn directly to values and beliefs and appropriate linguistic behaviours, influence can be exerted in a subtle way. It is frequently reported that gender-appropriate behaviours are encouraged covertly throughout the formative years of children's development. For example, parents tend to use prohibitives such as 'no' and 'don't' more often with boys than girls; they tend to initiate conversation with girls when they are engaged in helping or general activity while they tend to do so with boys during play activities (for a review, see Ely and Gleason, 1995).

Language socialization is pervasive. In terms of contexts, it can take place at home, at school or in the community in which children are growing up or with which they identify. In terms of sources, influence can come from a range of social networks that are significant to children: parents, grandparents, caregivers, siblings, peers, teachers, community members, playgroups, friends, neighbours, clubs, and so on. In terms of channels, language socialization can take place through conversation or any activity or medium that involves the use of language, such as story books, television, newspapers, Internet-mediated communications (Club Penguin, Facebook, etc.), adverts, songs, and so on.

A language socialization perspective offers us an analytical lens to explore the interface between language development and social development. In particular, it helps us understand the interpersonal and cultural dimensions of language acquisition, and, above all, the child's role in the process of language development.

- *Interpersonal dimension.* Language acquisition is more than a process of learning to put linguistic forms together. It entails learning when and how to use linguistic forms to achieve communicative goals in a way appropriate to a community. Children are motivated to accomplish these tasks out of the need to communicate and socialize with people around them.
- *Cultural dimension.* The cultural dimension of language acquisition is manifested in two ways. One is in the form of a cultural account of language acquisition. Learning to speak a language involves conveying and displaying sociocultural knowledge through language use. This emphasis on the cultural reality of language acquisition is very much in line with linguistic relativity. The other takes a cross-cultural comparative approach and argues that different cultures and communities have different values and beliefs as well as norms on the appropriateness of language use. Therefore, although the very idea of language socialization is universal, the content and process of socialization varies across cultures. For example, Ochs (1986) points out that cultures differ in assigning communicative roles to infants: in the Anglo middle class,

infants will be engaged in communicative activities such as greeting, while among the Kaluli of Papua New Guinea, caregivers will talk about or speak for infants but do not talk to them. Considering the process of socialization, we discussed various features associated with child-directed speech in the previous section. But we need to be aware that 'although prompting a child what to say appears wide-spread, expanding children's utterances, using leading questions, announcing activities/events for a child, and using a simplified lexicon and grammar to do so are cross-culturally variable' (Ochs, 1986: 6). Traditional Western Samoan mothers, for example, do not follow these characteristics.

- *The child's role in the process of language development.* Until recently, children were seen as passive recipients who need to be moulded and guided by people and society during language development (see discussion and criticism in Cromdal, 2009; Lanza, 2007). Recent language socialization studies have broadened to include older children, adolescents and adults in bilingual and multilingual settings and have examined a wide range of linguistic resources available and their impact on the ways in which children, adolescents and adults are socialized into a community (for a review, see Baquedano-Lopez and Kattan, 2007; Duranti, Ochs and Schieffelin, 2012). What emerges from these studies is a greater understanding of the dialogic nature of language socialization and the child's role in language development. We now know that language socialization takes place reciprocally and bi-directionally. Children play an active role in social activities and language practices. They can help to shape their own learning experience by their interactive response even if they are at a very early stage of language development. Moreover, language development is a dual process of identity formation. Through learning to use a language appropriately, children, as active and creative social agents, not only construct and negotiate their own identities, but also shape and impact on the identities of those around them (Zhu, 2010).

To sum up, language socialization is inseparable from the study of language acquisition. It brings social development and language development together by viewing them as an integrated process. It foregrounds the drive behind language acquisition, that is, the need to communicate and socialize and to assimilate into the community. It also offers a different perspective on the role of input: child-directed speech is not just about providing support and feedback needed for language development, but about making children aware of the sociocultural appropriateness of their language and social behaviour.

2.7 Summary

First language acquisition study investigates the situation where children learn to speak their mother tongue(s), as opposed to second and additional language learning in which children learn to speak another language in addition to their mother tongue(s). In this chapter, we discussed the facts and problems of first language acquisition and the role of input with evidence from monolingual children and bi/multilingual children acquiring their first language(s), either in normally or atypically developing conditions. We then further looked into the issue of the interaction between innateness and input from a cross-linguistic perspective. Finally, through the concept of language socialization, we examined the interface and interaction between language development and social development.

Study Questions

1. Find a video or audio recording of a child's speech from your own family collection, YouTube, the media or an existing database such as CHILDES. Listen to the child's speech and identify features in the speech that are different from those of adults. They could include the way a word is pronounced, words are put together, or conversation is initiated and organized, or any other aspects of language use.

2. What are the main features of child-directed speech?

3. What role do you think innateness and input play in first language acquisition and why?

4. Compare the unique features of first language acquisition of monolingual children and bi/multilingual children. What are the similarities and differences?

5. How do cross-linguistic studies help us understand language acquisition in general?

6. What is language socialization and what does it tell us about social, cultural and pragmatic development in first language acquisition?

Recommended Reading

Bayley, Robert and Sandra Schecter (eds.). 2003. *Language Socialisation in Bilingual and Multilingual Societies*. Clevedon: Multilingual Matters. This contains a collection of articles investigating language socialization among multilingual children.

De Houwer, Annick. 2009. *Bilingual First Language Acquisition*. Bristol: Multilingual Matters. This explores the issues of how children learn to understand and speak two or more languages.

Lindner, Katrin and Annette Hohenberger (eds.). 2009. Concepts of development, learning and acquisition. A special issue of *Linguistics* 47 (2), 211–511. This provides an up-to-date review of various models and theories of language development.

Lust, Barbara. 2006. *Child Language: Acquisition and Growth*. Cambridge: Cambridge University Press. This provides a comprehensive introduction to child language acquisition in a highly accessible and reader-friendly way.

Schieffelin, Bambi and Elinor Ochs (eds.). 1986. *Language Socialisation across Cultures*. Cambridge: Cambridge University Press. This is a collection of articles exploring how children from different cultural and linguistic backgrounds are both socialized through language and socialized to use language in culturally appropriate ways.

Zhu Hua and Li Wei. 2005. Bi- and multilingual language acquisition. In Martin Ball (ed.), *Clinical Sociolinguistics*, 165–179. Oxford: Blackwell. This provides a succinct review of routes to bilingualism.

There are many excellent guide books on childhood bilingualism (i.e. how children learn to speak bilingually or multilingually). For example, Colin Baker's various editions of *A Parents' and Teachers' Guide to Bilingualism* published by Multilingual Matters.

chapter 3

Second and Additional Language Acquisition

Jean-Marc Dewaele

Chapter Outline

3.1 Introduction
3.2 What Makes Somebody a 'Good Language Learner'?
3.3 Age Effects and the Critical Period Hypothesis
3.4 Previously Learned Languages
3.5 Instructional Environments and Authentic Use
3.6 Conclusion
3.7 Summary

Learning Outcomes

After reading this chapter, you should be able to

- describe the characteristics of the 'good language learner';
- discuss key debates on the contribution of psychological, biographical and educational variables in second and foreign language acquisition (SLA);
- describe the memory systems involved in SLA;
- explain why there is so much variation between learners;
- carry out a small-scale analysis on learners' perceptions.

Applied Linguistics, First Edition. Edited by Li Wei.
© 2014 John Wiley & Sons, Ltd. Published 2014 by John Wiley & Sons, Ltd.

Key Terms

- Affordances
- Age of onset of acquisition
- Aptitude
- Attitudes
- Automaticity
- Critical period
- Emic/etic perspective
- Explicit–implicit learning
- Foreign language anxiety
- Interlanguage
- Investment
- L2 socialization
- L2 user
- Motivation
- Multicompetence
- Naturalistic acquisition
- Personality
- Pragmatic competence
- Sociolinguistic competence
- Ultimate attainment
- Washback effects

3.1   Introduction

The main character of Pascal Mercier's novel *Night Train to Lisbon*, Raimund Gregorius, is an erudite Swiss-German teacher of Latin, ancient Greek and Hebrew with little interest in modern languages (although he speaks French). His former wife, Florence, was a fluent speaker of Spanish, but he has an intense dislike of the language. His attitude to modern languages changes radically one morning as he is on his way to school in driving rain. He encounters a mysterious woman about to jump off a bridge. He manages to distract her and, after an initial conversation in French, he asks her what her mother tongue is. The answer: '*Português*' has the effect of a magical formula on him: 'The *o* she pronounced surprisingly as a *u*; the rising, strangely constrained lightness of the *é* and the soft *sh* at the end came together in a melody that sounded much longer than it really was, and he could have listened to all day long'. The moment marks a milestone in his life and the start of his passion for Portuguese. He buys a bilingual German-Portuguese dictionary, a grammar of Portuguese, a mysterious book in Portuguese, and that same evening, sitting in his favourite chair at home, he listens to the first record of a Portuguese language course and repeats the same sentences again and again 'to narrow the distance between his stolid enunciation and the twinkling voice on the record'. He is exhilarated and experiences a great liberation from self-imposed limitation. His rapid progress in Portuguese also alters his perception of the language: what he had first perceived to be a distant inaccessible land suddenly becomes a 'palace whose door he had just pushed open'. Gregorius abandons his former life and embarks on a journey to Lisbon, where he is forced to quickly develop his basic Portuguese interlanguage in order to 'survive' and to find out more about the author of the amazing second-hand book he bought earlier in his hometown. He manages to overcome his communicative anxiety in Portuguese and becomes both braver and wiser as a person.

   The story of this sudden, intense 'foreign language acquisition' by a mature language learner is an excellent illustration of the complex interaction of affective and instructional variables, as well as sheer coincidence, that determine the rate and success in the learning of a new language.

Study Activity 3.1

Read out a text extract in your L1 for 30 seconds (use a stopwatch), and calculate how many words you have read. Repeat the experiment with a text extract in one of your foreign languages, calculate the number of words read, and compare your speech rate in the L1 and the foreign language. Why do you think the speech rate is lower in the foreign language?

The interlanguage, which can be a second language (L2) or a foreign language (FL) is usually defined as a language acquired after the native language(s) (L1s), typically after the age of three. Proficiency in the interlanguage can range from minimal to highly advanced and can in some cases be indistinguishable from the speech produced by native speakers of a similar socio-economic background.

In Gregorius's case, Swiss-German is the L1, French the L2 or FL (if a language is present in the learner's environment it can be referred to as the L2; if contact with the language is limited to the classroom only, it can be defined as a Foreign Language). Gregorius's extensive knowledge of two dead languages, Latin and ancient Greek, as well as Hebrew, represents a rich linguistic capital on which he can draw in his sudden quest to master Portuguese.

In the present chapter we will ask four questions related to Gregorius's learning of Portuguese by referring to the SLA research literature:

- Does his sudden passion for Portuguese make him a better language learner?
- Does his age have an effect on the speed at which he progresses?
- Does his knowledge of several other languages facilitate his learning?
- Does the learning method (self-tuition with books and records followed by total immersion) have an effect on his progress?

—— 3.2 What Makes Somebody a 'Good Language Learner'?

One of the baffling questions in SLA is why some learners take off from the start while others struggle to get airborne in the foreign language. Equally puzzling is why some learners manage to become indistinguishable from native speakers in the foreign language while others are identified as non-native speakers from the moment they open their mouth, even after spending years in the target language environment. Interestingly, the parable of the tortoise and the hare also applies to SLA: those who make quick progress early on in the learning process are not always the ones who end up being most proficient in the foreign language. Is it possible then to draw a profile of the prototypical 'good language learner'? This has been attempted by a team of Canadian researchers (Naiman, Fröhlich, Stern and Todesco, 1978) who looked at a group of 72 Canadian high school students learning French as an L2. The authors looked at 'good language learners', that is, the participants who scored highest on the Listening Test of French Achievement and an Imitation Test, to see if they had any distinctive psychological profile. Naiman and his colleagues found nothing conclusive, but that has not stopped further research in this direction (Griffiths, 2008). Since the difference between individuals with an apparent talent for learning foreign languages and those who lack such a talent originates in the brain, some researchers have looked to see whether pathological language talent was related to increased growth of particular brain areas (Geschwind and Galaburda, 1985). The findings of such studies are often disappointing, as no clear and straightforward conclusions can be drawn from the observations. The fact that the neurological basis for language talent or ability cannot be identified does not alter the fact that some individuals seem to possess higher levels of 'ability' (both intelligence and language aptitude) and motivation, which together seem to constitute the primary individual difference variables involved in language learning (Gardner, 2006).

The problem in SLA research often lies in the definition and operationalization of concepts. While all of us understand the meaning of terms like 'ability' or 'aptitude', it is really difficult to come up with an empirical way of measuring it. How can a person's language aptitude be captured without reference to that person's actual language performance? Because, if we used that person's linguistic performance to judge her language aptitude, and then linked it to some other linguistic data, we would be stuck in a circular definition where the high aptitude person would be defined as somebody who scores highly on a linguistic test, and these scores would miraculously correlate with other linguistic performance data. In other words, we would be saying something like 'fast runners are people who run fast', instead of measuring some independent biological characteristic like 'people with lower heart rates tend to be good long-distance runners'. Some tests do not attempt to measure performance in the L2 to determine language aptitude, but rely on the L1 to predict success in the L2. The best-known test is the Modern Language Aptitude Test (Carroll and Sapon, 1959), which covers areas such as vocabulary memory, syntax, coding of symbols and sounds in the L1 in order to predict talent at learning an L2.

Some SLA researchers have wondered whether such a thing as 'language aptitude' actually exists and whether it is just a number of cognitive factors making up a composite measure that can be referred to as the learner's overall capacity to master a foreign language (Dörnyei, 2006). Some of these factors constitute the nebulous 'language aptitude', such as working memory (Biedron and Szczepniak, 2012) and pronunciation talent, which has been found to correlate with personality traits such as musicality, empathy, conscientiousness and agreeableness (Nardo and Reiterer, 2009; Xiaochen Hu and Reiterer, 2009).

More recent research has confirmed that it seems just as difficult to find what successful SL learners have in common as it is to establish the psychological profile of millionaires (Dewaele, 2009). Beside some general characteristics, such as a willingness to invest oneself passionately in the task at hand – which is what Gregorius does – no single personality trait has been uncovered that could be a global cause for quick progression and ultimate success in the foreign language. Some traits such as openmindedness and self-confidence have been linked to more frequent use of the L2 and higher levels of self-perceived competence, but the amount of variance they explain is only modest (Ożańska-Ponikwia and Dewaele, 2012).

STUDY ACTIVITY 3.2

List the things Gregorius does to learn Portuguese and compare that list with what you do in your own foreign language classes. Compare the benefits of the two approaches.

Recent research on individual differences in SLA has shown that internal characteristics of the learner do play a role, but only in complex interaction with the (potentially infinite and unpredictable) context (Dewaele, 2012). In other words, SL learners with similar personality profiles may differ enormously in their progress and ultimate attainment because one may have experienced a 'trigger event' that suddenly pushed the learning of the foreign language to the number one priority for that individual, while the other may not have experienced such an event and therefore muddled on at a much slower pace and without too much worry about the ultimate attainment. We could wonder, for example, whether Gregorius's passion for Portuguese would have been as overwhelming if the episode on the bridge had happened 10 years earlier, when he was less dissatisfied with his life. Would the trigger word *'Português'* have had a similar effect on him if it had been uttered in less dramatic circumstances by a bland male character rather than by this mysterious, emotional female, about to jump off the bridge in the driving rain? Metaphorically, one could say that there needs to be a spark at the start of a potential learning process. Depending on the terrain and the climatic circumstances, the spark may fail to light any fire, it may also cause some smouldering, or just light a little campfire, or, in extreme cases, it could cause a raging firestorm. It is hard to predict whether a spark will catch, or not. A foreign language teacher could thus be seen as the person who provides the initial spark, and who is responsible for nurturing the fire in the heart of the learners. Arnold (2011) has pointed out that positive affect is the fuel for the learning process, while negative affect is like cold water dousing the emerging flames.

3.2.1   Multicompetence

Learners who develop a sudden passion for a foreign language do not just exist in novels. Kinginger has described the journey of such a language learner, Alice, a mature American student of working-class origin at Penn State, whose desire to learn French and live in France was a bid for access to a life of cultured refinement and a way out of extreme personal and financial difficulties (Kinginger, 2004). Kinginger takes the view that identity is a site of struggle as learners attempt to map images of self onto the resources for self-expression made available to them as study abroad participants. Alice dreamed of becoming fluent in French and meeting refined, interesting, cultured people who would, in turn, be interested in her (Kinginger, 2004). Alice's motivation was thus related to an idealized, imagined community of practice (Norton, 2001). Alice's study abroad programme proved disappointing, the gap between the imagined and the real French community of practice being too large. On her return, Alice stopped attending French classes. Yet, the conversations with French friends had made her much more politically aware and critical of US policy. So, although from a linguistic point of view Alice's stay abroad could not be labelled a great success, it was a beneficial experience for her. Kinginger describes Alice's language learning journey as 'a bid to break free of the confining circumstances of a peripatetic, working-class childhood and to become a person she can admire' (2004: 240). The parallel with our fictional Gregorius is striking. It also shows that the learning of a new language can have a dramatic impact on learners' perception of the world and of themselves. Cook (2002) argues that the mind of L2 users differs from monolingual speakers not only by the presence of a second language, but by the emergence of a unique multicompetence that is more than the sum of two monocompetences: 'Acquiring another language alters the L2 user's mind in ways that go beyond the actual knowledge of language itself' (2002: 7). Multicompetence affects the cognitive representation of grammatical and lexical categories of bilinguals with languages that have very different categories (Cook and Bassetti, 2010). Recent socio-psychological studies have confirmed that the knowledge and active use of several languages is linked to a different psychological profile. Young London teenagers knowing more languages obtained higher scores on the personality dimensions Openmindedness and Cultural Empathy, and lower scores on Emotional Stability (Dewaele and Van Oudenhoven, 2009). In a follow-up study, Israelis with advanced knowledge of several languages, which they used frequently, were found to score higher on Social Initiative, Openmindedness and Cultural Empathy compared with Israelis knowing fewer languages – and using them less frequently (Dewaele and Stavans, 2012). In other words, multicompetent multilinguals seem more aware and appreciative of the diversity in the world, able to consider it through the prism of their different languages and cultures, but – in some cases – also more nervous.

Gregorius's revulsion at Spanish illustrates the opposite attitude towards a foreign language. Real-life examples of such extreme negative attitudes are equally abundant. Richard Watson, an American academic, could read French but not speak it. After an invitation to give a paper at a conference in Paris, he decided it was time to learn to speak French. However, despite six months of conversation classes, his progress was so limited that the conference presentation turned out disastrously. He mentions the fact that French sounded 'syrupy' and 'effeminate' and a language that 'Real Men' would not speak (Pavlenko, 2005), hence his lack of enthusiasm for learning French.

3.2.2 Motivation

At the heart of the SLA process thus lies an affective factor, which has been variously described as 'motivation' (Dörnyei, 2005; Dörnyei and Ushioda, 2009; Gardner, 1985; Ushioda and Dörnyei, 2012) or 'emotional investment' (Kinginger, 2008; Norton, 2001).

Obviously, this affective factor does not emerge out of nothing; it can grow in any direction depending on how the individual with his/her unique personality and preferences reacts to the pedagogical, social, historical, political and cultural environment. Individual contexts are inextricably linked to social contexts, that is, the intergroup climate in which interlocutors evolve and which has a stable, long-term influence on the learner (e.g. intergroup relations, gender, social class) (MacIntyre et al., 1998). The importance of the global context for SLA can be illustrated through a few simple examples. Students from countries like France, Poland, Hungary or China realize that proficiency in at least one foreign language (typically English) will boost their chances in the job market because the rest of the world does not speak their language. In officially multilingual countries like Switzerland, Belgium or Canada, workers are typically expected to master at least two of the national languages. Despite tensions between the linguistic groups, students understand that they cannot remain monolingual if they want a well-paid job. Mastery of the second official language but also the knowledge of English, and maybe a fourth or fifth language, increases their chances of finding a good job. The motivation to acquire a foreign language for some benefit has been called 'instrumental', distinguishing it from integrativeness, that is, 'an openness to the target language (TL) group and other groups in general linked to one's sense of ethnic identity' (Gardner, 2006: 236). Gardner argued that attitudes and motivation can be measured quantitatively and in 1985 he published the Attitude Motivation Test Battery (AMTB), which presents a list of statements relating to possible reasons why a participant wants to learn a second language ('Studying the L2 can be important for me because it will allow me to travel to L2 areas; (…) it will allow me to learn about myself; (…) it will help me find a better job; (…) it will allow me to appreciate L2 minority problems'). The participant is expected to tick his/her agreement with the statement on a five-point Likert scale. These items are linked to 11 scales (integrative orientation, attitudes towards the target group, interest in foreign languages, teacher evaluation, course evaluation, motivational intensity, desire to learn the language, attitudes towards learning the language, language class anxiety, language use anxiety and instrumental orientation). These scales form the basis of five constructs, namely, integrativeness, attitudes towards the learning situation, motivation, language anxiety and instrumentality (Gardner, 2006). Once the data have been collected, the researchers calculate the score of each participant on the different scales, and hence provide a unique quantitative motivational profile of that person. These scores will then be used as independent variables – in other words, complex statistical analysis will be used to see whether these independent variables are significantly linked to the dependent variables, which could be any performance measure in the L2. A typical finding is that higher levels of motivation and lower levels of language anxiety are linked to better performance in the L2.

3.2.3 Motivation as a Dynamic System

Gardner's model has been criticized for being too static. Indeed, motivation levels have been shown to vary constantly, even in the course of the language class, hence the view that motivation is a 'dynamic system that displays continuous fluctuation, going through certain ebbs and flows' (Dörnyei, 2006: 51). Dörnyei has argued that a distinction needs to be made between different levels of motivational processes, some of which are linked to the enduring social context (e.g. the integrative motive) while others are more localized, such as the motivation to engage in effortful, task-related behaviour within a situation (Dörnyei, 2005).

Dörnyei (2006) has also wondered whether it made sense to talk about 'integrative motivation' outside bilingual countries, in other words in contexts without any realistic opportunity for direct integration. He has therefore suggested abandoning the term 'integrative' and focusing more on the identification aspects and on the learner's

STUDY ACTIVITY 3.3

Design your very own ideal foreign language learning environment. This may include special furniture for the classroom.

'L2 Motivational Self System' (Dörnyei, 2006; Dörnyei and Ushioda, 2009; Ushioda and Dörnyei, 2012). The central idea is the equation of the traditional 'integrative motivation' with the 'Ideal L2 Self'. The latter refers to the L2-specific facet of a learner's 'ideal self', namely, 'the representation of all the attributes that a learner would like to possess (e.g. hopes, aspirations, desires): If one's ideal self is associated with the mastery of an L2, that is, if the person that we would like to become is proficient in the L2, he/she can be described – using Gardner's terminology – as having an "integrative" disposition' (2006: 53). Gregorius's Ideal L2 Self would probably be a fluent speaker and reader of Portuguese, bolder and emancipated, wiser and enlightened, liberated from the shackles and prejudices of his former self.

3.2.4   Epistemological Choices

Any SLA researcher who wishes to tackle the thorny question about the characteristics of the 'good language learner' will have to make some difficult epistemological choices. We have seen that one way to look at it is through an etic, almost clinical perspective, where the researcher develops a research instrument to gather quantitative data from learners in order to uncover some universal relationship between some social psychological factor and a dependent variable. The validity and reliability of the research will be judged by the size of the sample of learners, the internal consistency of the questionnaire and the appropriate use of statistical analysis.

The advantages of such an approach in attitude and motivation research are obvious: it is 'systematic, rigorous, focused, and tightly controlled, involving precise measurement and producing reliable and replicable data' (Dörnyei, 2007: 34).

However, such an etic, quantitative, approach has one severe limitation, namely, its limited general exploratory capacity. A participant is forced to conform to the format of the questionnaire, and is thus unable to attract the researchers' attention to potentially relevant information that could help the researchers understand the bigger picture (Dörnyei, 2007). An emic approach, where the opinion of participants is heard, and which is typically based on qualitative methods, through the study of diaries and interviews, broadens the repertoire of possible interpretations and permits longitudinal examination of dynamic phenomena. Indeed, if Gregorius had filled out Gardner's questionnaire before and after the encounter on the bridge, it would have given an incomplete understanding of his attitude towards modern languages and his sudden motivation to study Portuguese. Alice's score on motivation scales after her stay in France would have been radically different from that on departure (cf. Kinginger, 2004). In other words, motivation is not stable in nature and although some aspects can be measured objectively, their value is relatively limited. There is growing agreement among SLA researchers that learners are more than mere bunches of variables stripped of intentionality and individuality (Barcelos, Kalaja and Menezes, 2008; Dörnyei and Ushioda, 2009; Lantolf and Pavlenko, 2001).

3.2.5 Summary

We set out with the story of Gregorius and his acquisition of Portuguese, and wondered whether he possesses some inherent characteristics that make him a 'good language learner'. Looking at the SLA research we found that the very term 'good language learner' is problematic. Etic – quantitative research based on test results and questionnaires, involving large samples, typically fails to uncover the complete profile of the good language learner. High levels of motivation and positive attitudes towards the L2 are clearly linked to faster acquisition and maybe to ultimate attainment, but as recent research shows, motivation levels are dynamic and other factors may cancel out the positive motivation. Emic – qualitative SLA researchers focused in great detail on cases of individual learners, following them over a period of time and considering their emotional investment in the learning of the new language. Here again, the variability in level of investment over time is striking. Some life events trigger high levels of commitment; other events might cancel them out completely. Maybe the category 'good language learner' is the fruit of wishful thinking on the part of L2 teachers and researchers. Some learners can be 'good' at certain times, at certain confluences of life events, when the spark falls on fertile ground. It is a little bit like falling in love, impossible to predict, but when it happens, it sweeps away all former barriers and gives the individual a sense of newfound freedom and exhilaration.

————— 3.3 Age Effects and the Critical Period Hypothesis

Could the fact that our fictional Gregorius is middle-aged have had an effect on the rate at which he acquires Portuguese and the level of proficiency he attains? Would he have progressed faster and become more proficient if he had started as a teenager, a pre-teen or as a child? The question is purely theoretical since it is impossible to test this question experimentally. Ideally, researchers would study Gregorius's development in Portuguese at a very young starting age before 'resetting' him (i.e. magically erasing all traces of knowledge of Portuguese), and have him start again when he was slightly older to see whether his development would be faster and would reach a higher level. Such a method, which belongs to science fiction rather than true science, would allow researchers to find whether there is such a thing as a 'critical period' (CP), defined as the age beyond which it becomes difficult to fully acquire a language.

The core idea of the CP is that 'automatic acquisition from mere exposure' seems to disappear after a certain age (Lenneberg, 1967: 176). It does not apply to rate of acquisition but rather to end-state attainment in grammar and pronunciation.

3.3.1 Research on the CPH

The seminal works on the Critical Period Hypothesis (CPH) date from the 1980s. Younger starters (i.e. with a lower age of onset of acquisition – AoA) obtained higher scores on grammaticality judgement tasks (Johnson and Newport, 1989). Studies on immigrants in the US showed a significant decline in scores on English tests with increasing AoA. Separate analyses on the groups of younger and older arrivals revealed a very strong negative correlation between AoA and English proficiency in the young group (AoA under 16) but a non-significant negative relationship emerged in the group of late arrivals (Johnson and Newport, 1989). In other words, the differences in test scores of 18-year-old starters and 50-year-old starters were much smaller than the differences between the five-year-old starters and the 12-year-old starters. The Johnson and Newport (1989) study was replicated by DeKeyser (2000) with a sample of Hungarian-speaking immigrants who had resided for at least 10 years in the US. He found a strong negative correlation between AoA and score on the grammaticality judgement test. DeKeyser argues that this is a clear indication that a low AoA confers an absolute advantage to that person. He argues that somewhere between the ages of 6 and 17, learners lose the 'mental equipment required for the implicit induction of the abstract patterns underlying a human language, and the critical period really deserves its name' (DeKeyser, 2000: 518). DeKeyser's views are not shared by all, and many researchers claim to have reported counter-evidence to the CPH. The counter-evidence comes from learners who had demonstrably attained native-like proficiency in the foreign language despite having begun exposure well after the closure of the hypothesized CP (Birdsong, 2009). Abrahamsson and Hyltenstam (2008) studied near-native adult L2 speakers of Swedish (who could pass for Swedish native speakers). The authors argue that these exceptionally talented language learners had an unusual ability to compensate for maturational effects 'and, consequently, that their nativelikeness per se does not constitute a reason to reject the critical period hypothesis' (2008: 481). Moreover, when asked to complete 'a battery of 10 highly complex, cognitively demanding tasks and detailed measurements of linguistic performance, representation, and processing, none of the late learners performed within the native-speaker range' (Abrahamsson and Hyltenstam, 2009: 249).

3.3.2 Possible Neurobiological Causes for Age Effects

Paradis (2004) has suggested that age effects are caused by the decline of procedural memory for late L2 learners (i.e. a more limited capacity to learn implicitly), which forces these learners to rely on explicit learning instead. Paradis argues that the upper age limit varies with respect to the component of the implicit language system that is being acquired through exposure to language interaction. Prosody precedes phonology, which is then followed by morphology and syntax. Since the learning of vocabulary is subserved by declarative (explicit) memory, it is not susceptible to the age effects.

3.3.3 CPH and Learning Context

Some researchers have pointed out that the effect of AoA varies according to the learning context (Muñoz, 2008). While the AoA effect seems quite robust in *naturalistic* foreign language acquisition, that is, when the learner is immersed in the foreign language environment, it is often much weaker in *formal* foreign language acquisition, that is, when the learner's only foreign language input comes through classroom instruction. Muñoz (2008) argues that the amount and quality of the input have a significant bearing on the effects that AoA has on foreign language learning. She claims that research findings from naturalistic learning contexts, typically immigrants with a wide age range and no knowledge of the language of the host country where the younger ones outperform the older immigrants, have been hastily generalized to formal learning contexts (Muñoz, 2008).

A related argument is that the fact that it is harder for anyone acquiring an L2 after about the age of 12 to speak the L2 without a foreign accent does not automatically imply that foreign language instruction should be initiated in childhood. Indeed, a large-scale project of AoA in formal foreign language teaching in Catalonia has revealed that earlier exposure (ages eight to nine) to English L3 in a classroom did not result in better performance but that length of exposure to English had a positive effect on performance (Muñoz, 2006). A group of learners who started English at age 11 and a third group who started at age 14 were found to progress more quickly than early learners but, after a similar number of hours of exposure, the differences between the groups were limited, with older starters having a slight advantage.

3.3.4 Summary

Most researchers agree that in SLA there are 'general age factors', where younger starters in L2 naturalistic contexts seem to outperform older starters, but there is disagreement on the existence of cut-off points (i.e. the term 'critical'), as some exceptional L2 learners seem to have been able to attain native-like levels of performance. Age effects seem to be much weaker in classroom L2 learning contexts. It has been pointed out that CP is not the only maturational effect to play a role as individuals go through gradual physical and psychological changes of all kinds all through their life (DeKeyser and Larson-Hall, 2005). These changes and other confounding variables such as individual aptitude, ability, learning context (Birdsong, 2009) are superimposed on the CP phenomenon and further complicate the analysis.

Coming back to Gregorius, we could wonder whether he might have made quicker progress and attained a higher level of proficiency in Portuguese if he had been much younger. The question is purely hypothetical of course. If he had moved to Lisbon as a child, he would probably have become indistinguishable from the native speakers around him. Defenders of the CP hypothesis would have pointed to his low AoA to explain his success. Sceptics of the CP hypothesis would have underlined the fact that his massive exposure to the L2 would have guaranteed native-like proficiency.

We could finally wonder whether it would have mattered to Gregorius himself. As an L2 user, his aim was to communicate freely with Portuguese interlocutors, but that did not entail a loss of his complex identity as a Swiss-German language teacher. He did not have to be indistinguishable from the native speakers of Portuguese in order to fulfil his dream. Similarly, L2 learners strive to become proficient in the target language but unless they need to blend in completely in the L2 community, there is no need for them to totally conform to native-speaker behaviour.

3.4   Previously Learned Languages

Does prior language knowledge or prior language learning make a difference in additional foreign language learning? Referring back to our fictional language learner, Gregorius, whose knowledge of Latin, ancient Greek and Hebrew is unsurpassed, and who has Swiss-German as a first and French as a second language, we can imagine that the Latin and French would be particularly helpful in the learning of Portuguese.

3.4.1   Stepping Stones

Research has shown that a high level of proficiency in the first language is already an advantage in the learning of a second language (this is Cummins's Developmental Interdependence hypothesis). Cummins (1979) argued that learners must reach a first threshold level in order to avoid the cognitive disadvantages associated with bilingualism and must reach the second level to enjoy the benefits of improved cognitive functioning. Cummins was specifically talking about immigrant children in Anglophone Canada, for whom English was an L2.

Some researchers have expanded the scope of the hypothesis to multilinguals. Indeed, the Developmental Interdependence hypothesis could also predict that multilingual learners may transfer the skills developed in the L1 or in any other language to another foreign language (Lasagabaster, 1998). A learner of an L4 with a high level of competence attained in the L1, L2 and L3 is more likely to attain a high level of competence in the L4 than somebody with an L1 and a basic knowledge of an L2. The former learner may acquire the L4 more quickly and maybe follow a different route of acquisition.

Studies with multilingual learners generally establish a positive association between bilingualism and additional foreign language achievement (De Angelis 2007; Rivers and Golonka, 2009; Le Pichon *et al.*, 2009), but several researchers have also pointed out that positive effects tend to emerge only in specific learning contexts. Differences between bi/ multilinguals and monolingual learners of a third language are only significant if the bilinguals have acquired literacy skills in both their languages (Cenoz, 2003). Swain *et al.* (1990) looked at precisely this question. The researchers looked at children in an English/ French bilingual immersion programme in Canada. Some of these children spoke a heritage language at home but did not have literacy skills in that language, while the heritage speakers who had also acquired literacy skills by attending heritage language programmes

---

STUDY ACTIVITY 3.4

Write your own linguistic autobiography, including your contacts with various dialects, sociolects and languages, the ups and down of your language learning and your hopes for the future.

---

outperformed the first group in tests measuring their writing, reading, speaking and listening skills in French L3. The authors found that bilingualism has a positive effect on third language learning, but only when coupled with the acquisition of literacy skills.

The knowledge of more languages has been linked to a capacity for grasping the grammar faster in a new language by applying a wider variety of learning strategies (Kemp, 2007), a stronger inclination to pursue the study of foreign languages (Dewaele and Thirtle, 2009) and more metalinguistic awareness and cross-linguistic awareness (Jessner, 2006).

3.4.2   Non-Linguistic Effects

Bilingual children have been found to outperform their monolingual peers on nonverbal control tasks such as the 'Simon task' (Bialystok, Craik and Luk, 2012). The bilinguals' superior performance has been linked to extensive practice with two active languages, which constantly requires the activation of one language and the inhibition of the other language, and switching between the languages (Bialystok *et al.*, 2012). As a consequence, bilingual children are better able to ignore irrelevant stimuli. More recent research has found that the effect extends to trilingual children (Poarch and Van Hell, 2012).

The positive effect of knowing more languages has been more consistent in the area of affective factors. The knowledge of more languages has been linked to an increased Cognitive Empathy and Tolerance of Ambiguity (Dewaele and Li Wei, 2012, 2013). Adults knowing more languages have been found to suffer less from foreign language anxiety than adults knowing fewer (typically two) languages (Dewaele, Petrides and Furnham, 2008). One possible explanation for this phenomenon is that trilinguals and quadrilinguals have become better communicators as a result of their multilingualism and that their self-confidence, as well as their self-perceived communicative competence, has grown as a result. Knowing more languages may give the multilinguals a little bit more confidence in their ability to avoid linguistic icebergs (Dewaele *et al.*, 2008).

The effect of the knowledge of more languages in additional language learning has recently been considered in the light of the theory of affordances. Heft (2001) is often quoted for his excellent metaphor for affordances:

> An affordance is the perceived functional significance of an object, event, or place for an individual. For example, a firm, obstacle-free ground surface is perceivable as a surface on which one can walk. In contrast, a boggy surface or a surface cluttered with obstacles (e.g. a boulder field) is typically perceived as impeding walking.
>
> (Heft, 2001: 123)

Multilingual language learners and users not only have larger overall linguistic repertoires, but also more of such potential affordances available to them than monolingual language users (Singleton and Aronin, 2007). This observation is linked to that of Ringbom (2007), who observes that cross-linguistic and intralinguistic knowledge can be highly relevant when learning a new language. Just how relevant such prior linguistic knowledge is depends on the proximity of the target language and any languages known: 'If you learn a language closely related to your L1, prior knowledge will be consistently useful, but if the languages are very distant, not much prior knowledge is relevant' (2007: 1).

Developing this idea about the effect of typological proximity and affordances, and the overall effect of multilingualism (and possible superior sociocognitive fitness), Dewaele (2010) tried to determine the effect of the knowledge of more languages in general, and, more specifically, languages belonging to the same language family as the target language (in this case French L2, L3 or L4), on self-perceived communicative competence and communicative anxiety in that language. Both affordances and, to a lesser degree, multilingualism were found to have a significant effect on the dependent variables. Affordances had the strongest effect on French L2 and L3, for which participants reported medium to advanced levels of proficiency, but it had no effect on French L4, for which participants reported extremely low levels of proficiency. A possible explanation for this difference between L2/L3 and L4 is the capacity to combine intralinguistic reflection with linguistic knowledge of other Romance languages, to compensate for gaps in the knowledge of French. However, if the level of French is too low (L4), the basis is too weak to benefit from a transfer of linguistic knowledge from other Romance languages. Affordances could thus be seen as a crutch for some learners, providing extra support for those with one functioning leg, but less useful for those without legs.

Recently, researchers have investigated whether it is multilingualism per se or rather the specific experience of learning a new language that leads to increased metacommunicative awareness (Le Pichon, de Swart, Vorstman and van den Bergh, 2009). The researchers suggest that children with previous language learning experience are more expert than bilingual children (who had not yet learned a foreign language through classroom instruction) in understanding, treating and solving a communication problem in a situation of communication in which interlocutors did not share the same languages.

3.4.3   Washback Effects

Biliteracy is not the only factor facilitating foreign language acquisition. Having a third language in the school curriculum can enhance the achievement in the second language. Griessler (2001) compared German L1 students studying in three different Austrian schools. The first group of students went to an English immersion school, the second group went to a school where English was part of the curriculum and where French was also taught early on in the programme, and the third group attended a regular Austrian secondary school where English was the only foreign language taught. Unsurprisingly, the first group of students scored highest on all measures of English proficiency. The second group of students outperformed the third group and, since the only difference between these two groups was the presence of French in the curriculum, Griessler concluded that French had boosted the second group's proficiency in English. Berthele and Lambelet (2009) found that highly proficient multilingual learners of a new unknown target language belonging to the same family as their L1 and L2 were particularly good at interlingual inferencing, possibly because of more 'perceptive tolerance' (i.e. an increased sensitivity to possible and potential correspondences between two or more related systems).

3.4.4   Cross-linguistic Influences

The knowledge of other languages – not necessarily the L1 – is also a source of cross-linguistic influences in the target language (De Angelis, 2007; De Angelis and Dewaele, 2011; Jarvis and Pavlenko, 2008). Recent research has focused on the identification of factors that affect L2 learners' reliance on previously learned languages and constrain the type and amount of influence on the target language. Among the most important factors, De Angelis (2007) lists language distance, target language proficiency and source language proficiency, recency of use, length of residence and exposure to a non-native language environment, order of acquisition, and formality of context.

3.4.5 Summary

To conclude, the learning of a third or an additional foreign language seems to be facilitated by a number of factors related to the linguistic history of the learners. Learners who have already mastered different languages seem to benefit from general cognitive advantages, such as the ability to ignore irrelevant information, a skill that might derive from the multilingual learner's ability to activate and inhibit different languages. Metaphorically, one could say that multilingual learners possess a bigger toolset that allows them to build the linguistic system of the new language more quickly and more efficiently. Learning typologically related languages also offers learners stronger affordances; in other words, they have the capacity to tackle a problem in the target language through interlinguistic comparisons and reflection. Literacy in a heritage home language seems to make a positive difference, as well as the knowledge of more languages, and especially languages belonging to the same linguistic family. The experience of learning languages in a formal context seems to be an asset in additional foreign language learning. Indeed, these experienced learners deploy a wider range of learning strategies. It is not just the learning of the additional language that is facilitated but also the authentic use of that language. Multilinguals and experienced language learners seem to have a better strategic competence in tackling communication problems, and they also have more metalinguistic and metacommunicative competence. Additional language learners who know several languages already also feel more confident about their communicative abilities and experience less communicative anxiety in their different languages.

—————— 3.5 Instructional Environments and Authentic Use

Gregorius, Mercier's fictional foreign language learner, creates his own unique instructional environment to acquire Portuguese. He starts with self-study, using a grammar, a bilingual dictionary and a course book with accompanying audio material. He studies grammar rules, memorizes word lists and imitates the voice of the speaker on the record. After having moved to Lisbon to continue his quest to find out more about the mysterious author whose book he is deciphering, his instructional environment changes completely. The language comes to life and becomes a tool for communication rather than an abstract object of study. With the language being used in its original environment (Lisbon), with its inhabitants, comes additional information on cultural practices, on the history of the place and the people, on food, architecture and climate. The amount of information to take in overwhelms Gregorius at some point and he locks himself in his hotel room, wondering whether he should return to Bern and abandon his quest into unfamiliar territory.

3.5.1 Types of Instructional Environment

SLA researchers have always been interested in the effect of different types of instructional environment, that is, 'a setting in which a content area or skill is organized, presented, and explained to the learner' (Pica, 2009: 473). The L2 can be the content or skill that is instructed as well as the medium through which the instruction is offered. The samples of L2 speech and text that learners access through the instructional environment allow them to develop their interlanguage system, and to modify and reconfigure it (Pica, 2009). Housen *et al.* (2011) showed that learners studying a target language that is widely used outside the language classroom (a typical L2 context) outperform learners in contexts where the target language is less prominent outside school (a typical FL context).

In their overview of studies that considered the effects of instruction, De Graaff and Housen (2009) concluded that both instructed and naturalistic (non-instructed) learners follow the same acquisition orders. Instruction propels learners faster along the natural route of development compared with non-instructed learners. Instructed learners ultimately reach higher levels of grammatical accuracy than non-instructed learners though they are not necessarily more fluent.

A crucial distinction is made between an explicit and an implicit approach to teaching languages. In the explicit approach, accuracy and grammatical knowledge are given priority. The linguistic input is structurally graded and simplified. Learners' attention is drawn to language form, where 'form' stands for grammatical structures, lexical items, phonological features and even sociolinguistic and pragmatic features of language (Housen and Pierrard, 2005). This approach is also characterized by frequent explicit correction and recasts. Learners are thus encouraged to speak or write the second language correctly from the beginning.

In contrast, the implicit approach is based on incidental, inductive learning through communicative interaction between teacher and learners. Classroom environment and activities should be meaningful and relevant, ideally mimicking real life. The teacher focuses on communication and avoids interrupting learners' output to correct them. Grammar is only discussed to disambiguate meaning in interactions. Learners are therefore encouraged to induce rules from the context in which the language is used and create their own hypotheses. The theoretical basis for this approach is Krashen's (1982) Input Hypothesis according to which the L2 is acquired through exposure to 'comprehensible input', in other words, language the learners can understand but that is slightly ahead of their current state of grammatical knowledge. The implicit teaching approach privileges meaning over form. Learners are encouraged to communicate quickly and efficiently without worrying too much about morphological and syntactical errors. Comprehensible input is mostly generated by learners themselves. As a consequence, linguistic hypotheses are built on the basis of their own interlanguage utterances. Successful communication coupled with a lack of corrective feedback may lead learners to falsely believe that their speech is grammatically accurate (Lightbown and Spada, 1994). Subsequently, the lack of corrective feedback risks reinforcing learners' conviction of the accuracy of their speech and may lead to fossilization (i.e. a cessation of development) of their interlanguage (Han, 2009).

The effect of implicit versus explicit teaching on the development of interlanguages is the topic of SLA research that has crucial implications for foreign language teaching. It has thus fuelled rich research. Several experimental studies which have investigated the effectiveness of L2 learning under explicit and implicit conditions have shown an advantage for explicit learning (DeKeyser, 1995; Ellis, 2004).

A comparative study of the effectiveness of Focus on Form (i.e. the communicative implicit approach with incidental focus on form) versus Focus on Forms (i.e. the more traditional explicit approach) on learning two grammatical structures, showed that the more traditional approach to language teaching has a significantly more positive effect on students learning the two grammatical structures than does the communicative approach (Sheen, 2005).

A study on the effect of explicit grammar instruction on complexity and accuracy in the L2 revealed that explicit instruction has a beneficial effect on learners' mastery of grammatical structures when used productively and that this beneficial effect is even more observable in unplanned speech (Housen, Pierrard and Van Daele, 2005). This implies that explicit instruction may, in fact, promote not only explicit but also implicit knowledge. The authors thus suggest that by directing the learners' attention towards previously discrete items it increases awareness and noticing.

In a large meta-analysis of SLA studies that considered four types of instructional environment, Norris and Ortega (2001) found that explicit, form-focused instructional environments were linked to greater accuracy and development in the L2 compared with the environment that relied on implicit approaches. Norris and Ortega (2001) did point out that the superiority of the explicit, form-focused approach could have been the consequence of the research design. Many of the studies that considered the effects of explicit, form-focused approaches had short-term treatments and compared two discrete points in the development of the interlanguage. Progress in explicit knowledge is more likely in this context than progress in implicit knowledge, which increases over longer time-spans.

3.5.2   The Nature of Learners' Linguistic Knowledge

A rich field of cognitively oriented SLA research has focused on the nature of the learners' linguistic knowledge. Does explicit instruction lead to explicit knowledge? In other words, knowledge that a person knows that they know, and which they can use intentionally to control actions, including verbal report (Williams, 2009). The mirror question is whether implicit learning leads to implicit knowledge. Implicit knowledge is commonly defined as the knowledge that a person has without knowing that they have it (Williams, 2009) and which is deployed automatically. Neurolinguists have argued that explicit and implicit knowledge are supported by different brain regions. Paradis (2004) distinguishes implicit (or procedural) knowledge, such as motor skills (cycling, walking) or a first language, which is rooted in the frontal and basal ganglia, and explicit (or declarative) knowledge, which is rooted in the medial and lateral temporal lobe structures. Researchers have pointed out that it is extremely difficult to operationalize implicit knowledge as it relies on assessment of subjective mental states, namely, measurements of awareness (Williams, 2009). Greater speed may point to automaticity and implicit knowledge, but some researchers have shown that explicit knowledge can also be accessed very quickly and result in very fluent speech (Segalowitz, 2003).

Another question concerns the link between implicit and explicit knowledge. Krashen (1981) argued that what had been learned could not become part of the

STUDY ACTIVITY 3.5

Compare the following one-minute extracts of French interlanguage by Danny and Dirk (Dutch L1 speakers). Focus on accuracy and fluency.

DANNY: Euh, alors je m'appelle Danny. J'habite à Schelle. C'est près d'Anvers. Je suis euh, j'ai dix-neuf ans. J'ai étudié des sciences biologiques. C'est ma première candidature ici euh. J'ai ni de soeurs ni de frères. J'ai un chien et euh j'avais un chat. Euh, il est mort, c'est tout.

INTERVIEWER: Et qu'est-ce que tu voulais faire?

DANNY: Ah, j'ai toujours eu envie d'aller dans les politiques. Mais on m'a dit à la maison c'est plus mieux que vous choisirez une direction dans l'Athénée qui est, laquelle est difficile parce que vous avez une base. Et là vous pouvez choisir si vous changez, parce que quand j'étais dans la troisième euh j'avais envie de venir vétérinaire.

DIRK: Je suis Dirk. J'habite Wezembeek Oppem et j'étudie ingénieur commercial, euh à l'ULB. Et je l'ai fait parce que je crois que dans l'économie il y a du futur, il y a de l'avenir dedans.

INTERVIEWER: Qu'est-ce qu'il y a qui te plaît, qu'est-ce qu'il y a qui te plaît moins?

DIRK: C'est pas une question de ce qui me plaît pas, c'est une question de si je sais suivre ou non hein. Euh, quand je, j'ai choisi j'ai euh pris cette direction parce que c'est une direction qui demandait une connaissance très polyvalent. Et je n'étais pas trop bien en maths ou en autres matières. Alors j'ai pris cela. Le programme est plutôt bien, mais c'est beaucoup, très beaucoup. Ça exige presque tout mon temps.

INTERVIEWER: Tu as des hobbies?

DIRK: De la guitare classique et la percussion, du sport, les scouts. J'ai tout dû euh laisser tomber.

acquired system. This is known as the non-interface theory and has been strongly criticized. The main objection is one of falsifiability, as Krashen did not provide evidence that (explicit) learning and (implicit) acquisition are separate systems. Other researchers have defended the view that explicit knowledge can become implicit, and vice versa, through practice (DeKeyser, 1997; Sharwood Smith, 1994). The basic idea is that in learning a sport or a foreign language, one progresses from knowledge *that* (explicit) related to some skill or behaviour to knowledge *how* (implicit), which becomes increasingly automatized (DeKeyser, 1997). This is the so-called strong interface position. The weak interface position, on the other hand, maintains that explicit knowledge serves as a facilitator of implicit knowledge by helping learners to attend to linguistic features in the input. Both types of knowledge are 'dissociable but cooperative' (Ellis, 2005: 305). This is illustrated by walking but also by speaking a native language; both happen automatically until an unexpected obstacle arises and explicit knowledge is needed to solve the problem.

3.5.3 The Transition From L2 Learner to L2 User

L2 learners who acquire their L2 through formal instruction tend to be monostylistic at first, choosing a speech style in the middle of the continuum, both for oral and written production. As a result they sound too formal when speaking and too informal when writing. As they become L2 users, they gradually start to explore both the more formal and the more informal ends of the continuum (Dewaele, 2007). L2 learners in these early stages typically use one sociolinguistic variant (generally the formal one) categorically. The monostylistic L2 repertoire has been linked to restricted access to sufficiently diverse linguistic input. Instructed L2 learners are mainly exposed to formal speech styles from their teachers and to written material. Once L2 learners become L2 users they start to pick up the linguistic characteristics and variation patterns of L1 users of their chosen target language. At that point alternation between two sociolinguistic or pragmatic variants starts to emerge. The variants can be phonological, such as the glottal stop in English; they can be morphosyntactic variants, such as the omission of the preverbal particle 'ne' in French negations or the choice of pronouns of address in languages where speakers have a choice; they can also be syntactic variants, such as particular word orders in French interrogative sentences (i.e. with or without subject–verb inversion). At first the choices of learners are non-systematic, oscillating between overuse or underuse of particular variants compared with native speaker norms (Regan, Howard and Lemée, 2009). However, once L2 users engage in intense contact with members of that speech community, they develop sociolinguistic and pragmatic competence and may start to conform to native speaker variation patterns (Howard, Mougeon and Dewaele, 2013; Preston and Bayley, 2009). L2 users become able to identify and reproduce gender-specific, social or generational speech patterns used by groups of native speakers with whom they may wish to identify.

However, L2 users may also consciously decide not to adopt certain variation patterns from the target language community if they judge them to be in conflict with their own ideological and cultural beliefs or sense of self. They might also refrain from using these variants (swearwords for example) if they feel that these words signal 'in-group' membership and that their use might have unwanted illocutionary effects given the fact that their foreign accent marks them out as not belonging to that in-group (Dewaele, 2008).

Examples of the growth of sociolinguistic, sociocultural and pragmatic competence are presented in Kinginger's (2004, 2008) and Kinginger and Blattner's (2008) comprehensive qualitative studies on the linguistic development through social interaction of American students studying in France. Kinginger, who works within a sociocultural framework, considered the results in relation to participants' own accounts of their experience through diaries, logbooks and interviews. Her credo is Kramsch's statement that 'language learners are not just communicators and problem solvers, but whole persons with hearts, bodies, and minds, with memories, fantasies, loyalties, identities' (Kramsch, 2006: 251).

One of Kinginger's main findings was that students who remained within the American group made little, if any, progress while those who actively engaged in L2 socialization through contact with native speakers of French made significant personal and linguistic progress. Progress was particularly clear in the awareness and use of sociolinguistic variants and colloquial forms. We have already mentioned the case of Alice, who displayed a fierce determination to speak French and cultivated social networks with Francophones. She encountered challenges to her lack of interest in world politics that initially affected her self-image but she resolved it by becoming more politically aware and by developing her sense of purpose as a future educator. By the end of her stay, she was 'the Queen of France', having 'these long philosophical conversations using big long French words' (Kinginger, 2004: 236). At the opposite end of the spectrum is Deidre, who during her final month of stay in Montpellier claimed that she wasn't talking French except in minimal service encounters. Her goal seems to have been to survive the ordeal. After her return to the US, she declared that she was no longer interested in taking any more classes and expected to start losing the little French she had learned (Kinginger, 2008).

Large-scale investigations of adult multilinguals have shown that frequency of use of foreign language was a stronger predictor of self-perceived competence and foreign language anxiety than variables such as type of instruction or AoA. High frequency of use of the foreign language results in higher levels of self-perceived competence in oral and written communication and lower levels of foreign language anxiety in different situations (Dewaele et al., 2008).

The potential boost that authentic use of the target language can give a L2 learner/user should not obscure the fact that useful work can be carried out in the L2 classroom. A large meta-analysis of quantitative studies that considered the development of L2 pragmatics in classroom settings showed that pragmatic instruction was effective, especially if it lasted for more than five hours. This finding was in sharp contrast to the time needed to teach aspects of grammar where short time-spans sufficed for significant progress to occur (Jeon and Kaya, 2006). For a recent overview of L2 pragmatics research, see Kasper (2009).

3.5.4   Summary

The instructional environment clearly plays an important role in the development of learners' interlanguages. Formal instruction seems to have an edge over naturalistic learning in the area of grammar but not necessarily fluency. Teaching approaches also have differential effects on different aspects of the interlanguages. Approaches range from purely implicit, inductive communicative approaches, which focus on fluency over accuracy, to explicit instruction methods, which are more deductive and typically focus more on accuracy. Cognitively oriented SLA researchers debate about the nature of the knowledge acquired by the learner and the precise location of that knowledge in the brain. The frequent use of an interlanguage in authentic communicative situations was found to benefit not only grammatical but also sociolinguistic, sociocultural and pragmatic competence. Participation in social networks in the target community not only boosts linguistic skills but also pushes L2 users to reflect on their identity, beliefs and practices. Just as Gregorius sees his hometown, Bern, differently when he is in Lisbon, Kinginger's students in France realize that their worldview is not necessarily shared by their French interlocutors. Some embrace this opportunity to expand their horizon, reporting a sense of liberation, while others seek refuge with compatriots to escape the sense of being lost in a foreign land and culture.

STUDY ACTIVITY 3.6

Does someone using a foreign language feel like a different person? Compared with when they use their L1, do they feel more anxious? More logical? More emotional? More serious? More fake? More funny? More free? Design a short questionnaire with five-point Likert scales (ranging from 'absolutely disagree' to 'absolutely agree') based on the feedback for every item. Calculate the means. Use a paired t-test to see whether the difference is significant between the L1 values and the values for the FL.

3.6   Conclusion

We set out on this overview with the account of a fictional language learner, Gregorius, in his quest to master Portuguese in order to decipher a mysterious book. He becomes an entirely different person through the abrupt end of long-established routines and the sudden immersion in a foreign language and culture. He establishes new and completely different social networks, becomes fluent enough in Portuguese to hold complex conversations and daring enough to question some of the decisions he has made earlier in his life. To the reader it becomes clear that Gregorius's journey to Lisbon is also a journey of self-discovery. Gregorius's creator, the author Pascal Mercier, has done good research in the preparation of his novel. The story strikes a chord with anyone who has learned a second language and has stayed in a foreign country. We wondered whether Gregorius fitted the profile of a good language learner. The SLA literature revealed that 'good' language learners, just like 'bad' language learners, come in all forms and shapes, but that what 'good' language learners have in common is a positive attitude towards the language, motivation to learn it, and sufficient passion and dedication to overcome the difficulties in mastering the foreign language. We then wondered whether Gregorius might have been at a disadvantage because of his age. Might he have passed a certain critical period to an age that would prevent him from attaining native speaker levels in his Portuguese? While there is agreement in the SLA literature that age effects exist, especially in naturalistic acquisition, where younger immigrants typically reach higher levels of proficiency in the L2 than older immigrants, researchers are divided about the existence of clear cut-off points beyond which it would be impossible to reach native speaker levels. Indeed, some studies have shown late starters attaining native-speaker levels in their second language on some tasks. The next question we considered is whether Gregorius's knowledge of three dead languages and two modern languages facilitated his acquisition of Portuguese. The multilingualism literature suggests that experienced foreign-language learners, and children who grew up as multilinguals, do indeed seem to have an advantage in acquiring a new language depending on a number of variables, such as literacy in the different languages. It seems that multilinguals have a better 'meta'-understanding of various aspects of language, and can use their previous knowledge to form hypotheses about the target language. This seems to make them more confident communicators and language learners. In the final question, we wondered about the cognitive aspects of SLA and multilingualism, namely, the relationship between instructional context and the nature of linguistic knowledge (implicit or explicit) as well as its location in the brain. We concluded by looking at the effect that Gregorius's sudden immersion in Portuguese society might have had on his linguistic skills. Sociolinguistic and pragmatic competence are typically difficult to acquire without intense exposure to – and use of – the target language. We considered the literature on students during their study abroad, and found huge individual variation, linked to the enthusiasm with which students engaged in L2 socialization and showed a willingness to adapt to the new environment.

3.7 Summary

This chapter has looked at the factors that have been linked to successful acquisition of second or foreign languages. We have identified psychological and biographical factors such as age of onset of acquisition and the knowledge of other languages. We have also considered the effects of type of instruction and the opportunities to use the language in authentic communication on second or foreign language acquisition and use. Finally, we have considered the cognitive, psychological and social effects of second and foreign language learning.

Study Questions

1. List the languages you know, and reflect on aspects of one language that helped you acquire an aspect of another language.
2. Why do you think everybody can become fully proficient in their L1 (if they have no pathological problems), while very few ever become fully proficient in a foreign language?
3. What keeps you motivated in your foreign language learning?
4. Have you ever been unintentionally rude in a foreign language? What happened and why did it happen?
5. Which aspects of the foreign language do you find most difficult and why?
6. What might be the characteristics of the 'bad language learner'?

Recommended Reading

Gass, Susanne M. with Jennifer Behney and L. Plonsky. 2013. *Second Language Acquisition: An Introductory Course*, 4th edn. New York and London: Routledge. An excellent updated overview of research in SLA, this includes actual learner data, in several languages, inviting the reader to reflect on methods of analysis, on hypothesis building and on interpretation.

Gass, Susanne M. and Alison Mackey (eds.). 2011. *The Routledge Handbook of Second Language Acquisition*. London: Routledge. Fifty leading international SLA researchers contributed to this state-of-the-art overview. It covers a wide range of topics: language in context, linguistic, psycholinguistic and neurolinguistic theories and perspectives, skill learning, individual differences, L2 learning settings, and language assessment.

Herschensohn, Julia and Martha Young-Scholten (eds.). 2013. *The Cambridge Handbook of Second Language Acquisition*. Cambridge: Cambridge University Press. This is a comprehensive 31-chapter handbook. It offers a multi-perspective synopsis of recent developments in SLA research and covers cutting-edge and emerging areas of enquiry such as third language acquisition, electronic communication, incomplete first language acquisition, alphabetic literacy and SLA, affect and the brain, discourse and identity.

Housen, Alex, Folkert Kuiken and Inneke Vedder (eds.). 2012. *Dimensions of L2 Performance and Proficiency: Complexity, Accuracy and Fluency in SLA*. Amsterdam: John Benjamins. This 11-chapter volume presents research into complexity, accuracy and fluency (CAF) as basic dimensions of SL performance, proficiency and development. It showcases current research on CAF by bringing together 11 contributions from renowned international researchers in the field. These contributions bring new research findings to light and address fundamental theoretical and methodological issues.

Mercier, Pascal. 2008. *Night Train to Lisbon*. New York: Grove Press. Great philosophical and linguistic novel.

Ritchie, William C. and Tej K. Bhatia (eds.). 2009. *The New Handbook of Second Language Acquisition*. Bingley (UK): Emerald. The work is divided into six parts: (1) a recent history of methods used in SLA research and an overview of currently used methods; (2) chapters on Universal Grammar, emergentism, variationism, information processing, sociocultural, and cognitive-linguistic; (3) overviews of SLA research on lexicon, morphosyntax, phonology, pragmatics, sentence processing, and the distinction between implicit and explicit knowledge; (4) an examination of the neuropsychology of SLA, child SLA, and the effects of age on second language acquisition and use; (5) a consideration of the contribution of the linguistic environment to SLA, including work on acquisition in different environments, through the Internet, and by deaf learners. Finally, (6) chapters concerning social factors in SLA, including research on acquisition in contact circumstances, on social identity in SLA, on individual differences in SLA, and on the final state of SLA, bilingualism.

Robinson, Peter (ed.). 2012. *Routledge Encyclopedia of Second Language Acquisition*. London: Routledge. This is a user-friendly, authoritative survey of terms and constructs that are important to understanding research in SLA and its applications. It was written by an international team of specialists. It is designed for use as a reference tool by students, researchers, teachers and professionals with an interest in SLA. It contains 252 alphabetized entries and cross-references to related entries in the Encyclopedia . It has nine survey entries that cover the foundational areas of SLA in detail: Development in SLA, Discourse and Pragmatics in SLA, Individual Differences in SLA, Instructed SLA, Language and the Lexicon in SLA, Measuring and Researching SLA, Psycholingustics of SLA, Social and Sociocultural Approaches to SLA, and Theoretical Constructs in SLA. The remaining entries cover all the major subdisciplines, methodologies and concepts of SLA.

chapter 4

Language and the Brain

Marjorie Lorch

Learning Outcomes

After reading this chapter, you should be able to

- describe how different aspects of communication are revealed by studying language impairment;

Applied Linguistics, First Edition. Edited by Li Wei.
© 2014 John Wiley & Sons, Ltd. Published 2014 by John Wiley & Sons, Ltd.

- explain how language impairments reflect the interaction and independence of linguistic processes and other cognitive domains;
- appreciate the variation in language functions with maturation for young children, teens, adults and the elderly;
- discuss aspects of language disorders that are differentially manifest in speech as compared with reading and writing;
- describe the different patterns of impairment that are found in people who speak more than one language.

Key Terms

- Agrammatism
- Agraphia
- Anomia
- Aphasia
- Dyslexia

- Neurolinguistics
- Paraphasia
- Pragmatic impairment
- Specific Language Impairment

——— 4.1   Introduction to Language Processing in the Brain

At the age of 18 George Harris fell ill while travelling in Bratislava. He retells the story of his sudden difficulty in speaking and long-term recovery in a personal history article for the national UK newspaper *The Guardian* entitled 'I woke up with a Russian accent' (9 May, 2009). George recalled having suffered pains in his lower jaw and mouth and then falling unconscious. 'When I came out of the coma I couldn't speak. In my head I felt normal, and I was so desperate to tell everyone around me what I was thinking; to ask what had happened to me. I thought I had died. But I would open my mouth and just groan. ... Within a few weeks my speech had progressed – but the voice still wasn't mine. The grunts had, inexplicably, developed into a thick Russian accent. In my head my voice was normal, but the words came out strangely. I would even structure sentences in a Russian way: instead of saying, "Can you put the kettle on?" I would say, "Put kettle on." I would also get simple words confused – "coffee seeds" instead of "coffee beans". But at that point I was just glad I could talk at all' (Harris, 2009).

This autobiographical account captures the dismay and frustration often experienced by people who suddenly have difficulty communicating through serious neurological illness. It also captures specific aspects of speech and language that can be selectively impaired after neurological impairment. He expresses dismay at the change in the sound of his voice and his manner of speaking. As discussed in the chapter Language in Interaction, in this volume, we know that aspects of speech and language are crucial aspects of a person's social identity. This was clearly undermined by his difficulties in articulation and led him to feel that he did not sound like an English person any more. George's account of the stages of his recovery of speech also highlights some significant linguistic distinctions: first, the difficulty producing any speech sounds; next, the distortion of articulation; later, a specific difficulty with word retrieval, and finally, residual difficulty with sentence structure. This personal account provides a good illustration of the way in which the type of difficulties George experienced can provide a window on the mental architecture of language function.

The study of acquired language disorders has provided major evidence for how language is organized in the brain. Studies of children with Specific Language Impairment or SLI (Leonard, 1998) and other developmental disorders that affect language, such as Williams Syndrome, Down Syndrome and autism, provide other sources of important evidence (Jenkins, 2000). In the chapter Language in Development, in this volume, we see that the acquisition of language is a dynamic process that unfolds over a long period of time. Language capacity develops in an individual through maturation with multiple sources of variation from both genetics and the environment over the lifespan. The study of how language fails to develop successfully in some children is another source of evidence that contributes to our understanding of how language is organized in the brain.

Until recently there was no way to directly inspect the functioning human brain to learn about how language is understood and produced. Because the ability to talk and understand other people is an automatic and unconscious process, we cannot learn about how we are able to accomplish the remarkable feat of having words come out of our mouths to produce coherently formed messages. Indeed, George did not actually know how his brain damage had affected his ability to talk, although he did try to reflect on this. For 150 years our main source for learning how language was organized in the brain came from studying the behaviour of people who had suffered some kind of impairment in neurological function that affected their ability to speak and understand. Although this research strategy has been likened to trying to study how radios work by taking out different components, a great deal has been learned through this approach.

The most common type of acquired disorder is aphasia. It results from damage to the parts of the brain that contain language. Aphasia may cause problems in any or all modalities of speaking, understanding, reading and writing. There is what is called laterality with respect to language function. Only damage to the left side of the brain causes aphasia for most right-handers and about half of left-handers. Because of this, the left hemisphere of the brain is said to be dominant for language. Individuals who experience damage to the right side of the brain may have additional difficulties beyond speech and language with the social use of language. Some people with aphasia have trouble using words and sentences (expressive aphasia). Some have problems understanding what other people are saying to them (receptive aphasia). Severely affected people may struggle with both producing and understanding speech (global aphasia).

These kinds of acquired difficulties with language are incredibly common and are thought to affect approximately 1 in 250 people (Anonymous, www.aphasia.org). Research is being carried out in order to understand the different components of language processing and find ways to rehabilitate those with acquired disorders and assist children with developmental language problems. Cross-linguistic research is being carried out to determine the ways in which the structure of different languages may be reflected in specific symptoms and how people who speak more than one language may be differentially affected. Ultimately, research on language disorders can assist in revealing how the human capacity to use language to communicate is a product of interactions between subcomponents of a highly complex neural system.

In the previous chapters you learned about how language develops in children and how people learn to speak more than one language. In this chapter you will discover how people who have suffered various types of language impairment can help us understand the components of language and the functional architecture of the brain systems that support speech.

Many different parts of the nervous system are involved in our ability to hear speech sounds, listen to and understand what people are saying to us, interpret and remember the meaningful aspects of the message being conveyed and formulate and produce a spoken response. There are separate but connected processes involved in reading and writing that also share some aspects of abilities such as number calculations and appreciating and making music.

William James, the nineteenth-century Harvard professor, described babies' experience of the world as a 'buzzing confusion'. However, children soon hear what is said to them as series of meaningful words as the nervous system learns the distinctive properties of human speech sounds and the particulars of the language(s) spoken around them. The processing of sound begins in the cochlea inside the ear, passes through several different stages of processing and is then received by the primary area of the brain that is specialized for hearing. The neural coding of speech is a complex process that allows us to identify individual speech sounds and put them together into words and phrases with grammatical properties, as well as aspects of discourse meaning. An area in the left hemisphere is primarily responsible for this. Linguistic processing involves the integration of information about what we have heard with our experience of the movements involved in how those sounds are produced. This is combined with other knowledge we have about our language, our world and the person we are speaking with. It is quite complex but also automatic, extremely rapid, typically effortless and occurs without our awareness of how we actually achieve this skill. Various regions of the brain concurrently contribute to this process.

When we talk we draw upon a range of linguistic and other cognitive, social and emotional abilities as well. When we think of something we want to say we need to conceive of a message that will be tuned to the situation and speaker we are addressing. This involves areas deep in the brain involved in memory and emotional responses as well as higher-level structures in the frontal regions involved in planning. An utterance needs to be formed according to the grammatical and phonological structure of our language(s) to create a string of words and phrases which are processed primarily in the central regions of the left cortex. This in turn is then converted into articulations through the coordination and timing of movements of the muscles of your tongue, jaw, lips, larynx and breathing by an area of the motor cortex specialized for speech. The network of areas of the brain involved in understanding and producing language has been studied through a number of methods to help us see how this complex process unfolds.

—————— 4.2   How Does Communicative Function Fractionate Through Selective Impairment?

It is a curious fact, one that has been recognized for over one hundred years, that if someone suffers acute brain damage from a stroke in a particular spot below their left temple they will have difficulty speaking. They will not be mute, but will talk in short strings of

Figure 4.1 The Cookie Theft picture (Goodglass and Kaplan, 1983). Copyright permission granted by Pro-Ed, Inc., Texas.

words with visible effort. If the damage is below the top of the left ear, on the other hand, they will speak fluently but not appear to make much sense or understand what others say to them. These two extreme patterns of language disorder, termed Broca's aphasia and Wernicke's aphasia, reflect the way the knowledge of one's language is organized in the brain.

You can appreciate the way in which the speech of a person with Broca's aphasia has been impaired in their attempt to describe what is happening in this picture of three people in a kitchen, known as the 'Cookie Theft' picture.

BROCA'S APHASIC: Wife is dry dishes. Water down! Oh boy! Okay Awright. Okay ...
Cookie is down...fall, and girl, okay, girl...boy...um...
EXAMINER: What is the boy doing?
BROCA'S APHASIC: Cookie is...um...catch.
EXAMINER: Who is getting the cookies?
BROCA'S APHASIC: Girl, girl.
EXAMINER: Who is about to fall down?
BROCA'S APHASIC: Boy...fall down!

Example of a Broca's aphasic speaker
describing the Cookie Theft picture
(cited in Avrutin, 2001: 3).

As you can see, the utterances produced by the Broca's aphasic are very short and use simple words without using full sentences. Contrast this with the following sample of a person with Wernicke's aphasia attempting to describe the same picture:

WERNICKE'S APHASIA: Uh we're in the kermp kerken kitchen in in the kitchen and there's a lady doing the slowing. She's got the pouring the plate watching it with with um. The water is balancing in the sink the (?) of the sink and the water is pouring all over the bowing bowing all over it.

> Example of a Wernicke's aphasic speaker describing
> the Cookie Theft picture (Edwards, 2005: 5).

Here the Wernicke's aphasic is producing long utterances which are difficult to make sense of and words are used in unusual ways. The following is a sample from someone with word-finding difficulty, termed anomic aphasia, asked to describe the same picture.

First of all this is falling down, just about, and is gonna fall down and they're both getting something to eat...but the trouble is this is gonna let go and they're both gonna fall down...but already then...I can't see well enough but I believe that either she or will have some food that's not good for you and she's to get some for her too...and that you get it and you shouldn't get it there because they shouldn't go up there and get it unless you tell them that they could have it. and so this is falling down and for sure there's one they're going to have for food and, and didn't come out right, the uh, the stuff that's uh, good for, it's not good for you but it, but you love it, um mum mum (smacks lips)...and that so they've...see that, I can't see whether it's in there or not.

> Example of an anomic aphasic speaker describing
> the Cookie Theft picture (cited in Avrutin, 2001).

Not only can the linguistic system be impaired; all levels of communication can be seen to suffer selective impairment in other types of acquired neurogenic disorders. Related patterns are also seen in children with developmental difficulties in acquiring language. Selective difficulty with the grammatical elements of language is seen in children with Specific Language Impairment who develop normally in all other cognitive domains. (This topic will be developed in detail in the next section.)

STUDY ACTIVITY 4.1

1. Reflect on the three aphasic language samples given above. Consider how they reveal aspects of phonological, morphological, lexical and syntactic aspects of aphasic impairment.
2. Imagine what it would be like to have a conversation with one of these people. How would you communicate successfully with them?

The examples given above illustrate difficulties with syntactic and semantic aspects of language. At the other end of the communicative spectrum there are people who have difficulties producing particular aspects of speech sounds rather than linguistically meaningful units. Some have difficulties with the rhythm, timing or shape of articulatory movements, termed dysarthrias. There are those who have uncontrollable spasms of their vocal cords whose speech sounds hoarse and have difficulty conveying the emotional tones that normally colour our speech rather than the words themselves. Applied Linguists can be trained to carry out diagnostic assessments on such difficulties, which in turn inform clinical decisions on intervention. Intervention and treatment, though, need to be carried out by clinically qualified speech and language therapists rather than linguists.

A rare difficulty in control of particular muscles involved in articulation may lead someone to sound like they have acquired a foreign accent. In the excerpt at the beginning of the chapter, George describes himself as having developed a Russian accent. This is really a pseudo-accent since it is the impression of the impaired place and manner of articulation in the ear of the listener rather than a result of an adult's second language learner pronunciation.

Case Study 4.1

In the 1950s and 1960s a group of clinicians (initially founded by Harold Goodglass with Norman Geschwind, and later joined by dozens of others) founded a research centre based in Boston dedicated to investigating various aspects of language disorder informed by recent developments in the field of generative linguistics championed by Noam Chomsky and colleagues, who were nearby at the Massachusetts Institute of Technology (MIT). This research was facilitated by the availability of research subjects at the Veterans Administration Hospital, which provided a large homogeneous group of aphasics who were in long-stay chronic care. This unique medical context, which was replicated in a number of centres both in the USA and Europe, created the opportunity to take detailed quantitative measurements of performance of spared and impaired language, speech and voice functions in hundreds of people, which were correlated with neurological and psychological data. It was at the Boston VA Hospital Aphasia Unit that the first controlled psycholinguistic studies of aphasic language, focusing on the production and comprehension of syntax and morphology, were carried out (Goodglass and Blumstein, 1973). While previous work on aphasic disorders in the 1950s had been carried out primarily on individual cases, Geschwind and Goodglass instituted a new methodological approach employing controlled group studies to provide large-scale analyses of the statistical characteristics of aphasic speech. Novel standardized assessment techniques were developed such as the Boston Diagnostic Aphasia Exam and the use of materials such as the 'Cookie Theft' picture (Goodglass and Kaplan, 1983). Theoretical models derived from correlations between clinical and neurological deficits (Goodglass and Gescwhind, 1976; Goodglass, 1993) were supported by innovations in neuroimaging techniques (e.g. Naeser and Hayward, 1978; Naeser and Palumbo, 1995). For over 30 years, these patients were studied by an interdisciplinary team of researchers who had the benefits of insights from theoretical developments in linguistics to investigate aspects of grammatical impairment (e.g. Kean 1985; Grodzinsky, 1990) and the lexicon (e.g. Goodglass and Wingfield, 1997).

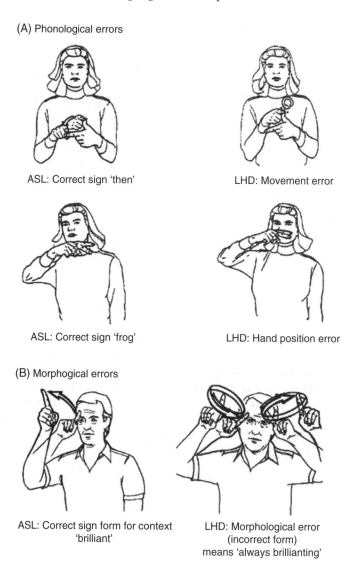

(A) Phonological errors

ASL: Correct sign 'then'   LHD: Movement error

ASL: Correct sign 'frog'   LHD: Hand position error

(B) Morphogical errors

ASL: Correct sign form for context   LHD: Morphological error
'brilliant'   (incorrect form)
                                          means 'always brillianting'

Figure 4.2 Examples of paraphasias in deaf left-hemisphere damaged (LHD) signers. In phonological errors **(A)** the correct American Sign Language (ASL) phoneme is substituted for an incorrect one. In paragrammatic errors **(B)** an illegal combination of ASL morphemes or signs is used (Hickok, Bellugi and Klima, 1998). Copyright permission granted by Elsevier.

Communication disorders in people who speak more than one language display every possible combination of interactions between their linguistic systems. Not only are particular aspects of spoken language seen to break down in people with neurological impairments, those who have acquired deaf sign language show similar types of difficulties in their visual gestural communication. The study of such aphasic disorders reveals particular properties of the grammar of language. Selective impairments have been recorded in the syntax of the language through difficulties with word order and inflections; in the semantics of the language through difficulties within and between lexical classes of words; and in the sound system of the language with impaired phonological processes.

4.3   How Does Language Interact with Other Cognitive Domains, Or is It Independent of Them?

The relation between language and thought is an old conundrum which has recently taken on new meaning in the context of work in cognitive science. If you are asked to consider if you can think without language or have language without thought you might have some introspective notions of these possibilities. New understanding of the modular design of the brain, and the cognitive capacities processed by it, has underscored some of the ways language and thought are both independent and interrelated. Some important evidence for addressing this philosophical question comes from the study of a number of different types of acquired and developmental phenotypes for language and other types of behaviour.

In the section above we introduced the possibility of losing linguistic abilities because of suffering damage to particular parts of your brain. In many cases of acquired aphasia the difficulty may be isolated only to language while other abilities, to count, sing, gesture, way-find, joke, play games, use tools and so on, may be unimpaired. In fact, each of these abilities mentioned above, as well as many others, can be selectively impaired. Not only can this happen in previously healthy adults who had achieved levels of skill in these areas, but these kinds of patterns can also be seen in developing children.

Children with Specific Language Impairment (SLI) appear to develop typically as infants. Once language begins to develop they appear to exhibit difficulties. Assessments of other aspects of learning are normal for their age group but as they get older their difficulties with language become more evident.

A four-year-old child with SLI is looking at a set of pictures and asked to make up a story about them:

EXAMINER: This is Jim. Tell me a story about Jim.
CHILD: Him going fishing. Jim hold …water. And go fish. And [unclear].
EXAMINER: I didn't hear this [last] one.
CHILD: I don't know.

For another picture the same child said:

CHILD: Kathy brush teeth. Her eat. And her get clothes on.

Examples of a child with SLI describing
two pictures (Leonard, 1998: 4).

STUDY ACTIVITY 4.2

1. Compare the linguistic difficulties you identified in the sample of a Broca's aphasic with that of the child with SLI speech.
2. Reflect on the similarities and differences you might find in the speech of these individuals as compared with that of someone who is a second language learner with low proficiency.

Although these children go to school and may develop good skills in a range of activities, the dependence on language understanding and expression is so central to our education system that some with persistent difficulties begin to fall behind academically. It is not that these children don't learn how to speak but rather that their progress in developing language is slow and they speak ungrammatically. They may produce verb forms without the appropriate ending, fail to mark plural nouns or leave out little grammatical words. It is often the case that you can get the sense of what they are saying even though it is not well formed.

The following utterances were produced by a 16-year-old boy with SLI:

- 'The grandmother look for son in room.'
- 'When the man plowing the field, her sister go to school that morningtime.'
- 'Now us have lot of snow at … around this house.'
- 'That man in a dark room.'
- 'Those are businessmen talking for a building to build in that city.'

Examples from the speech of a teenager with SLI
(from Weiner, 1974, in Leonard, 1998: 21–22).

Other children with SLI have more difficulties in comprehending others' speech. For these children, listening to someone talking must be a bit like having a conversation in a very noisy restaurant where you nod and smile but do not catch what the other person is saying.

On the other hand, children born with Down syndrome have very slow development which affects their general learning and motor development as well as their language. However, not only do these children learn to use language quite effectively, some learn to read and write successfully despite their general learning difficulties. This is somewhat surprising as literacy skills are very demanding cognitive tasks. Another, much more rare, genetic disorder called Prader-Willi syndrome also leads to general learning difficulties and slow development overall. While these children also acquire language, the developmental path they take is somewhat different from those with Down syndrome. The study of these various atypical developmental trajectories reveals the many ways that language is independent of, but involved in, various other mental abilities.

These children can be contrasted with others who have a genetic disorder called Williams syndrome. These children appear to develop language normally and are typically very chatty. However, they have serious learning difficulties. They represent the opposite side of the paradox. Children with Williams syndrome acquire grammar very well but fail to grasp the underlying concepts and relations. Although they talk, their conversations lack meaning. If you listened to them speaking in another room so that you couldn't hear the actual words, they would sound fine. Only when you try to have a meaningful conversational exchange does it become obvious that there is a lack of meaning attached to the words being used. It is a bit like a very small child mimicking a word used by a grownup without really understanding the actual meaning of the word or its appropriate usage.

Beyond difficulties with language per se are difficulties with the social aspects of language use, termed pragmatics. People who have suffered from diffuse damage to the front of the brain from, for example, hitting their head in a car accident, often have lasting problems because of their inability to use language appropriately in particular communicative social contexts. They may have difficulty providing sufficient information for communicative intention or be unable to produce coherent responses, shifting topics in a confusing way.

Here is a conversational speech sample from a person who suffered a traumatic head injury:

'I have got faults and . My biggest fault is . I do enjoy sport . It's something that I've always done . I've done it all my life . I've nothing but respect for my mother and father and . My sister . and basically sir . I've only come to this conclusion this last two months . And . As far as I'm concerned , my sister doesn't exist.'
                    Example of speech from a person with traumatic head injury (from Perkins,
                              Body and Parker, 1995: 305, cited in Perkins, 2007: 16).

Although people with traumatic head injuries can generally express themselves, they may also be communicatively inappropriate, speaking impolitely or too casually, sometimes with swearing or joking, without the ability to modify the register of their language in more formal social interactions. A developmental form of pragmatic impairment can also be seen in some children with autistic spectrum disorders.

STUDY ACTIVITY 4.3

Examine the extract above taken from Perkins (2007: 16). Appreciate that the hesitant quality of the speech is indicated by [.] in the text. Consider how this conversational extract fails to create a coherent, meaningful and socially appropriate message.

In Section 4.2 I introduced some of the types of aphasia that are seen with neurological damage to the left side of the brain. It is significant that impairments to language processing, both the comprehension and production of the grammatical aspects of language, typically only occur when the damage suffered is on the left side. So what happens when someone has a stroke that affects only the right side of the brain? Interestingly, these people speak fluently and are able to express and understand literal language but have difficulty interpreting and using more affective or metaphorical aspects of language. They may have difficulty understanding the tone of someone's voice or whether someone is being sarcastic.

This is an example of a person who suffered a right-hemisphere stroke describing the same Cookie Theft picture:

'Looks like a lady washing dishes and the sink is going over. And that looks like a drive and that's a window and that's a curtain. And the faucet, and a kitchen cupboard. There's a cookie jar. And a girl, and a boy on a stool. There's a bunch of trees here and long grass. That's it.'

> Example of a speaker with right-hemisphere damage describing
> the Cookie Theft picture (Myers, 1997: 204).

As you can see, instead of a narrative description relating the people and elements of the scene, this is merely is a listing of individual items. There is no attempt to relate what is happening in the scene.

Those suffering from psychotic disorders such as schizophrenia may produce fluent speech in which words are strung together in ways that make it difficult to understand the speaker's intended meaning. These people are considered to have a thought disorder, which is reflected in their speech, rather than a language disorder per se.

Here is an example of conversational speech from a person suffering from schizophrenia:

'I'm a catholic, but I don't believe in fishes. The water in the gutter is not the master of civilization.'

> Example of schizophrenic word salad (Andrewes, 2002: 433).

In some contrast to this is the case of autism, a developmental difficulty with the understanding of what others know and how social aspects of meaning affect communication. Such people often have problems with narrative meaning and inferring the significance of messages. Their difficulties involve the emotional, social and pragmatic aspects of interactions that go beyond their often relatively good ability to process the lexical and grammatical content of language. For example, if someone points to a cup and says, 'This is a shoe', children as young as two years will say that they are joking or pretending. This reflects their ability to appreciate another's mental state and use that to interpret the extralinguistic meaning of communication. However, children with autism will typically say that they are simply wrong. While they appreciate that the word does not correctly match the object they may fail to consider why someone might have said such a thing and the possible nonliteral meaning it might convey.

4.4   What Effect Does Maturation Have on the Manifestations of Language Impairment?

As people age many experience increasing problems with their memory, which often show themselves as word-finding difficulty. The thoughts that they wish to express are clear in their own mind but they have increasing difficulty retrieving the specific words needed to express those thoughts. This experience is also common in healthy people who are temporarily suffering from stress, fatigue or other types of altered mental states. What are called 'normal speech errors' reflect a functional disruption of the language production system without any impairment to thought processes. For example, someone might say 'I caked a bake' when they intended to say 'I baked a cake'.

'Tip of the tongue' experiences commonly show that you may have difficulty saying a word that you are thinking of but may be able to recall a lot about the word you are having trouble retrieving. You may be able to say something about this word's meaning, other related words, and aspects of how it sounds – such as what letter it starts with or number of syllables, and will recognize it if someone else says it.

In contrast, people with memory disorders (from, for example, Alzheimer's dementia) will continue to communicate using grammatically well-formed speech until very late stages of the illness but will have increasing difficulty retrieving the particular words they need to express precise and contentful meaning. Their word-finding difficulties are compounded by other cognitive problems with monitoring, attention and general recall of experiences and information.

Here is a description of the Cookie Theft picture produced by a dementia sufferer:

'Well/let's see/over that way/well it looks to me like uh/the/like here/there's a couple of 'em/but uh/but by the time they really/use you know use them or something/they probably run down already some/but then again/the it's not that bad/now this/this woman here/she's/got/that's her hand I know there/and she's got a little here/yes/there/s a lot to it/to keep you going/and keep things straight.'

Example of a speaker with dementia describing
the Cookie Theft picture (Myers, 1997: 247).

STUDY ACTIVITY 4.4

Examine this description of the Cookie Theft picture from a person with dementia and compare it with the extracts from the three different types of aphasic speakers in Section 4.1 and the person with right-hemisphere damage in Section 4.3.

1. What grammatical features are similar or different?
2. What lexical choices are similar or different?
3. What overall impression do you have of the success of these communications?

Their speech is empty of meaning and sudden changes of topic make it hard to follow. However, even severely impaired people with Alzheimer's dementia will continue to maintain appropriate social and pragmatic conversational conventions for some time after their semantic and syntactic performance has degraded. They will correctly maintain eye contact, appropriately take turns in conversational exchanges, and automatically respond to greetings and expressions of thanks.

4.5   What Can Be Learned about Language by Considering Impairments in Speech as Compared with Reading and Writing?

Up to this point our consideration of language has focused primarily on speech production and comprehension, with some mention of the parallels found in the visual gestural languages of deaf signers. In this section we will consider written language production and comprehension and the differences and similarities between spoken and graphical language. There is some common awareness that a certain minority of children have an inordinate difficulty in learning how to read in their early school years. In recent years a great deal of research has been carried out to investigate the neurological substrate of this problem and to understand the relationship between genetic factors, educational issues and orthographic demands which all appear to contribute to specific reading difficulties. The current picture suggests that this group of dyslexic children is not homogeneous and that it is likely that there are multiple sources for difficulty with this cognitively complex task related to language. Problems have been identified at both the visual (eye movements and eye dominance) and perceptual (letter form identities) levels; the role of short-term memory in dealing with serially ordered items has also been implicated.

In some ways similar to cases discussed in Section 4.2, these difficulties with written language processing appear to be modality specific and independent of general intelligence or spoken language abilities. However, reading difficulties may also be associated with a cluster of other cognitive learning problems involving numbers and arithmetic, visual-spatial skills, short-term memory and/or fine motor coordination. Most of the children identified as dyslexic will go on to become readers as they reach puberty; however, they may show residual difficulties with spelling or written text production. Like those with SLI who grow up to show few residual signs of spoken language difficulties, children with dyslexia do learn how to read as they grow older but may never be fluent adult readers nor error-free in their reading performance.

Interestingly, previously literate adults may lose the ability to read and/or write as a consequence of neurological illness. Many aphasic persons with difficulties in the production and comprehension of spoken language will experience parallel difficulties in the written domain. However, some may selectively suffer lasting impairments in only reading and/or writing after their spoken language problems have resolved. By studying the patterns of difficulties that different individuals had with reading after brain damage we have learned a great deal about the underlying processes involved in reading. There are two primary types of difficulties represented in those with alexia (acquired reading difficulty) and agraphia (acquired writing difficulty) which reflect the ways in which sounds are encoded into orthographic forms in a language.

In languages like English, which use an alphabet, some written forms represent a direct correspondence between a single letter (grapheme) and the individual sound (phoneme) associated with it. This allows words such as 'bed' to be pronounced by knowing the sounds represented by 'b', 'e' and 'd'. Other written forms do not have this one-to-one correspondence between the grapheme and the phoneme. Words such as 'yacht' must be learned as whole forms in order to be correctly pronounced. These two reading procedures must be used together in learning to read in English since our spelling system has a mixture of transparent grapheme–phoneme mappings and irregular spellings which must be learned as wholes.

STUDY ACTIVITY 4.5

In the passage above we described two different ways to map sound onto spelling: either by individual sound (phoneme) and letter (grapheme) correspondences or by whole word forms with irregular spellings that exist in English. Identify how these mappings work for individual sounds and letters and multiple sounds and letters considering different units such as syllables and morphemes.

Each of these procedures can be selectively impaired, resulting in some people finding it difficult to read new words that could be sounded out, such as 'flut', while others pronounce words with irregular spellings as if they were regular, such as reading 'said' as "sa-id". A third group of difficulties reflects a combination of problems in these reading procedures which results in words being read as phonologically unrelated synonyms, such as 'orchestra' being read as 'symphony'.

If we consider other written language systems apart from English we see a variety of different patterns of acquired reading difficulty which reflect the way a given language encodes the spoken form orthographically. Take Chinese and Japanese for example. In Chinese there are no individual letters that correspond to our alphabet. Words are represented in the form of characters with associated meanings which may be combined. There is little information encoded in the written symbols to provide phonological clues. There are many thousands of these characters which must be learned by children in their school years. Acquired reading difficulties in Chinese reflect this property of the system to visually represent units of meaning rather than sound. Difficulties occur typically at the level of whole-word reading in this language. In contrast, Japanese has a complex written language with several different orthographies which serve different functions and have different properties. Kanji, which is used to represent content words, is more similar to Chinese-style character writing, while two forms of kana, which are used to represent grammatical forms and loan words, are syllabic sound representations. In persons suffering from acquired disorders of reading and writing there may be difficulty with only kana or kanji selectively.

4.6   What Can Be Learned about Language by Considering Impairment in People with More Than One Language?

Many clinico-pathological patterns of aphasia are fairly consistent, such as the association of more anterior lesions with primarily expressive difficulties while more posterior lesions lead to primarily receptive difficulties. However, most of what we know about how language is organized in the brain comes from studying people who only speak English. A large majority of people in the world, however, typically have some knowledge or use of more than one language. In the chapter Second and Additional Language Acquisition, in this volume, we explore what it means to be bilingual or multilingual and the variety of ways in which people have knowledge and use of the different languages they have learned. We know that people who learn to use more than one language do so in many different ways and use them for different social purposes, and that their various languages have different significance in terms of their personal history and identity. These factors seem to have an effect on the mental representation of those languages.

Patterns of aphasia in people who speak more than one language are extremely variable. We might expect that if multiple languages were all processed the same way language impairments following brain damage would equally affect all the languages someone knows. Surprisingly, in a substantial number of cases the languages are differentially impaired. There may be different types of aphasic symptoms, different levels of severity of impairment or different rates of recovery in the different languages an aphasic person uses. This suggests that for some people who speak more than one language these may be represented in psychophysiologically distinct ways.

A number of different factors have been suggested to explain the patterns seen in impairment and recovery of bilingual aphasics: (1) the language learned first; (2) the language that is the most familiar; (3) the language that is most automatic; (4) the language with the strongest emotional association; (5) the language they use most in their daily life; (6) the language they can read and write in; (8) the language of the clinical environment and of therapy delivery.

STUDY ACTIVITY 4.6

Think about when and how you were exposed to another language, whether in school, on holiday or as part of a new community.

1. List all the details about this language learning experience and consider how they might have consequences for the neurolinguistic representation of that language capacity.
2. Draw up a list of questions you might wish to ask about the language history of a bilingual aphasic person that might be used to explain their difficulties.

Although there has been a great deal of psycholinguistic research that suggests that age and/or manner of acquisition and level of proficiency will have consequences for how a second language is represented in the brain, there has been little in the way of consistent patterns of findings for either of these variables in bilingual aphasia (Ijalba, Obler and Chengappa, 2004). There are other paradoxical patterns demonstrated by bilingual aphasic speakers, such as only being able to speak their weaker or less dominant language, unusual translation, switching or mixing of languages. These patterns have also been found in multilingual speakers suffering from dementia.

Case Study 4.2

Modern bilingual aphasia research was instigated by a number of researchers in the 1970s including Michel Paradis (1977) studying the bilingual culture in Montreal, Canada, and Loraine Obler and the multilingual researchers in Boston (Albert and Obler, 1978). Throughout the next two decades, there was a great deal of research activity investigating bilingual aphasia. However, huge variability was documented in the relative quality and severity of impairment in an individual's languages which frustrated attempts to develop an explanatory account for bilingual aphasia. An alternative approach to developing a neurolinguistic account for the human language faculty was initiated in the 1980s. A number of researchers began to realize that aphasia research that focused exclusively on English-speaking monolingual individuals would not provide a comprehensive picture of language organization in the brain. Paradis and colleagues first investigated the patterns of spoken and written language impairments found in Japanese aphasic people (Paradis, Hagiwara and Hildebrandt, 1985). Later international research collaborations gathered characterizations of aphasic individuals who were speakers of a broader range of languages to allow cross-linguistic comparisons of grammatical impairments (Menn and Obler, 1990). At the same time, there was growing interest in the neurolinguistic properties of visual-gestural languages with the growth in social prominence of the Deaf communities (Poizner, Klima and Bellugi, 1990). In addition, there have been attempts to understand the variety of ways in which a person might become multilingual within a framework drawing on current models of working memory. Paradis (2001) carried out a review of over one hundred cases of bilingual aphasia published between 1985 and 2000. He found that while the majority had parallel recovery of both languages, approximately one quarter showed various patterns of differential recovery including language mixing, selective impairment in one language with respect to the other(s), or successive recovery of their languages. Having intensively investigated these patterns throughout his research career, Paradis concluded that all the variables that had previously been proposed could not account for this pattern of results: 'Neither primacy, automaticity, habit strength, stimulation pre- or post-onset, appropriateness, need, affectivity, severity of aphasia, type of bilingualism, type of aphasia nor structural distance between the languages could account for all the non-parallel recovery patterns observed' (Paradis, 2001: 77). New developments in both the neuroimaging of bilingual speakers and psycholinguistic processing models of activation and inhibition of nodes in networks have helped further attempts to characterize patterns of language impairments in bilingual aphasic speakers. More recently, Paradis (2009) has put forward a model based on the idea that first language learning is served by procedural memory systems while later second language learning relies on declarative memory systems which are known to be neuroanatomically distinct.

The picture of how language is organized in the brain is complex and incomplete. This is even more confusing when trying to account for speakers of multiple languages. One of the tools for learning about patterns of language abilities as a consequence of neurological deficit comes from a variety of elicitation and testing techniques. These tools allow us to gain a window on implicit aspects of language processing and components. However, they can also be misleading, as demonstrated by the mislabelling of children who spoke a non-standard variety of English or were speakers of English as a second language (as in Labov, 1982). Many of the 'black' and 'Asian and Latino' children were labelled as learning disabled, mentally handicapped or hard of hearing because the word discrimination tests used items that were not phonologically distinct in their vernacular. In this instance, the assumption that everyone speaks Standard English, and that knowing another language is not relevant, led to the conclusion of language pathology rather than that of healthy psycholinguistic differences in language representation.

4.7 Summary

In this chapter we have considered the ways in which the study of individuals with language difficulties reveals processes of linguistic organization. Both acquired neurological illnesses and developmental difficulties may lead to problems with specific aspects of speaking, listening, reading and/or writing. Aspects of sound, meaning and grammatical structure may be independently affected. Neurolinguistic research has also demonstrated the ways in which language is related to, but independent from, other psychological functions such as memory and reasoning. Linguistic impairments may selectively affect aspects of literacy. Patterns of difficulties experienced by multilingual speakers also reveal interesting details about the way language functions are organized in the brain.

Study Questions

1. Outline the ways in which different aspects of language can be impaired.
2. Outline the different modalities of language function that can be independent from each other, using examples from this chapter.
3. In this chapter we have considered how age affects the language system. Compare the ways in which language is impaired in developmental and acquired disorders over the lifespan.
4. Consider how the study of language impairments sheds light on the relationship between language and thought.
5. Discuss the ways in which the study of language impairments is illuminated by considerations of literacy and the learning of more than one language.

———————————————— Recommended Reading

Ahlsén, Elizabeth. 2006. *Introduction to Neurolinguistics*. Amsterdam: John Benjamins. This provides an overview of the different components of language through evidence from aphasia.

Chiat, Shula. 2000. *Understanding Children with Language Problems*. Cambridge: Cambridge University Press. This explores the phonological, morphological, lexical and syntactic aspects of atypical language development.

De Bot, Kees and Sinfree Makoni. 2005. *Language and Aging in Multilingual Contexts*. Bristol: Multilingual Matters. This provides a perspective on healthy aging and dementia, exploring their impact on multilingual communication.

Denes, Gianfranco. 2011. *Talking Heads*. Hove: Psychology Press. This presents an introduction to the functional processing of language in the brain.

Fabbro, Franco. 1999. *The Neurolinguistics of Bilingualism: An Introduction*. Hove: Psychology Press. This considers aspects of the language-processing systems in the brain and how they are organized in speakers of multiple languages.

part II

Language in Use

chapter 5

Language in Interaction

María Elena Placencia

Chapter Outline

Learning Outcomes

After reading this chapter, you should be able to

- understand key concepts and the basics of some theories employed to describe language use in interaction;
- recognize the role of context in language use;
- identify and categorize different kinds of speech actions;

Applied Linguistics, First Edition. Edited by Li Wei.
© 2014 John Wiley & Sons, Ltd. Published 2014 by John Wiley & Sons, Ltd.

- distinguish between directness and indirectness levels in speech act realization and explain the Cooperative Principle and how hearers understand implied meanings;
- identify some of the ways in which language is used in managing rapport and interpersonal relationships;
- explain in basic terms how conversation is coordinated and organized in interaction.

Key Terms

- Adjacency pairs
- Conversation/talk-in-interaction
- Implicature
- (Im)Politeness

- Indirectness
- Openings and closings
- Speech acts
- Turn-taking

5.1 Introduction

A university tutor (A) wrote an email to a colleague (B) asking if B could possibly send A a copy of the outline of a particular course. B replied, 'I would be happy to meet up with you later this week and answer any questions you have about the course.' By declaring himself ready to do something that A was not in fact asking for, B was indicating, by implication, that he was unwilling (or unable) to let A have the course outline that she was requesting. Through his choice of words, however, B avoided refusing A's request directly, which would almost certainly have given a negative impression, and he was nevertheless able to express his position in unambiguous terms. His strategy was to let A draw her own conclusions.

Letting our interlocutors draw their own conclusions rather than conveying our message in a direct or explicit manner is a practice in which we all engage in our daily lives: for instance, in order to express negative feelings or make a refusal as in the example above, or perhaps for purposes of humour; to add interest to what we are saying; not to hurt other people's feelings or to protect ourselves, or both.

How implied meanings are understood is precisely one of the aspects of language use that we will explore in this chapter. But first we will consider the notion of language as action and the role of context in the interpretation of meaning. We then move on to look at (in)direct ways of performing actions through language, as well as *why* people often avoid saying what they mean directly. Next, we will consider (im)politeness phenomena. The use of indirectness has not infrequently been linked to the notion of politeness; however, as we will see, indirectness can be more or less appropriate depending on both the situational and the sociocultural contexts in which it is used.

Finally, we will look at some aspects of the organization of conversation or talk-in-interaction, including how participants exchange and take turns in talking, and the overall level of organization of conversation that relates, for example, to the mechanisms that conversationalists employ to coordinate, step by step, the opening and closing of conversations.

The above are all aspects of language use in interaction examined within the broad field of pragmatics, which is the focus of this chapter. Language use in the workplace, in service encounters and in a multiplicity of other settings is central to Applied Linguistics. In dealing with problems of language use in intercultural interactions, for example, Applied Linguists have drawn extensively on the concepts and theories presented in this chapter. Likewise, studies of language use in real-life contexts have had an impact on theorizing on language use in interaction.

5.2 Language as Action and the Role of Context in the Interpretation of Meaning

In the example in the previous section, by saying 'I would be happy to meet up with you later this week …', the speaker is not simply making a statement but performing an action: uttering a refusal by means of an offer. Utterances have the power to transform reality, and it is in this sense that *language* is *action*, or *saying* is *doing*. For instance, an apology can have the effect of repairing a relationship when its balance has been upset by an offence or a blunder. Likewise, the 'I do' that the bride and groom (may) utter as part of their marriage ceremony has the social effect of transforming their civil status from a single to a married one.

The idea of language as action is closely linked to *speech act theory*, a theory that was put forward and developed by two language philosophers, John Austin (1962: 17) and John Searle (1969, 1975), and that, together with the theory of implicature (see section 5.4), is one of the cornerstones of pragmatics.

In *How to Do Things with Words*, published posthumously in 1962, Austin noted that language is used not only to describe the world through statements to be judged in terms of whether they are true or false, an objective emphasized in some philosophical circles in the 1950s, but also to do things. Some of these actions can be expressed explicitly, as when we say, for example, 'I apologize', 'I promise', and they are referred to as *explicit performatives*; other actions, however, cannot, as in the case of insults (*'I insult you'). Sometimes, on the other hand, the explicit performative does not really correspond to what it says. For example, when a parent tells a child, 'If you call your brother names again, I'll take your iPad away, I *promise*', this is more a threat than a promise.

Within speech act theory, the smallest unit through which we do things with language is the *speech act*. Through speech acts we make requests and we accept them or reject them; we make promises, extend invitations, and give advice; we compliment or criticize others; we agree or disagree with them.

Our actions, however, are not always *felicitous* or successful because, for example, we may not have the power to execute a particular action or we may fail to do the action appropriately. The manager's threat in the third example of Study Activity 5.1 would not work if she did not have the power to convert the kitchen into an office. The term 'felicitous' alludes to Austin's (1962) *felicity conditions* for the successful performance of speech acts. With reference to ritual actions, Austin notes that there are conventional procedures

STUDY ACTIVITY 5.1

Consider the following utterances and identify the action(s) that each performs (e.g. a request):

1. A politician after an email scandal: *'I'm sorry for the damage I did to the Government.'*
2. A sign left by contractors in a street: 'Tree works on 10 Sept, 8 am-6 pm. *Any car parked in the coned area is subject to removal.'*
3. Email from a manager to her employees: *'… I found the staff kitchen in a mess this morning and had to spend a good hour tidying it up!!* I write to ask that anyone using it please make an effort to keep it pleasant for everyone. *As you all know, we are very tight for space in this building and that kitchen would make a pretty spacious office…'*
4. Exchange taken from *Yahoo!Answers, UK & Ireland*:
    QUESTION: 'My upstairs neighbour is driving me mad with the noise…? How do I avoid this turning into a feud?'
    ANSWER: *'Report him to the HA and Environmental Health. They can't tell him legally who complained so just deny all knowledge if challenged!'*
5. A newly appointed research fellow to an administrator: *'Thank you for the letter confirming my appointment. Could I trouble you to put the original into the post for me?'*

that need to be followed but that also require the right people to execute them (e.g. not everyone can officiate at a wedding ceremony or declare a court case adjourned), as well as the right circumstances (e.g. inappropriate premises for the ceremony may render a marriage invalid). Likewise, in ceremonies, the actual words we use can be very important. Answering 'I suppose so' rather than 'I do' to the canonical question 'Do you take …?' in a marriage ceremony, for example, does not count.

Going beyond ceremonies, in a highly publicized case, the British public found out through the hostile tabloids that the then Prime Minister Gordon Brown had written a letter of condolence to the bereaved mother of a British soldier. His intentions were obviously good; however, they were negated by the fact that the letter was riddled with what appeared to be spelling mistakes. In the circumstances, the mother found the letter highly offensive. The Prime Minister attempted to rectify the offence his letter had caused by offering an apology over the phone. From transcripts of this call printed by the tabloids, one could see that, despite his repeated expressions of regret, his intended action was again infelicitous. It took a press conference the following day, where the Prime Minister reiterated his apology, for it to be accepted by the bereaved mother. In an interview she gave, she indicated that at the press conference 'he [the Prime Minister] looked sincere, he looked humbled', whereas on the phone, although he had said sorry repeatedly, he 'didn't sound apologetic' (Jacqui, 2009).

This example shows that it is not enough to say 'I'm sorry' for an utterance to count as an apology, but it is also important how and where you say it; paralinguistic (e.g. intonation) as well as nonverbal (e.g. gaze, gesture) cues can be vital. Also, with public figures, apologies often need to be made in the public arena for them to be successful.

This example also serves to illustrate two levels of meaning that can be distinguished in any speech act:

1. the surface or literal meaning; and
2. the intended/underlying meaning also referred to as *illocutionary force.*

Within speech act theory, these two levels of meaning are encapsulated in the notions of *locutionary* and *illocutionary* acts, respectively. However, Austin and Searle also distinguished a third act – the *perlocutionary* act – to refer to the effect that a particular speech act can have on an audience (e.g. the Prime Minister's letter of condolence in the example above was intended as an expression of sympathy; however, as we saw, it was perceived as offensive).

While sometimes the illocutionary force of an utterance corresponds to its literal meaning, often it does not. In fact, one of the characteristics of language use is its indeterminacy: there is no one-to-one natural correspondence between an utterance and its meaning or function. Utterances can have multiple meanings or functions, and it is for the hearer to determine what a person means by what he/she says on a particular occasion. And yet, in our everyday interactions within our own sociocultural environment, we normally manage to negotiate meaning rather painlessly by drawing on specific features of the context of the interaction. Consider the following example:

(1)   A woman comes into a university building and hurriedly approaches the attendant sitting at the reception desk:
      WOMAN: I've come to give a talk for the German Society.
      ATTENDANT: Through the double doors, turn left and then right, room 119.

While 'I've come to give a talk for the German Society' is simply a statement about the woman's intended activity, the attendant appropriately interprets this utterance as a request for information and tells the woman where to go. The key features of context that helped him understand the woman's utterance as a request for information include:

• the physical setting: the interaction took place in the reception area with the attendant sitting at the information desk; and
• the type of activity that they were engaged in – a service encounter – together with knowledge of the social roles associated with service encounters, namely, those of customer and service provider, and of the rights and obligations attached to these roles. Part and parcel of an attendant's role, for example, is to give enquirers information about places, events and where people can be found.

Yet another kind of knowledge the attendant needed to have in order to interpret the woman's query appropriately is knowledge about what people do at universities, what talks are taking place, and so on. Such knowledge is part of what is referred to as *shared knowledge.*

Finally, the co-text or exchanges in which an utterance is embedded also play a role. There is no preliminary talk in the example above, suggesting a lack of previous knowledge between the interactants and, given the setting, pointing to a customer–service provider category of interaction. However, if we imagine, for example, that the attendant knew the woman because she used to work in the building, he may engage in social talk and ask, for instance, 'What brings you here?' In this case, 'I've come to give a talk for the German Society' would be a response likely to be interpreted as an item of information only.

Context, however, should not be taken as a given or as predetermined. For instance, while the physical setting is important, in itself it does not necessarily contribute to defining an activity as a specific type of encounter. This is, to a large extent, accomplished by the participants' joint actions within a given setting. Attendants at reception desks, for example, do not only or always engage in service talk; as in the imagined scenario above, they can very well engage in social talk, or in a combination of service and social talk. The result is that the physical setting can sometimes be irrelevant.

5.3   Indirectness: Avoiding Saying Directly What You Mean

In formulating a speech act, we have the choice of employing forms that convey our intent or illocutionary force with more or less clarity. In self-service tills, for example, supermarkets tend to use *direct* forms that are unambiguous for customers. When you are about to pay, you are told, 'Insert cash or select payment type'. The use of the imperatives *insert* and *select* in this example illustrates prototypical instances of directness (cf. Blum-Kulka, House and Kasper, 1989).

Requests of the 'can/could you ...?' type, on the other hand, employed in other contexts, illustrate paradigmatic instances of *indirectness*, that is, cases where there is a mismatch between the literal or surface meaning of an utterance and its underlying social meaning (Stubbs, 1983). Still within the supermarket setting, when you are making a payment at a counter and you insert your bank card into a chip and pin device, the cashier might prompt you with the utterance, 'Can you type in your pin number?' On the surface, this is a question about your ability to type in your pin number; however, its underlying meaning is normally that of a request similar to 'please type in your pin number'. Likewise, in a different setting, a man informing his partner, who is in the habit of reading in bed until late at night, 'I'm going to work really early tomorrow', is not simply stating his plans for the following day, but is indirectly asking his partner to switch off the bedside light. This and the previous example would therefore be cases in which one illocutionary act is performed indirectly by way of performing another (Searle, 1975).

These two examples also show the distinction that has been proposed between two basic types of indirectness – *conventional* and *nonconventional* (Searle, 1975). 'Can/could you ...?' would be an example of conventional indirectness, since it is through convention that the structure 'can/could you ...?', unlike 'are you able to ...?', has come to be associated with requests in English. On the other hand, the utterance 'I'm getting up really early tomorrow' is not immediately associated with a request, except perhaps, for the couple in question, if it is employed repeatedly in the same context. Utterances of this type are, rather, instances of nonconventional indirectness, or the kind of indirectness that involves giving hints that need to be picked up and deciphered (Tannen, 1979; Weizman, 1989).

Pragmatics, however, is not only concerned with describing *how* people use language, but also with *why* they use language in the way they do, that is, with the motivations behind people's linguistic choices. In the case of nonconventional indirectness, it has been suggested, somewhat paradoxically, that it can serve the interests of communicative efficacy

STUDY ACTIVITY 5.2

Examine the request and compliment utterances in the examples below and decide whether they illustrate cases of directness, conventional indirectness or nonconventional indirectness.

1. A note from a neighbour placed through the letterbox:
    A very much loved cat called Rosy who lives on this street has been missing since the evening of Saturday 4th July. It's not like her to go far and we are concerned. Could we kindly ask that you check your sheds or garages to see if she is trapped inside? If you have seen her, can you please call me on one of the numbers below? Thanks very much for your help.
2. Compliments made by friends on Facebook in reaction to posted photos:
    a.   On friend's holiday photo of a sunset: 'Do you work for Jamaica's tourism and travel board?'
    b.   On female friend with boyfriend: 'you look Beautiful!!!!'
                        (Facebook examples taken from Placencia and Lower, forthcoming)

since, in some contexts, indirectness may be the only way to say what we want to say. This is because some thoughts or feelings are ineffable (Dascal, 1983). 'I'm on fire' is, for example, how Speech Debelle (2009: 27), a rapper, metaphorically describes how she feels when she is in a creative mood, writing her songs in the middle of the night. It would be difficult to convey that same feeling, and with the same impact, in a literal way. Indirectness can therefore add interest to an utterance, and increase its impact (Thomas, 1995).

On the other hand, it has been proposed that politeness is one of the main motivations behind the use of conventional indirectness (cf. Searle, 1969; Brown and Levinson, 1987 [1978]) since indirectness increases options for the hearer (Leech, 1983), who may otherwise feel coerced or restricted in his/her freedom of action. The example of the request above relating to the missing cat illustrates the use of conventional indirectness, in conjunction with mitigating devices such as *please* aimed at achieving a politeness effect.

However, indirect forms are not always, or not necessarily, polite or appropriate and may not be effective either. In certain commercial environments, for example, in order to drive a hard bargain, indirectness may not get you very far. The advice given to Britons by TV presenter and consumer 'champion' Dominic Littlewood (2009: Y4) is to avoid saying things like 'I don't suppose you could give me a discount?' but, instead, to say something along the lines of 'I like those … get the price down and I'll buy them today.' It is clear in these examples that if customers show serious doubts about getting a discount, then it is unlikely that they are going to get it; hence, a direct formulation such as 'get the price down …' followed by an offer or a promise ('I'll buy them today') might prove to be more effective in such situations. Similarly, if someone is in immediate danger, a brief and to-the-point 'watch out!', for example, is certainly going to be more useful than a 'polite' 'could you possibly watch out?' (cf. Brown and Levinson 1987 [1978]).

On the other hand, our choice of (in)direct forms also depends on the rights and obligations associated with particular roles/activities, and whether we are asking for something
that goes beyond participants' rights and obligations or not. For example, in service
encounters in bars at breakfast time in Seville, Placencia and Mancera Rueda (2011a)
found that while direct forms were commonly used when customers were placing their
order, as in Example (2), below, requests for a glass of water were normally produced
using conventional indirectness, as in (3):

(2)   Media tostadita.
      'Half a toast+diminutive'

                                                                              (2011a: 502)

(3)   Severino / ¿me puedes dar un vasito de agua?
      'Severino /can you give me a glass+diminutive of water?'

                                                                              (2011a: 501)

This can possibly be explained by taking into account the fact that requests for tap water,
because it is not paid for, go beyond the standard transaction. The use of conventional
indirectness can be taken as an acknowledgement of this state of affairs.

The appropriateness of (in)directness, however, not only varies situationally, but also
cross-linguistically and across varieties of the same language (cf. Placencia, 2011).

Requests (and other speech acts) have been examined in numerous languages and
language varieties. In most studies, conventional indirectness has been found to prevail
across situations too; nonetheless, the cultural embeddedness of request realization has
also become apparent in these studies through variation manifested in the choice of
sub-strategy and the use of mechanisms such as politeness formulas that mitigate the
force of a request. For instance, Breuer and Geluykens (2007), who studied requests
among British and American university students, started out with the hypotheses that the
British informants would produce more indirect requests and that they would make more
use of mitigating devices than their American counterparts. However, they found that
conventional indirectness was preferred across both varieties of English. Interestingly,
and contrary to their expectations, the American corpus showed a slightly higher use of
conventional indirectness, and the British corpus of directness and nonconventional

---

Case Study 5.1

In a classic study, Blum-Kulka and House (1989) analysed requests in several languages
including Australian English, Hebrew and Argentinean Spanish in a range of situations
varying in terms of the degree of social distance and social dominance obtaining between
the participants, as well as the weight of the imposition represented in the request. Despite
some situational variation, they found conventional indirectness to predominate across
the languages that they examined. Nonetheless, they found that in certain situations in
some languages (i.e. Argentinean Spanish and Hebrew) direct forms were a great deal
more frequent than in others (e.g. Australian English); thus certain languages show more
tolerance of impositions.

---

indirectness. The authors, nonetheless, did find that the British used more mitigating devices than their American counterparts.

The appropriateness of (in)directness may also change over time. This is a phenomenon some scholars have examined from a historical perspective. An interesting finding that has emerged, for example, by looking at play texts and trial procedures from past periods is that conventional indirectness, prevalent in contemporary English, was not so in seventeenth- and eighteenth-century English (Culpeper and Archer, 2008).

5.4   From Expressed to Implied Meanings

In the introduction to this chapter we looked at an example that illustrates how people can say something and yet convey something else: the tutor, by indicating that he was happy to answer questions about the course, indicated that he was unwilling to let his colleague have the course outline that she had requested. Consider this other example:

(4)   A male reader's comments on Cormac McCarthy's book *The Road*:
      'I started reading your book after dinner and I finished at 3.45 the next morning ...'
                                                                  (Jurgensen, 2009: 1)

In this example, by offering a description of when he started and finished reading McCarthy's book, the reader is also conveying another meaning: he is expressing an assessment of the novel – how it was so gripping that he felt compelled to continue reading until he finished it in the early hours of the morning.

The implied meanings highlighted in these two examples serve to illustrate the notion of *conversational implicature*, which we explore in this chapter. We owe this notion to H. Paul Grice (Grice, 1975 [1967]), another language philosopher working in the 1950s and 1960s who sought to explain mismatches between what is said and what is meant, and how hearers arrive at implied or *implicated* meanings.

Implicated meanings or conversational implicatures, as in the two examples above, are derived from the context of the utterance. To explain how such meanings are derived, Grice proposed the existence of a conversational principle – the Cooperative Principle (CP) – and maxims to which conversationalists orient in interaction. The CP operates on the assumption that, in order to attain their goals, people approach the conversational endeavour in a rational way, and that conversation is a joint activity that requires cooperation. Adhering to the CP means

> mak[ing] your conversational contribution such as is required, at the stage at which it occurs, by the accepted purpose or direction of the talk exchange in which you are engaged. (Grice, 1975 [1967]: 45)

The maxims, most of which have subsets, serve to clarify what cooperating in conversation involves:

The maxim of quantity:
* Make your contribution as informative as is required (for the purposes of the exchange).
* Do not make your contribution more informative than is required.

The maxim of quality:
- Try to make your contribution one that is true.
- Do not say what you believe to be false.
- Do not say anything for which you lack adequate evidence.

The maxim of relation:
- Be relevant.

The maxim of manner:
- Be perspicuous.
- Avoid obscurity of expression.
- Avoid ambiguity.
- Be brief (avoid unnecessary prolixity).
- Be orderly.

(Adapted from Grice, 1975 [1967]: 45–46)

According to Grice, observance of these maxims results in maximally effective exchanges of information. This can be seen in the following example:

(5)   At a library help desk
      LIBRARY USER: What time does the Library close during the holidays?
      LIBRARIAN (pointing to a sign):   At 6 pm.

In responding, the librarian in this example provides the customer with sufficient information that is accurate, relevant, to the point and unambiguous.

On the other hand, nonobservance can result in *flouting* of the maxims. This refers to cases where the nonobservance of one or more maxims is blatant or obvious to the hearer. This can be seen clearly in the course outline example in the introduction where B's reply is not very relevant on the surface, providing more information than requested – A never asked if B could answer questions about the course. So B is failing to observe the maxims of relevance and quantity. Likewise, in *The Road* reader's comments example, by providing his reading times, the reader seems to be giving more information than needed and information that is, on the surface, not relevant either, giving rise to conversational implicature.

In other words, when hearing blatant nonobservance of a maxim, hearers are alerted to the fact that the speaker is wishing to convey more than what he/she is expressing, and this conclusion is possible because the hearer assumes that the speaker is abiding by the CP.

Maxims can also be *infringed*, and this happens when speakers inadvertently fail to observe a maxim (Thomas, 1995). As Thomas (1995: 74) explains, this can occur when speakers have an imperfect command of the language, as in the case of young children or foreign language learners, for example, or because of a cognitive impairment.

Regarding foreign language learners, problems can, in fact, be anticipated in Intercultural Communication when Grice's CP and maxims are adhered to in different ways by different cultural groups, and when participants in an interaction are not aware of these differences. For example, in his study of cross-cultural differences in doctor/healer–patient interaction in Spain and Senegal, in the context of Western and traditional medicine in Spain and rural Senegal, respectively, Raga Gimeno (2005) observes that patients who

Study Activity 5.3

Consider the following examples and decide which maxims are being flouted and what the implicated meanings might be. Also consider the communicative impact the flouting of these maxims has.

1. Interview with sculptor Dylan Lewis (Meeke, 2009: 10):
   INTERVIEWER: Are you happy?
   SCULPTOR: *I have happy days. As I get older, I'm getting more honest with myself: what I want to do, who I am.*
2. Elliot Conwan, an actor, was asked if he had a girlfriend. This was his reply (White, 2009: 18):
   'I am unencumbered.'
3. Interviewer to Jane Horrocks, actress, married, mother of two (Greenstreet, 2009: 10):
   INTERVIEWER: What or who is the greatest love of your life?
   JANE HORROCKS: *Who can say?*
   INTERVIEWER: How often do you have sex?
   JANE HORROCKS: *Never, I'm still not sure where those kids come from.*

visit a healer or *marabout* in Senegal do not reveal much information about their condition. This is because they perceive it as the healer's task to find out what is wrong with them, and this involves the healer, rather than engaging in a question-and-answer consultation session with the patient, looking at external signs in the patient as well as using his powers of divination. On the other hand, in a Western-style medical consultation, doctors are expected to ask questions, and patients, to answer them. In this context, a patient providing too little information is likely to be perceived as uncooperative.

In relation to speech disorders among children, Bishop and Adams (1989), for example, identify giving too much or too little information (i.e. an infringement of the maxim of quantity) as one of the features of the so called Semantic-Pragmatic disorder. The following is one of the examples that they provide to illustrate a case of too much information:

(6)   95 A: is that a good place to break down?/
      96 C: the answer whether it's a good place to break down is no, because if see if anybody broke down cos there's no telephone to telephone, there's no telephone for the breakdown/

                                                                        (1989: 252)

In defining the CP and maxims, Grice noted, however, that achieving a maximally effective exchange of information might not necessarily be the aim of conversationalists who may, for example, want to influence or direct the actions of others, and that there are probably other maxims in operation: some social in nature, such as *Be polite*, and others of an aesthetic or moral character. This suggestion was taken up by scholars such as Leech

---

STUDY ACTIVITY 5.4

Read this email written by a foreign student to his project supervisor (names changed) in a British university, close to a submission deadline, and consider which maxim or maxims were infringed by the student.

Dear Robert,

I do hope you are well. I am writing to inform that my project is still in progress and it will be done before the deadline for a certainty. I thought you might be worried due to the lack of contact from me. However, I don't think I will be able to send to have a look of it as it is going to be done probably next Friday or during weekend. It is a pity that I didn't have chance to show my work and get guidance from you due to my laziness. I apologise for this irresponsibility of mine. But as mentioned above, it will be done on time. I hope you are gonna enjoy this weekend and see you soon.

Best wishes.

Tim

(1983), who proposed adding a Politeness Principle (PP) to the CP in order to explain phenomena like indirectness, as we will see in the next section.

While Leech proposed expanding Grice's CP and maxims, others have supported reductions instead. For instance, Sperber and Wilson (1986) focused and built on Grice's maxim of relation, developing Relevance Theory; this is an alternative and more sophisticated theory that also attempts to explain how implicit meanings are communicated and interpreted through inferencing processes.

—— 5.5 (Im)Politeness: Language Use in the Management of Rapport and Interpersonal Relationships

Grice's theory of implicature paved the way for our understanding of how we interpret implied meanings in communication. It was left to others to explain the social motivations behind the use of indirectness and related phenomena, and to look at the use of language not only for the maximally effective exchange of information, but also in the pursuit of interpersonal goals and the management of rapport (cf. Spencer-Oatey 2008[2000]) and interpersonal relationships. This is a task that various linguists first undertook in the late 1970s and the 1980s, putting forward the first theories of politeness. Leech (1983), mentioned in the previous section, was among the first.

Closely building on Grice's CP and maxims, Leech proposed a Politeness Principle (PP) and maxims to complement the CP as part of an interpersonal rhetoric intended to account for the effective use of language in communication. His maxims include, for example, *tact* (minimize cost to other; maximize benefit to other); *agreement* (minimize disagreement between self and other; maximize agreement between self and other), and *modesty* (minimize praise to self; maximize dispraise of self). These maxims relate to a number of scales, such as the *cost–benefit* scale, relevant to requests and other *directives*. For instance, requests often involve some kind of cost to the hearer. In the cat example above, the cost to the addressee is obvious as the woman writing the missing-cat note is asking strangers to do something for her. Hence her use of various politeness strategies when she writes, 'Could we kindly ask that you check your sheds or garages to see if she is trapped inside?' Example (7) below, on the other hand, illustrates adherence to Leech's modesty maxim since, by saying that she did not prepare the dessert, the woman is minimizing self-praise:

(7)   Response a woman gave to a compliment that she received on a dessert that she
       offered with a meal:
       'I'm glad you like it. I'll tell you something, it comes from the local supermarket.'

The opposite can be seen in this other example, where self-praise is maximized, the speaker thus seemingly violating the maxim of modesty:

(8)   Colin Murray in an interview with Ian Burrell (2009: 44):
       'I have confidence in my presenting … I think I'm a talented broadcaster.'

   Leech's (1983) PP and maxims have been found useful in explaining certain differences in communicative style across languages and cultures. For example, when comparing responses to compliments among Americans and Mandarin Chinese speakers from mainland China, Chen (1993) found that the Chinese, unlike the Americans, favoured rejection, that is, that they displayed an orientation to Leech's modesty maxim; for Americans, on the other hand, the agreement maxim seemed to prevail. Leech's maxims, however, have been criticized by some for their ethnocentricity, since their formulation (e.g. minimize cost to other; minimize praise of self) favours certain behaviours that are not necessarily going to be applicable across different situations, languages and cultures.
   Another theory building on Grice's CP is Brown and Levinson's (1987 [1978]). This, in fact, has been one of the most influential theories in the study of politeness phenomena. Brown and Levinson share Grice's (1975 [1967]) view that language use is purposive and that people use their rationality to achieve their goals. Nonetheless, they place the notion of *face*, which they borrowed from the writings of the American sociologist Erving Goffman, at the centre of their theory. Face, for Goffman (1972 [1955]: 319) is 'the positive social value a person effectively claims for himself by the line others assume he has taken during a particular contact'. Face is something you can lose in social interaction – hence the expression 'to lose face' – and that you normally wish to protect.
   Brown and Levinson see face as consisting of two aspects which are in conflict with each other: the need to be liked and approved by others (*positive face*), and the need to be free from imposition (*negative face*). On the other hand, the authors suggest that, in the course of reaching our goals in interaction, we might lose face or threaten other people's face. As a matter of fact, Brown and Levinson are of the view that most actions that we perform are face-threatening and that, therefore, the use of politeness strategies is required to redress

the negative effect of the face-threat. They propose five options in terms of the strategies that people can use when dealing with face-threatening acts (FTAs). We illustrate them with reference to a potential request – asking someone to open the window:

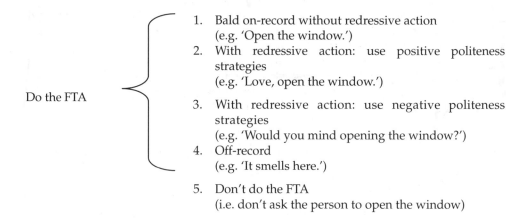

Do the FTA

1. Bald on-record without redressive action
   (e.g. 'Open the window.')
2. With redressive action: use positive politeness strategies
   (e.g. 'Love, open the window.')
3. With redressive action: use negative politeness strategies
   (e.g. 'Would you mind opening the window?')
4. Off-record
   (e.g. 'It smells here.')
5. Don't do the FTA
   (i.e. don't ask the person to open the window)

Moreover, Brown and Levinson provide an extensive list of positive and negative politeness strategies that they had identified and that are intended to be of universal application. For example, indirectness, giving deference and using impersonalizing mechanisms appear as negative politeness strategies in their model, and employing in-group markers, seeking agreement and exaggerating interest or approval as positive politeness strategies.

Assigning a politeness value to utterances out of context, however, can be problematic. As we saw above, indirectness, for example, cannot always be equated with politeness. The value of an utterance as (im)polite needs to be determined from the context in which it is employed (cf. Eelen, 2001). For example, certain address forms that may convey respect or affiliation in certain contexts may result in impoliteness in others. For instance, the Spanish address form *doña* (literally 'lady') tends to be associated with respect. However, in a study of service encounters in public institutions in La Paz, Bolivia, Placencia (2001) found that this form acquired negative connotations when service providers employed it in addressing indigenous women, as in the following example:

(9) In address to an indigenous female customer:
    SERVICE PROVIDER: ¿*Casada eres doña?*
    'Are you [you familiar] married *doña*?'

                                                                    (Placencia 2001: 208)

In the same context, Placencia found that service providers employed the familiar *you* forms *vos/tú* with indigenous people, as in (9), whereas they used the formal form *usted* with white-mestizos (Placencia 2001: 206). Using *vos/tú* is appropriate and desirable as it conveys affiliation in contexts of true familiarity; however, in the context examined, the use of these forms had the effect of expressing condescension or lack of respect, since the customers and service providers concerned were not known to each other. In brief, and echoing the Ann Arbor case that exemplifies institutionalized discriminatory practices

STUDY ACTIVITY 5.5

With reference to Brown and Levinson's framework, compare the politeness orientations reflected in the strategies employed by the producers of these texts:

1. Email message from an academic to a book series editor in the US:

    Dear Bob,

    In the 4th of July spirit, full of joy and good wishes, I wanted to ask you something. My colleague X and myself would like to know if you would be interested in publishing a book on x in your series. We have the proposal ready and I could send it to you tomorrow.

    Hope to hear from you soon, and have a wonderful 4th of July weekend!!!!

    Silvia

2. Note from a milkman to one of his customers:

    Dear Mr Potts,

    I note from our records that we are no longer delivering milk to your home at the moment. However, I must bring to your attention the fact that your account with us is still outstanding to the sum of £9.59. If there is some reason why this account has not been settled I would be obliged if you could contact me so that we can discuss settlement. Otherwise, could I please ask you to give this matter your urgent attention and settle your account within 7 days?

    Thank you for your cooperation.

    Yours sincerely

towards certain groups in society (see Chapter 1), Placencia's study illustrates how language can be used to construct certain groups as different and inferior through address and other forms.

While Brown and Levinson's theory has been highly influential, it has also received numerous criticisms. For example, it has been criticized for offering a pessimistic view of human nature given Brown and Levinson's formulation of politeness as conflict avoidance in the face of face-threatening acts. Kerbrat-Orecchioni (1997), among others, has highlighted the importance of face-enhancing acts in social interaction.

Moreover, their model has also been criticized for its ethnocentricity. For instance, in relation to their notion of face, one of the criticisms is that their focus is on the individual rather than the group's wants (cf. Matsumoto, 1988). Also, certain speech acts such as requests that are presented as face-threatening in their theory have been found not to be necessarily so in a number of sociocultural contexts (cf. Sifianou (1992) with respect to Greek and Fitch (1998) in relation to Colombian Spanish). In fact, it has been proposed that the avoidance of imposition at the core of Brown and Levinson's model may be central to Anglo-Saxon politeness systems, but not necessarily to other systems.

Other frameworks that have been put forward within the past decade aim to avoid ethnocentrism by catering for individual and group wants as well as for individual and cross-cultural variation (cf. Spencer-Oatey, 2008 [2000]; Locher and Watts, 2005); they also represent more encompassing models than Brown and Levinson's as they aim to account for not only politeness, but also impoliteness. Additionally, in these more recent models, a one-to-one correspondence between particular utterances and a politeness value is no longer assumed; rather the role of context and the co-text in the production and interpretation of (im)politeness phenomena is highlighted.

5.6   Language in *Inter*action: The Study of Conversation or Talk-in-Interaction

Conversation is an everyday activity through which we develop and maintain our relationships with others (Liddicoat, 2011). While being something quite mundane and ordinary, conversation is a highly organized activity requiring skilful coordination between at least two participants at various levels. This is something a group of sociologists noticed and set out to study in the 1960s and 1970s (cf. Sacks, Schegloff and Jefferson, 1974) giving rise to *Conversation Analysis* (CA) or the study of talk-in-interaction.

One of the levels of organization of talk-in-interaction is *turn-taking*, which refers to how conversationalists exchange turns at talk. Consider this extract of a service encounter in a bar in Seville:

(10)   A and B are both middle-aged males; A is the bartender and B is a customer:

>   [...]
>   03 A: ¿Qué pasa con esa cara↑? ¿Tenemos mal día↑?
>   'What's with the long face? Are we having a bad day?'
>   04 B: Sí/ mal día↓...
>   'Yes, a bad day ...'
>   05 A: ¿Y eso↑?
>   'And why's that?'
>   06 B: Una multa↓
>   'A fine'

(Placencia and Mancera Rueda 2011b: 201)

This extract illustrates a typical pattern for the exchange of turns in dyadic conversations: ABAB. It also illustrates the use of *adjacency pairs* – questions and answers in this case – as a mechanism employed for the smooth exchange of turns. Adjacency pairs are, as the name indicates, pairs of utterances occurring in adjacent positions where the production of the first part makes the production of a second part relevant: a question (e.g. 'Are we having a bad day?'), for example, creates the expectation of an answer (e.g. 'Yes, a bad day'). The adjacency pair is a basic unit of the *sequential organization* of conversation which attempts to explain how utterances are tied to each other.

Other normally paired actions include compliments and compliment responses, requests and invitations and their corresponding acceptance or rejection, and so forth. Within CA, adjacency pairs are regarded as the minimal unit in the analysis of talk-in-interaction, unlike speech act theory where the focus is on isolated utterances (see above). For conversation analysts, it is important to see the response or second part of an adjacency pair in order to find out how the initial utterance was interpreted (see Example (1) above).

Going back to the turn-taking system, the exchange of turns involves knowledge of when to start a turn, for instance, or how to indicate that one's turn is coming to an end. In spoken languages, the latter is done through issuing a mixture of cues of a linguistic, paralinguistic and nonverbal nature, such as completing a sentence or phrase, a drop in volume and a change in gaze direction. In sign language interaction, on the other hand, gaze plays a central role in turn-taking, but the speed of signing, hand 'rests' and head tilts have also been found to constitute important cues in, for example, American Sign Language interaction (Baker, 1977).

At every *transition-relevant place* (TRP) or possible completion point of a speaker's turn, turns can be exchanged. In conversation, this can be done through self-selection or other-allocation, that is, the current speaker may continue speaking, or he/she may allocate the floor to another conversationalist, or a different conversationalist may self-select and start talking. In other kinds of activities, such as chaired discussions, there are specific turn-taking rules according to which speakers are not expected to self-select but need to wait to be allocated a turn.

A smooth exchange of turns typically involves no gap between turns and little or no overlap. In some languages and cultures, silences between turns tend to be taken as problematic and requiring further action. In others, however, they may be more common and even expected (cf. Lehtonen and Sajaavara 1985; Scollon and Scollon 1981). Likewise, overlaps and interruptions may also be more common or expected in some sociocultural contexts, such as the Spanish vis-à-vis the Swedish context (cf. Fant, 1992).

STUDY ACTIVITY 5.6

Record a television or radio talk show with three or more participants and examine the exchange of turns. See if you can determine a turn-taking pattern. Consider the following: Who allocates the turns and how? Can speakers self-select? How do speakers mark that their turn is coming to an end? Look at linguistic, paralinguistic and nonverbal cues if available.

Conversations and other types of interaction can also be described at the *overall level of organization* or section by section, since many conversational activities have beginnings, middles and ends. A focus on this level of organization highlights the fact that conversations are not simply opened or closed but that participants have to coordinate entry and exit.

In landline telephone conversations, two initial sequences that have been identified in the opening of these conversations are the *summons–answer* and the *identification–recognition* sequences (Schegloff, 1979). The following examples illustrate these sequences:

(11)   01   ((Telephone rings))   }   Summons–answer sequence
        02 ANSWERER: *hello*

        03 CALLER: Hi Maggie (.) it's Pete.   }   Identification–recognition sequence
        04 ANSWERER: oh hi how are you

The summons–answer sequence (lines 01–02) is constituted by the telephone ring (01) that acts as a summons and the 'hello' of the answerer upon picking up the phone. The second one is the identification–recognition sequence, where participants deal with the identification and display of recognition of each other: In this example, the caller displays recognition of the answerer by producing a greeting + name. The pause that follows, marked by '(.)', however, shows that the caller was also possibly expecting recognition from his voice sample. Since this did not happen, the caller identifies himself ('it's Pete'). In 04, the answerer now displays recognition of the caller through the greeting and the how-are-you inquiry. The 'oh' in this utterance also plays a role: it indicates a change in state from lack of recognition to recognition.

Interestingly, despite technological developments, the same sequences of actions have been found in mobile phone conversation openings, albeit with some variations that relate to the sophistication of the technology. Nonetheless, a new type of sequence that has been identified for mobile phone interactions is the *locational enquiry* sequence (Hutchby and Barnett, 2005), which is linked to mobile phone portability. Hutchby and Barnett (2005: 165) provide the following example, which illustrates how this sequence is initiated (lines 6 and 8):

(12)   1.   ((summons))
       2.   KISHA: Hullo
       3.   SB: Kisha?
       4.   KISHA: Yeah
       5.   SB: Wots gwa:rnin?
       6.   KISHA: Where are you
       7.   SB: Hah?
       8.   KISHA: Where'r you
      Recording cut off

It has been observed that particular openings can give rise to particular communicative activities. In medical consultations with a general practitioner in England, for example, utterances such as 'how are you' and variations of 'what can I do for you' have been identified as two basic types of openings in follow-up consultations and new consultations, respectively (Gafaranga and Britten, 2003). However, the nature of the consultation is in practice negotiated by the participants in the interaction; in other words, while the general practitioner may open an interaction as a follow-up consultation, its nature might be changed by the patient if he/she brings up a new concern. This can be seen in the following example, where the doctor starts with a how-are-you inquiry (line 3), that is, he starts treating the consultation as a follow-up consultation; nonetheless, the patient transforms it into a new consultation with '… but mainly erm I've been getting really bad headaches …' (line 6).

(13) 1. DOCTOR: Sorry to keep you waiting so long
      2. PATIENT: That's all right
      3. DOCTOR: Behind this afternoon (0.2) *How are you?*
      4. PATIENT: Okay. Erm (could see) a couple of things
      5. DOCTOR: Mm
      6. PATIENT: And about my knee again but mainly erm I've been getting really
                    bad headaches [basically
      7. DOCTOR: [right
      8. PATIENT: couple of weeks ago I banged my head and gave myself
                    concussion
                                              (Gafaranga and Britten, 2003: 244)

While the complexity of the coordination in and out of an interaction goes unnoticed by most of us in our daily lives, some studies on children's telephone interactions, for example, such as Bjelic's (1987) on telephone talk among four- and five-year-olds, show that coordinating exit from a conversation is a social skill that takes time to acquire. Likewise, some cross-cultural studies of telephone conversations among adults show potential difficulties in the handling of openings and closings in telephone and other interactions when it comes to Intercultural Communication. For example, Pavlidou (2000), who studied telephone openings and closings in Greek and German among people who are familiar with each other, found that Greeks produce longer openings since they engage in more phatic exchanges, such as how-are-you enquiries, before getting to the reason for the call. Germans, on the other hand, tend to proceed more swiftly from the opening to the reason for the call.

STUDY ACTIVITY 5.7

With the permission of participants, record a telephone conversation and analyse how it is opened and closed, turn by turn. Alternatively, examine a number of openings and closings of email or text messages and, without overlooking features of context or the co-text, see if you can identify any recurrent elements.

5.7   Summary

In this chapter we have explored some key topics within pragmatics. We started with the notion of language as action encapsulated within speech act theory, one of the founding theories of the discipline, and moved on to considering the indeterminacy of utterances and the role that context plays in the production and understanding of language use. We then considered some aspects of indirectness, including how it has been characterized, some of the motivations behind its use, and situational and cross-linguistic variability in how it is used. Next we looked at how implied meanings are generated with reference to Grice's CP and maxims, and how these notions have been employed to shed light on cross-linguistic variability in compliment responses and medical consultations, for example. We then examined how some scholars, building on Grice's CP, went on to propose theories of politeness that attempted to account for the social motivations behind the use of indirectness and other strategies. We also reflected on a number of issues that have come up in the study of (im)politeness phenomena and that have resulted in proposals for amending some of the seminal theories as well as in new theories that attempt to reflect the complex and dynamic nature of rapport management in interaction. In the last section we looked at how conversation is coordinated by participants at various levels, stressing the notion of language as *inter*action rather than action alone. We also highlighted the interest in the study of the organization of conversation/talk-in-interaction for understanding, for example, how particular communicative activities are constituted through talk. Gaining knowledge of the concepts and theories considered in this chapter will help you understand some of the developments and empirical work undertaken in various areas of Applied Linguistics, such as second-language acquisition and Intercultural Communication.

Study Questions

1. Observe and take notes of examples of requests or compliments as they are formulated in a particular context (e.g. at home or at work; on a social-networking site) and examine the use of (in)directness and mechanisms employed to mitigate or intensify the force of the utterance, if any. Consider the features of context that appear to play a role in the way the requests or compliments that you are examining are formulated.

2. Reflect on instances of Intercultural Communication that you have observed where a conversational maxim was infringed: consider which maxim was infringed as well as the consequences of the infringement.

3. Attempt to provide a definition of (im)politeness and discuss in what ways Brown and Levinson's model may be adequate for Anglo-Saxon cultures, but not for other cultures. Consider whether it is possible or desirable to develop a universal model of politeness.

4. Some authors have proposed that some speech acts are inherently

polite and others inherently impolite. Do you agree with this view? Explain.

5. In the Ann Arbor case (see Chapter 1), as you will recall, it was established that Black English Vernacular had certain morphosyntactic and phonological features that distinguished it from other varieties of American English. In the characterization of language varieties, the focus has traditionally been precisely on such features. Not much attention, however, has been given to (socio)pragmatic features. Think of examples of regional variation across varieties of English (or another language) that suggest variation in turn-taking, speech act realization or the use of forms of address in interaction, for example.

Recommended Reading

The following textbooks provide useful introductions to the topics covered in this chapter:

Cruse, Alan. 2010. *Meaning in Language: An Introduction to Semantics and Pragmatics*, 3rd edn. Oxford: Oxford University Press. Chapters 18 and 20 offer a good introduction to speech act theory and conversational implicature, respectively.

Cutting, Joan. 2008. *Pragmatics and Discourse: A Resource Book for Students*, 2nd edn. London: Routledge. In Section A of this book you will find a clear introduction to key concepts in pragmatics. If you want to further explore the application of some of these concepts to naturally occurring data, you will also find Section C useful as it provides such data for analysis.

Johnstone, Barbara. 2008. *Discourse Analysis*, 2nd edn. Oxford: Wiley-Blackwell. This book, which offers a clear and thoughtful introduction to Discourse Analysis, explores, in Chapter 7, speech act theory and conversational implicature in terms of people's intentions and goals in interaction. It also considers in what contexts the application of such theories can be useful.

Liddicoat, Anthony. 2011. *An Introduction to Conversation Analysis*, 2nd edn. London: Continuum. This book is recommended for those interested in the organization of talk-in-interaction. Chapters 5 and 6 focus on turn-taking, Chapter 7 on adjacency pairs and preference organization, Chapter 8 on expanding sequences, and Chapters 10 and 11 on openings and closings, respectively. If you find Conversation Analysis a little daunting, you may want to start with Paltridge (2012) (see below).

Paltridge, Brian. 2012. *Discourse Analysis: An Introduction*, 2nd edn. London: Continuum. This book offers an accessible introduction to speech acts, implicature and politeness in Chapter 3, and the organization of conversation in Chapter 5.

chapter 6

Intercultural Communication

Zhu Hua

Chapter Outline

Learning Outcomes

After reading this chapter, you should be able to

- give three examples of the main concerns of Intercultural Communication as a field of study;
- explain why there are breakdowns in Intercultural Communication;
- outline culture-specific ways of communication;

Applied Linguistics, First Edition. Edited by Li Wei.
© 2014 John Wiley & Sons, Ltd. Published 2014 by John Wiley & Sons, Ltd.

- understand the concept of interculturality in intercultural encounters;
- define Intercultural Communicative Competence and the ways of developing and measuring it.

Key Terms

- Culture
- High context
- Intercultural Communicative Competence

- Interculturality
- Low context
- Schema

6.1   Introduction

Swedish diplomat insults Iran's Islamic president by exposing soles of his shoes.

This news headline appeared in many English-language newspapers in December 2012. It was alleged that the newly appointed Swedish ambassador to Iran, Peter Tejler, insulted Iranian President Mahmoud Ahmadinejad by 'exposing the soles of his shoes' when he was sitting with his legs crossed during a formal meeting. *The Atlantic Wire* went one step further and invited an expert from the University of West Florida to explain that it was a taboo in the Muslim culture to show soles, because soles are 'considered dirty, closest to the ground, closer to the devil and farther away from God'. However, a number of Iranian students and scholars I talked to following the incident found the news headline bewildering to say the least. They attested that, as in many other cultures, it was nothing unusual to sit with legs crossed in their home culture and, whether exposing soles or not, was not a problem at all. With their help, I traced back to the Arabic newspaper, *Asriran*, where the news first appeared. It turned out that the Swedish diplomat was frowned upon, not because he exposed the soles of his shoes, but because he breached a diplomatic etiquette by sitting too comfortably and crossing legs in a formal diplomatic meeting.

There are many issues to be drawn from the above incident. Most relevant to the theme of this chapter are the problem of stereotypes in understanding the culture and practice of 'others' and factors behind mis- or non-understanding in Intercultural Communication. In this chapter, we first look into the main themes of Intercultural Communication as a field of study and then examine some of the key issues in Intercultural Communication that are closely related to the way we use language.

6.2   What is the Field of Intercultural Communication Concerned With?

The field of Intercultural Communication was founded by Edward Hall in the 1950s to solve a practical challenge of preparing American diplomats for their overseas posts. Intercultural Communication refers to the situation where people from different cultural backgrounds come into contact with each other. Although some would differentiate Intercultural Communication from Cross-Cultural Communication (i.e. comparative studies of communication patterns in different cultures), more and more people now use 'Intercultural Communication' as an umbrella term to include both interactions between people of different cultures and comparative studies of communication patterns across cultures. Nowadays, Intercultural Communication has become a highly interdisciplinary field, drawing insights from several different disciplines such as communication studies, psychology, anthropology, business management, Applied Linguistics, cultural studies, and so on. A number of overarching themes and strands are outlined below.

6.2.1   Strand 1: The Cultural Value Approach

Different cultures have different values and beliefs. Defined as assumptions about how things ought to be in a group, values and beliefs influence the way we behave and communicate. Some psychologists have proposed a number of cultural values in their attempt to categorize national and ethnic cultures. Among widely cited models, one is Hofstede's five cultural dimensions (i.e. individualism vs. collectivism; high vs. low power distance; masculinity vs. femininity; high vs. low uncertainty avoidance; and long-term vs. short-term orientation; see Hofstede, 2001). Other scholars following a similar approach include Trompenaars and Hampden-Turner (1998), Schwartz (1992, 1994), and Kluckhohn and Strodtbeck (1961). Underlying the work of the cultural value approach is an assumption that culture values have a determining effect on an individual's style of communication. For example, people from an individualistic culture are often associated with explicit or direct verbal communication style and the wants, needs and desires of the speaker are embodied in the spoken message. In contrast, people from a collectivistic culture tend to communicate indirectly and within the group itself; interpersonal harmony and cooperation are important purposes of communication. Over the years, cultural value studies have been criticized for their essentialist and over-generalized view of culture, that is, members of a cultural group are treated as the same, sharing definable characteristics whatever the context may be (e.g. McSweeney, 2002). Nevertheless, the classification systems proposed by various scholars do act as a convenient, albeit rather simplistic, tool in revealing the cultural differences in values and beliefs. The studies following this particular line of enquiry are still widely cited in business and organization management studies and applied in intercultural training.

6.2.2   Strand 2: Intercultural Communication as Interpersonal and Intergroup Communication

While cultural value researchers were discovering and comparing the values and beliefs of different cultures, a group of scholars turned their attention to the process of Intercultural Communication and brought general communication theories into the study of interactions between people of different cultures. The bulk of this work was done in the 1980s, and the leading researchers included William Gudykunst, Stella Ting-Toomey, Young Yun Kim and Guo-Ming Chen, to give a few examples. They considered Intercultural Communication as a specific case of interpersonal and intergroup communication, and by doing so they tried to theorize the process of Intercultural Communication in general communication terms (e.g. Gudykunst, 2005; Gudykunst and Kim, 2003; Chen and Starosta, 1998; Ting-Toomey, 1999). The specific topics these scholars addressed range from cultural adaptation, communicative effectiveness and competence, conflict management and anxiety/uncertainty management to the communication accommodation theory, identity negotiation and management, and cultural diversity and intercultural ethics.

6.2.3   Strand 3: Discourse Approaches to Intercultural Communication

Although the relevance of discourse studies to Intercultural Communication seems obvious, it was not until the 1980s that the connection began to materialize in systematic analyses of the discourse patterns of speakers from different cultural and linguistic backgrounds. The discourse approaches provide in-depth and systematic investigations of interactions either in Intercultural Communication situations or from a comparative perspective in a way that no previous studies have been able to do. An impressive number of studies have emerged that have examined various aspects of language use which may vary from culture to culture and from language to language, such as address terms, turn-taking, discourse markers, topic management, and speech acts of request, apology, greeting, refusals, and so on. These studies have made an important contribution to raising awareness of cultural differences in the way people communicate. When interpreting either Intercultural Communication breakdown or cross-cultural differences in interactional patterns, the discourse approaches often appeal to notions such as politeness and face whose analytic capacity is limited by their culturally relative definitions. Examples of discourse approaches to Intercultural Communication include Gumperz (1978, 1982), Gumperz and Tannen (1979), Gumperz, Jupp and Roberts (1979) and Scollon and Scollon (2001).

6.2.4   Strand 4: Intercultural Learning and Intercultural Communicative Competence

To many people, the ultimate goal of Intercultural Communication is to gain an understanding of people from different cultural backgrounds and to develop abilities and skills to communicate with them. Since the 1950s, there have been a number of studies that explore the ways in which Intercultural Communicative Competence (ICC, the ability to communicate effectively and appropriately in intercultural encounters) can be more effectively developed. The earliest influential theory was the Contact Theory proposed by Allport (1954), who specified four conditions for optimal intergroup contact, including equal group status within the situation, common goals, intergroup cooperation and authority support. Since the 1980s, numerous conceptualizations of ICC have been proposed, including, for example, Spitzberg and Cupach (1984), Gudykunst (1994), Chen and Starosta (1996), Byram (1997) and Fantini (2000).

6.2.5   Strand 5: Language Learning and Teaching

According to Kramsch (2001), *Linguistics Across Cultures* by Robert Lado (1957) was the first book to link culture and language in the context of language teaching and learning.

Since then, significant progress has been made, from the traditional language learning and teaching approaches which very often reduced culture to 'foods, fairs, folklore, and statistical facts' (Kramsch, 1991: 218), to the integration of cultural values and practices in language teaching and learning. It is now generally accepted that one cannot be a competent user of a second language without a good knowledge of the L2 culture. In the meantime, once a person begins to learn a new language and culture, the new language and culture will have an impact on the learner's first language and culture as well. A new identity and set of cultural values will develop alongside the development of linguistic knowledge.

6.2.6 Strand 6: Intercultural Communication in Context

As a field that was born out of a concern for real-world problems, Intercultural Communication is interested in intercultural encounters in different contexts and sites, such as business, politics, law, the media, health, the workplace, service encounters, marriages, tourism, education, the Internet, and so on; and in genres such as small talk, meeting, telephoning, humour, job applications, business writing, and so on. Recent years have seen an increasing number of studies that examine Intercultural Communication in connection with multilingual and translanguaging practice (Buhrig and ten Thije, 2006; Meyer and Apfelbaum, 2010). By looking at how Intercultural Communication takes place in a specific context, these studies explore the interplay of cultural, contextual, organizational, (multi-)linguistic factors, and norms and general expectations in the way intercultural interactions are conducted.

These strands, among others, represent concerted effort by intercultural scholars from a number of adjacent disciplines and at different times. The spectrum of these different strands highlights diversity in the disciplinary backgrounds that have provided input to the field and its potential for engaging with and ultimately impacting on a wide range of theories and models.

6.3   What Are the Key Factors Behind Mis- or Non-understanding in Intercultural Communication?

The success or non-success of Intercultural Communication is subject to many factors. Some of the factors are generic and not limited to communication between people from different cultural backgrounds. For example, in everyday communication, misinterpretation of the meaning of certain words, mishearing of what is said, ambiguity in implicature or mismatch in knowledge and expectation between the speaker and hearer can happen to anyone. Other factors, on the other hand, such as language proficiency and mistranslation, may be specific to Intercultural Communication in which people very often communicate in their non-native languages. We will focus on the second type of factors in the following discussion.

6.3.1 Different Norms of Interaction

As Example (1) shows, different cultures have their own rules of interaction regarding appropriateness and effectiveness in communication. These rules, or norms of interaction, range from paralinguistic cues (i.e. how something is said, such as stress, intonation, rhythm, etc.) to politeness features (i.e. how to address each other's 'face want' in conversation, in particular with reference to power, social distance and familiarity between interactants); from turn-taking to nonverbal aspects of conversation (silence, eye contact, gestures, proxemics, etc.). They regulate the way we communicate in intercultural encounters and set up our expectations towards the other party with whom we communicate. Differences in the norms will lead to clashes in Intercultural Communication.

(1) A former Japanese Master's degree student who has studied Spanish and lived in Mexico for approximately six years once commented on her experience of adapting her speech to the local culture:

'First thing I noticed in Mexico is the difference in the types of voice we use. In Japanese society, especially young women, use a relatively high-pitch voice and tend to speak in a somehow 'childish' way. 'Childish' behaviour of a woman, not only the type of voice, but also her behaviour itself, is considered as something 'cute' or 'favourable', and very widely accepted in our society. In Mexican society, however, they use a lower and deeper tone of voice than in Japan; … In Mexican society, to use a childish voice, as many Japanese women do, could be a disadvantage, not something 'favourable'. After living in Mexico for a couple of months, I noticed about this fact and started to try using a different kind of voice, deeper and softer one, so that I could be treated as an adult person (especially because an Asian woman looks much younger than a Latin American woman!).'

6.3.2 Language Matters

In Intercultural Communication, sometimes one or both parties in the interaction speak in a language other than their native languages. This is known and researched as lingua franca communication. A key feature of lingua franca communication is its heterogeneous nature, since it is very often the case that lingua franca participants speak the shared language with different degrees of proficiency. Does language proficiency matter? The answer is yes and no. Yes, because we know that sufficient proficiency always helps, particularly in the situation when a message needs to be communicated precisely or appropriately. No, because language is not the only means of communication. We have other resources such as nonverbal communication, common sense, schemata, and so on. In fact, in various models of Intercultural Communicative Competence (see the next section) linguistic ability does not feature centrally. The assumption is that language skills alone are not enough to prepare anyone to be a competent intercultural communicator. Cultural awareness, attitude and the ability to use knowledge, attitudes and skills under the constraints of real-time communication and interaction play important roles.

Research evidence has also indicated that speakers are generally cooperative in lingua franca communication and employ a range of clarification and repair strategies to prevent, signal and resolve misunderstanding and to negotiate meaning.

6.3.3   Discrepancies in Beliefs, Values, Shared Knowledge and Reference Points

When drawing inferences from conversation, we very much rely on shared knowledge as reference points. The shared knowledge includes our understanding and assessment not only of the local context, but also of the world. The latter, referred to as schema, is the knowledge that we have learned, accumulated and stored in our memory. It helps us with the process of anticipating and interpreting social events, situations and other people and their situations, guides our attention to certain things and ultimately influences the way we understand the world. For example, if someone says that the weather is really nice back home, we may have different interpretations, depending on schemata. If we know that 'home' refers to Toronto and at the time of conversation it is as hot as 40 °C, then we can infer that the speaker is being sarcastic. The lack of relevant and shared schemata can lead to communication breakdown in the conversation.

The point made in the last paragraph is important to our understanding of Intercultural Communication in that it shows that *not all breakdowns in Intercultural Communication are caused by the mere fact that the people involved in interactions are from different cultures.* Some scholars argue that it is lack of knowledge about professional and institutional discourse systems and mismatches in contextualization, rather than *ethnicity per se,* that sometimes lead to failures or breakdowns in Intercultural Communication and put specific ethnic groups or outsiders in a disadvantaged position (e.g. Roberts, 2011). Other scholars challenge the practice of regarding cultural differences as something static. For example, Piller (2011) proposed a progressive account of cultural differences and used examples of intercultural marriage to argue that cultural differences between intercultural partners may become less prominent over time.

—— 6.4   What Are Culture-specific Ways of Communication?

Cross-cultural differences exist in many aspects of discourse and communication, ranging from communication style to variations in speech acts, from discourse organization to choices of means of communication, from verbal to nonverbal communication. This section will introduce some key concepts in the search for culture-specific ways of communication.

6.4.1   Culture-specific Communication Style

A number of dichotomies have been employed to describe differences in communication styles between cultures. Up to now the most widely cited terms are *high* vs. *low* context, coined by Edward Hall (1976). As an anthropologist, Hall noticed that there are differences between cultures in how much information is carried in context. In some cultures, such as the German, information exists in explicit and tacit messages, while in cultures such as those of East Asia much of the information exists in the actual setting or the environment and the listener needs to work it out. Some studies of Intercultural Communication have investigated the linguistic features of cultures which have a preference for high-context style. Sachiko Ide's work on Japanese honorifics and *wakimae* (Ide, 2005) is such an example. Ide argued that in high-context cultures such as the Japanese, there are three levels of communication. The first level is 'meta communication', which considers whether or not to say it, who is to speak, when and where to speak and how to take turns. The second level is 'meta pragmatics', where the speaker needs to consider 'territory of information' (i.e. who, between the speaker and hearer, knows more about the information) and to acknowledge the distinction by means of modal expressions of evidentials (i.e. grammatical elements in a language which specify the source of information such as *it is alleged*). The speaker also needs to consider situational factors such as the relationship between the speaker and the hearer and the formality of the situation. Appropriate use of modal expressions such as honorifics, person referent terms and sentence-final particles is obligatory. On the listener's part, constant back-channelling or some other means of making the discourse pragmatically appropriate is expected. The third level is propositional communication in which the speaker says the propositional content.

Gudykunst and Ting-Toomey (1988) proposed four verbal communication styles. These are direct vs. indirect, elaborate vs. succinct, personal vs. contextual, and instrumental vs. affective:

- Cultures differ in the degree of directness whereby speakers disclose their intentions through communication: direct style is very often used in low-context, individualistic cultures where speakers express their intentions and needs overtly, while indirect style is associated with high-context, collectivistic cultures where intentions are hidden or hinted and ambiguous and vague expressions are preferred. 'Dugri' talk, translated as straight or direct talk and dominant in the discourse of native-born Israelis of Jewish heritage, is a typical example of a direct communication style.
- Cultures also differ in the quantity and volume of talk. The elaborate style is often associated with many Arabic, Middle Eastern and Afro-American cultures, while in some cultures, a succinct style is preferred. The frequent use of silence among Finnish people as cited in some studies is an example.
- Personal vs. contextual communication styles differentiate the extent to which speakers' roles, social status and relationship are emphasized. A number of linguistic features are very often used as evidence of contextual communication style; for example, the use of familiar and formal forms of 2nd person pronoun and address terms in many languages, such as French, German and Swedish, honorifics in the Japanese and Korean languages, kinship terms in the Chinese language.
- Instrumental vs. affective styles differ in the goal of communication. The former is goal-oriented while the latter is primarily intended to initiate, develop and maintain social relationships and therefore is very much listener-oriented.

These cross-cultural communication styles illustrate some broad cultural preferences in communication. However, it is important to bear in mind the risk of overgeneralization that these communication styles often incur.

6.4.2   Cross-cultural Variations in Speech Acts

CCSARP (the Cross-Cultural Study of Speech Act Realization Project) was set up in the 1980s to investigate cross-linguistic similarities and differences in the realization patterns of the speech acts of requests and apologies in eight languages. Since then, numerous studies have compared realizations of specific speech acts across cultures, such as requests, apologies, greetings, refusals, and so on.

6.4.3   Discourse Organization

Information flow may occur in different manners in languages. In business communication in English, people tend to put the most important information first and leave the least important information last in the fashion of an inverted pyramid. The differences in information flow (also known as rhetoric) are illustrated in the following activity.

STUDY ACTIVITY 6.1

An assistant to a CEO has drafted two versions of an email message to announce the appointment of a new communications chief. What are the three most important messages in each version? Which version would you prefer and why? Which version resembles the way information is presented in a different culture or language you are familiar with? The activity is based on Flynn and Flynn (2003).

1. Jane Tomm, a graduate of City University, with a master's degree in journalism and a bachelor's degree in English, is an integral member of the health department's public relations team, serving initially as a public information officer then as a manager of special projects. A civil servant for 12 years, Jane has also published two books on children's fiction and is a volunteer tutor with the city schools, teaching writing skills to secondary school students. Effective today, Jane has been named communications chief for the regional health department. All please plan to attend tomorrow's 9 am staff meeting to learn more about Jane's promotion and her plans for the department.

2. Effective immediately, Jane Tomm has been named communications chief for the regional health department. All supervisors, managers and staff will now report to Jane. Please plan to attend tomorrow's 9 am staff meeting to learn more about Jane's promotion and her plans for the department. For those who are unfamiliar with Jane, she is a 12-year civil servant and an integral member of the Health Department's public relations team, where she served first as a public information officer, then as manager of special projects. A graduate of City University, with a master's degree in journalism and a bachelor's degree in English, Jane has published two books of children's fiction and is a volunteer tutor with the city schools, teaching writing skills to secondary school students.

6.4.4   Choice of Means of Communication

With the growing use of technology, more choices of means of communication become available. However, cross-cultural differences exist regarding what is the preferred and appropriate means of communication, when to use it and with whom. For some cultures, technology-mediated communication such as emails can appear to be too businesslike for interpersonal communication. A student from Ecuador cited in Thatcher (2004) once commented,

> I lost all the emotion on email and the internet … I cannot communicate all that I want to. It is really difficult.

However, the lack of a personal touch associated with technology-mediated communication can work to one's advantage. Some people from cultures which value in-group solidarity may find it easier to discuss and debate controversial issues online, since it reduces face threat.

6.4.5   Nonverbal Communication

Nonverbal communication involves all the nonverbal stimuli that are meaningful either intentionally or unintentionally to the people concerned. It includes body movement (such as posture, gestures, facial expressions), paralanguage, personal space, silence, and so on. Cultural norms differ on how, when and to whom nonverbal communication is displayed. The same stimuli might mean completely different things to people from different cultures. For example, some cultures (e.g. Mediterranean cultures) do not shy away from showing or even exaggerating signs of sadness. In these cultures, it is not uncommon to see men and women crying in public. However, in some cultures a reticent approach is preferred. 'I feel stupid crying in front of the camera' was the comment made by the father of one of the two Soham girls (UK) murdered by their school caretaker, when he reflected on the event two years later.

STUDY ACTIVITY 6.2

Hall (1966) suggests that generally speaking there are four levels of personal space among middle-class Americans: intimate distance (0–46 cm) among close family members; personal distance (46–121 cm) for informational conversation between family members or friends; social distance (121–366 cm) for more formal conversation; and public distance (366 cm and above) for the most formal occasions such as a speech.

Observe the space between yourself and different conversation partners in different contexts and activities: lectures, home, train, workplace, informal get-together, and so on. Do you think that Hall's observations apply?

To sum up, we described some culture-specific communication styles in this section. In doing so, we followed the traditional approach and took culture-specific communication style as the norm shared by a group of people. During the discussion, we have taken care not to assume that cultural values have a determining effect on an individual's style of communication. We argued along the line that some communication styles are culture-specific and associated with a particular culture.

──────── ## 6.5   What Does 'Interculturality' Mean in Multilingual and Multicultural Communicative Contexts?

Recent years have seen a growing use of the term interculturality (IC) in public discourse, when contact, interaction and dialogue between different cultural groups are promoted as a way to achieve better understanding of different cultures in an increasingly globalized world, and as a social ideal for a better society. For example, the International Network on Cultural Policy (INCP), which has a membership of over 70 countries and regions, defines IC as

> the interaction between cultures, exchange and communication where the individual recognizes and accepts the reciprocity of the other's culture.
>
> (INCP website: http://www.incp-ripc.org/index_e.shtml)

In such a context, the notion of interculturality refers to a 'state of being intercultural', the situation where participants from different cultures interact with each other.

As a research paradigm, interculturality represents a line of investigation moving away from the traditions seen in the works of many social psychologists and cultural anthropologists. As reviewed in the previous sections, there is a growing body of studies that are predominantly concerned with providing a cultural account for mis- or non-understanding in interaction or different styles of communication. These studies often assume that in intercultural interactions, cultural values determine speakers' discourse strategies and cultural differences are a source of intercultural miscommunication. Although this line of investigation has many followers across various fields, in particular business communication and training, language teaching and learning, concerns have been raised by many scholars (e.g. Sarangi, 1994; Scollon and Scollon, 2001). They questioned the validity of defining culture solely in terms of nationality and treating cultural values as something shared homogeneously among a group, as well as the practice of applying national character to the interpretation or prediction of behaviour of an individual coming from that culture.

Our experience also tells us that people from the same culture do not always behave in the same way, and predicting how someone is going to interact according to the cultural account is neither reliable nor feasible. Mis- or non-understandings in interactions are not necessarily always the result of cultural differences between participants. Sometimes, mis- or non-understandings occur between people from the same culture, speaking the same language.

Against such a background, a new research paradigm that problematizes the concept of interculturality emerged. These studies (e.g. Nishizaka, 1995) challenge practices whereby participants' cultural differences are taken for granted and used to explain an individual's behaviour. Instead, they argue that 'being intercultural' is a socially constructed phenomenon and needs to be studied through fine-grained analysis of inter-action on a case-by-case basis. These studies argue that an individual belongs to several different categories, but not all the categories are equally relevant or salient at a given point. On some occasions, 'foreignness' is deliberately brought into practice or interaction – for example, tutors are addressed as Sensei in karate practice. On other occasions, how-ever, cultural differences are irrelevant to the conversation. This is very likely to happen in a highly controlled genre such as 'saying prayers', when there is strict restriction on when and what participants can say, or in a situation, such as giving a lecture on research methods, where one's cultural background is less relevant:. There are also times when only some aspects of the participants' cultural and ethnic backgrounds are salient. For example, a well-travelled American who has some cultural knowledge about Japan may align himself with the Japanese interactants rather than American students in a conversa-tion (Mori, 2003).

Some recent works on interculturality place an even greater emphasis on the emer-gent, discursive and dynamic nature of cultural differences. Echoing the arguments put forward by scholars who have examined the fluidity and multiplicity of social identities (e.g. Antaki and Widdicombe, 1998), they believe participants' sociocultural identities are neither *a priori* (something knowable independent of experience – for example, the assumption that a Westerner tends to be direct in making a request while an Eastern Asian person tends to be indirect), nor static. Instead, participants' sociocultural differ-ences are constructed and negotiated through interaction. Therefore, these studies see cultural differences as a process rather than an end product. Take, for example, the translated transcripts shown in Study Activity 6.3 of a radio programme interview with a foreign student in Japan (Nishizaka, 1995).

In the extract, the interviewer A was Japanese and the interviewee B was in fact a Sri Lankan living in Japan. The interview was conducted in Japanese and transcribed broadly. During the interview, which aimed to discover the view of a 'foreigner' on living together with Japanese people, the interviewer did not make his Japaneseness relevant to the interaction. Rather, he deliberately distanced himself from 'Japanese people' by repeatedly referring to Japanese as 'Japanese people' or 'they'. In doing so, the interviewer made salient his conversational role as an interviewer rather than his Japaneseness. The interviewee followed the lead and tried to establish himself as a rep-resentative of foreigners living in Japan. He confirmed the interviewer's assertions in almost every turn by saying 'yes' and elaborating occasionally (e.g. Turns 23, 25). In Turn 23, he used the word 'foreigners' as if he was talking about a group of people, not about himself.

In sum, studies on interculturality show that cultural differences cannot be assumed to be relevant to or the cause of all the mis- or non-understanding in intercultural interac-tion. Participants in Intercultural Communication can make use of a range of interactional resources to establish and negotiate their sociocultural identities. In some cases, the pro-cess can build rapport and create a sense of common ground among the participants. The process of negotiating cultural differences also constitutes an important element in the socialization of younger generations of diasporic communities (Zhu, 2010). However, interculturality can also have a negative impact on the participants, since it simultane-ously creates a sense of subordination and prevents the conversation participants from learning about and from each other (Axelson, 2007).

STUDY ACTIVITY 6.3

Read the following extract of an interview on a radio programme from Nishizaka (1995: 304).
Could you tell who is Japanese and who is a foreigner and why?

```
1    A:   One thing I want to ask you is: when Japanese people talk in
2         Japanese, they are sometimes only diplomatic,
3    B:   Yes.
4    A:   [they] are just apparently sociable,
5    B:   Yes.
6    A:   [they] are sometimes so, aren't//[they]?
7    B:   Yes.
8    A:   For example, 'Well, Shiri-san, come to my home uh next holiday,'
9         say [they] very easily.
10   B:   Yes.
11   A:   If you actually go there on the next holiday, [they] will say, 'Oh?
12        For what have you come here,' ma(h)//y(h)be(h).//.hhhh
13   B:   hhhhhhhhhhhh
13a       Yes.
14   A:   I mean, what [they] say and
15   B:   Yes.
16   A:   what [they] mean seem different,
17   B:   Yes
18   A:   this way Japanese often
19   B:   Yes.
20   A:   talk,//don't [they]. [they] often talk so.
21   B:   Yes.
21a       Yes.
22   A:   How about this.
23   B:   This is a little troublesome to foreigners, //[they] th-
24   A:   It's troublesome, isn't it.
25   B:   Yes, wrongly, [they] will take what is said for what is meant,
```

6.6   How to Develop Intercultural Communicative Competence?

Intercultural Communicative Competence (ICC, also known as Intercultural Competence),
broadly speaking, refers to the ability to communicate effectively and appropriately in
intercultural encounters. Although different studies may have various conceptualizations
of what ICC constitutes and how it is measured and assessed, there is increasing consensus

on its core components. The following synthesis is based on the available existing literature, in particular Lustig and Koester (2003).

- *Cultural awareness and knowledge*: information, understanding, mindfulness and critical evaluation of cultural, group and individual differences as well as one's own values, beliefs and practice (self-awareness).
- *Attitudes and motivations*: openness, curiosity, tolerance, empathy and readiness to learn about something different and new, and willingness to cooperate.
- *Skills*: the ability to operate under the constraints of real-time communication and interaction. For example:
  - interpersonal and relationship-building skills;
  - skills to listen and observe, and to gather and assess information promptly and actively;
  - skills to manage anxiety and ambiguity;
  - skills to transfer and adapt skills from one culture to another;
  - skills to make use of one's interactional resources, even if limited, to achieve one's goal;
  - skills to interact appropriately, ranging from the appropriate choice of channel of communication, style, register, discourse management and strategies, to nonverbal communication skills;
  - skills to interact effectively to accomplish one's goals, such as relaying a message clearly, persuading an audience, relationship-building, and so on.

With the increase in the number of intercultural exchanges or study abroad programmes, there have been a growing number of studies that investigate the impact of the experience on the participants' ICC. These studies suggest that ICC is not something one either has or does not have, but something that one develops over time through intercultural experience. Some aspects of ICC seem to benefit more from direct contact than other aspects. For example, some studies suggest that intercultural experience can increase participants' knowledge of the host culture, improve fluency in the language of the host country, reduce anxiety in interacting with people from different cultures, develop sensitivity towards cultural differences and increase efficacy. Participants also develop greater intercultural networks and friendships with people from different cultural backgrounds.

Most ICC assessments, such as the Intercultural Development Inventory (Hammer, Bennett and Wiseman, 2003) and YOGA Form (Fantini, 2000), take the form of multiple-item questionnaires. In a typical questionnaire type of assessment, a respondent is asked to rate his or her own level on various components of ICC. A profile of the respondent's ICC can then be extracted based on their own self-assessment. Questionnaires are also used to monitor the changes that occur to individuals. However, recently there is some debate on comparability and reliability of self-ratings by respondents. Several longitudinal studies reported that, after participating in study abroad programmes, respondents gave themselves a lower rating than at the beginning, possibly because their reference points changed during the experience, thus resulting in a paradox that is best summarized by the phrase 'the more you know, the more you realize that you don't know'.

A Sample Question From YOGA Form (Your Objectives, Guidelines and Assessment) Designed by Fantini (2000)

Level I: Educational Traveler – I demonstrate awareness of:

- differences across languages and cultures   0 1 2 3 4 5
- my negative reactions to these differences
  (fear, ridicule, disgust, superiority, etc.)   0 1 2 3 4 5
- how a specific context affects/alters my interaction with others   0 1 2 3 4 5
- how I am viewed by members of the host culture   0 1 2 3 4 5

Study Activity 6.4

Below are some sample questions from *Autobiography of Intercultural Encounters*. Try to answer these questions about yourself and about an intercultural encounter in which you were involved.

- How would you define yourself? Think about things that are especially important to you in how you think about yourself and how you like others to see you.
  In describing the encounter,
- Give the encounter a name which says something about it.
- What happened when you met this person/these people?
- Where did it happen?
- What were you doing there?
- Why have you chosen this experience?
- Describe any other reactions and say what you think caused your reaction.

An assessment tool that departs from the method of quantifying ICC is *Autobiography of Intercultural Encounters* (AIE), designed by Michael Byram, Martyn Barrett, Julia Ipgrave and their colleagues for the Council of Europe (AIE, 2009). It takes the form of a series of questions and prompts carefully designed to guide the learner's reflections on his or her intercultural encounters. In doing so, it provides the learner with a structure to analyse the incidents and consider what they learned from the encounters.

Compared with the prolific pool of ICC assessment tools, how to teach or learn culture has received very little attention. The following offers a brief summary of influential theory and models.

6.6.1   Learning Culture Through Contact

The earliest influential theory on culture learning is Allport's intergroup contact theory (1954), which postulates that the positive effect of intergroup contact requires four key conditions: equal group status within the situation; common goals; intergroup cooperation; and authority support. This theory has received attention among policy makers and practitioners in racial integration and equality, racial conflict resolution and the intergenerational gap. It, together with Kolb's experiential learning theory (1984), has also been used as the rationale for creating opportunities for intercultural experience, such as study abroad, exchange programmes, overseas expeditions, and so on.

6.6.2   Learning Culture Through Acculturation

Acculturation describes the process whereby someone new to a culture learns to adapt to the host culture. Some people experience a negative reaction, sometimes referred to as 'culture shock', that is, a feeling of anxiety or loss, when living in a new culture. As described in the U-curve and the W-curve hypotheses, the process of learning a culture can take many turns: from excitement at the moment of arrival in the host country to anxiety when excitement wears out; from being lost to recovery of confidence and getting used to the system in the host country; from the joy of returning to the home culture to disappointment at re-entry when discovering that familiar things are not there any longer; from the feeling of loss in one's home culture to recovery and reintegration into the home culture.

6.6.3   Learning Culture as Socialization and Identity-making

Learning a new culture is also a process of being socialized into the new culture and learning how things are done in the host culture while developing and constructing one's social cultural identity. Although the application of language socialization to studies of Intercultural Communication is only emerging, the perspective has much to offer for understanding intercultural learning.

6.6.4   Learning Culture Through Language Learning

Language and culture are intertwined. There is a growing body of empirical evidence demonstrating that learning to speak a language is not just about learning to put grammatically correct sentences together. It is about learning what to say in a culturally appropriate way and about developing and constructing a new sociocultural identity. However, traditional language learning and teaching approaches very often fail to acknowledge the importance of culture, which is frequently reduced to 'foods, fairs, folklore, and statistical facts' (Kramsch, 1991: 218). Byram and his colleagues in their series of publications (e.g. Byram and Morgan, 1994) have called for an integrated method of language and culture teaching in which the culture of the target language is made explicit in the curriculum.

Recent years have seen increasing discussion on adopting the sociocultural approach to language learning. In this approach, language learning is seen as a social activity in which the learner not only learns how to take actions with words, but also acquires the knowledge needed to be a fully participating member through the guidance of more experienced members. This knowledge ranges from a framework of what constitutes the concept of 'knowledge' to the sociocultural significance of the activity, from the roles one plays in social activity to understanding that roles are constructed through social action.

6.7 Summary

As a rapidly developing field of study, Intercultural Communication is concerned with a wide range of topics and comes with a variety of perspectives. In this chapter we focused on a small selection of key issues in the study of Intercultural Communication, including factors behind mis- or non-understanding in Intercultural Communication, culture-specific ways of communication, the notion of interculturality, the concept of Intercultural Communicative Competence (ICC) and ways of developing it. Recent years have seen a prolific output of textbooks, handbooks, readers and research monographs in the field. The recommended reading list for this chapter is a good starting point for a more comprehensive overview of the field.

Study Questions

1. Describe an event from your own experience of studying, living and travelling abroad where there were mis- or non-understandings in communication. What do you think were the causes? Was culture a factor?
2. Select a culture and research the literature about communication styles associated with that culture. Are there any culture-specific communication styles and what are they?
3. Discuss the concept of interculturality and explore why it is important to think of cultural differences as socially constructed by interactants through interaction.
4. What is Intercultural Communicative Competence and how can we develop and assess it?

Recommended Reading

Jackson, Jane. 2012. *The Routledge Handbook of Language and Intercultural Communication*. London: Routledge. This contains 35 review articles on a wide range of topics in the study of language and Intercultural Communication.

Paulston, Christina Bratt, Scott. F Kiesling and Elizabeth S. Rangel. 2012. *The Handbook of Intercultural Discourse and Communication*. Oxford: Wiley-Blackwell. This offers a number of review articles in the study of intercultural discourse and communication.

Piller, Ingrid. 2011. *Intercultural Communication: A Critical Introduction*. Edinburgh: Edinburgh University Press. This provides a critical overview of the field of Intercultural Communication from a combined discourse-analytic and sociolinguistic perspective.

Spencer-Oatey, Helen and Peter Franklin. 2009. *Intercultural Interaction: A Multidisciplinary Approach to Intercultural Communication*. New York: Palgrave. This provides an overview of the key concepts and practices in the field of Intercultural Communication from a number of perspectives including Applied Linguistics, discourse studies, international business, psychology and anthropology.

Zhu Hua (ed.). 2011. *The Language and Intercultural Communication Reader*. London: Routledge. This contains a selection of articles under six research themes related to the study of language and Intercultural Communication, with notes for students and instructors.

Zhu Hua. 2014. *Exploring Intercultural Communication: Language in Action*. London. Routledge. This explores real-world intercultural issues in classroom, the workplace, business, family, study abroad and tourism, ways of effective and appropriate communication and key theoretical models and conceptual issues.

chapter 7

Literacy and Multimodality

Li Wei, Lisa J. McEntee-Atalianis
and Marjorie Lorch

Chapter Outline

Learning Outcomes

After reading this chapter, you should be able to

- describe different aspects of literacy acquisition and performance for both the individual and society;
- appreciate the different ways reading and writing systems vary across languages;
- appreciate the various ways in which reading and spelling skills are taught;
- discuss the issues surrounding second language literacy and biliteracy;
- discuss issues of social literacy;

Applied Linguistics, First Edition. Edited by Li Wei.
© 2014 John Wiley & Sons, Ltd. Published 2014 by John Wiley & Sons, Ltd.

- describe the various new modalities for representing language and serving communication;
- discuss whether sign language competence aids literacy development in deaf children;
- discuss issues of multimodality and multimodal communication in society.

Key Terms

- Biliteracy
- Bimodal bilingualism
- Common Underlying Proficiency/ Interdependence Hypothesis
- Deaf/deaf
- Grapheme
- Linguistic landscape
- Literacy

- Metalinguistic skills
- Multimodality
- Orthography
- Phonological awareness
- Script
- Sign language
- Social literacy

Jorge is a five-year-old Venezuelan boy, newly arrived in London with his parents, who are studying at a British university. He attends a nursery school in south London. He speaks Castellano Venezolano and is beginning to learn English. One day, as he was doing a spelling exercise at home, Jorge asked his mum why the English word *quick* is spelled with *qu*, not *kw*. The mother was puzzled and said to Jorge, 'Of course it is spelled with *qu*, it's *quick* and that's how English is spelled.' Jorge said to his mum, 'But Kwik Fit is spelled with *kw*, and daddy said, when we went to the garage the other day, it is the same as *quick*.' The mother paused a little and said, 'That's just a name of the garage. It's not correct spelling.' 'You mean they spelled it wrong in the garage?!' Jorge questioned. 'At school, you need to write *qu*, *i*, and *ck*,' the mother said to Jorge. Jorge looked at his spelling book and pronounced it like the Spanish *qué*. The mother stopped him and said, 'No, Jorge, it is *k-w-i-k*.' She pronounced the sounds slowly. Jorge looked at his mum, even more puzzled. 'So the garage is right!'

7.1   Introduction

UNESCO defines literacy as the 'ability to identify, understand, interpret, create, communicate, compute and use printed and written materials associated with varying contexts. Literacy involves a continuum of learning in enabling individuals to achieve their goals, to develop their knowledge and potential, and to participate fully in their community and wider society' (UNESCO, 2004: 13). This definition only refers to the traditional domain of printed text but more recently the concept of literacy has expanded to include new technologies and the forms of visual representation they provide. These new literacies based on the development of digital technologies have been an area of growing research interest since the beginning of the twenty-first century.

Typically, the social notion of functional literacy was based on the ability to read a newspaper and fill out forms, but increasingly there is a more significant need to use Internet-based media and telecommunications, including blogs and text messages. The social value and prevalence of literacy vary greatly around the world. Widespread literacy did not exist in Western countries before the mid-nineteenth century. Historically, in some societies the ability to sign one's name was taken as an indication of basic literacy. At the same time, the ability to read does not necessarily imply the ability to write. Someone who is able to read is referred to as being literate, an illiterate is someone who did not have the opportunity to learn how, while a dyslexic is a person who has inordinate difficulty in learning how to read (see Chapter 4 for more on disorders of reading and writing). The mastery of traditional reading and writing and the new literacies is increasingly becoming a vital capability linked to social, economic and political empowerment.

This chapter begins with a brief outline of the basic components of literacy. It then discusses literacy in a cross-modal bilingual context, before exploring the notions of social literacy and continua of biliteracy. The concept of multimodality as it is discussed in Applied Linguistics is then outlined. Links between modality and literacy are also discussed in this section.

7.2   Basic Components of Literacy

There are a number of subcomponents and skills involved in learning to read:

phonological awareness, decoding, fluency, comprehension and vocabulary.

An orthography is the symbolic communication system used to graphically represent a spoken language comprised of letters, characters or symbols. The set of these elements is called the script. In computer mediated communication we can also vary the font in which the letters are presented. So, for example, English is written using an alphabetic orthography with Roman letters; there are upper- and lower-case forms for both printed and cursive scripts which are used in handwriting, while typed forms have various fonts; the font you are reading this in is called 'Palatino'.

There is a long history of how writing systems came to be developed for different languages at different times. The invention of writing is considered one of the great technological human achievements. This is because it provides the opportunity to preserve records which do not rely on any one individual's oral memory. While the great majority of the languages in the world exist only in spoken form, the ability to read and write in one of the global languages, such as English, Chinese, Arabic or Spanish, is becoming more important for gaining access to knowledge. Languages of the Deaf, such as British Sign Language, are produced in a visual gestural form and do not have written counterparts except for conventions for fingerspelling proper nouns and loan words from spoken languages.

Alphabetic orthographies used in languages such as English and Hindi (Devanagari) represent individual speech sounds (phonemes) with individual characters (graphemes) though they use different scripts. The writing systems used for Arabic and Hebrew represent the consonants and typically do not include written symbols for vowels, which are determined by morphosyntactic context. Other orthographic systems use individual symbols to represent larger speech sound units such as syllables (Korean) or morphemes (Chinese). Orthographies used in languages such as Chinese are referred to as logographic to indicate that one symbol can be used to represent a whole word. Some languages are written with more than one orthography, such as the kana and kanji in Japanese, and some languages may be written with more than one script, such as Punjabi. Most orthographies are linear, but while English is written from left to right, Arabic is written in the opposite direction and logographic languages such as Chinese were typically written vertically until recent digital influences changed this convention to left-to-right writing. There are also tactile writing systems, such as Braille for the blind and manual alphabets for the deaf.

The regularity of the mapping of graphemes to morphemes varies from language to language and is described as degrees of orthographic transparency. Some languages, such as English, have little regularity in this mapping. Letters can have several different pronunciations and sounds can be represented by various letter spellings. Because of this, English has many heterographic homophones, which are pronounced the same but differ in spelling and meaning, such as 'piece' and 'peace', and homophonic homographs, which are words that are spelled the same but differ in meaning, such as 'bear' (the animal or to carry). Heterographic homophones also occur in non-alphabetic languages such as Chinese. In contrast, languages such as Finnish are said to be orthographically transparent; each letter typically has only one pronunciation. This type of variation in the mapping between the spoken and written form of a language has implications for the way children learn to read and for variations in attainment. The symptoms displayed in dyslexic children are language specific (Ziegler and Goswami, 2005).

While it is the case that any spoken utterance can be represented accurately in written form, there is an acknowledged difference between spoken and written communication. There are a number of formal conventions in written language which have to do with punctuation and paragraphing. In addition, text-level organization and structure are typically more complex because of the opportunity to edit and revise written communications (Biber and Conrad, 2009).

The written form of the language typically reflects the standard spoken form and conventions which are particular to writing texts. People who speak Standard English, for example, may not perceive any differences. They have acquired the conventions of written English through formal education instruction. However, those who speak non-standard varieties such as African-American English in parts of the USA or Scouse in the Liverpool region of the UK will be aware of the large divergence between their spoken language and the written language used in public documents. There is a growing appreciation of vernacular literacy which recognizes the desire of people to produce writing in their non-standard variant. A more significant variation between the spoken form and written form occurs in Arabic, where regional spoken varieties are relatively mutually intelligible dialects of one language, as compared with the situation with Chinese, where one orthography is used for languages that are more divergent in their spoken form.

While speaking is a naturally developing ability in all healthy children, reading is a skill that requires explicit instruction, typically included in formal primary education. There is great diversity in the way children learn to read in different languages and in different societies. There are also huge differences in the age at which the formal teaching of reading commences. Languages with non-transparent mapping between the written and spoken forms may be taught over a period of many years. So there is weekly assessment of

Case Study 7.1

In order to overcome limitations associated with script incompatibilities, Greek users of the internet have developed *Greeklish*, a transliterated version of Modern Greek using Roman characters. This Greek-to-Greeklish conversion (broadly termed as transliteration) relies either on the phonemic or the graphemic overlap of a given Greek letter with a Roman one. For the subgroup of letters that sound and look the same across the two alphabets (e.g. *o*), and for script-specific graphemes that map onto the same phoneme (e.g. *φ-f*, which map onto /f/), the output of the Greek-to-Greeklish transliteration does not vary. However, a reduced set of Greek letters can map on different Roman letters, such as the Greek letter *ω*, that can be mapped onto *o* on the basis of the phonemic overlap, or onto *w* on the basis of a graphemic criterion. Therefore, Greeklish transliterations usually have extensive phonemic overlap (e.g. *μῆ´λο-milo* [apple] are pronounced like /milo/) while the degree of graphemic overlap can vary from very limited (e.g. *ζύμη*-zymi-zymi [barm]) to almost complete (e.g. *σοκάκι*-sokaki [alley]). Technically, the term transliteration refers to the act of representing a given string in a language with a formal representation from a different code (e.g. script) following the phoneme-to-grapheme conversion rules of this new code. If the relations between graphemes and phonemes are similar in both codes, transliterations are considered to be transcriptions. Accordingly, Greeklish conversions with high graphemic overlap with respect to the Greek base words, for which the Roman graphemes sounding the same as the Greek graphemes are visually similar, are better defined as transcriptions. In contrast, when the Roman graphemes associated to the phonemes do not visually resemble those graphemes from the Greek alphabet, the Greeklish conversions are characterized as transliterations. A well-known instance of transliteration can be found in languages using different writing systems, such as Katakana-Kanji transliterations of Japanese with extensive phonemic overlap but null graphemic overlap. A transcription-transliteration distinction similar to the Greeklish-Greek one is found in the Cyrillic-Roman correspondences that guide Serbian script alternations; while some of the Roman and Cyrillic graphemes that map onto the same Serbian phoneme are visually very close or identical (transcribed letters like a-a, b-б), others are visually distinct (transliterated letters like l-л, c –ц).

In order to ensure the fluidness of the intended virtual communication, it is expected that experienced users of Greeklish would have developed a series of highly internalized processes to perform Greek-to-Greeklish and Greeklish-to-Greek conversions. Using the masked priming paradigm, Dimitropoulou *et al.*'s study examines the level of automaticity of these conversion processes in Greeks who are exposed to Greeklish on a daily basis. They designed two lexical decision experiments using Greeklish primes with different degrees of graphemic overlap with their corresponding Greek targets. Results show that Greeklish primes were effectively processed and transliterated to their Greek counterparts. Larger masked priming effects were found as a function of increased prime-target graphemic overlap. Interestingly, these Greeklish priming effects were in all cases of smaller magnitude than the pure Greek identity priming effect. The findings suggest that extensive experience with a recently developed artificial writing system leads to its non-effortful processing, but that even for highly experienced Greeklish users the Greeklish-to-Greek conversion is modulated by the graphemic properties of the input stimulus.

(Dimitropoulou, Duñabeitia and Carreiras, 2011)

spelling vocabulary in children up to the age of 12 in the USA, while in places that use transparent orthographies, such as Spain, school children are simply instructed in the grapheme–phoneme mappings for the alphabet.

Reading instruction may use a variety of techniques to train young children to learn the mappings between the spoken and written form. The so-called phonic approach emphasizes the association between written characters and sounds while the so-called whole language approach involves acquiring words or phrases without analysing the smaller units that compose them. The phonic approach focuses on training the child to automatize a number of decoding skills. For languages that rely on an alphabetic writing system, children must first become aware that the sound stream that comprises spoken language can be analysed as being made up of smaller units of sound such as syllables and phonemes. This ability is called phonological awareness and is thought to be a prerequisite for learning how to read (Anthony and Francis, 2005). The notion of phonological awareness has been the subject of a great deal of recent research. It has become evident that there are several distinct skills involved and that phonological awareness arises out of early reading experience rather than being a precondition (Neuman and Dickinson, 2011).

7.3 Literacy in Cross-modal Bilingual Contexts: Does Sign Language Competence Facilitate Deaf Children's Literacy Development?

The discussion so far has focused on a consideration of the development of literacy in individuals or populations whose communication skills are primarily developed and supported through competence in a spoken modality. However, for some children access to spoken language is limited or severely restricted. Estimates vary widely, but approximately one in every 1,000 babies born in the UK is deaf, and few of these children later succeed in reaching the levels of literacy achieved by their hearing counterparts on leaving school. Some report that over 90% of profoundly deaf school-leavers attain a reading age of approximately nine years of age, making even the tabloid press difficult to access. Only 2% are reported to leave school able to read at an appropriate level. Many of the errors found to perseverate in the writing of deaf learners are noted to be similar to the types of errors made by hearing second language learners (L2), for example, omissions or over-generalizations, and are reported to be a consequence of the limited 'quality' and 'quantity' of the input in educational contexts (Plaza-Pust, 2008: 76).

Understanding why deaf children experience so much difficulty in reading and writing is complex. This is largely due to the diversity of the Deaf[1]/deaf population in terms of their hearing status as well as diversity in their linguistic, cultural, familial and educational experiences. In addition to this, there is a paucity of research on the natural acquisition of sign language and bimodal bilingualism (involving both auditory-vocal and visual-manual channels) internationally, compared with research on spoken language acquisition/learning and bilingualism. One obvious (often cited) general explanation for poor literacy development in deaf children is that writing is a graphic representation of a spoken language and since spoken language is inaccessible to congenitally deaf children, literacy skills are difficult to acquire. However, as noted by Ardito et al. (2008: 140), writing is not simply a graphic representation of a spoken form but a 'semiotic system with its own

STUDY ACTIVITY 7.1

1. Reflect for a moment on factors that may influence deaf children's ability to read and write.
2. How might a deaf child's learning experience in the classroom be different from that of a hearing child? How might/should teachers accommodate to their learning needs?

characteristics and learned through a complex series of linguistic and metalinguistic processes'. Many advocate that the natural language of the deaf is sign language, which serves as a strong platform on which to build cognitive, linguistic and metalinguistic skills necessary for reading and writing. However, only about 10% of deaf children are born to Deaf signing parents and enter school with productive sign language competence.

Cummins (1991), researching literacy development in minority children learning a majority second language, suggests that establishing a strong foundation in a first language (L1) enhances literacy development in the L2 owing to the prior establishment of linguistic and cognitive skills in L1. His 'Common Underlying Proficiency/ Interdependence Hypothesis' has been applied in many contexts and attention has recently been paid to its consideration in cross-modal bilingual contexts. Researchers have sought to establish whether deaf children are better able to become literate in a majority language if their learning is supported by a sign language and whether the relationship between sign language and spoken/written languages is bidirectional in literacy development, and, if so, at what levels – linguistic/metalinguistic/cognitive? What components of sign language impact on literacy development and how do learners cross modalities?

Over recent years, many hypotheses have been proposed about the relationship between sign language and spoken/written language in the sequential bilingual development of deaf children. It has been suggested that there are three levels at which the languages might interact: the linguistic level (e.g. lexical/morphosyntactic/narrative structures); the metalinguistic level (knowledge about language), and the metacognitive level (cognitive structures necessary for language acquisition) (Plaza-Pust, 2008). Three dominant positions prevail in the literature about the facilitative or debilitating influences of cross-modal interaction in bilingual development:

*   *the interference hypothesis*, which proposes that sign language competence has a negative impact on the acquisition/learning of written forms (e.g. Maeder, 1995, cited in Plaza-Pust, 2008);
*   *the double-discontinuity hypothesis*, which suggests there is no direct relationship between the sign language and written language skills (e.g. Mayer and Akamatsu, 1999, 2000); and
*   *the hypothesis of a positive relationship between L1[2] and L2* leading to direct or indirect transference of linguistic or metalinguistic knowledge (e.g. Hoffmeister, 2000, cited in Plaza-Pust, 2008).

STUDY ACTIVITY 7.2

What evidence might be brought to bear to support or refute each of the hypotheses listed above?

In proposing the 'Interference Hypothesis' researchers have drawn on persistent and common errors in the writing of deaf children and adults, particularly syntactic errors (Niederberger, 2008). They have found, for example, that the syntax of sign language transfers to sentence word order in writing and that, in reading, spatial and time references can be difficult to process when based on spoken language word order. Researchers differ in their interpretations of these phenomena: some suggest that it is a consequence of differences in cognitive framing (e.g. Vincent-Durroux, 1992, cited in Niederberger, 2008); others that written language is filtered and processed through sign language (e.g. Sero-Guillaume, 1994, cited in Niederberger, 2008), although the latter hypothesis has been objected to in light of the similarity in the errors produced by deaf children and adults who do not know sign language (e.g. Wilbur, 2000, cited in Niederberger, 2008). Plaza-Pust (2008) also points out the benefits of sign language in providing children with a grammar which they can temporarily 'borrow' for literacy tasks.

In contrast to the 'Interference Hypothesis', other researchers suggest that there is no interference from sign language in the development of literacy. The 'Double-Discontinuity' Hypothesis is based on a consideration of linguistic phenomena. Mayer and colleagues. (Mayer and Akamatsu, 1999, 2000; Mayer and Wells, 1996, cited in Niederberger, 2008), studying deaf children/adolescent literacy in America, argue that the linguistic structures of English and of American Sign Language (ASL) are too dissimilar to be influential. They suggest that linguistic transfer can only occur from oral to written languages through two possible routes: (i) L1 oral language > L1 written > L2 written, or, (ii) L1 oral language > L2 oral language > L2 written. They argue that since the majority of deaf children and adolescents are not sufficiently competent in spoken English they are unable to use oral language skills to acquire written skills. Moreover, since there is also no written form of ASL, linguistic transfer between ASL and written English cannot occur – there is therefore 'double discontinuity'. Niederberger (2008) argues, however, that far from leading to deficit, ASL can facilitate the acquisition of literacy as demonstrated through a comparison of the role of ASL with English-based sign systems in facilitating reading.

The final position is at variance with the former two hypotheses. Drawing on the socio-cultural theory of Deafness, in which the Deaf are viewed as a minority social and linguistic grouping (see for example, Ladd (2003), and Cummins's (2000) suggestion that academic skills in L1 can be easily transferred to L2, his 'Common Underlying Proficiency' model), this hypothesis supports the view that there is a positive relationship between sign competence and literacy and so early and sustained exposure to sign language should be encouraged for deaf children. Researchers suggest that the ability to sign improves children's metalinguistic ability, enabling them to think about and deconstruct linguistic forms and structure – skills necessary in L2 learning. Moreover, experience of genre – for

Case Study 7.2

Burman (2008) reports on a teaching programme for deaf primary school children designed to improve their ability to decode and produce English words through an understanding of English morphology. Literacy assessments for school teachers to measure signing children's morphological development were also developed. These instruments were based on a cross-linguistic comparison of British Sign Language (BSL) and written English and drew on the ability of deaf children to visually code English words. Children were taught to decode English words in reading and to use 11 different classifications of English morphemes (e.g. plural -s; regular past tense –ed, etc.) to spell. For example, the research targeted the difference between plurality in BSL and English. In BSL the noun form remains uninflected but plurality is marked through the use of the quantifier, as opposed to English, in which plurality (in regular forms) is marked by the addition of 's' as represented as the following gloss:

BSL = 1 hat; 2 hat
English = 1 hat; 2 hats

Children were taught to recognize and reproduce this distinction in reading and writing, and appreciate the relationship between morphology and grammar in written English.

example, narratives and poetry – enhances the opportunity for linguistic transfer to a written form and reading comprehension (Niederberger, 2008). Wilbur (2000, cited in Niederberger, 2008) proposes that in writing English, ASL users transfer their knowledge of narrative structures in sign to the written form – for example, establishing background information such as character descriptions and details about the setting. Others also (e.g. Padden and Ramsey, 2000, cited in Niederberger, 2008) suggest that at a lexical level finger-spelling acts as an important tool in the teaching of lexis and spelling and that sign language competence also enables children to develop world knowledge, necessary for comprehending meaning in text.

In the development of these hypotheses researchers have focused on different phenomena both in analysis and interpretation, and on different linguistic structures, making it difficult to arrive at a general conclusion about the interaction between sign and literacy development. Research to date on various sign languages suggests that there is a direct beneficial influence of sign language competence on literacy skills in relation to: finger-spelling; comprehension of synonyms and antonyms; and production of narratives. However, there is limited support for the beneficial influence of morphosyntax, although there may be indirect benefits in the form of cognitive or metalinguistic development. Further, researchers have found that instruction that exploits sign language as an explanatory or cross-comparative tool has a positive effect on reading/writing skills, as structures in the L2 can be compared with similar forms in the L1.

Further research is necessary to disambiguate the linguistic, metalinguistic and cognitive influences of sign language on literacy and vice versa. Nevertheless, findings to date suggest that exposure to and acquisition of sign language and the introduction of bilingual education programmes that provide a good quality and quantity of language input are beneficial to literacy development and can have positive consequences for literacy skills in a majority language.

—————————— 7.4   Social Literacy and the Continua of Biliteracy

Sociolinguists, such as James Gee (e.g. 2011), have problematized the tendency to define literacy as a singular knowledge or developmentally ordered skill set, as unvarying across contexts and situations, and as primarily cognitive. Instead, they have demonstrated that literacy entails much more than the ability to read and write. In particular, they have shown that literacy practices are enmeshed within and influenced by social, cultural, political and economic factors, and that literacy learning and use vary by situation and entail complex social interactions.

There are at least two reasons why we should consider literacy in broader terms than the traditional conception of it as the ability to read and write. First, in our world today, language is by no means the only communication system available. Many types of visual images and symbols have specific significances. We will discuss the notion of multimodality in Section 7.5. Second, as Gee argues, reading and writing, or the 'meat' of literacy according to the traditional notion of the term, are not such obvious ideas as they first appear. 'After all,' Gee states, 'we never just read or write; rather, we always read or write something in some way' (2008: 14). In other words, according to which type of text we read, there are different ways in which we read depending on the 'rules' of how to read such a text.

Literacy, according to Gee, even if it is the traditional print-based literacy, should be conceived as being multiple, or comprising different literacies, since we need different types of literacies to read different kinds of texts in ways that meet our particular purposes for reading them. A simple example would be that we read a novel in a different way from how we read a cookery recipe. This sociocultural approach to literacy has come to be known as the New Literacy Studies, which emphasize studying language-in-use and literacies within their contexts of social practice. One of the areas on which researchers in New Literacy Studies have been focusing is the literacy practices of bi- and multilingual language users. Early scholars of biliteracy, such as Goodman, Goodman and Flores (1979), defined biliteracy as mastery of reading and writing in two languages. Some scholars, retaining the notion of literacy as singular, did not refer to the term biliteracy and spoke instead of *literacy and bilingualism* (Williams and Snipper 1990) or of *literacy across languages and cultures* (Ferdman, Weber and Ramírez 1994). Most of these studies, as García, Barlett and Kliefgen (2008) pointed out, focused on the acquisition of literacy in a powerful second language. Reyes (2001: 98) also defined biliteracy as mastery, but she extended the concept to mean

> mastery of the fundamentals of speaking, reading, and writing (knowing sound/symbol connections, conventions of print, accessing and conveying meaning through oral or print mode, etc.) in two linguistic systems. It also includes constructing meaning by making relevant cultural and linguistic connections with print and the learners' own lived experiences ... as well as the interaction of the two linguistic systems to make meaning.

Hornberger offers an even broader definition and describes biliteracy as 'the use of two or more languages in and around writing' (Hornberger, 2003: xii) or 'any and all instances in which communication occurs in two or more languages in or around writing' (Hornberger 1990: 213). She adapts the definition of 'literacy event' given by Heath (1986: 83) as 'any occasion in which a piece of writing is integral to the nature of participants' interactions and their interpretative processes' in a bilingual context. But because bilingualism and biliteracy are so complex, Hornberger speaks of biliteracy 'instances', encompassing not only events, but also 'biliterate actors, interactions, practices, activities, programs, situations, societies, sites, worlds' (Hornberger 2003: xiii; Hornberger and Skilton-Sylvester 2000: 98; Hornberger 2000: 362). For Hornberger, biliteracy is much more than what is learned in schools or other formal educational contexts, but also develops in families, homes and communities. Children and adults surrounded by different scripts in out-of-school settings often acquire the ability to read and write in two languages in functionally appropriate ways, as the example at the beginning of the chapter illustrates. They also acquire different attitudes and values about different literacy practices, including how these are associated with particular situated identities and social positions. The inclusion of more than one language system also points to power differentials and potential tensions about linguistic rights.

Hornberger proposes a multi-faceted model of 'continua of biliteracy' to draw attention to the continuity of experiences, skills, practices and knowledge stretching from one end of any particular continuum to the other. Specifically, the continua model depicts the development of biliteracy along intersecting first language–second language, receptive–productive, and oral–written language skills continua; through the medium of two (or more) languages and literacies whose linguistic structures vary from similar to dissimilar, whose scripts range from convergent to divergent, and to which the developing biliterate individual's exposure varies from simultaneous to successive; in contexts that encompass micro to macro levels and are characterized by varying mixes along the monolingual–bilingual and oral–literate continua; and with content that ranges from majority to minority perspectives and experiences, literary to vernacular styles and genres, and decontextualized to contextualized language texts (Hornberger, 1989; Hornberger and Skilton-Sylvester, 2000).

STUDY ACTIVITY 7.3

1. Find a bilingual or multilingual family and ask them if any of the family members engage in reading and writing different languages.
2. Do they encourage the children to be literate in all the languages of the family? Is any particular language preferred with regard to literacy development?
3. Do all the languages of the family receive equal support with regard to literacy – for example, reading resources available in different languages, learning opportunities and opportunities for using different languages?
4. Is literacy in any of the family languages affected in any way by socio-political factors such as school language policies and community relations?
5. What does the family need to support its biliteracy or multiliteracy development and practice?

7.5 Multimodality

Concepts such as *social literacy* and *biliteracy* have broadened the scope of literacy studies beyond conventional, print-based literacy. Bi-modal and sign language communication, as described in Section 7.3, further extended the scope by bringing modality into consideration. As a result, we have shifted our attention to what Bailey describes as '(a) the simultaneous use of different kinds of forms or signs and (b) the tensions and conflicts among those signs, based on the sociohistorical associations they carry with them' (2007: 257). While acknowledging that linguistic signs remain the primary semiotic tools for human communication, the new focus is on the highly multimodal nature of communication, or 'communication in the widest sense, including gesture, oral performance, artistic, linguistic, digital, electronic, graphic and artefact-related' (Pahl and Rowsell 2006: 6).

The theoretical underpinnings of multimodality studies can be traced to linguistics, in particular Halliday's social semiotic theory of communication (Halliday, 1978). Multimodal social semiotics, as it is widely referred to nowadays, focuses on signs of all kinds, in all forms, the sign makers and the social environments in which these signs are produced (Kress *et al.*, 2005: 22). It is argued that 'sign makers' can make meaning through drawing on a variety of modes that do not occur in isolation but always with others in ensembles. Moreover, different modes may share similar and/or different 'modal resources' (e.g. writing has syntactic, grammatical and graphic resources whereas image has resources that include the position of elements in a frame, size, colour and shape). These differences in resources have important implications for the ways modes can be used to accomplish different kinds of semiotic work, which means that 'modes have different affordances – potentials and constraints for making meaning' (Bezemer and Kress, 2008: 6). The discussion of different modes for meaning making and their affordances needs to be considered together with the medium of distribution involved (e.g. print, electronic, digital).

Multimodal social semiotics views linguistic signs (both monolingual and multilingual) as part of a wider repertoire of modal resources that sign makers have at their disposal and that carry particular sociohistorical and political associations (Lytra, 2012: 522). Such an approach has inspired new work on multilingual literacy which has extended our understanding of the ways multilingual language users combine different modes and media across social contexts and negotiate social identities. Kenner, for example, reports on how bilingual/biliterate young children learn different writing systems (Chinese, Arabic and Spanish) at home, in the complementary school context and in the mainstream primary school. Her work illustrates how a focus on different modes, including the children's sets of linguistic resources, can foreground the different culture-specific ways multilingual children mesh the visual and actional modes (i.e. make use of shape, size and location of symbols on the page, directionality, type of stroke) in the process of learning how to write in two languages (2004: 75). Moreover, such a focus shows the different ways multilingual children combine and juxtapose scripts as well as explore connections and differences between their available writing systems in their text making. By drawing on more than one set of linguistic and other modal resources to construct bilingual texts in settings where multilingual communication was encouraged, Kenner argued, children could 'express their sense of living in multiple social and cultural worlds' (2004: 118).

From the multimodal social semiotic perspective, electronically mediated communication (EMC), which is increasingly dominating our everyday social life in the twenty-first century,

---

Case Study 7.3

Lytra (2012) examines the way a group of 10-year-old boys of mainland Turkish and Cypriot-Turkish heritage combined and juxtaposed the use of different sets of linguistic resources with other semiotic resources to engage in music sharing and to evaluate shared songs mediated through mobile phones in a London Turkish literacy class. She looks at how the participants drew on strips of talk, their bodies, the material structure in the surroundings, in particular their mobile phones, the sequential organization of their talk and action, participation frameworks and the encompassing Turkish literacy activities to negotiate their media engagement, construct their interpersonal relationships and display different forms of knowledge and expertise in the complementary school setting.

Turkish literacy teaching in the complementary schools is characterized by whole-class teacher-fronted instruction, heavily relying on the traditional I-R-F (initiation–response–follow-up) sequence, substitution drills and the reading of texts on worksheets followed by sets of reading comprehension questions. Classroom discourse tends to encourage decontextualized knowledge, modelling and chorus-style responses to teacher prompts. The default mode of classroom interaction with the teacher during Turkish literacy teaching tends to be (standard) Turkish, whereas off-task talk among peers tends to be English. Generally, the use of English and vernacular forms of Turkish during Turkish literacy teaching is frowned upon, although occasionally deemed necessary for communication purposes.

The boys' media engagement is low-key. It is triggered and sustained by their mobile phones, usually stowed away in a school bag casually lying on the desk next to school worksheets but within easy reach or kept in their hand or pocket throughout the duration of the lesson. The mobile phones allow them to 'stay connected' across space, both inside and outside the classroom. Boys usually sit along the back rows, sometimes sitting on their own or in pairs, whereas girls sit in close proximity to each other, in two long rows, occupying the front right of the classroom. In this context, mobile phones radically transform the classroom environment both physically and socially; they provide opportunities for communication across classroom space and for different forms of peer interaction (e.g. sharing and listening to music during the lesson, evaluating shared songs, comparing features of mobile phones). Lytra provides specific examples of how the boys dip in and out of sharing songs and talking about their mobile phones as they read silently an assigned text and complete a series of reading comprehension questions on their worksheets. In particular, the music-sharing episodes occur as a backdrop to pedagogic routines and practices occupying the official classroom space (e.g. doing an assigned task, reading silently, writing the answers to a set of reading comprehension questions on the whiteboard). They also emerge during 'liminal' moments seen as transition points outside normal social structures during which the boys passed from one social status to another (e.g. when the lesson has been put on hold and the teacher is going around checking coursework). Thus, music sharing commonly took place in the periphery of the main classroom talk and activity, resembling what Maybin has called literacies 'under the desk' to capture 'a range of unofficial literacy activities which appeared to be clearly "off-task" in terms of institutional norms' (2007: 519).

The boys draw on different sets of verbal and nonverbal linguistic resources (i.e. standard and vernacular forms of English and Turkish as well as singing, humming and prosody) to frame the music-sharing activities mediated via their mobile phones. Some of these English linguistic resources used in the music-sharing episode include: the dropping of the copula, the dropping of word-final consonants, the use of slang terms ('bro', 'man') and of medium-specific vocabulary ('accept', 'hacking') as well as singing and humming of tunes, repetition and manipulation of prosodic cues. The frequent use of vernacular forms of English and Turkish in peer talk more generally is in contrast to the use of more or less standard forms of Turkish and occasionally English in official teacher–pupil talk. The boys' different sets of linguistic resources are intertwined with the manipulation of their mobile phones (e.g. sending, accepting or rejecting music files, 'hacking into' each other's mobile phones) as well as actively listening to, singing and humming raps in English and Turkish. Their media engagement occurs in parallel with their on-going engagement with the assigned task (e.g. reading a text silently and completing the reading comprehension questions) and the manipulation of artefacts associated with Turkish language learning (e.g. worksheets, notebooks, pens and pencils). The boys' engagement with music sharing and evaluating shared songs while the lesson is in full swing raises the question of what happens when such informal out-of-school practices travel into the classroom setting.

---

presents an exciting area for Applied Linguistic research. There is a whole range of EMC modes, both synchronous – for example, text chat, instant messaging, voice over Internet protocol (e.g. Skype), videoconferencing, online games and virtual world – and asynchronous – including email, online bulletin boards, e-forums, wikis, blogs, SMS texting and social networking sites (e.g. Facebook, MySpace). In terms of their linguistic features, the interactive and fragmentary nature of chat and instant messaging make them seem somewhat speech-like. Yet the bulk of EMC is still written via keyboard. So unlike spoken communication, the binary on/off nature of the medium does not allow back-channelling (e.g. uh-huh, right, yeah), for instance. Kern (2011) suggests that 'the relative leanness of EMC creates a different dynamic from that of spoken communication, and this difference may well be significant for language learning contexts that are exclusively EMC-based (e.g. tandems or 'key-pal' projects) (2011: 203). Moreover, most forms of EMC leave an enduring trace, allowing them to be searched, sorted, reviewed, forwarded and recontextualized. While this may potentially benefit language learners, for the exchanges can be mined for vocabulary, structures, discourse markers, and so on, for teaching and learning purposes it does raise issues of privacy, ownership and the 'semiotic power' of the languages and other signs being used for EMC.

EMC is often constrained by the alphabetization of the users' languages and the social conventions for written usage in their respective speech communities. Their impact on multilingual practice becomes obvious in postcolonial settings, where written discourse still depends on a former colonial language, whereas the indigenous and/or Creole languages that serve as spoken vernaculars may lack standardized orthography. Studies by Hinrichs (2006) on Jamaican Creole/English code-switching and Lexander (2010) on French/Wolof code-switching in Senegal suggest that, in these settings, language choices and code-switching patterns that are unmarked in spoken usage are turned into marked ones in digital writing, precisely because the spoken and written partitions of participants' linguistic repertoires are differently structured. Digital media offers new opportunities for writing vernaculars. But linguistic insecurity may inhibit a transfer of spoken vernacular into writing, making language users stick to the language they write (rather than speak) best. A further implication of literacy constraints relates to the orthographies and scripts that are available to networked writers. In post-migrant and transnational settings, language users may lack access to the written representation of minority or migrant languages. An example is the romanized writing of languages such as Hindi, Farsi or Greek on the Internet, which is common in post-migration Europe. Such vernacular romanization can variably reflect technological constraints, a lack of acquisition of the respective non-roman script, or a more or less conscious script choice in discourse. It may seem ironic that, as Georgakopoulou (1997) suggests, the lack of familiar cue in EMC (e.g. tactile, olfactory, auditory, as well as visual channels, operating in parallel) 'results in an increased reliance on code-centered contextualization cueing, which would be otherwise delegated to different signals' (1997: 158). In order to accomplish pragmatic work that would draw on eye contact, context perception, gestural and prosodic information in ordinary spoken conversation, digital interlocutors manipulate written signs and transcend orthographic boundaries. This reliance increases the indexical load of spelling, punctuation, and the graphic shape of language generally. However, studies also show that online language users can exploit their digital literacy repertoires, creating linguistic forms that blur and cross boundaries of scripts and orthographies, and drawing on the resulting contrasts to create pragmatic and language-ideological meaning (Androutsopoulos, 2006). For instance, whenever two or more scripts or orthographies are available to online writers, the choice among them can be deployed as a resource for script-focused translanguaging, or 'trans-scripting', whereby features of one of the available languages are represented in the spelling or script of another. Hinnenkamp (2008) describes a deliberate and reflexive 'mixing of alphabetic conventions' among German-Turkish chatters, whereby 'German words and even phrases get a kind of Turkish wrapping' (Hinnenkamp 2008: 262, 266), as in the word *Deutsch* (German orthography) being spelt *Doyç* (Turkish orthography).

The multimodal social semiotic approach to language and communication has also prompted the birth of a new area of Applied Linguistics research, known as Linguistic Landscape (LL), which Shohamy describes as studies of 'the presence, representation, meanings and interpretation of language displayed in public places' (2012: 538). The display of language in public space, usually in the visual modality, can have functional as well as symbolic purposes, offering rich and stimulating texts on multiple levels: single words with deep meanings and shared knowledge, colourful images, sounds and moving objects, billboards and graffiti, as well as a variety of text types displayed in cyber space,

---

STUDY ACTIVITY 7.4

Choose a virtual reality multiplayer game and find out:

1. Who are the participants?
2. How many languages are being used, and are there specific linguistic forms that are different from the way language is used in ordinary face-to-face conversation?
3. Do the participants use other signs, symbols and communicative means?
4. Can the game be used in any way to enhance language learning – for example, improving listening skills, turn taking, picking up multiple cues, raising cultural awareness?

open without being physically present. These displayed languages are 'closely related to people as people are the ones who hang the signs, display posters, design advertisements and create websites. It is also people who read, attend to, decipher and interpret these language displays, or at times choose to overlook, ignore or erase them' (2012: 538). Linguistic Landscape studies therefore not only focus on signs per se but also on how people interact with them. The main goal of Linguistic Landscape studies, according to Shohamy, is to 'describe and identify systematic patterns of the presence and absence of languages in public spaces and to understand the motives, pressures, ideologies, reactions and decision making of people regarding the creation of public signage' (2012: 538).

Many Linguistic Landscape studies focus on examining the role of displayed language in rapidly changing urban spaces (e.g. Shohamy, Ben Rafael and Barni, 2010), as summarized in Shohamy (2012). Du Plessis (2010) has, for example, documented the transformation of linguistic landscapes in the post-apartheid cities in South Africa, which is occurring as part of a wider process involving the standardization of orthographic conventions for writing place names. Leeman and Modan (2010) studied the linguistic landscape of Washington, DC, where public language display is being constructed as part of official city policy to commodify it and to drive the symbolic economy. Lou (2010), also writing about Washington, DC, shows how the values accorded to various forms and varieties of the Chinese language in Chinatown are contingent not only on spatial scales but also on the discursive reconstruction of Chinatown, which involves conjuring up contemporary China and simultaneously disconnecting Chinatown from its original history as an immigrant enclave. Another study by Jaworski and Yeung (2010), based on different neighbourhoods in Hong Kong, focuses on the ways in which the nature and form of linguistic landscape are shaped by economic factors. Waksman and Shohamy (2010) examined how the municipality of Tel Aviv used various types of LL in public spaces to deliver a redefinition of the city as part of preparations for its centennial.

Some of the linguistic landscape researchers have studied graffiti in public spaces. Graffiti involves the creation of hybrid forms of text and pictures. Moreover, it draws on multimodal resources that have both global and local meanings. Pennycook (2009) argues that local instances of graffiti need to be interpreted as part of a transgressive semiotics, within a global flow of practices. He raises questions about why some signs have more importance than others, how and why signs are made, how they are read and interpreted and how different linguistic resources are used. Graffiti is not only illegal (in most cases), it is also about production, about learning skills, about style and identity, as well as about different ways of claiming space by interacting with it.

Other linguistic landscape researchers have explored the connections with language planning and language policy research (see Chapter 10, this volume). One example of studies in this area is that by Pavlenko (2010), which describes linguistic landscape in Kiev, Ukraine. Pavlenko shows that, despite the government's efforts to relegate Russian to the status of a 'foreign language' and to promote the Ukrainian language, top-down imposition of linguistic policies in linguistic landscape is not all-powerful; Russian still occupies a very prominent public space. Other studies of the role of linguistic landscape in language policy have been conducted in places as diverse as Canada, Japan, Belarus, Czech Republic, Israel, Slovakia, Ethiopia and Italy. For example, it has been shown that people constructing linguistic landscapes often defy formal and explicit policies. New words and new orthographic conventions are created and displayed in public spaces and we see the emergence of hybridized language forms and fusion of local and global varieties. Thus, in some linguistic landscapes in public spaces, we see the creation of what Shohamy (2012) calls 'language policy from below'. This is especially noticeable when examining language in cyber space. There, mixing of languages is commonplace, and new linguistic rules of syntax and spelling are applied (see the Greek-Greeklish example above), often combined with other semiotic modes such as sounds and images.

The expansion of multimodal social semiotic studies of linguistic landscape has recently begun to include the role of displayed languages in language learning. Immigrants and tourists coming to new places are often drawn to signs in their primary encounters with new cultural practices. As the example at the beginning of this chapter shows, they also use public signage as they try to make sense of new environments and the messages they convey. Thus, linguistic landscape can serve as a powerful tool for learning languages and for language awareness. Dagenais *et al.* (2009) are engaged in a large study in Quebec and Vancouver where elementary school students are documenting their contacts with a variety of languages in their local communities. They are describing how children co-construct representations of languages, language speakers and language learning through these language awareness activities. These researchers recommend the use of linguistic landscape as a tool for increasing language awareness. They show how children engaging in multilingual awareness activities can develop a critical perspective on language diversity and literacy practices, especially in socially and politically contested areas. Other studies also show how linguistic landscapes can serve as resources for teaching languages and for raising cultural and linguistic awareness. For example, Sayer (2009) showed how linguistic landscape can be used for pedagogical purposes via a study in Mexico. He involved students as language investigators employing multiple research methods to analyse the social meanings of public signs where English was used. He presents a framework distinguishing between intercultural and intracultural uses, and between iconic and innovative uses of English on signs. He argues that the project is useful both for thinking about the innovative ways people use the language in local contexts and as a template for a classroom-based project that teachers can implement. This is a means of engaging English-as-a-foreign-language students in investigating and talking about social aspects of language use. Hanauer (2009) focused on the LLs of educational institutions. He presented a study of the different genres incorporated in the wall display of a microbiology laboratory. This laboratory was part of a project where high school and undergraduate students were brought together to engage in joint microbiological inquiry. Wall space was used to facilitate the flow of knowledge throughout the laboratory and to illustrate

Study Activity 7.5

Choose a neighbourhood and spend a little time observing the public signs and listen to the conversations of passers-by who are either on a mobile phone or face-to-face with other people.

1. How many different languages can you observe?
2. Is there any mixing between different languages?
3. Is there any mixing between different scripts and signs?
4. Is there a dominant language on display?
5. Is there any informal, non-standard writing on display?

the procedural aspects of conducting scientific inquiry. Hanauer used genre analysis and multimodal analysis to show how an understanding of this type of linguistic landscape can promote the scientific and educational aims of learning and knowledge exchange. All these and many other studies of multimodality and linguistic landscape are described and discussed in Shohamy (2012).

7.6 Summary

While the basics of literacy lie in the ability to decode the written word, the concept goes beyond reading and writing and includes thinking critically about what is written, how it is written and what it may represent. It may also include the ability to understand the consequence of reading and writing on the individual and the society. In the twenty-first century, literacy and multimodality are closely interconnected. Technological advancement pushes the notion of literacy to include the media and electronic text, in addition to alphabetic and number systems. Evolving definitions of literacy may cover all the symbol systems relevant to a particular community and encompass a complex set of abilities to understand and use the dominant symbol systems of a culture for personal and community development.

Study Questions

1. What is the role of phonology in reading different kinds of script?
2. How does the concept of continua of biliteracy apply to the community you are familiar with?
3. In what way can schools help to develop children's social literacy?
4. Which hypothesis – interference, double discontinuity or a positive relationship between L1 and L2 – do you favour in the consideration of deaf children's literacy? Provide argumentation from other sources to support your viewpoint.
5. How might research into literacy development in deaf children inform our understanding of literacy development in other minority populations? What factors (e.g. research methodology, outcomes) might be similar and what might be different in studying different populations?
6. What roles does multimodality play in everyday communication?
7. How does multimodality impact on language status?

Notes

1. The conventions of the D/deaf distinction are adhered to here. 'Deaf' (with a capital 'D') refers to those who are culturally, linguistically and politically associated with the Deaf community, advocating the rights of the Deaf as a minority group with a minority language (sign language). The term 'deaf' (with a lower case 'd') refers to the audiological state.
2. Where L1 is considered as the first language of the D/deaf, despite differences in age and environment of acquisition compared to hearing children.

Recommended Reading

Baynham, Mike and Mastin Prinsloo (eds.). 2009. *The Future of Literacy Studies*. Basingtoke: Palgrave. A collection of articles by leading researchers in the field of literacy studies, examining the roles that literacy texts and practices play in social activity of various kinds, including digital literacies.

Brueggemann, Brenda Jo (ed.). 2004. *Literacy and Deaf People: Cultural and Contextual Perspectives*. Washington: Gallaudet University Press. This edited volume contains diverse contributions from scholars reporting on different educational and cultural contexts. All contributors advocate a reframing of 'Deaf literacy' to incorporate a consideration of Deaf cultural identity.

Cain, Kate. 2010. *Reading Development and Difficulties: An Introduction*. Hoboken: John Wiley & Sons, Inc. This textbook provides a clear and accessible introduction to the stages of development in the acquisition of literacy in childhood.

Crystal, David. 2008. *Txtng: The Gr8 Db8*. Oxford: Oxford University Press. A popular and fun introduction to the language of text messaging.

Gee, James Paul. 2011. *Social Linguistics and Literacies: Ideology in Discourses*. London: Routledge. Provides useful historical context on current debates and discussions on literacy; describes and illustrates a sociocultural approach to literacy.

Hornberger, Nancy. 2003. *Continua of Biliteracy: An Ecological Framework for Educational Policy, Research, and Practice in Multilingual Settings*. Clevedon: Multilingual Matters. Offers a comprehensive yet flexible model to guide educators, researchers and policy makers in designing, carrying out and evaluating educational programmes for the development of bilingual and multilingual learners, each programme adapted to its own specific context, media and contents.

Jewitt, Carey (ed.). 2009. *The Routledge Handbook of Multimodal Analysis*. London: Routledge. A comprehensive 'research tool kit' for multimodal analysis, covering a wide range of theoretical and methodological issues. Detailed multimodal analysis case studies are included, along with an extensive glossary of key terms, to support those new to multimodality and allow those already engaged in multimodal research to explore the fundamentals further.

Kress, Gunther. 2009. *Multimodality: A Social Semiotic Approach to Contemporary Communication*. London: Routledge. Packed with photos and illustrations to demonstrate the methodological points made, the volume sets out to locate communication in the everyday, covering topics and issues not usually discussed in books of this kind, from traffic signs to mobile phones.

Shohamy, Elana and Durk Gorter (eds). 2008. *Linguistic Landscape: Expanding the Scenery*. London: Routledge. Written by Applied Linguists from different parts of the world, the volume analyses linguistic landscapes in a range of international contexts. Dozens of photographs illustrate the use of language in the environment – the words and images displayed and exposed in public spaces.

Smith, Frank. 2012. *Understanding Reading: A Psycholinguistic Analysis of Reading and Learning to Read*, 6th edn. New York: Routledge. This book presents a comprehensive description of the psychological aspects of the reading process. It is considered a fundamental text on the topic written by one of the leading researchers on literacy for the past three decades.

Street, Brian and Adam Lefstein. 2007. *Literacy: An Advanced Resource Book for Students*. London: Routledge. This introduces students to a broad range of approaches to understanding literacy in educational contexts and in society, integrating psychological, educational and anthropological perspectives.

van Leeuwen, Theo. 2004. *Introducing Social Semiotics*. London: Routledge. Using a wide variety of texts including photographs, adverts, magazine pages and film stills, the volume explains how meaning is created through complex semiotic interactions. Practical exercises and examples, as wide-ranging as furniture arrangements in public places and advertising jingles, provide readers with the knowledge and skills they need to be able to analyse and also produce successful multimodal texts and designs.

part III

Language in Society

chapter 8

Language Diversity and Contact

Penelope Gardner-Chloros

Chapter Outline

Learning Outcomes

After reading this chapter, you should be able to

- understand the reasons for studying languages in relation to the society/ies where they are used;
- classify languages/varieties depending on both their linguistic characteristics and their functions;

Applied Linguistics, First Edition. Edited by Li Wei.
© 2014 John Wiley & Sons, Ltd. Published 2014 by John Wiley & Sons, Ltd.

- compare notions, including social network, speech community, Community of Practice, and so on, that are used in sociolinguistic research in relation to both monolingual and bi/plurilingual settings;
- describe the differences between language change and language shift and the attendant linguistic phenomena, notably societal bilingualism and inter-individual code-switching;
- appreciate why some varieties are more powerful than others and how the power balance may change.

Key Terms

- Accent
- Code-switching
- Community of Practice
- Language
- Language shift

- Linguistic community
- Pidgin/creole
- Standardization
- Synchronic/diachronic
- Variety

8.1 Introduction

Figure 8.1 shows an article which appeared in the *News of the World* newspaper in March 2009 that highlights a number of issues to do with languages and the societies where they are spoken. It raises the question of the link between language and ethnic/national identity. Deva believes that speaking English is an essential element in being British – and while this is not specified, it seems likely that his idea of 'English' would not include anything except the standard. Second, it makes us think about whether Britain is actually a monolingual or a multilingual country: Deva won't serve people 'until they can speak English'. This appears to be regardless of whether he understands the language they are speaking or not, so the practical issue of being able to communicate is secondary. Third, there is an implied view that minority languages should not be encouraged or protected, but that we should favour assimilation or, at the very least, bilingualism – though this is not explicit. Further implications include the connections between language and religion (we are told that 'a few muslims' (*sic*) didn't like his message); politics (he has been 'slung out' of the Liberal Democrat party for his attitude); and militarism (he does not want British soldiers to be booed). The journalist writing clearly supports Deva's stance, referring repeatedly to his courage and clearly approving of his 'patriotism', which manifests itself also in flying the Union Jack and teaching his children the national anthem.

The tone of the article is quite emotional, as is Deva's own stance – he is presented as little short of a martyr ('Many Britons are afraid to speak out. And now, tragically, he sees why.') A more dispassionate approach would have involved simply stating the facts of the case: that Deva refused to serve people who did not speak English in his Post Office, on the basis that he, a Sri Lankan immigrant, had managed to assimilate linguistically and in other ways to his country of adoption, and thought others should do the same.

STUDY ACTIVITY 8.1

Consider the issues listed below, which arise from this article:

1. Does emigrating to a country mean that you must speak that country's language (regardless of the reasons and circumstances of your emigration?). What level of linguistic proficiency should be expected? Who should take this decision and who should decide what is an adequate level of proficiency? Should it be a condition for citizenship to pass or attain a certain level?
2. Given the number of people from linguistic and ethnic minorities in the UK, Britain is effectively a multicultural and multilingual nation. Should there therefore be provisions for various languages other than English to be used – as there are, for example, on benefits forms? What is the role of education?
3. Regardless of whether you believe that immigrants should learn the 'national language', is it right to refuse to serve them in an essential public service context such as the Post Office, if they are unable to do so? What are the alternatives?

In what way could the political and religious issues that are hinted at in the article be relevant to the linguistic questions? For example, how is it relevant that they were 'muslims' who forced him out of his job?

These questions all highlight the essential links between language and society. Languages and varieties are rarely all equal, and some tend to be considered superior or more appropriate than others, depending on context. This is not a linguistic judgement properly speaking, but a social one. Here, the implication is that the minority languages are all right in their place (i.e. in the home), but not in public places. For a child – whose parents might insist on the mother tongue being spoken at home – this could be quite a confusing situation. The article presents the linguistic choices as black and white ones, and makes no mention of bilingualism. Yet this is arguably the essential issue. The second generation in immigrant communities is normally bilingual, but the first generation is not necessarily so. Our choice is whether – and how – to accommodate to the fact that we all speak differently – different languages, dialects, accents and idiolects.

There are cases, of course, where language diversity and its consequences are not just a matter of personal or political choices but have life and death implications. We need look no further than Europe for grave consequences to occur. In heavy fog in Tenerife in 1977, the senior Dutch pilot of a KLM 747 plane said he was 'at take-off', meaning he was *in the process of* taking off. The Spanish air traffic controller interpreted this small deviation from Standard English to mean that he was simply positioned at the take-off point on the runway. At the same time the Dutch pilot failed to understand the air traffic controller's

CAROLE MALONE

Email Carole at carole.malone@notw.co.uk

Sri Lankan Brit
shows true grit

IT SEEMS shameful that the first person in a long time to make me feel patriotic and remind me what a great country Britain can be is a Sri Lankan postmaster who lives in Nottingham.

Deva Kumarasiri, who came to England 17 years ago, loves Britain so much he has a huge Union Jack flying outside his house and another in the back window of his car.

He believes absolutely that this is the best country in the world and because of that he has taught his two daughters every word of the national anthem. So great is his love of this country and all it stands for he even took citizenship exams.

And that is why he is now adamant that people who come into his Post Office and can't speak English won't be served until they can.

Deva isn't being racist or rude or divisive. He's actually just being respectful to a country he loves and which has allowed him to prosper.

But predictably, Deva has paid a high price for his courage and his patriotism. In a country that champions free speech he has now been forced out of his job at the Post Office by threats and slung out

of the Lib Dem Party.

And all because a few muslims didn't like the fact he told them they had to learn English in a country they had made their home.

Just two days ago Deva made his brave stand telling people: "This is the best country in the world. All I'm doing is telling people who want to be in Britain to be British.

Punished

"Don't boo our soldiers. Don't live here without embracing our culture. And don't stay here without making the effort to learn our language."

Deva said what he said because he understands that integration is only possible if people learn the language of the country they live in, see that country as home and embrace its ways, (which doesn't mean they have to forsake their own).

And he said all that because he knows that too many Britons are afraid to speak out. And now, tragically, he sees why. I

hoped Deva wouldn't be punished for what he'd said because **HE** was an immigrant and because he understands and has overcome the problems they face.

But no, he too has paid the price for saying what he believes to be right thanks to a vicious campaign by muslims who believe they must not ever be criticised for **ANY** reason—even one as funda-

Figure 8.1 'Sri Lankan Brit shows true grit' by Carole Malone, *News of the World*, 22 March 2009. Permission granted by The Newspaper Marketing Agency, www.nmauk.co.uk.

mental as rejecting the country that protects and takes care of them.

What has happened to Deva is what happens in a dictatorship. And it's a damned disgrace. Because what made his argument so powerful wasn't just that he was right—it was his passion, his love, his gratitude to a country where, 17 years on, he still feels privileged to be living.

How many of us see Britain that way? How many of us possess his sense of belonging? How many of us believe we're lucky to live here?

The only time I ever feel vaguely patriotic is when one of our football teams or athletes does something amazing.

But for Deva every day living in this country is a bonus. He didn't come here expecting a free ride and a life on benefits. He wanted to contribute. And he has.

Already, because of his stand, immigrants coming into his Post Office who didn't speak English are now saying Please and Thank You and trying to construct short sentences.

PATRIOTIC: Deva

"Our laws are written in English, our culture is chronicled in English. How can anyone understand those things if they don't speak English?" he says.

"We have a terrible problem in Britain. We don't know who our neighbours are. And if your neighbour doesn't speak the same language you get lack of understanding, and fear, and so often racism."

How right he has proved to be. This government is always telling us all races and cultures must be respected. What it actually **MEANS** is all races and cultures—except the British culture.

Forcing a man who stands up for Britain to move to a predominantly white area—how racist is that!

It's time we stopped pandering to bigots. They see our tolerance as weakness and it has to stop. Free speech can't just be free for the ethnic minorities who make the most noise.

Because the nightmare scenario is already happening. In coming elections it is predicted the BNP will take control of five councils and win seven EU seats. And that will be because the frustrations of the majority are being ignored.

We have to decide what we want from our immigrants. Do we want them to be like Deva—workers, contributors, true Brits? Or do we want them living in their own communities, isolated and not being able to communicate with the rest of us.

Deva understands that **REAL** immigration is about belonging. He is British to the core and proud of it.

And for that he's not just being punished for it—he fears for his life.

Figure 8.1 (*Continued*)

discussion with the English-speaking pilot of another aircraft, which indicated that the runway was not clear. The result was a collision between the 747 and the other passenger plane, in which almost 600 people died.

8.2 Classifying Varieties

The term *variety* is a catch-all term which covers different languages, dialects, accents, registers and styles of speech. The need for such a neutral term arises because the way we *designate* different ways of speaking is tied up with how they are evaluated and valued – remember Molière's comic character, the social climber Monsieur Jourdain, who was deeply flattered to be told he had been speaking 'prose' all his life? Even the term 'language' is not as neutral as one might think. It is often taken as referring to *standard* languages which are associated with particular nation states (as in 'English and French are the languages spoken in Canada'); hence the need for a neutral term that carries no implications of size, number of speakers, standardization or other attributes. There are written and spoken varieties, standard and non-standard ones, varieties used for communication between people who do not share a mother tongue (*lingua francas*) and varieties that develop between people who have no common language at all (*pidgins and creoles*).

This toolkit of terms is important for linguists because most of these terms are ideologically loaded. For example, a 'dialect' is often seen as inferior to a 'language'. It generally has connotations of being (i) purely regional, or (ii) spoken rather than written. In fact, there is no reason to think that dialects are spoken by very few people compared with languages – on a worldwide scale, more people speak non-standard than standard varieties. The other 'myth' about dialects is that they are in some way impoverished compared with languages – that they have a reduced vocabulary, no grammatical rules, or that they are somehow 'incorrect'. None of these is in fact the case. In reality, dialects can normally express subtle and complex thoughts as easily, or even more easily, than standard languages. They generally fulfil the role of *vernaculars*, that is, popular speech forms for everyday interaction, and are therefore the repository for popular wisdom and for comment on day-to-day matters. Yet another misapprehension is that their use is confined to spoken interaction. In reality, there are many examples of poetry and literature in dialects. A historic example is the troubadour literature in various Romance dialects of the Middle Ages; a more modern one would be poetry and songs in Jamaican patois. Sometimes languages and dialects are distinguished in terms of mutual comprehensibility: it is thought that people speaking different *languages* cannot understand one another, whereas those speaking different dialects of the same language can. Once again, this distinction fails in practice: the Scandinavian *languages* (Swedish, Norwegian and Danish) are largely mutually comprehensible, but dialects – even of a world language like English – often are not (broad Geordie or Scottish English are opaque to a Southern English speaker, and even more so to someone from the United States or Australia!).

In multilingual contexts, owing to contact between different varieties, new forms of communication develop and sometimes grow into fully fledged languages in their own right. This explains the genesis of *pidgin* and *creole* languages, which arose mainly in colonial and ex-colonial settings as a result of contact between the colonizers' language – for example,

English, French or Spanish (the *superstrate*) – and the languages spoken by their population of slaves, who were often imported from different areas and did not even share a language among themselves (the *substrates*). These languages are much studied by linguists, because they show how a language can gradually transform itself from a basic mode of communication, with a highly simplified grammar, into a fully fledged idiom (e.g. Caribbean creoles in Jamaica, Martinique, St Lucia, etc., or Tok Pisin in Papua New Guinea; see Sebba, 1997). In other, rarer, contact situations, varieties emerge with the grammatical structure of one language and the vocabulary of another (e.g. Media Lingua in Bolivia, a mixture of Spanish and Quechua, or Michif, a mixture of French and Cree, an Algonquin language, in Canada). All these processes come about through a pooling of linguistic resources and apply to different dialects as well as different languages. Thus common dialects can arise through the process of *koineization* between dialects that started off far apart from one another (Kerswill, 2001). This process can also be observed in the modern-day *levelling* between non-standard British English dialects, which results in so-called *Estuary English*. Sociolinguists are intrigued by the influence of varieties spoken by communities of immigrant origin on these new forms of English (Cheshire, 2009; Rampton, 1995). Although Estuary includes traditional 'Cockney' features, in other ways it is distinct (for example, it does not generally include *h*-dropping in words like *house*).

Within given languages, how should we distinguish between different *types* or *levels* of language? These give rise to quite different results in terms of lexical choice, accent/pronunciation and even grammatical structure. *Register* is one important subcategory, which refers to the type of language that is appropriate for particular situations (*formal* vs. *informal* register). It is often associated with particular specialized fields – for

---

Study Activity 8.2

Below are some examples of features of 'Multicultural London English' as studied by Cheshire, *et al.* 2011. These embody a range of systematic differences from Standard British English. Do you use any of these forms yourself? If so, have you always done so or are you aware of having picked them up at some stage?

Phonology	Intervocalic *t* realized as glottal stop (*be'er* for better)
Lexis	*yard* for home
	Intensifiers (*bare*)
	sick = good
Syntax	Omission of prepositions: '*I'm going college*'
Morphology	New regular plurals: *mans* for men
	-dem plural: *one of the boydem*
Verb modifications	Levelling of *was/were*
Discourse	Extenders (*and stuff*)
	Replacement of 'you know' with '*you get me*'

example, the legal register – and implies the use of a specialized vocabulary. Although in the first sense its meaning is close to that of the term 'style', 'style' tells us nothing about the use of a specialized vocabulary. Although linguists have not always used these terms consistently, generally speaking style is seen more as a matter of personal initiative and less as dictated by the situation. Bell (2009) has developed a theory of style as being connected to 'Audience Design', that is, he claims that people tailor their speech according to how they want to come across to their audience. *Genre* is another closely related term, but tends to relate to written texts rather than to spontaneous speech, and *modality* refers to the channel of communication, whether spoken, written, broadcast or signed. These terms are not watertight but often overlapping – in effect they are different ways of apprehending the same linguistic phenomena, and it would be tedious to enumerate all the terms that arise. To give an example: in 1959 the linguist Charles Ferguson identified a small set of languages, including Modern Greek, Swiss-German and Haitian Creole, which he termed *'diglossic'*. By this he meant that each of them comprised two related forms of the language (which he called the *High* and the *Low* varieties) with differences of vocabulary and grammar, each of which was appropriate in different *domains* or areas of life – for example, at worship, for literature, for informal speech to children, and so on (Ferguson, 1959/2000). Much has been written about how watertight the two forms actually were in the cases he selected and in other, comparable cases. It has been argued that what he called *High* and *Low* could also be designated as formal and informal registers, or different styles, and that the two forms were also partly distinguished by the modalities in which they were used, with the *High* being more appropriate in writing, or speech that is closely modelled on written forms. So although these terms are useful as a shorthand to

---

Case Study 8.1

In *London Jamaican*, Sebba (1993) shows how speakers can alternate between different varieties of the same language within a single conversation, each of those varieties carrying different connotations *or* identifying different types of discourse. He gives the example of two London teenagers of Jamaican descent, Andrew and Barry, discussing an incident that occurred while Andrew was serving in a grocery shop and which involved a difficult customer. Andrew predominantly uses a variety of London English, but switches occasionally into Creole, for example when he is quoting the customer, or to highlight various parts of his narrative. The Creole passages are mainly identified by a different pronunciation. The intervention of the manager of the shop to defuse the incident is in an RP 'posh' voice, indexing authority or 'the voice of the law' (1993: 119–120).

Similarly, Rampton (2006) analyses the varieties used in an inner-city high school in London by pupils and teachers. He shows how the teenagers use traditional British class accents (notably 'posh' and 'Cockney') strategically to 'draw lines', that is, to differentiate between 'high' and 'low' spheres of activity and to mark their attitudes towards people within the school. Rampton concludes that the class boundaries underlying these accents are still part of the pupils' awareness, but that the accents are subverted and used in a variety of stylized ways. This demands a revision of traditional sociolinguistic ideas about the 'linguistic insecurity' of non-standard speakers.

describe different linguistic situations, we should be wary of 'essentializing' them, that is, believing that the terms themselves hold some sort of truth about the varieties they designate. We need to confront categories distinguished in academic research with the – often less tidy – real-life facts.

8.3 Choosing a Target Group and a Suitable Speech Sample

The first question to ask when you set out to study language is, 'What is it about language that interests me?' Theoretical linguists in the Chomskyan tradition consider language to be the product of an innate 'programme' in the brain and use data derived from *introspection*, that is, they use themselves as guinea pigs to decide what is correct – or *grammatical* – language. Since this innate programme is common to all humans, there is no need to consider variation. As Chomsky famously wrote: 'Linguistic theory is concerned primarily with an ideal speaker/listener, in a completely homogeneous speech-community' (1965: 3). Sociolinguists, by contrast, are interested in exactly those aspects of language that do vary from group to group, from individual to individual and from situation to situation. They can be considered 'Applied Linguists' because they apply linguistic theory to various forms of concrete empirical data.

However, they too run the danger of idealizing the behaviour of the speakers they observe. For example, early studies of gender differences often assumed that there were immutable – and therefore fairly predictable – differences between men's and women's speech. In the study of bilingualism, it used to be thought that 'proper' bilinguals kept their languages rigorously separate and spoke each of them as a monolingual would. Weinreich, an early scholar of bilingualism, considered that 'The … ideal bilingual switches from one language to another according to appropriate changes in the speech situation (interlocutors, topics, etc.) but not in an unchanged speech situation, and certainly not within a single sentence' (1953: 73–74). The problem with studying such 'perfect' monolinguals or bilinguals is that they are more theoretical than real. Men and women, whether bilingual or monolingual, make use of the varieties available to them in various ways according to circumstances. They alternate between – and combine – languages, dialects, registers and styles much as a cook combines the same finite list of ingredients differently in order to produce different dishes.

So having answered the first question above, the next question is, 'Whose language will I study, when and how?' The aim is to define the object of linguistic enquiry in as representative a way as possible, and to study how people actually speak, rather than how they might do in an idealized world. In the 1960s and 1970s, William Labov gave linguistics a new direction by pointing out the advantages of studying language through the observation of representative samples of speakers in cities, rather than in rural locations as traditional dialectologists had done. This is because it is in cities that language variation and change can be identified most accurately, taking account of socio-economic groupings, gender, ethnic identity and other factors. He was one of the first to use the notion of a *speech community*, a group of people who may not all speak in the same way, but who share a set of social attitudes towards language. For example, in New York City, where he did much of his research, he showed that speakers of different ages and social classes could be distinguished according to whether – and in what contexts – they would pronounce the *r* after a vowel in words like *arm* or *there* (the standard British pronunciation of these words being *r*-less). Despite considerable variation in their actual behaviour, New Yorkers shared the same set of attitudes about how correct, or prestigious, it was to pronounce the postvocalic *r* (1972: 150–152) – unlike speakers from out of town. The New Yorkers could therefore be considered a speech community according to Labov's criteria. Even here, though, there remains a danger in assuming that speakers are more consistent and/or homogeneous in their behaviour than they actually are. In reality, people are part of several communities simultaneously (through neighbourhood, occupation, gender, class, religious affiliation, and so forth). Their behaviour therefore varies in different contexts. To account for this, various models have been exploited or developed to describe and explain the linguistic patterns that develop in any social grouping.

One of the best-known of these models is the application of Social Network Theory to language (Milroy, 1987). In a study of the speech of various groups in Belfast, Milroy showed how people's socialization patterns determined how closely they stuck to local *vernacular norms* – for example, the pronunciation of the vowel in *good* to rhyme with the vowel in Standard English *food*. Dense networks, where people interacted intensively with the same people in different capacities or in different contexts (e.g. as neighbours, colleagues and friends) gave rise to converging vernacular norms. These were typical of working-class speakers, whereas middle-class speakers tended to have a broader range of contacts. The network model has successfully been applied to bilingual communities by Li Wei (1994), who showed, for example, that the maintenance of Chinese by second- and third-generation speakers on Tyneside was closely related to the type of network ties of different speakers.

More recently, models seeking to explain patterns of usage, such as particular sets of choices of vernacular or less vernacular variants, have tried to describe and explain how the same speakers can vary in their speech at different times. Le Page and Tabouret-Keller's (1985) *Acts of Identity* model proposes that the speech of individuals varies according to the group with which they wish to identify at a particular time (see Chapter 9). Bell's *Audience Design* model (2009) suggests that much of the variability can be explained with reference to the intended audience – as he demonstrates, for example, in relation to a travel agency employee and a radio programme presenter. Once again, monolingual and bilingual variations are shown to be two sides of the same coin – similar findings to those of Bell were described by Wei Zhang in relation to a Chinese radio programme (2005). Perhaps the most popular recent model, however, has been the Communities of Practice (C of P) model (Eckert, 2000; Meyerhoff, 2001), which provides a way of linking the micro-analysis of variation with the macro-analysis of sociolinguistic groupings. Eckert has shown how people's linguistic practices may vary according to whether they are core or peripheral members of various groups. She studied the way in which adolescents in four high schools in Detroit fell into categories that corresponded with numerous lifestyle choices as well as linguistic features (the groups were called 'Jocks', who identified with school values, 'Burnouts', who identified more with working-class values from outside school, and 'In-betweens'). The fact that people do not either belong or not belong to different groupings, but belong to them *more or less*, explains, for example, why categorizing Black English as distinct from other working-class varieties was originally so controversial. The C of P model is particularly useful in relation to our understanding of gender differences in language. Rather than seeing gender as an inescapable aspect of identity that is bound to result in different practices, the question of why men and women

Study Activity 8.3

Think of the people with whom you interact on a daily basis – family, friends, work colleagues, neighbours, and so on. What different ways of speaking can you distinguish either *within* or *between* these groups (different accents, dialects, use of vocabulary or slang)? If you belong to a bilingual community or social group (e.g. students from the same country), perhaps some of your acquaintances code-switch (i.e. mix languages) whereas others do not.

What factors would seem to you to explain the different groupings? These might be broad sociolinguistic differentiators – age, gender, social category/class – or communities of interest or practice. Which of the models described above accounts best for the differences that you have noticed?

behave – or speak – differently is viewed from the perspective of the practices in which they engage, in the particular communities to which they belong. These can lead to greater or lesser differences between the sexes, depending on how *gender* is constructed in the particular setting or society.

To recap, there are many ways to identify the object of study in sociolinguistics:

- a *speech community* is a group of speakers who share some aspects of their speech behaviour – if not a particular variety then at least common attitudes towards the varieties spoken;
- a *social network*, in this context, is a group of people who associate with one another in various capacities and who are therefore likely to share linguistic practices also;
- *audience design* refers to the process whereby speakers adapt their way of speaking to their audience, whether a single interlocutor or a bigger group;
- the *communities of practice* approach cuts across groupings based on external factors like social class and instead seeks common linguistic practices that reveal which speakers identify with which other speakers.

New ways of explaining the underlying systematicities in speech behaviour at a social level continue to emerge. For example, it is now recognized that, apart from belonging to – or reacting to – socially defined groupings, speakers also adjust their speech as a flexible response to further aspects of context/speech situations, so as to represent themselves and their personal style in particular ways; this is known as linguistic 'stance' (Jaffe, 2012).

8.4   Language Change and Language Shift

One of the puzzles that exercises sociolinguists most is why and how languages change. On a broad historical scale, we all know, for example, that we no longer speak English like Chaucer did in the fourteenth century, like Shakespeare did in the sixteenth and seventeenth or like Jane Austen did in the eighteenth and nineteenth – and none of them spoke like one another. Even if we look less far back, we can record noticeable changes in the last 50 years in Britain. Surprisingly, this affects not only the type of non-standard language, of which some examples were given above, but even RP (Received Pronunciation), otherwise known as the Queen's English or BBC English. In an article which examined how the Queen's own pronunciation has changed over the last 50 years in her Christmas broadcast, it was found that over this period her vowels had become noticeably more 'democratic' and shifted in the direction of speakers of Standard Southern British English (see Harrington, Palethorpe and Watson 2000).

From the research by himself and others on such questions, Labov extracted a number of principles concerning the origins and spread of linguistic change – sound change in particular. In simple terms, at any given time, there is a range of ways to pronounce any given phoneme within a language, that is, an average pronunciation and several 'outliers'. According to Labov, women, young people, less conformist members of society and the upwardly mobile all tend to use the pronunciation that is further away from the average pronunciation, as a way of differentiating themselves from the conservative 'standard'. In time, the wheel turns, the 'outlying' pronunciation becomes widespread, and new speakers start the process all over again. It must be said, however, that studying this poses considerable methodological problems and the process is still not well understood. Ideally, it should be studied diachronically rather than synchronically – if you compare different generations at a given time as a shortcut to understanding change, you cannot be sure that the way the adolescents speak now is representative of how they will speak as mature adults in 30 years' time.

Studying language change in a monolingual context may, in fact, obscure the role of *contact* between different varieties, and many of the historical changes that used to be considered the result of internal developments are now ascribed to the effects of contact instead. Understanding the role of contact between varieties of English was crucial to the analysis made by linguists in the Black English case (Labov 1982). An important reference for this is Thomason (2001: 1), who defines contact very simply as 'the use of more than one language in the same place at the same time'. The most dramatic development is when, following a period of bilingualism, one language is entirely replaced by another. This has been the case for many minority languages that have been colonized by major vehicular languages. One example is East Sutherland Gaelic, which was still spoken in remote fishing villages in Northern Scotland 30 years ago, but which has now been effectively replaced by English (Dorian, 1981, 2010). This language and its gradual disappearance have been studied on and off throughout this period by Dorian, who first went to these villages as a research student and who has continued to monitor the situation over the years. Her insights from long-term participant observation in the community are highly important for our understanding of minority language situations in general. For example, she identified the category of *semi-speaker*, meaning people (usually adolescents and young people) who know a great deal about when and how to use the dying language but only possess a restricted range of its grammatical forms (and vocabulary). She also drew attention to the effects of a language being used for the private sphere only, which can change the speakers' whole sense of what the language is for, and lead to its impoverishment for formal and abstract purposes. Recently, the subject of *language death* – that is, the death of the last active speaker of the language – has become highly topical, with the appearance of several books on the subject. The work of the sociologist of language Joshua Fishman (2001) on language revitalization – that is, what steps can be taken to revive a language before it disappears altogether – is also very significant.

8.5   Code-switching among Bilinguals

One of the most characteristic developments that is found among bilingual speakers is *code-switching*, the alternate use of two or more varieties in the same conversation or sentence. This occurs not only in situations where one variety is clearly in decline, but in a wide variety of settings (see Gardner-Chloros, 2009). It is found among small bilingual communities (e.g. migrants) as well as in well-established language contact situations. It is traditionally considered a spoken, informal mode of speech but can also be found in writing (Sebba, Mahootian and Jonsson, 2012). As illustrated in the Italian-Sardinian case below, when language shift is occurring, code-switching allows less competent speakers to keep on speaking the ancestral language at least to some extent, and so contributes to it not being abandoned so quickly.

Code-switching has been extensively analysed from the point of view of its linguistic make-up, with different grammatical patterns of switching being characteristic of different sociolinguistic settings and different language combinations. When the varieties are closely related, for example, sentences can contain numerous code-switches without any disruption of the grammatical template. However, it appears that the sociolinguistic parameters are even more influential. Relatively stable bilingual situations give rise to simple alternation, in which one language may appear to be the *matrix* into which elements of the other are slotted; in situations where the bilingual speakers (e.g. migrants) are dominated by a monolingual majority, the type of code-switching is often more intense and involves convergence between the two grammars.

In the following example, we can see that code-switching is closely connected with borrowing, since the English verb *to pick up* is integrated into French with a French infinitive ending, *-er*.

Tu peux me pick-up-*er?*
You can me pick up-INF suffix
'Can you pick me up?'

(Gardner-Chloros, 2009: 86)

We also see from this example that code-switching can occur in positions where the word order differs between the two languages (note the position of the French direct object *me*; the English 'me' would be after the main verb). One of the functions of code-switching is clear here – there is no direct French equivalent of the English 'to pick up' so the code-switch is fulfilling a 'lexical need'.

Code-switching patterns can be diagnostic in multiple ways. They can be indicative of what is being lost when a language is threatened by another, and linguistic analysis may help us discover which of the two grammars is prevailing. But code-switching also occurs in relatively stable bilingual contexts – whether immigrant or indigenous – where it fulfils specific functions. We then need to consider what it *buys* speakers to use two varieties when they could, in many cases, use one at a time. In some cases, being bilingual is an important aspect of people's identity, and code-switching is overall the best way to express that. But as Conversation Analysis has shown us, it also provides a set of tools for structuring interaction. In classrooms, teachers can use one variety for the formal part of the lesson and another (usually the vernacular) for

Case Study 8.2

Code-switching should not be seen as a symptom of linguistic incompetence. In a study carried out with a large group of bilingual English-Spanish speakers in the Puerto Rican community in New York, Poplack (1980) found that fluent, balanced bilinguals code-switched *more* than those who were less competent in one of the languages.

Rindler-Schjerve (1998) studied the use of Italian and Sardinian dialect in Sardinia, where, as with other Italian dialects, a shift is occurring towards more use of standard Italian and away from the local dialect. This leads to an increased use of code-switching between the two. However, Poplack (1988) found that it was the more balanced bilinguals who switched most. According to this study, code-switching speakers 'contribute to the maintenance of Sardinian in that they change the Sardinian language by adapting it to the majority language, thus narrowing the gap between the two closely related codes' (1998: 246). In the following exchange, the Italian expression *secondo me* (=in my opinion) is inserted in a Sardinian sentence, but adapted to Sardinian phonology to minimize the transition (*segunnu me*). Its function is to highlight or separate the parenthetical expression 'in my opinion':

Non m'an giamadu 'e veterinariu ma segunnu me *fi calchicosa chi a manigadu*
They didn't call a vet but *in my opinion* it was something which it has eaten (1998: 243).

Rindler-Schjerve claims that although the switching occurs in a context of language shift, it 'should not be seen as a mechanism which *accelerates* the shift' (1998: 247).

informal explanations or for disciplining. In everyday conversation, balanced bilingual speakers can play one language off against the other, changing languages to show their displeasure or 'dispreference' when the conversation takes a turn they do not like, as in the following example (Li Wei, 1998: 171–172):

A is an eight-year-old girl, and C is A's 15-year-old brother. B is their mother who is in her forties.

A.	Cut it out for me (.) please
B.	(2.5)
A.	Cut it out for me (.) mum.
C.	[Give us a look
B.	[**Mut-ye?** ('**What?**')
A.	Cut this out.
B.	**Mut-ye?** ('**What**'?)
C.	Give us a look. (2.0)
B.	**Nay m ying wa lei?** ('*You don't answer me?*')
A. (To C)	Get me a pen.

Here we see code-switching being used in addition to pausing – another indication of dispreference. So although monolinguals can generally achieve the same effects, code-switching provides a further set of conversational tools for bilinguals.

STUDY ACTIVITY 8.4

Consider the following news story and what it tells us about the purposes of code-switching. Can you think of any comparable examples, especially if you have come across code-switching in other communities?

On 19 May 2009, BBC Radio 4 news reported that President Rajapaksa of Sri Lanka had announced that, after many years, the national army had defeated the Tamil Tigers. The Tigers had been fighting for a separate state for Tamils in the north and east of Sri Lanka since the 1970s. The speech, we were told, started in Sinhala, the official language of Sri Lanka: 'Today we have been able to liberate the entire country from the clutches of terrorism,' he said. 'We have been able to defeat one of the most heinous terrorist groups in the world.'

After speaking in his native Sinhala, President Rajapaksa then switched to the language of the Tamil minority, saying ethnic and religious divisions should end. 'We must find a homegrown solution to this conflict. That solution should be acceptable to all the communities.' He then switched back to Sinhala again to say: 'Let us all be united'. The President's switching back and forth is significant, and it is also interesting that this was remarked upon by the BBC news reporter, who clearly understood that the code-switching was functional. One of the well-documented functions of code-switching is specifying whom one is addressing, who is included, who is excluded, and who is specifically targeted.

8.6 Powerful and Less Powerful Varieties

Power is exercised not only through physical force or the threat of physical force but also through language. Some languages are more 'powerful' than others because they are associated with powerful groups in society. The sociologist Bourdieu talked of languages having a value in the 'linguistic marketplace', like other commodities. Powerful languages tend to be: (i) standard languages rather than regional or social dialects, and (ii) major world languages rather than those spoken in small or economically deprived nations. Wealth is one aspect of power, and a connection between GDP and the impact of various languages on the world stage can be established. English, the language behind some 30% of the world's GDP, is also the most widely learned second language worldwide.

Governments and institutions almost invariably use standard languages, though non-standard languages can gain acceptance and even supplant the standard ones in

Study Activity 8.5

Fairclough (1989: 18) gives the following example of an interview at a police station involving a policeman who is interviewing a witness to an armed robbery. Consider how the inequality in the power relationship is expressed in the form the conversation takes:

P: Did you get a look at the one in the car?
W: I saw his face, yeah.
P: What sort of age was he?
W: About 45. He was wearing a…
P: And how tall?
W: Six foot one.
P: Six foot one. Hair?
W: Dark and curly. Is this going to take long? I've got to collect the kids from school.
P: Not much longer, no. What about his clothes?
W: He was a bit scruffy-looking, blue trousers, black…
P: Jeans?
W: Yeah.

cases where they fulfil a strong identity function for their speakers. Examples of non-standard languages becoming increasingly 'institutionalized' include Swiss-German in Switzerland – formerly considered a dialect and subservient to High German; and Tok Pisin in Papua New Guinea, where this variety of pidgin has gradually gained ground as the country has achieved a greater degree of autonomy from its colonial past.

Within a given language framework, different types of discourse may also be more powerful than others. In Study Activity 8.5, above, we give an example of how power can be exercised through language by individuals in a position of authority.

Another category of people who exercise control through language is politicians. In 1948, George Orwell famously pointed to the dangers of euphemisms ('*extermination*') the use of slogans for political ends ('*War is peace*', '*Freedom is slavery*') and other linguistic manipulations in his novel *1984*. More recently, Fairclough, from whom the example above was taken, has analysed the language of contemporary politicians, in particular the 'New Labour' politicians in Britain, including Tony Blair, Peter Mandelson, John Prescott and Alastair Campbell, who became known in the 1990s for delivering 'spin' – clever talk in response to difficult questions, which skims over dissensions within the party in power and delivers a message which, superficially, appears to satisfy all possible concerns. Phrases like 'traditional values in a modern setting' were held to be particularly characteristic of this approach (2000: 3). This ability is not exclusive to the British Labour Party and has been identified in many powerful figures, including the right-wing Margaret Thatcher. In more extreme forms, it is a feature of totalitarian regimes all over the world. The analysis of speech and written texts from the point of view of the presuppositions that underlie them and the messages they try to put across covertly is known as Critical Discourse Analysis.

STUDY ACTIVITY 8.6

Critical Discourse Analysis is applied to many fields other than politics, in particular institutional discourse, but also to our understanding of humour and advertising.

Consider the unspoken assumptions (you should find at least three) about women and men – and their relationship – underlying an advertisement used by a French DIY company – the tellingly named Monsieur Bricolage ('Mr DIY') – in which the caption beneath a recumbent and scantily clad woman holding a power drill reads: 'Bien conseillée, je peux!' ('With good advice, I can!').

One way in which power relations are systematically – and, in many cases, unavoidably – encoded in language is through terms of address. In a large number of the world's languages – present-day English being an exception – plurality, especially of the pronouns used to address people, denotes politeness or respect. Thus in French, Italian, German and many other languages, there is a choice between the informal 2nd person singular pronoun and the more formal 2nd (or 3rd, for German) person plural (see Brown and Gilman, 1972; Clyne, Norrby and Warren, 2009). Brown and Gilman considered that the choice of pronoun with a given interlocutor was determined by two principal dimensions: power and solidarity. In past, less socially egalitarian times, it was common for the more powerful individual in a relationship to address their inferior with the singular (*tu*) form, but to receive the polite (*vous*) form in exchange. In the twentieth century, they claimed, the solidarity ethic became much more marked and mutual use of pronouns became much more common. The decision as to whether to use mutual *tu* or mutual *vous* remains a matter for case-by-case evaluation in languages that provide this type of option. In languages that do not use pronouns to encode such relations, there are many alternatives (e.g. the use of last name and title, as in *Mr. Brown*, as opposed to first name, *John*, or diminutive/nickname, e.g. *Johnny*).

The last type of power relationship encoded in language that will be considered here is the power relationship that may exist between women and men, with men traditionally being the more dominant and powerful members of society. There is a considerable literature now on gender differences in language (Coates, 2004: Coates and Pichler, 2011) and, nowadays, an increasing focus on language and sexuality more generally (Cameron and Kulick, 2006). Traditionally, language and gender questions are considered under two main headings: (i) how gender relations are encoded in the language itself, and (ii) the differences between male and female speech (or indeed language productions in other media, e.g. in writing or electronic communication). Regarding the first category, many if not all languages make a distinction in how they treat women and men, thereby reflecting – and perpetuating – social inequalities. In British English for example, women are still implicitly asked whether they are married or not more or less every time they give their name to a stranger ('*Is that Miss or Mrs?*'). In the US, the neutral alternative *Ms* is more widespread. This is tantamount to a power inequality because the interlocutor immediately has more knowledge about a woman than about a man, regardless of whether that knowledge is relevant. There are also inequalities encoded in the lexicon – think of the connotations of *mistress* as opposed to *master* – and in the grammar –, English, like many languages, uses the masculine pronoun as the inclusive one, rendering women linguistically invisible: *Each to his own preferences*, though alternatives, such as using the plural *their*, are increasingly tolerated.

There is more to be said – and more active research – on the question of how women's and men's language differs. It is not possible to do justice to the variety of work on this issue here, so a couple of examples will have to suffice. Most are taken from Coates and Pichler (2011), which brings together a significant collection of the important works in this field.

Based on early – and not very scientific – work by Lakoff in 1975, a number of features supposedly typical of 'women's language' were identified in English – including hedges (e.g. *sort of; kind of, I guess*); (super) polite forms (e.g. *would you please … I'd really appreciate it if …*); frequent use of tag questions to indicate hesitancy or a need for approval; hypercorrect grammar and pronunciation; question intonation in declarative contexts, and others. Some of these features may have been more common in the language of (certain) women than in that of their menfolk at that time, but since then there have been many challenges to the idea that there is anything intrinsically 'female' about such features. Instead, such features have been seen as defining 'powerless' language. Different – but not always clear – results are found where the normal power balance found in Western societies is reversed, and women are in a position of power over men. A study by O'Barr and Atkins (1998) involving witnesses in American courtrooms found that female expert witnesses spoke in the assertive way normally associated with men, and concluded that such features were a function of power differentials rather than of gender as such. On the

---

STUDY ACTIVITY 8.7

Coates (1996) studied the differences between conversations in single-sex groups among her women friends (British, middle class) and in male friendship groups. With respect to interruptions – often taken as a sign of conversational dominance – she found that the women interrupted one another a great deal, that there was a high proportion of overlapping speech and of finishing one another's sentences. However, this behaviour was in no way seen as competitive or aggressive; on the contrary, it was felt as cooperative and supportive. The men's groups were marked by longer stretches of uninterrupted speech, each one taking his turn to be the 'expert' at a given moment.

What are the various factors that could explain the different interpretations of 'interruptions' in this study compared with the ones mentioned above? In what sense is it necessary to know more about the relationships involved or the underlying cultural conventions, in order to come to a conclusion about the significance of particular conversational features? How do Coates's findings compare with your own experience of single-sex conversations?

other hand, West (1998) found that gender-dominance could override other factors; in a study of doctor–patient encounters, female doctors were interrupted by their male patients more than the other way round, despite their expert status in the relationship. Yet others have argued that the findings about female–male speech differences are culturally relative, noting, for example, that in the Japanese culture, interrupting and dominating a conversation, rather than being associated with a powerful role, is considered bad manners or immature (Wetzel, 1998). There are many other fascinating findings about the differences between male and female language, but more research is needed for us to understand the underlying reasons for such differences.

8.7 Conclusion

One of the preoccupations of linguists of a more social persuasion – they need not strictly speaking be 'sociolinguists' – has always been with the *relevance* of their work to society, or just to people in general. There are many reasons for this: one is a sense of duty to 'give back' something to those who have provided them with material for their research, and thereby supported their career as well as their interest in language; another is a desire to contribute to improving society by raising awareness of linguistic issues. This could help to support minorities, eliminate inequalities and make education, in particular, fairer; linguistic issues are not usually well understood by the public as linguistics is not a widely taught subject. Here is an example from Labov (1997):

In 1987, I had another opportunity to test the usefulness of linguistics on a matter that was vital to a single person. A number of bomb threats were made in repeated telephone calls to the Pan American counter at the Los Angeles airport. Paul Prinzivalli, a cargo handler who was thought by Pan American to be a 'disgruntled employee', was accused of the crime, and he was jailed. The evidence was that his voice sounded like the tape recordings of the bomb threat caller. The defense sent me the tapes because Prinzivalli was a New Yorker, and they thought I might be able to distinguish two different kinds of New York City accents. The moment I heard the recordings I was sure that he was innocent; the man who made the bomb threats plainly did not come from New York at all, but from the Boston area of Eastern New England. The problem was to prove this in court to a West Coast judge who could hear no difference between Boston and New York City speech!

All of the work and all of the theory that I had developed since Martha's Vineyard flowed into the testimony that I gave in court to establish the fact that Paul Prinzivalli did not and could not have made those telephone calls. It was almost as if my entire career had been shaped to make the most effective testimony on this one case. The next day, the judge asked the prosecuting attorney if he really wanted to continue. He refused to hear further statements from the defense. He found the defendant not guilty on the basis of the linguistic evidence, which he found 'objective' and 'powerful.'

Few linguists will have the opportunity to use their expertise in such a direct way as Labov did, both in this case and in the Black English trial (Labov 1982), to improve the lot of their fellow human beings. In a less immediate but no less important sense, however, they carry a responsibility to correct misinformation and prejudice about language and languages, which is likely to have wide-ranging consequences in society.

8.8 Summary

The chapter begins with a newspaper article about a Sri Lankan postmaster who refused to serve customers who did not speak 'proper English', pointing out the range of issues that his 'linguistic' judgement raises, including that of linguistic attitudes, normativeness, ethnicity and citizenship. In any given context, some varieties of language tend to be considered superior to others. One way in which this superiority is conveyed is by distinguishing between 'languages' and 'dialects', which, although they may be just as rich linguistically, do not benefit from standardization. Any dialect *can* be standardized, this being just one of the changes that linguistic varieties can undergo. There are also a number of ways in which varieties become transformed through – less deliberate – processes derived from contact with other varieties – for example, code-switching, pidginization, koineization and levelling. It is unusual for different varieties within a society to have neatly differentiated roles (as in classic *diglossia*), and sociolinguists now tend to study the complex interaction of varieties found in urban settings, such as *Multicultural London English*. These are certainly affected by contact, and develop differentially depending on the *social networks* to which speakers belong and on *Communities of Practice*, the spheres of activity that lead them to identify with particular groups. In bi- and multilingual settings, the role of contact may be even more marked and can give rise to code-switching. Bilingualism tends to be unstable and may lead to one variety – usually the economically powerful one – swallowing up another (known as *language death*). Other areas in which the relationship between language and power is studied include *gender differences* in language use, and *Critical Discourse Analysis*, which uncovers the hidden power agenda in, for example, political discourse. The chapter ended on a brief discussion of the researcher's potential role in these issues – for example, in forensic linguistics or in supporting minorities.

Study Questions

1. In your local community, how many linguistic subgroups can you discern (different languages, dialects, accents, etc.)? Try to describe both the linguistic and the social differences between them and describe how you think these differences arose.

2. Ask 10 people you know (not linguistics students!) what they think is the difference between a language and a dialect. To what extent do their criteria overlap with what was said above about this and to what extent do they agree among themselves?

3. Can you identify a minority with which you are familiar and explain what makes them a minority? Is it just sheer numbers or are there other factors keeping them apart from the rest? Are they linguistically distinct as well as being distinct in other ways? If so, is their distinctiveness being maintained or is it fading? Why?

4. Listen to an interview with a politician or a political discussion on the radio or TV. Are the politician's replies proper answers to the questions or are they evasive? If they are evasive, how do

> they achieve this in linguistic terms?
>
> 5. Set up a mini-debate with another student in which one of you has to argue that linguistics should be relevant to society – as Applied Linguistics purports to be – and the other argues that linguistic knowledge should be pursued for its own sake. What are the dangers of either approach?

Recommended Reading

Chambers, Jack, Peter Trudgill and Natalie Schilling-Estes. 2001. *The Handbook of Language Variation and Change*. Oxford: Wiley-Blackwell. This is a classic collection of 'variationist' sociolinguistic work, containing papers on each of the main factors underlying traditional sociolinguistic analysis from Labov onwards.

Cheshire, Jenny, Paul Kerswill, Sue Fox and Eiving Torgesen. 2011. Contact, the feature pool and the speech community: the emergence of Multicultural London English. *Journal of Sociolinguistics* 15 (2), 151–196.

Coates, Jennifer and Pia Pichler. 2011. *Language and Gender: A Reader*, 2nd edn. Oxford: Wiley-Blackwell. The most comprehensive collection of papers on the features investigated under the heading of language and gender/sexuality, which includes both investigations of specific assumed 'differences' between the sexes and theoretical discussions which help explain the evolution of the discipline.

Coupland, Nikolas and Adam Jaworski (eds.). 2009. *The New Sociolinguistics Reader*. Basingstoke: Palgrave Macmillan. This volume is a collection of 'classic' papers on a range of topics of interest to sociolinguistics in the broadest sense, covering both the macro and the micro ends of the spectrum.

Fairclough, Norman. 1989. *Language and Power*. Harlow: Longman. A seminal and inescapably 'political' analysis of how language is an intrinsic part of the exercise of power between individuals and groups, and of the construction of the relevant social distinctions.

Labov, William. 1982. Objectivity and commitment in linguistic science: The case of the Black English Trial in Ann Arbor. *Language in Society* 11 (2), 165–201.

Poplack, S. 1988. Contrasting patterns of code-switching in two communities. In Heller, Monica (ed.), *Codeswitching: Anthropological and Sociolinguistic Perspectives*, 215–245. Berlin: Mouton de Gruyter.

Thomason, Sarah G. 2001. *Language Contact: An Introduction*. Edinburgh: Edinburgh University Press. A scholarly introduction to the field, based on a wealth of historical and more contemporary examples, with a broad perspective and providing a bird's-eye view of language change.

Wardaugh, Ronald. 2010. *An Introduction to Sociolinguistics*, 6th edn. Oxford: Wiley-Blackwell. A thoroughly readable textbook which has been kept up to date and which surveys the principal monolingual as well as bilingual centres of interest with objectivity.

chapter 9

Language, Identity and Power

Lisa J. McEntee-Atalianis

Chapter Outline

9.1 Introduction
9.2 What is (Linguistic) Identity?
9.3 Is 'Identity' Something We 'Have' or Something We 'Do'?
9.4 How Do We Construct and Negotiate Identity through Narrative?
9.5 How and Why are Boundaries Constructed?
9.6 How are Identities Represented in and for the Media?
9.7 Summary

Learning Outcomes

After reading this chapter, you should be able to

- describe '(linguistic) identity';
- discuss key debates in the field, including a consideration of identity as a 'pre-discursive'/'stable' versus 'discursive'/'fluid' phenomenon;
- define the terms 'essentialism' and 'social constructionism';
- describe how boundaries are marked discursively;
- carry out a small-scale analysis of narrative, conversational and media texts.

Applied Linguistics, First Edition. Edited by Li Wei.
© 2014 John Wiley & Sons, Ltd. Published 2014 by John Wiley & Sons, Ltd.

> **Key Terms**
>
> - Crossing
> - Cultural ideologies
> - Cultural subjectivities
> - Discursive/pre-discursive
> - Essentialism
> - Performance/performativity
> - Social construction
> - Synthetic personalization
> - Variationist sociolinguistics

9.1 Introduction

At the first White House Correspondents' Association Dinner under the presidency of the newly elected Barack Obama, the popular stand-up comedian Wanda Sykes received rapturous applause when she heaped praise on Obama for his election to office as 'the first black President'. With comic-timing she went on to administer a pseudo-threat:

> – well that's unless you screw up! And then it's going to be 'What's up with the half-white guy, huh? … Who voted for the mulatto[1]? …'

The impact of her joke was felt by the audience on hearing the final two rhetorical questions. Superficially these raised a laugh because of the sensitive nature of the material and the juxtaposition, indeed the rise and fall, of praise so swiftly followed by scorn. But Sykes's joke also skilfully accomplished identity work through the construction and indexical marking of a stereotypical African-American speech style and attitude towards racial boundaries. The comedian shifted in an instant from the expression of a congratulatory in-group speech act, delivered as a fellow black American, to admonition, marking through reported speech a negative stance towards out-group 'half-white' identities. The joke was received in good humour, not only because of the context within which this exchange took place, but also, as with many good jokes, because of its currency. Obama's identity had become a key issue in his bid for election and continues to be exploited at the time of writing. Sykes played cleverly on this intertextuality. Additionally and significantly, the comedian was deemed able to express an opinion on this racially and politically sensitive topic because of her own heritage and professional standing.

This brief account serves only to bring into focus some of the issues that we will be exploring in this chapter, including: how we, and others, construct and represent our identity in different contexts; how and why identity is negotiated and shaped in discourse; who has the power to construct and 'position' identity/ies; and how and why ascriptions are resisted and boundaries marked between individuals or groups. It will become evident that language is fundamental to the formation and expression of identity, and others' perceptions of us. It is arguably the most malleable, powerful and ubiquitous channel through which we express our selfhood and the channel through which others also construct and manipulate our personal and social identity (Bucholtz and Hall, 2006).

We begin the chapter by defining 'identity' and consider how this term has taken on different meanings in Applied Linguistics. We will then explore how language is used to construct and 'perform' identity/ies and how it can be used as a marker of social inclusion or exclusion in different social contexts. We will finally consider how identity/ies are represented and con-structed in cultural products, such as the media and political speeches, and how these realiza-tions may lead to the creation of cultural subjectivities and the formation of cultural ideologies, which influence the way in which we think about individuals or social groupings.

9.2   What is (Linguistic) Identity?

If I asked you to reflect on your identity, it would probably take you more than a moment's pause. To answer comprehensively you might have to reference a number of diverse cultural and social/personal circumstances – for example, your personality; age/generation; ethni-city; religion; gender; social status; heritage; educational influences; your behaviour in differ-ent situations. You may privilege a few of these over others. If you found the question difficult to answer then feel reassured, many researchers argue that identity is not an objective fixed state but a complex multi-faceted phenomenon which changes throughout our lifetime and alternates on a daily basis as we encounter different situations. In other words, it is not static but may be formative, fluid and emergent, constructed by ourselves and others and negoti-ated (i.e. challenged and contested) over time and space (geographic and social).

In helping you to think about this initial definition of identity and its linguistic expression, consider the following:

Study Activity 9.1

1. Reflect on three different conversations that you have recently engaged in: a conver-sation in a public setting with someone you do not know very well (e.g. at the shops, or the doctor's surgery); a conversation with a very close friend; and a conversation at home with a member of your family. How did your behaviour and the structure and content of the conversation (e.g. accent, word choice, language choice, turn-tak-ing and topic management) differ in each context, and how was it influenced by the roles and identities of the people involved in the conversations?
2. Consider how you would describe your identity 10 years ago and today. What aspects of your identity appear to have remained the same and which have changed? (You may feel that over time some aspects of your identity have remained stable, e.g. your name and nationality, while others have been more prone to change, e.g. your educational/ professional status; your taste in clothes).

We have established so far that the task of defining identity is very difficult, but some have ventured to define its complex and multi-dimensional nature, marrying this with a consideration of language.

Different perspectives have been put forward – for example, sociolinguistic (Le Page and Tabouret-Keller's (1985) 'Acts of Identity'), social psychological (Tajfel and Turner's (1979) 'Social Identity Theory') and sociocognitive (Van Dijk, 1998). Tracy (2002) views identity from a sociocultural and rhetorical perspective and defines it in relation to four categories: 'master'; 'personal'; 'interactional' and 'relational'. These can be thought of in relation to two dichotomies: stable versus dynamic identities; and social versus personal identities.

'Master identities' and 'personal identities' constitute 'stable pre-existing' (2002: 20) elements: 'master' refers to elements of our identity which remain constant and steadfast – for example, our place of origin, our name, our sex. These aspects of identity reflect an embeddedness and membership within broader biological and/or social categories. 'Personal identities', in contrast, describe a characterization of the individual, based on others' perceptions of us, in light of their interpretations of our behaviour or conduct (e.g. kind, intelligent, honest), or characterizations based on references to indexical markers which denote an association between ourselves and other (social) categories – for example, using British Sign Language will index an association with Deaf culture and the Deaf community; speaking with a particular accent may indicate our place of origin. Personal identities are therefore unique to the individual and constructed both by the individual and by others with whom the individual comes into contact.

In contrast to these comparatively stable categorizations of identity, other aspects are more fluid and dynamic and may be realized differently in different situations. The exercise above asked you to think about the roles of different interactants in conversations. We all take on different interactional roles, or, as Tracy defines them, 'interactional identities', depending on the context and the people we are conversing with. I have a number of interactional identities, influenced by my familial, professional and social relationships. I am a daughter, sister, wife and mother; I am employed as a university lecturer and am therefore a teacher, a researcher and a colleague; but I also take on other interactional roles on a daily basis – I engage in conversations with shop assistants in which I am positioned as 'customer'; and I assume the role of patient while visiting the doctor, and so the list goes on. My interactional identity may influence my language use – for example, the medium through which I communicate (email, lectures, telephone, face-to-face); the subject matter; the degree and type of relational as opposed to transactional talk; the expression of politeness; the degree of control over the interactional encounter – but my role does not necessarily determine or prefigure the nature of the interaction itself or how it will evolve. My enactment of particular identity/ies in conversation is not 'fixed' but may be negotiated as the conversation progresses between myself and my interlocutor(s). This projection of identity/ies in conversation is what Tracy (2002) refers to as 'relational identity' and we witness the enactment of this in the following extract in which a doctor repositions her identity, from that of a medical professional (as determined by the institutional context) to that of a parent when breaking difficult news to parents (Maynard, 1989b: 64, cited in Arminen, 2005: 103):

DR. D: I think-you know I'm sure you're anxious about today and I know this has
         been a really hard year for you. And I think you've really done an extraordi-
         nary job in dealing with something that's very hard for any human being or
         any parent- and you know Mrs. Roberts and I can talk as parents as well as
MRS. R: True
DR. D: uh my being a professional. It's HARD when there's something not all right
         with a child, very hard.

This repositioning of her identity serves an important conversational function; it serves to lessen the distance between herself and the parents of her patient. In establishing a common 'parental' identity the doctor projects a shared understanding, crucially foregrounding and mitigating the force of her subsequent difficult diagnosis.

Tracy's (2002) model provides a useful lens through which initially to view 'identity' and consider the role of language in its development and projection. It separates *personal/unique* ('personal' and 'relational') and *social categories* ('master' and 'interactional') while reconstituting these to illustrate the comparatively *stable* ('master' and 'personal') versus *dynamic* ('interactional' and 'relational') aspects of identity construction.

―――――――――――――― 9.3   Is 'Identity' Something We 'Have' or Something We 'Do'?

Tracy (2002) combines two apparently contradictory aspects of 'identity' – stability and fluidity – and hints at larger ideological and ontological differences in the historical and current treatment of identity in the research literature. Theories and investigations of identity have been influenced by different conceptualizations, motivated broadly by different aims and assumptions: identity as a 'pre-discursive' or 'enduring' state or property of the individual or society, in which the relationship between language and social variables is seen as stable; and identity as an external 'construction' determined through social interaction and discourse. The former perspective may be referred to as an 'essentialist' or 'realist' perspective and the latter as 'postmodern/social constructionist' and 'post-structuralist'[2] perspectives.

The earliest accounts of identity are reported to have appeared in the sixteenth century, focusing on individual self-determination and interpretation (Benwell and Stokoe, 2006). These studies conceived of 'identity' as being under the control and understanding of the individual, as a product of the mind.

Some researchers view identity as an internalized and/or stable property of individuals and social groupings, which determines and reflects biological, psychological and social reality. The individual, and social structures, are conceived as independent forms, individuals being influenced by social structures via socialization leading to the internalization of social influences. Researchers have used identity categories as analytical tools and have been at pains to determine, for example, how they can distinguish individuals and groups from each other and the relationship between identity and language variation and change/shift. Work within the social sciences has given rise to discrete demographic/identity labels considered to represent pre-existing or stable biological, psychological and social structures, such as age, sex, social class and ethnicity, and these classifications have been used by researchers as explanatory variables or attributes, to index and predict linguistic behaviour by speakers.

The emergence of variationist sociolinguistics in the mid-twentieth century is an example of this work. Researchers within this tradition have used discrete and predetermined category classifications – for example, male/female, working class/middle class/upper class – as important variables against which to correlate individual or group behaviour, considering identity as an attribute of the individual/group rather than the context. The relationship between an individual's/group's identity and their language use was seen as causal and reflective. For example, it might be hypothesized that coming from a working-class background will determine greater use of the glottal stop [ʔ] in words like 'button' or 'mutton' in certain dialects of English. Similarly, researchers who apply Tajfel's (1979) 'Social Identity Theory' in their investigation of the ethnolinguistic vitality of groups in language contact situations also assume a correlation between a speaker's social identity and their language attitudes and use.

Variationist sociolinguistics has developed significantly since the mid-twentieth century. Researchers typically gather data over an extended period of time through participant-observation, ethnographic and interview methods, often recording their informants while engaging in everyday ('naturalistic') activities (e.g. while at play or at meal times). Having transcribed the data gathered, researchers calculate the incidence of the specific linguistic variable(s) under investigation (e.g. phonological, lexical, morphosyntactic or discourse variables). The linguistic variable(s) are then correlated with the demographic variables.[3]

Some researchers criticize and challenge the view of identity as 'stable' or 'pre-existing' and instead conceive of it as an external (social) rather than an internal (private), pre-discursive phenomenon. Identity is considered to be an inter-subjective

---

Case Study 9.1

A well-known study in the variationist tradition is Susan Gal's (1978, 1979) account of language shift in the Austrian town of Oberwart. Through observation, Gal noticed that language shift was taking place in the community from Hungarian to German-dominant language use. She was interested to determine the reasons for this change and the protagonists responsible for language shift. Aware of the community's history – it's change, post-World War I, from Hungarian to Austrian administration and the consequent changes to language policy, including, for example, the shift from Hungarian to German as the language of education – and also aware of socio-economic and geographic changes – in which Oberwart transformed into a city and industrial setting, away from an agricultural lifestyle – Gal designed a participant-observation study, in which she observed the language choices of citizens conversing with different interlocutors in different contexts. She classified her participants into discrete analytic categories – male/female; age groupings and peasant/non-peasant status – and hypothesized that language choice was dependent on these identity variables and the values that the participants associated with the different codes. She noted that Hungarian had come to symbolize a peasant status in the community whereas German, owing to the evident sociohistorical and cultural changes, had come to symbolize prestige, a 'worker' status, distinct from the peasant/agricultural status of the native inhabitants. Gal found three dominant factors influencing language choice: speaker age, sex and social network. The older informants, men and those mixing with peasants spoke more Hungarian than German; however, the young, women and those mixing predominantly in non-peasant networks were German-dominant. Since 'mixed-marriages' were also commonplace, children in the community were increasingly using more German at home and this, allied with the official status of German in the community, was leading, Gal suggested, to a permanent shift to German. Gal's study viewed participants' language choices as strategically and socially meaningful and asserted a direct correlation and causal link between speaker identity (as defined by the analyst) and language choice.

construction, dependent on discursive enactment and accomplishment, something *brought about* in the conversation or situation. It is not a predetermined individual or social reality, a 'fixed' uniform state *brought to* the conversation, but is complex, fragmentary, and may be multiply constructed or transformed in and through discourse and other semiotic systems. It is a resource through which subjects are created and projected. Drawing on various theories, for example critical, cultural theory and theories of performativity (Benwell and Stokoe, 2006), social constructionists argue that category labels (such as male/female, peasant/non-peasant) are inexact, broad, fixed and crucially determined *a priori* by researchers, thereby influencing analysts' interpretation and conceptualization of 'identity'. They further argue that correlations between demographic categories and language use may be fallacious; just because an individual drops their 't's, for example, does not necessarily index a 'working-class' identity. They assert instead that 'identity' is not something we 'have' – a stable property or 'essence' (in time and space) determined by the individual or the analyst – but something we 'do' and co-construct in social action, in order, for example, to persuade, or to joke (as in the Obama examples above and below) or to construct in-group/out-group dichotomies. Through this 'performance' we can conceive of identity in a far more complex way: as something mobile, fluid and negotiable. Identity 'work' may be different on different occasions and influenced by personal and social circumstance. This being so, 'group identity and subject positions become (conversational) categories that may be invoked as a resource in discursively produced identities' (Benwell and Stokoe, 2006: 29).

Recent research has given rise to both micro- and macro-analyses of identity formation and representation. Researchers approach the study of identity from different methodological and ideological bases. For example, micro-analyses of conversational data motivated by the ethno methodological and conversational analytic (CA)

STUDY ACTIVITY 9.2

In considering the different approaches and theoretical underpinning of Conversation Analysis (CA) and Critical Discourse Analysis (CDA), review the doctor/patient extract in Section 9.2, above, and attempt the following:

1. From a CA perspective, discuss the construction and representation of identity/ies in this extract. How do the interactants display an orientation to (an awareness of) the interactional order and the identities of the interactants? For example, consider turn-taking and floor-apportionment – who is in control? Who speaks longest?
2. From a CDA perspective, consider the discourse of 'parenthood' as invoked by the doctor in this short extract, that is, how does the doctor construct the identity of 'parent' through her account? How does she position the parents and herself with respect to this, and what are the consequences of this positioning?

approaches examine how identity is displayed and discursively constructed through 'talk-in-interaction'. Researchers are less interested in historical, political or cultural influences than in how identity is made relevant and 'oriented to' procedurally by speakers in conversation, and how it is used as a resource by participants. For example, in the analysis of the doctor–patient extract above we would refrain from categorizing the speaker as a 'doctor' until such time as her identity is made relevant in or through the discourse. Conversation Analysts are interested in how participants draw on, or challenge, normative features and categorizations in the casting or alter-casting of identity/ies through interaction. In contrast, Critical Discourse Analysts adopt a more ideologically and politically motivated approach and are keen to iden-tify powerful agents and discourses that serve to regulate and control social ideology and the construction, performance and positioning of certain identities. Their work aims to highlight unequal or oppressive attitudes or practices as they investigate which representations and discourses (i.e. ways of talking about issues, e.g. women's rights; immigrant groupings) are produced and reproduced, and the motivations behind these constructions – for example, to discriminate against women/minority groups.

9.4   How Do We Construct and Negotiate Identity through Narrative?

A great deal of work in the social constructionist paradigm has focused on gender identity. Judith Butler (1990) proposed a theory of 'performativity' which conceives of identity as a discursive production and accomplishment. Jenny Coates, a well-known gender theorist, has illustrated how men and women 'perform' their gender identity in all-male and all-female story-telling. She argues (as Barbara Johnstone (1993) before her) that through the act of story-telling men and women build different 'story worlds' which both reflect and construct women's and men's 'psychological, social, and cul-tural worlds outside their stories' (Johnstone, 1993: 67–68, cited in Coates 2003: 107). She illustrates how men perform 'hegemonic masculinity', while women 'ideal femi-ninity' through narration.

STUDY ACTIVITY 9.3

Examine the extracts that follow, taken from Coates (2003: 107–109), and determine:

1. if there are any similarities and differences between the stories;
2. how the narrators 'perform' masculinity and femininity.

(1)   The Fight
      [Three men in their twenties in a pub, talking about an engineer at work who was an
      alcoholic]
      1.   he came in this one time
      2.   drunk,
      3.   and he started ordering me about.
      4.   With kind of personality I've got
      5.   I told him to piss off,
      6.   I wasn't taking any of it.
      7.   So I was making these um alarm bell boxes, the alarm boxes,
      8.   you put this bell on and you wire these-
      9.   can't remember how to do it now anyway but-
      10. wiring these up,
      11. and he come out,
      12. and he sss, sss, sss, <MIMICS NOISE>
      13. what he did was he threw the knife at me,
      14. this is honest truth,
      15. threw a knife at me,
      16. and then- and there was this cable,
      17. you know um like on the workbenches where you connect the cables into these
           three points,
      18. a bare wire,
      19. he fucking chased me with it,
      20. and I thought, 'Fuck this',
      21. and he kept like having a go and teasing me,
      22. and I just smashed him straight round the face with a bell box in front of the
           boss,
      23. crack,
      24. got away with it as well,
      25. I said 'Look', I said, 'he's thrown knives at me',
      26. it sounds like something out of a film but it's honest truth.
      27. […]
      28. Honestly it was unbelievable.

(2)   Sardines in Aspic
      [Context=discussion of narrator's eccentric mother]
      1.   Actually when I first took Martin up there
      2.   when Martin and I-<LAUGHS>my husband- [yes] ex-husband and I were first
           going out together
      3.   and it was all new and really embarrassing you know <LAUGHS> [yeah]
      4.   he only ever used to like traditional English food like-
      5.   cos he was steak and kidney pie shepherd's pie and roast dinner on Sunday
           [yeah]
      6.   and that was all he'd eat,
      7.   give him anything foreign [yeah] and he'd have hysterics, [yeah]

8.   so I phoned my mother up before we went up for our very first visit
9.   and I said 'He only likes plain food so just don't go mad', [*yeah*]
10. cos she always goes mad, [*yeah*]
11. 'Don't go mad,
12. just cook something really ordinary',
13. *she does, makes nice food though, really nice food.*
14. So we got there late at night
15. and she said 'I've made something for you to eat',
16. and she'd made sardines in aspic<LAUGHTER.>
17. and beetroot in natural yoghurt, <LAUGHTER>
18. plain food<LAUGHTER>
19. *did she do it on purpose?*
20. I don't know, probably.
21. *what did he say?*
22. he wasn't very impressed<LAUGHTER>
23. he kept hauling me down to the little chip shop in the village<LAUGHTER>
24. cos he was hungry,
25. he wouldn't eat anything she made. <LAUGHTER>

While cautioning against over-simplification and over-generalization, Coates points out some similarities between the two tales, including, for example, the ability of the story-tellers to take the conversational floor and engage their audience (as reflected by their audience's compliance and continued indications of listenership), and the fact that the stories successfully reflect the well-known subgenres of 'heroic' and 'humorous' story-telling, so commonly heard in Western cultures. She notes, however, that the differences between the two stories are marked. 'The Fight' can be characterized as an 'action' story in which the teller is positioned as the heroic protagonist in a public setting apparently dominated by men. In contrast, in 'Sardines in Aspic', the story-teller positions herself in relation to other familial relationships, her mother and her former husband. Her story is set in the privacy of the home, involving both male and female company and the world that she depicts reflects 'sensitiv[ity] to the complexity and difficulty of human relationships' (2003: 111).

Caution must be exercised when viewing such examples as these, as Coates acknowledges. Although such analysis is concerned to identify the enactment of gender identity, the categories of 'male' and 'female' must not be treated by analysts as *a priori* explanatory variables. Other work in the field has been at pains to report on the heterogeneity of gender identity and to discuss intra-gender difference, as well as inter-gender similarity.

Narratives not only build and reflect individual and group identities but are also sites of negotiation and contestation. They allow us to position ourselves in relation to others (individuals and groupings) and to cultural and social norms and events. Moore (2006: 625) illustrates this in her account of a long-term ethnographic study of a group of girls in a high school in Bolton, north-west England. Through her analysis of one narrative, in which two girls, Ellie and Meg, are reporting on a recent night out in which Meg had been duped into drinking urine from a beer bottle and had subsequently smashed the bottle over Ellie's head in fury, she illustrates how stories are jointly constructed and negotiated, and how they serve to establish personal identities and a shared understanding of events. We pick up the story when the two girls offer individual accounts of the event:

```
69   ELLIE:                        ~ And then she ran off down
     MEG:     (0) That looks really bad. ~
70   ELLIE:    the road, and everyone was like – (0) it all went
71   ELLIE:    (X_black_X) - -
     MEG:                        Yeah. (0)Cos the second I did it – Right.
...
84   ELLIE:    Oh = shit. And er- [Sadie started] and went, What the fuck
     MEG:                        [(H) (C)]
85   ELLIE:    have you done? (0)She goes - -
     MEG:                              No, they were all – (0)all
86   MEG:      the Year 10s were all standing round me in a massive
87   MEG:      circle,..and they all went, What've you done?
...
92   MEG:      (H) And then, they all went, Yeah, I know. (0)Started
93   MEG:      pushing me-<A_They're all in a circle. I was going
94   MEG:      like this – (0)going <Q_Ahh!_Q>_A>And then, I was stood
95   MEG:      there, against this green box thing, and Sally went
96   MEG:      <Q_Poo!_Q>' Oh and just whacked me one. I went, My eye!
97   ELLIE:    ~And [then, even] though she'd bottled me, and I saw
     MEG:      ~       [<@(Hx)@]
98   ELLIE:    everyone started on her, I le=gged it down, and I
99   ELLIE:    pushed everyone away, and I stood in front of her –
100  ELLIE:    <F_like the little hero I am - - _F>
.......
```

[beginning of first overlap   ] end of first overlap   - self-interruption
~ interspeaker latching   = lengthened syllable   ( ) timed pause   (C) cough
(S) sniff   (H) breath in   (Hx) breath out   @ laughter

The extract depicts a co-narration. Moore describes how Ellie and Meg each bid to tell their version of the story. Ellie (line 69) begins to tell of the events following the bottling, the point at which Meg is moving away from the scene of her crime, but she is interrupted by Meg, who (in line 71) begins a slightly different account which situates events in a different time and space – at the moment of the bottling and immediately afterwards. Both girls continue to tell their own version of the story, focusing on different issues. It is not until line 85, the point at which Meg indicates her disagreement with Ellie's account, that their stories begin to coalesce. This contestation is marked linguistically by the negative particle 'no' when Meg reasserts her right to the floor and narrates events leading up to her abuse by the Year 10 crowd. Meg relinquishes the floor at line 97 to Ellie, who concludes the story and enacts her 'heroic' identity.

This brief extract illustrates how identities and experiences may be self-presented, co-constructed and contested through personal narratives. It also illustrates how narrators cast and altercast their own and others' subject positions, building a picture of allegiance, or animosity in this instance, and subject roles as active agents or passive recipients. Note, for example, how Sadie and all the Year 10s are brought into the narrative through the rhetorical use of reported speech which serves to add validity to the narrative by implying a 'factual' reporting of events. It is at this point that Meg shifts roles from attacker to victim, an impression supported by Ellie's final account.

In the next section we extend our discussion to consider how linguistic resources are brought to bear in the marking of multiple identities and group boundaries.

9.5   How and Why are Boundaries Constructed?

We have established so far that being the 'same' as or 'different' from someone else or another grouping may be socially and situationally motivated. Identity ascriptions vary according to circumstance and motivation. We all have multiple allegiances and subjectivities and we enact selective versions and characteristics of these in different contexts: constructing, positioning and repositioning boundaries between ourselves and others. But how are these identities realized, and why? And how does this boundary marking differ across different communities and circumstances? And how is it explained by researchers coming from different research traditions?

At a simplistic level we may adopt the behaviour (including linguistic) of the person/ group(s) with which we identify in any situation. This may include, for example, dressing in a certain way, shifting to another language or adopting a particular accent, or using slang terms. Terms of address may be determined by our culture but these, too, mark personal/social identification(s) within a particular context and also indicate symmetrical/ asymmetrical relationships or social distance. For example, it is common practice in schools in the UK for pupils to address teachers by their title and surname (e.g. 'Miss Jones'), while in Greece pupils refer to their teachers by their title and first name (e.g. 'Miss Elena'). These differences denote ethnic and cultural boundaries between the British and Greek nations. However, the fact that in both contexts the teacher is always referred to by her title, and the pupil by their first name, serves to mark an asymmetrical power relationship between the interactants.

We categorize ourselves and are categorized by others through the use of labels which serve to denote both personal and social identification. Sometimes, of course, the ascriptions

---

STUDY ACTIVITY 9.4

Compare and contrast Eckert's study with that of Labov (see Case Study 9.2). What are the differences between the ascriptions afforded to the groupings in each context? What are the consequences of these ascriptions and how does the notion of 'power' play into this?

Case Study 9.2

Some years before Eckert's study, William Labov (1963) demonstrated how changes to the social and economic circumstances of a community can lead to subtle patterns of linguistic variation between in- and out-group members of a community, and ultimately to longer-term language change. He investigated language use on the small island of Martha's Vineyard (off the coast of New England). The island had been predominantly inhabited by Native Americans and descendants of old English and Portuguese families; however, at the time of his study Labov reported that it was increasingly experiencing an influx of wealthy tourists from mainland America. He noticed changes in the pronunciation of certain sounds by some of the local inhabitants and subsequently carried out interviews with speakers of different ages, ethnic backgrounds, occupations and places of residence, investigating their pronunciation of a range of phonetic variables. In his investigation of the pronunciation of certain diphthongs – for example, [ai] (as in KITE) – he noted that some members of the community were changing their pronunciation from the standard form (also used on the mainland), to a more centralized pronunciation, [əi]. Quantitative analyses of the pronunciations of a variety of forms revealed an interesting pattern of stratified language use within the community. He noted in particular that among the 31–60-year-old age group the centralized island pronunciation was increasing in use and this was particularly marked in the speech of one occupational and geographic grouping, the fishermen of Chilmark, who Labov identified as being passionate protectors of their industry and island lifestyle. Labov concluded that the changes in the linguistic repertoire of the relatively poor island inhabitants had been motivated by the presence of the tourists and the subsequent changes to the island economy and lifestyle. He noted that changes in pronunciation reflected a symbolic boundary marking between the inhabitants and the tourists, an expression of island identification, born out of difficult economic and social circumstances, in which the island inhabitants were battling to retain their community and island life. In contrast, he notes that the younger generation (14–30 year olds) was less affected by these circumstances, with some even wishing to study or work on the mainland, and this was reflected in their maintenance of standard forms.

we choose for ourselves are not the same as those chosen or imposed by others! Penelope Eckert (2000) describes a group of high school children in Detroit, USA, who self-ascribe and are identified by others as belonging to oppositional social groups: the 'Jocks', who are characterized as actively participating in school events and culture and who aspire to a college education and subsequent 'white collar' employment; and the 'Burnouts', who reject school culture, integrate within the local community and ultimately aim for 'blue collar' occupations. These identifications and aspirations are described by the pupils themselves but also enacted symbolically through differences in dress and speech. The Jocks are reported to use more conservative language forms, such as standard pronunciation and limited use of obscenities, in contrast to the Burnouts, who adopt local vernacular forms and frequently swear.

Globalization has certainly brought about great social change, facilitating real and virtual contact between diverse communities. This has led, in some instances, to the construction of multiple and 'hybrid' identities which may be expressed stylistically. All identities and identifications index lifestyles and some people choose to 'cross' into the identity/ies of others in order to enact a different lifestyle or identity from the group with which they are conventionally associated. In London, for example, teenagers from diverse ethnic groupings (e.g. Bangladeshi, Pakistani and white) appropriate the speech style of Caribbean Creole speakers. Through interactional work they strategically perform a 'cool' adolescent identity, garnering covert prestige and dissolving interethnic boundaries in their creation of an alternative youth culture to the mainstream groupings (Rampton, 1995).

Speech styles and codes become resources, therefore, that are exploited in conversations and enact particular identities. These, in turn, mark group boundaries. Multilingual speakers draw on an array of varieties in their identity performance. For example, second-generation Dominican-Americans, resident in Providence, Rhode Island, are described as 'Hispanic, American and largely of African descent' (Bailey, 2001: 190). They are reported to use different varieties of Spanish and English, including Standard and Vernacular Dominican Spanish and English, African American Vernacular English (AAVE) and hybrid forms, exploiting these in their construction of and resistance to ethnic and racial boundaries, as shown below:

Two girls, Isabella and Janelle, are chatting in high school after lunch. Isabella ate at a nearby diner and is describing the sandwich she ate (2001: 195–196):

J: Only with that turkey thingee   //ya yo (es)toy llena.
                                         'I'm already full'
I: //Two dollars and fifty cent.
J: That's good. That's like a meal at //Burger King
                                    // That's better than going to Burger
     King, you know what I'm saying?
....
I: //But it's slamming, though, oh my God, mad ['a lot of'] turkey she puts in there

Although the author reports that the conversation was predominantly in English, we witness the switching between Spanish and English and the appropriation of AAVE vocabulary commonly associated with African-American youths. The combination of these codes sets these girls apart as belonging to the Dominican-American community.

Bailey accounts for 'three nested levels' (2001: 192) of boundary marking in this community and reports on how Dominican-Americans are able to:

1.   construct 'non-white' identities and establish solidarity with other non-white (low-income and minority) groupings, through the use of AAVE and the mocking use of white English varieties;
2.   perform a 'non-Black' Dominican identity through the use of Spanish, thereby creating a boundary between themselves and others of African descent and an identification with a 'Dominican-American' ethnolinguistic ascription; and
3.   mark intra-group boundaries between those Dominican-Americans born in the United States and more recent immigrants from the Dominican Republic.

Subtle power relationships can often be played out through the adoption of stock phrases or linguistic forms from other groupings. Hill (cited in Bucholtz and Hall, 2006) asserts that

Anglo-Americans humorously appropriate expressions such as 'No problemo' when, for example, agreeing to a request. Hill argues this does more than reflect a jovial stance; it also serves to index an attitude and identity that are set apart from, even in opposition or superior to, the Spanish-speaking community. These appropriations and associations between language and identity in turn lead to the formation of cultural stereotypes, such as the 'laid-back Mexican', which may contribute to the formation of essentialized cultural ideologies.

In the final section we take forward the consideration of cultural and social ideologies in our discussion of how people and events are represented and constructed in the media, and how the media contribute to the creation of subjectivities and ideologies that may influence the way in which we think about individuals or social groupings.

9.6   How are Identities Represented in and for the Media?

Critical linguists argue (e.g. Fairclough, 1989, 1995; Van Dijk, 1989) that the media has the power to represent, construct and challenge particular identities: both the identities of the individuals/communities they are reporting on and the identities of their imagined 'target' audiences. The media, they argue, function ideologically in their production of meanings and their construction of power relations, selecting what to emphasize and include, or reject and silence. They therefore have the linguistic power to mediate and represent events and people in particular ways. As audiences we engage with these positions, not always consciously or critically, but we frequently accept, and less frequently challenge or reject, the positions proffered. In the latter case the discourse takes on widespread currency and acceptance and subsequently becomes 'naturalized', so that the way that we talk about events or people is accepted as 'common sense', 'neutral' or the 'norm'.

In this section we will consider how both cultural identities and individuals are represented in and through media texts and images. Drawing on the work of Litosseliti (2006) we initially consider how masculine and feminine identities are constructed and how journalists influence the way we think about identities and power relations. We will then briefly return to our discussion of Barack Obama and consider how his identity has been put to rhetorical effect and publicized through Western media.

Litosseliti argues that the media often present an essentialized, exaggerated and binary conceptualization of male and female subjectivity, often limiting discussion of the similarities between men and women or the differences within gender categories. Quoting Ballaster et al. (1996: 87) she suggests that '[t]he world of the magazine is one in which men and women are eternally in opposition, always in struggle, but always in pursuit of each other'. Moreover, the discourse of magazines, she argues, helps to construct a 'code of femininity/[masculinity]' and a community, a 'synthetic sisterhood (Talbot, 1995)' (1996: 97) or 'brotherhood', achieved through the exploration of certain subject matter and the invocation of such linguistic features as personal pronouns, inclusive phrases (e.g. 'many of us') and colloquial expressions, used to mark in-group solidarity and identification.

Since the 1980s some male magazines have constructed and targeted the identity of the 'new man': a man responsive to and interested in female concerns and subject matter (Litosseliti, 2006). These magazines similarly sport articles on, for example, health, beauty and fashion. However, in presenting this identity Litosseliti (2006) notes that there is a tension between more traditional and more progressive male discourse. In an attempt to manage this tension, journalists construct and appeal to an identity that is set apart from an essentialized female or homosexual identity. This is achieved through the use of particular heterosexualized discourse and imagery, including, for example, the use of irony or overtly heterosexual imagery. For example, the men's magazine *Esquire* (August 2009: 125) can be found to employ instructive discourse in a 'self-help' column, entitled 'How to wear aftershave'. Here the journalist tackles the progressive subject of male grooming by appealing to the 'imagined' consumer as a 'traditional man', a man usually unconcerned with his appearance, ready to 'break the rules' – a tough, and yet ambitious, individual heading for success:

> For those looking to ditch their dusty bottles of Denim, or others newly converted to the fragrance world, follow these rules for the smell of success:
>
> 1. If you're still wearing the stale stuff you used at school to hide the smell of cigarette smoke, trust us, it's time for a change. ...

Here we witness the commodification of an identity drawing on the discourses of 'the traditional man' and 'the schoolboy'.

STUDY ACTIVITY 9.5

Can you find evidence of the creation of 'synthetic sisterhood' in this editorial from *Good Housekeeping* (August 2009: 5) by Lindsay Nicholson?

THE FEATURE that has got all of us talking in the office this month is Tame Your Inner Cavewoman ... While we were editing this feature ... I invited some friends over for a barbecue at home. Cue extreme hunter-gatherer behaviour ... The men ... stood around the glowing coals poking at the meat with sticks and drinking beer ... that would suggest they had hunted down a wildebeest themselves ... Meanwhile, and despite the fact that I am by no means a girlie-girl, the women sat inside the cave ... nibbling on nuts and berries and talking about relationships. ... the children climbed all over the sofas ...

STUDY ACTIVITY 9.6

1. What benefits are bestowed on the media industry through their construction and exploitation of these essentialized identity representations?
2. How might media discourse influence the way in which we talk about and view our gender identity? How might this impact on our behaviour and attitudes?

Indeed, the semiotic meanings constructed and reflected in advertising similarly draw on an essentialist ideology, often constructing polarized and simplified categorizations of men and women as revealed in the strap line for an advert for vitamins for men in the same magazine. The advert carries the strap line 'because men and women will always be different' (*Esquire*, August 2009).

We have argued so far that the media has the power to influence the way in which we think and talk (individually and collectively) about identities. Their representations may become part of our natural discourse. The semiotic resources employed have political overtones, therefore: they may enhance or constrain representations of who we and others are and this may lead to advantages for some or discriminatory consequences and social/cultural disadvantages for others. Sometimes these representations may be put to rhetorical effect (as we saw at the beginning of the chapter) and may even be exploited by the subjects of the media reports themselves for personal or political gain, as in the case of Barack Obama.

Certainly, Barack Obama, his staff and journalists have variously and repeatedly made reference to and exploited his complex master and personal identities. He has been described as 'the first African-American President of the United States of America', born in Hawaii to parents of American and Kenyan descent, and subsequently influenced by diverse cultural upbringings in both Indonesia and the United States of America. Different categories and constellations of his identity are rhetorically peppered throughout speeches and news articles fielding national and international political issues. On his first official visit to the Middle East he delivered the now famous 'Cairo' speech. In this short extract we witness how Obama attempts to create rapport with his audience by emphasizing shared master and personal identifications. His identity is constructed and exploited to accomplish social action: to persuade his audience of his authenticity and sincerity.

> I am a Christian, but my father came from a Kenyan family that includes generations of Muslims. As a boy, I spent several years in Indonesia and heard the call of the azaan at the break of dawn and at the fall of dusk. As a young man, I worked in Chicago communities where many found dignity and peace in their Muslim faith.
>
> As a student of history, I also know civilisation's debt to Islam. …
>
> Much has been made of the fact that an African-American with the name Barack Hussein Obama could be elected president. (Applause.) …
>
> There is also one rule that lies at the heart of every religion – that we do unto others as we would have them do unto us. (Applause.) This truth transcends nations and peoples – a belief that isn't new; that isn't black or white or brown; that isn't Christian, or Muslim or Jew.
>
>   http://news.bbc.co.uk/1/hi/world/americas/8082862.stm

While acknowledging differences between himself and his audience in the Middle East, Obama strategically attempts to transcend these and create rapport by appealing to shared ethical and religious principles. It is, however, mainly through vicarious associations, reconstructed selectively and chronologically from his personal and professional experiences, that he attempts to demonstrate a life-long respect, empathy, understanding and interest in the traditions, history, religion and culture of the Muslim world.

9.7   Summary

In summary, we began the chapter by attempting to define 'identity' and concluded that a simple definition is not possible. Many definitions have arisen from different theoretical, conceptual and disciplinary perspectives. We noted, however, that there are differences in perspective that broadly conceive of identity as a 'fixed/stable' state versus those that consider its enactment in discourse. Taking up the latter perspective, we examined the 'performance' of gender identity and the construction and negotiation of individual and group identity through narrative and further considered how and why boundaries are marked between identities in different communities of speakers. We finally considered how identity/ies is/are represented and exploited in and through media and political texts, and how these realizations may project and position cultural groups and individuals, and influence the way in which we talk about and view these subjects. We noted that the performance of identity in social interaction is a highly complex undertaking and may be strategically determined.

Study Questions

1. Extending Study Activity 9.1, record conversations involving yourself or a friend (with their permission and that of the other interactants) in three different settings. How does the structure and content of the conversations differ in each context and how is this influenced by the roles and identities of the people taking part in the conversations?

2. You have been asked to return to Oberwart, Austria to investigate the current status of Hungarian and German in the community. Consider how you would collect and analyse the data. How might your approach be different from that of Gal?

3. Record a friend/fellow student/ parent narrating a story about a past experience (approx. 10 minutes of recording). Carry out a brief narrative analysis. How does your subject construct their identity and that of any other actors in their story? Compare your findings with those of Coates.

4. How are boundaries marked politically, socially and linguistically between communities in your locality/nation? What are the consequences of these divisions and how are these used strategically by all parties to forward their arguments?

5. Collate a range of magazines targeting either a male or a female audience. Select a similar genre in each (e.g. adverts, editorials) and compare their representation of male or female identity. Are there differences/similarities? If so, what are they? Do you find support for Litosseliti's argument that the media often present an essentialized, exaggerated and binary representation of men and women?

Notes

1. 'Mulatto' is a pejorative term used to refer to individuals who have one black and one white parent.
2. Post-constructionism and post-structuralism are not synonymous. See Chapter 12 in Antaki and Widdicombe (1998) for an insightful account.
3. See Eckert (2012) for an account of historical developments in sociolinguistic variationist research.

Recommended Reading

Benwell, Bethan and Elizabeth Stokoe. 2006. *Discourse and Identity*. Edinburgh: Edinburgh University Press. This provides an overview of theoretical debates and various approaches to the study of identity taking an ethnomethodological and conversation analytic approach.

De Fina, A., D. Schiffrin and M. Bamberg (eds.) (2006) *Discourse and Identity*. Cambridge: Cambridge University Press. This edited volume explores various discursive studies of identity in different interactional contexts, communities and genres.

Edwards, John. 2009. *Language and Identity: An Introduction*. Cambridge: Cambridge University Press. This considers the relationship between identity, language, dialect and group membership, with special focus on national, ethnic and religious identity.

Litosseliti, Lia and Jane Sunderland (eds.). 2002. *Gender Identity and Discourse Analysis*. Philadelphia, PA: John Benjamins. This reviews critical debates in relation to gender identity and presents research on its discursive construction. The key sites of education, media, parenthood and sexuality are explored.

Llamas, C. and D. Watt (eds.). (2010) *Language and Identities*. Edinburgh: Edinburgh University Press. This edited volume is divided into four sections encompassing work by leading scholars on 'theoretical issues', 'individuals', 'groups and communities' and 'regions and nations'.

Thomas, Linda, Shan Wareing, Ishtla Singh *et al.* 2005. *Language, Society and Power: An Introduction*. London: Routledge. This provides a chapter overview of contemporary research on language and identity.

Tracy, Karen. 2002. *Everyday Talk: Building and Reflecting Identities*. London: Guilford Press. This takes a rhetorical and cultural approach to the discursive construction of identity in public and private contexts.

chapter 10

Language Planning and Language Policy

Li Wei

Chapter Outline

10.1 Introduction
10.2 Domains of Language Planning – Where is it Needed? Why is it Needed?
10.3 What is Being Planned? Status and Corpus Planning
10.4 What are the Social Motivations for Language Planning and Language Policy?
10.5 Who Makes Language Policies and Who Makes Them Work?
10.6 What are the Consequences of Language Policy and Language Planning?
10.7 Summary

Learning Outcomes

After reading this chapter, you should

- understand the main purposes of language planning and language policy;
- be familiar with key notions such as status planning and corpus planning;
- understand the key agents in language planning and policy making;
- appreciate the consequences of language planning and language policy.

Applied Linguistics, First Edition. Edited by Li Wei.
© 2014 John Wiley & Sons, Ltd. Published 2014 by John Wiley & Sons, Ltd.

Key Terms

- Acquisition planning
- Agents/agencies in language planning
- Bad language

- Corpus planning
- Family language policy
- Language attitudes
- Status planning

── 10.1 Introduction

Mr González is a senior engineer in a California-based power company which has many links with Japan. After several visits to the country, Mr González accepted a two-year posting by his company to the southern Japanese island of Kyūshū. He was very excited about it as he was able to take his family, who had always talked about going to Japan, especially his two sons, aged six and eight, who were mad about Japanese comics and electronic games. Mrs González was equally excited as she was an art teacher in an elementary school in California and was interested in Japanese art and design. They arrived in June 2010 in the city of Kitakyūshū. The company arranged a nice house for them to rent. The neighbours, all Japanese, seemed extremely friendly and helpful. However, they soon found that there were very few people in the neighbourhood who could speak English. Mr and Mrs González had planned to send their children to a local school with other Japanese children anyway, but when the school term started in August, they realized that everything was in Japanese. In fact, few teachers at the school felt confident enough to speak to the González family in English. There were English speakers at the company where Mr González worked, but they were not available to help the family with their everyday matters. Nevertheless, the González family remained positive and the children soon started making friends at school. Mrs González also learned to speak some Japanese and, within a couple of months, could manage brief conversations with the neighbours.

Something interesting happened at Thanksgiving. Mr and Mrs González arranged an international call to their relatives back in California via Skype. During the conversations, one of the aunties commented that she couldn't understand what Tommy, the six-year-old, was saying. The parents did not realize that Tommy had begun mixing his languages. Later that day, Mrs González asked her husband whether they should insist on the boys speaking English only with them. However, the González family are English-Spanish bilinguals and do often switch between the two languages.

Mr and Mrs González also noticed that both boys began to read books in Japanese only. Apart from the Internet, they had little suitable reading material for their ages in English. They used to write emails in English to their cousins and friends in California. But the contact gradually reduced, and they only wrote occasionally and very briefly.

10.2   Domains of Language Planning – Where is it Needed? Why is it Needed?

When the terms 'language planning' and 'language policy' are mentioned, most people automatically think of them as something that happens at a macro-societal level. After all, language planning and language policy are part of social planning and social policy, which tend to be managed by the government or other public institutions. Yet language planning and language policy are concerned with everyday language practices. As the example at the beginning of this chapter illustrates, families and individuals often need to make decisions as to which language to use to whom and when for a variety of reasons. They need to plan their language use. Sometimes their plan becomes a family language policy which is adopted over an extended period of time. This is particularly common among transnational families. Similarly, language planning and policy can take place in the workplace. In the contemporary globalizing world, multinational companies employ people from many different linguistic and cultural backgrounds. They often find themselves having to make decisions, as company policy, as to which language is allowed for formal meetings, for official records and in interpersonal conversations among the employees.

Table 10.1 gives a sample list of the domains in which language planning and language policy may occur. As we can see, language planning and language policy can occur in a variety of domains, from those that are immediate to our everyday life to the ones that have a broader scope involving institutional structures of various kinds. Applied Linguists who study language planning and language policy as their main topic ask questions such as who does the planning and makes the policy in a particular domain, and what the reason or purpose of the planning and policy may be. Such questions help to reveal the social forces and motivations behind language planning and language policy.

Take the family domain, for instance. Does everyone in the family have an equal say in which language should be used when and how? The answer is clearly not. In most cases, the parents of nuclear families (i.e. families of two generations: parents and children only) tend to decide what the children should do in terms of language use. If the two parents happen to come from different language backgrounds, they may decide to each use their own first language with the children, or they may use both languages interchangeably, or they may use only one of the languages. If it is the last option (i.e. use only one of the parents' languages), whose language gets chosen becomes an interesting question.

In extended families with three or more generations, language policy becomes much more complicated. It has been reported that many immigrant families maintain a particular language because they need to communicate with a monolingual grandparent who speaks that language. And when that grandparent passes away, the family then changes to a different language or adopts a more bilingual practice. This has been described as the 'grandmother factor'. Yet, the children may not always follow what the parents want them to do. Even in the family domain, other factors come to influence language planning and policy. For example, if the neighbourhood the family lives in is predominantly monolingual, members of the family will need to use the language of the neighbours in order to communicate with them. The school that the children attend also has significant influence on the children's language preference and language practice as well as the parents' language use. In order for the parents to communicate with the school, they will need to

Table 10.1 Domains of language policy

- Family
  - *Bilingual and multilingual families*:
    - One parent one language
    - One context one language
    - Additional languages
  - *Monolingual families*:
    - Standard language versus dialect
    - Second/foreign language
- School
  - National language
  - Minority languages
  - Second/foreign languages
- Religion and religious organization
  - Sacred language versus community language
  - National language versus local dialects
- Workplace
  - Standard language versus dialects
  - National language versus minority languages
  - Second/foreign languages
- Government
  - Standard language versus dialects
  - National language versus regional, community languages
  - Written language versus spoken language
  - Second/foreign languages
- Nation/state
  - Official languages
  - Regional languages
- Supernational grouping
  - National languages versus international languages
  - United Nations' 'Working Languages' and languages for translation/interpreting

use the same language. The family, in planning their language policy, will need to consider issues such as their relationships with the neighbours and the school, as well as the children's long-term development.

In a globalizing world such as today's, it is hard to find an organization whose workforce is entirely monolingual. Language policy of the workplace becomes an important issue. Very often, employers do not have explicit language policies for the workplace and no conscious language planning effort is made as to which language should or should not be used. If it is an American company, located somewhere in the United States, it is simply expected that everybody should be speaking English at work. Yet the reality may be quite different. Employees of different linguistic backgrounds may choose to use languages other than English with each other. And they may do so for a variety of reasons. For the employees whose first language is not English, speaking another language with their colleagues, be it Spanish, Korean or Swahili, gives them a sense of solidarity, confidence

Case Study 10.1

All 120 packers at the book dealer Waterstone's distribution depot in Burton upon Trent, Staffordshire, England, were told to use English during working hours and only use their native tongues at break time because it could 'isolate' colleagues who did not know languages other than English.

The workforce, mainly Poles and Latvians, has drawn up a petition against logistics firm Unipart, which runs the warehouse for the book dealer, claiming the ban discriminates against them.

Rick Coyle, regional officer for the Unite union, said: 'It is ridiculous to employ lots of people from other countries while insisting they must speak among themselves only in English. Unipart has a lot to learn about human nature and respect. Unite supports the workers' petition.'

A Unipart spokesman said: 'It is important both for good, clear communication among employees and also to ensure that our stringent health and safety standards are maintained that all employees speak a common language.

'Unipart requires all employees to communicate in English during working hours in the workplace. This does not apply during meal and rest breaks.

'We have also found that all employees speaking the same language when working together creates a better team environment.'

The Plain English Campaign said that using a common language at work 'would make it easier for all'.

> (http://www.metro.co.uk/news/ 875494-eastern-european-warehouse-workers-told-to-speak-in-english-only#ixzz1fBA FmZL5)

---

or informality. On the other hand, an organization may want to project a specific identity to the outside world by having a more explicit language policy. They may insist on all employees speaking the same language at work. Case Study 10.1 is one example where the employer has decided that the Polish and Latvian employees should be speaking English among themselves during working hours. The rationale behind this policy is said to be effective communication.

Questions can be asked as to who the so-called effective communication is meant for. Clearly it is not meant for the employees themselves, as the majority of them are Polish or Latvian. It is more likely to be meant for communication with the supervisors and the management of the company who do not understand these languages. So, as a result, the interest of certain groups within the company is protected while that of others is not. The policy may well also be meant for projecting a particular image of the company. Many businesses nowadays employ a highly multilingual workforce. Some choose to project an image of a global company whereas others may identify themselves with a specific history or heritage. Language choice can become part of the company's identity.

Language planning and language policy are concerned not just with which language is permitted in which domain but also with how a specific language should be used. It is interesting to observe that even in societies that have a long democratic tradition and among people who think of themselves as liberals, language use can arouse very strong feelings. If you read the Letters to the Editor column of a newspaper or a magazine in the United States, in Britain, in France or in China, it would not be very difficult to find complaints about certain pronunciation, spelling and grammatical use that some readers find objectionable. Here, we are not talking about the so-called 'political correctness' in language use. In fact, lots of the complaints are not about incorrect or bad usage either. Rather, they are about differences between what is perceived to be the standard or normal way of using a language and what has actually been used. In the 2010 general election in Britain, for example, there were people who objected to David Cameron and Nick Clegg, two former private school boys who later became the Prime Minister and Deputy Prime Minister respectively, pronouncing the word *create* as *crate*. The interesting question for the Applied Linguist is not what people are complaining about, but why they make such complaints in the first place. We will come back to this issue in Section 10.3, but there does seem to be a common, and fairly strong, desire for societal intervention in language matters. In countries such as France and China, there are national bodies that regulate language usage. In other countries, language planning and language policy are carried out more indirectly through schools, social services and employers. Exactly what these bodies do in terms of language usage is a question that we attempt to address in the next section.

10.3   What is Being Planned? Status and Corpus Planning

In the previous section, we talked about the domains in which language planning and language policy may occur. They are mainly social, situational or contextual domains. There are also specific linguistic domains where language planning and language policy take place. These may be an individual linguistic micro unit, such as a sound, a spelling or the form of a letter, a collection of units, such as pronunciation more generally, or a lexicon or a writing system, or a macro variety, such as a dialect or a specified, named language. Policies that are aimed at one linguistic domain inevitably affect other domains, because languages are made up of conventionally agreed, intersected sets of choices of linguistic units. Changing a lexical item is potentially a step towards changing a language variety.

The Norwegian-American linguist Einar Haugen (1966) described four stages of language planning: (i) selection of a norm for a particular language; (ii) codification of its written, or spoken, form, its grammar and its lexicon; (iii) implementation of the plan by making sure that it is accepted and followed by the target population; and (iv) elaboration or continued modification of the norm to meet the requirements of modernization and development. Heinz Kloss (1969), a German linguist who specialized in linguistic minorities, summarized the stages in terms of *status* planning and *corpus* planning.

Status planning is about planning the status, or standing, of a language vis-à-vis other languages within a community. It often refers to the official or juridical status of a language. A specific language can be the sole official language of a nation (e.g. French in France; Turkish in Turkey) or a joint official language with (an)other language(s) (e.g. English and Afrikaans in South Africa between 1984 and 1994; French, German, Italian and Romansh in Switzerland). The official status may be confined to a specific geographical or political area (e.g. Igbo is a regional official language in Nigeria; Marathi is a regional official language in Marathi in Maharastra, India). However, sometimes a language lacks official status on a national or regional level, but is promoted, and sometimes used, by public authorities for specific functions (e.g. Spanish in New Mexico; West African Pidgin English in Cameroon). One can assign the status of a language according to the function it fulfils. For instance, a community language functions as a common language among the members of a specific cultural or ethnic community, a school subject language is a language that is taught as a subject in an educational institution, and a religious language functions as a language for the ritual purposes of a particular religion (see Stewart, 1968, for a detailed list of language status and functional domains). Cooper (1989) summarizes the various statuses of language in three broad functional categories: statutory, working and symbolic. A statutory language is a language that a government has declared official by law. A working language is a language that a government uses as a medium for daily activities, and a symbolic language is a language that is merely a symbol of the state.

Various other factors can determine the status of a language. They include, for example, the ratio, or percentage, of users to another variable, such as the total population. This is sometimes described as *language vitality*. For example, if 90% of the total population of a community speaks a specific language, that language will have very high vitality, as opposed to, say, 20% of the population speaking it. Other factors may include the origin of the language, that is, whether a given language is indigenous or imported to the speech community, and the degree of standardization, that is, the extent of development of a formal set of norms that define standard usage. The last point about language standardization is also part of *corpus planning*.

Corpus planning is about the design of the structure of a particular language. It often involves three interrelated processes: codification, standardization and modernization. Codification, sometimes known as graphization, refers to the development, selection and modification of scripts and orthographic conventions for a language. The writing systems of the world's languages have evolved over time, often incorporating elements from different sources and adapting them to suit the features of the spoken languages. As new concepts and objects are invented, new words and phrases are coined in a specific language and then translated into other languages. The translation process may involve adaptation of the original form in a different language into a form that is more consistent with the recipient language. In the meantime, there are still communities in various parts of the world whose languages do not yet have a written form. Linguists are involved in developing writing systems for such languages. They have the option of using an existing system or inventing a new one. For instance, the Chinese language planners have devised the writing systems for several ethnic minority groups inside China who had no written language. Interestingly, the writing systems that are invented use a mixture of Latin and Cyrillic letters and a number of International Phonetic Alphabet (IPA) symbols rather than Chinese characters. The Ainu community of Japan developed their writing system on the basis of the katakana syllabary of the Japanese language. But in the course of development, a number of adaptations had to be made in order to accommodate the syllable structure of the Ainu language.

The use of writing in a speech community can have lasting sociocultural effects, which include easier transmission of material through generations, communication with larger numbers of people, and a standard against which varieties of spoken language are often compared. Charles Ferguson, who did a great deal of work on language standardization, made two key observations about the results of adopting a writing system. First, the use of writing adds another variety of the language to the community's repertory. Although written language is often viewed as secondary to spoken language, the vocabulary, grammatical and phonological structures of a language often adopt characteristics in the written form that are distinct from the spoken variety. Second, the use of writing often leads to a folk belief that the written language is the 'real' language, and that speech is a corruption of it, whereas in fact writing is a representation of speech, and not always a truthful one.

Another important aspect of corpus planning is standardization, whereby the uniformity of the structural norm of a language is enhanced through such activities as the creation of dictionaries and grammars. A pre- or co-requisite for language standardization is often the designation of one variety of a language as the formal, or standard, variety over other social and regional varieties of that language. The history of English provides an example of standardization occurring over an extended time period, which began when William Caxton introduced the printing press in England in 1476. This was accompanied by the adoption of the south-east England variety of English, especially that spoken in London, as the print language. Because of its use for administrative and literary purposes, this variety became entrenched as the standard norm for the English language. In this sense then, corpus planning and status planning are linked.

It is important to remind ourselves that the choice of which language takes precedence has important societal consequences, as it confers privilege upon speakers whose spoken and written dialect most closely conforms to the chosen standard. The standard that is chosen as the norm is generally spoken by the better-educated and more powerful social groups within society, and is often imposed upon the less privileged groups. Socio-economic mobility is often reinforced by the dominance of the standard language.

All languages need to elaborate and expand in order to fulfil different functions, especially in the written form. Part of the corpus planning process therefore is modernization of the language. Over the years, some languages, such as Japanese and Hungarian, have experienced rapid lexical expansion to meet the demands of modernization, while others, such as Hindi and Arabic, grow relatively slowly. Language modernization can occur

---

STUDY ACTIVITY 10.1

Think of the speech community to which you belong, and ask yourself the following questions:

1. What is the process of status planning and corpus planning?
2. Look at the historical development; has it always been the same language that is used as the common language for communication in your community?
3. What are the frequently used terms that are borrowed from other languages?
4. How are these borrowed terms adapted into the language?
5. What are the new inventions in the language?
6. Do people from the community ever complain about language change and particular usage of language? If yes, what kinds of complaints are they?

when a language undergoes a shift in status, such as when a country gains independence from a colonial power or when there is a change in the language education policy. But in most cases, the most significant aspect of language modernization is the expansion of the lexicon, which allows the language to discuss topics in modern semantic domains. Language planners generally focus on creating new lists and glossaries to describe new technical concepts. Technical vocabulary can expand either by using the language's own process of word formation or by heavy borrowing from another language. Hungarian, for example, has almost exclusively used language-internal processes to create new lexical items, while Japanese has borrowed extensively from English to derive new words as part of its modernization. It is also increasingly important to expand the language by incorporating new expressions that are typically associated with the younger generations within society and their sociocultural activities. Netspeak, mobile language, pop language, and youth language in general, are some of the most significant growth areas of language in the globalization era.

This last point of language modernization – youth language – relates to another process of language planning which some language planning researchers describe as *acquisition planning*, whereby a national, state or local institution aims to influence the learning of a language by specific groups within a community, usually through educational means. Often, acquisition planning is integrated into a larger language-planning process in which the status of a language is evaluated, the corpus built or revised, and changes made and introduced to society on a national, state or local level through education systems. This process of planning can lead to changes not confined to the language, such as an alteration in student textbooks, a change in methods of teaching or assessing an official language or the development of a bilingual language programme. Such changes may help to raise the status level of a certain language and increase its prestige. In this way, acquisition planning is often used to promote language revitalization.

Acquisition planning can also be done at a more micro level (e.g. within a family). The parents may decide which language(s) their children should learn, or if all of the family members should start learning and using a particular language. However, their decisions are most likely to be influenced by macro-level forces – for example, the language policy of the school, the language commonly used in public services within the community, employment prospects or migration intentions.

——————— 10.4 What are the Social Motivations for Language Planning and Language Policy?

Spolsky (2004) characterized the social motivations for language planning and language policy in terms of 'driving out the bad', 'pursuing the good' and 'dealing with the new'. The idea that language can be 'good' or 'bad' is an interesting one. It has more to do with people's perception or social evaluation of linguistic norms and practices than the actual forms of language. Swearing, for example, is generally regarded as 'rude'. But is 'rude language' also 'bad language'? After all, swearing has existed in every language and culture since the beginning of human civilization and is an integral part of everyday life. In terms of the linguistic form, it simply does not make sense to describe swearing as 'good' or 'bad'. But the practice, or act, of swearing is perceived as 'bad' in certain contexts (e.g. in public, in front of young children or by young people). We therefore see complaints in newspapers and online blogs from the general public about footballers, TV chefs and pop singers swearing, television stations bleeping out swear words, parents and teachers trying to stop children from swearing and the education secretary of the British government urging schools and parents 'to eliminate foul and abusive language from our schools and homes' (*The Times*, 28 April 2000).

Sometimes language can be perceived to be so bad that it is banned. In most countries, there are laws and regulations forbidding the use of obscene, blasphemous, racist and sexist language. The assumption seems to be that words can lead to action; specific use of language can incite prejudice and violence. One difficulty, as Spolsky points out, is that what is acceptable and what is offensive are in a constant state of flux. The American Psychological Association's Guidelines for Avoiding Racial/Ethnic Bias in Language, for example, note: 'Name designations of racial/ethnic groups change over time, and members of a group may disagree about their preferred name at a specific time.'

Within the sphere of language planning and language policy, 'bad language' often goes beyond the use of rude or offensive words and phrases and refers to what are seen as corrupt forms of the standard language. This ranges from pronunciation and word meaning to punctuation and politeness routines. There is a whole industry producing guides on how to use English correctly, for example. Many of them are produced in good faith, for instance, to help non-native speakers of English to learn the standard form of the language. While some of us enjoy singing 'It Ain't Necessarily So' or 'We Don't Need No Education', we may feel reluctant to use the same constructions when we have a conversation with other people in a real-life situation. We may love Winston Churchill's alleged response to an overzealous newspaper editor's attempt to rewrite what he had said: 'This is the sort of bloody nonsense up with which I will not put', but we still tell learners to avoid ending a sentence with a preposition. Upholding the standard of language seems to be a key social motivation in language planning and language policy.

There seems to be a particular concern about the written language when it comes to the use of non-standard forms. There was an uproar in certain quarters of British society when, in 2009, the Queen's English Society published a study of written work produced by final-year university undergraduate students. The study revealed that, on average, British students had 52.2 punctuation, grammatical and spelling errors per paper, compared with just 18.8 for the international students whose first language was not English. 'Bad written English is more than embarrassing', one newspaper headline declared. 'How frightening is that? People who do not know how to write their own language?' asked a woman who ran a business of helping companies to prepare written documents through her company blog. Several universities immediately set up writing classes for native English speakers and linked the 'correct' or 'proper' use of English to the employability agenda. The errors made by the undergraduates as revealed in the study included spelling errors, such as 'seperate' for 'separate', 'yeild' for 'yield', 'relevent' for 'relevant', grammatical errors, such as 'done by my partner and I', punctuation errors, such as 'the cows rectum' and 'the harem's of seals', and incomplete sentences or ambiguous statements, such as 'Barr bodies can be used to determine sex (present in females but not in males)', 'pass their X chromosome to half their son' and 'these colonies are then cross with another yeast strain'. The Queen's English Society, whose stated aim is to 'become the recognised guardian of proper English', blamed the errors on a 'widespread deterioration in standards' when it comes to promoting the English language in British schools.

STUDY ACTIVITY 10.2

Find examples of what you think is 'bad' language use.

1.   Why are they bad?
2.   What do you think can be done about them?

Case Study 10.2: Bad Language: The Use and Abuse of Official Language

House of Commons Public Administration Select Committee First Report of Session 2009–10

Summary

Politics and government are public activities, and so politicians and public servants should use language that people find clear, accurate and understandable. We undertook this inquiry because we were concerned that too often official language distorts or confuses meaning. This is damaging because it can prevent public understanding of policies and their consequences, and can also deter people from getting access to public services and benefits.

We conclude that bad official language that results in tangible harm – such as preventing someone from receiving the benefits or services to which they are entitled – should be regarded as 'maladministration'. People should feel able to complain about cases of confusing or misleading language, as they would for any other type of poor administration. Equally, government and public sector bodies need to respond properly to complaints about bad official language; and if they do not, people should be encouraged to take their complaints to the relevant Ombudsman.

Bad official language deserves to be mocked, but it also needs to be taken seriously. We hope that our conclusions and suggestions will encourage government to mind its language in future.

One of the most frequent complaints about bad language use, in both the written and the spoken form, is language mixing. It happens not only in large countries with an established national language and a strong government but also in smaller tribes and more complex communities. Stanley Newman (1955), who studied the Zuni Indians, claimed that they did not allow foreign words in their ritual ceremonies even though slang words were permitted. The Arizona Tewa has a similar ban on language mixing (Kroskrity, 1998). The Turkish language reform after the founding of the modern republic was intended to eliminate the many thousands of Arabic and Persian borrowings that had become entrenched in the language after the Turks became Muslim, creating a mixture of languages. Policies and efforts such as these that are aimed at preventing language borrowing and mixing come out of an ideology of linguistic purism. As Spolsky (2004: 23) remarks, 'Clean, uncorrupt, pure language is highly valued ideologically.' Despite the fact that borrowing and mixing have played a crucial role throughout the history of human language evolution, they are frowned upon by linguistic purists and generally regarded as sources of linguistic corruption rather than linguistic innovation. Even multilingual speakers themselves often deny the use of borrowing and mixing between languages thanks to the deep-rootedness of the ideology of linguistic purism.

Of course, language policy and language planning are not just about driving out the bad and pursuing the good, but are also about responding to and managing the changes in society that affect language structure and language use. The Turkish language reform is an interesting example of a language planning effort in dealing with the new, in this case a new national identity. The Japanese writing system reform during the Meiji period, in comparison, made borrowing from other languages such as English much easier by introducing a modern kana – a syllabic Japanese writing script system – combined with a simplified kanji – the Chinese characters system. In fact, most of the language reforms of different writing, including spelling, systems in the past represent 'something borrowed' for 'something new'. Countries tended to adopt or adapt an existing writing system to meet new needs, both linguistic and socio-political. Since the disintegration of the Soviet Union, the central Asian republics have passed laws raising the status of their own languages while embarking on an alphabet reform, abandoning the use of Cyrillic script and adapting the Latin alphabet to their languages, including inventing special letters. In Tajikistan, debate continues about the choice between Latin and Arabic script.

Whether it is for 'driving out the bad', 'pursuing the good' or 'dealing with the new', language planning and language policy are intrinsically tied up with language ideology. Language ideology refers to the perceptions held by people about a specific language or language in general, what language can do and how language should be used. Wolfram and Schilling-Estes (2006) define *language ideology* as 'ingrained, unquestioned beliefs about the way the world is, the way it should be, and the way it has to be with respect to language'. Irvine (1989) talks about language ideology in terms of 'the cultural system of ideas about social and linguistic relationships, together with their loading of moral and political interests'. Language ideology plays a highly significant role in language policy and language planning. For instance, standard language ideology often biases towards idealized national norms, as maintained and imposed by dominant social groups and institutions, and against minority language users.

Lippi-Green (1997) discusses the standard language ideology in the United States, which is biased towards an idealized homogeneous phonology and grammar of Standard American English and seeks to impose it as the official language on all ethnic groups while designating other languages as heritage languages. One of the consequences of such a language ideology is that Spanish is constructed as a resource for the professional advancement of middle- and upper-middle-class foreign language learners, while simultaneously being a detriment to the social mobility of heritage language users, that is, Latino Americans.

The case of Spanish versus English in the United States highlights the role language plays in sociocultural integration, social mobility, and economic and educational advancement, all of which are also influencing factors in language policy and language planning. Other cases in point include the spread of English as an international language and the increased popularity of Mandarin Chinese as a school subject language across the globe. Interestingly, different people have very different reactions to such phenomena.

The author Michael Erard, in an otherwise positive and entertaining discussion of what he calls 'free-form adoption of English' in China, claims that English is evolving into a language that its so-called native speakers may no longer understand (*Wired* 17.06). Members of the Chinese parliament, the National People's Congress, on the other hand, want to stamp out all English from newspapers, television and other state-controlled media, seeing it as an 'invasion' and an 'attack' on the Chinese language. In the meantime, huge investment has been made in compiling dictionaries and other reference books for different varieties of Chinese spoken in mainland China, in Taiwan and by Chinese communities overseas.

10.5   Who Makes Language Policies and Who Makes Them Work?

As we have seen in the previous sections, the process of language planning involves different stakeholders making decisions at different levels. Some have a more influential role in deciding on the status of a language. Others are apparently on the receiving end of decisions but can oppose and reject any decision imposed on them and make their own choice. In this section we ask two related questions: who makes language policies, and who makes language policies work in real-life situations?

The key stakeholders in language planning and policy making include both institutions and individuals, both of whom need to carry out their planning and policy through specific instruments. We mentioned earlier some of the language planning and policy instruments, such as dictionaries and textbooks. Together, institutions, instruments and individuals form what might be called a 'tripartite system of agency' in language planning and language policy. Let us look at the role each of the three agents plays in turn.

10.5.1   Institutions

When we think of institutions that are responsible for language planning and language policy, we tend to think immediately of language academies, such as L'Académie française, which have existed for centuries as language regulators. There is, indeed, a long list of language academies in different countries that regulate standard languages, ranging from the Bangla Academy in Bangladesh and Die Taalkommissie in South Africa to the Yoruba Academy in Nigeria and the Welsh Language Board in Wales. Many of them are motivated by linguistic purism and typically publish dictionaries and prescriptive grammars which purport to officiate and prescribe the meaning of words, pronunciations, standard sentence structures and punctuations. There are also international organizations for specific languages that are used in different nation states. For example, the Asociación de Academias de la Lengua Española is constituted by the Real Academia Española of Spain plus 21 other separate national academies in the Spanish-speaking world. It has produced a pan-Hispanic dictionary, a grammar and a standard orthography. The Zwischenstaatliche Kommission für deutsche Rechtschreibung, now known as the Rat für deutsche Rechtschreibung, has a particular focus on German orthography. It has council members from Germany, Austria, Switzerland, Italy, Belgium and Liechtenstein. Clearly, many of these institutions have the backing of the government or governments. But few of them have legal power to legislate the use of language. Instead they act as promoters of standard languages, mainly through education and the media.

Many of the language academies mentioned above originated in or have strong connections with religious organizations. Indeed, religion has always been a key institution in language planning and language policy as it adds a moral dimension to language use. As Spolsky (2009: 31) points out, the fact that Arabic is so widely used among the Muslim communities around the world today is at least in part due to the insistence of Islam that all religious services must be conducted in it. And Hebrew was kept alive for nearly two millennia after people stopped speaking it as a vernacular language through its continued use as a language of prayer and religious learning. In an interesting contrast, Christianity has been willing to translate it sacred texts into various vernacular languages, in fact quite active in doing so. Consequently, different languages are used in Christian churches around the globe. People of different faiths feel similarly obliged to follow the rules and standards set by their religion.

Another institution that plays an important role in language planning and language policy is the court of law. In some countries, there are specific laws and regulations on the status and use of certain languages. Even where there is no language law as such, the language use in legal contexts can have an immediate impact on the people involved. Many Applied Linguists have studied how in Common Law countries such as the United Kingdom, the USA and Australia, individuals who do not speak English as their first language can be disadvantaged in court and other legal contexts (Shuy, 1993, 1998; Berk-Seligson, 2002; Gibbons, 2003; Pavlenko, 2008; Eades, 2008).

The role of the various institutions in language planning and language policy clearly varies: language academies, for example, tend to focus on corpus planning by producing and promoting standards of the linguistic form, while religion and the law maintain or promote the status of certain languages.

In contemporary society, the media plays a highly influential role in language planning and language policy. For a long time, newspapers, the radio and the television have been held by the general public to be the standard-bearers as far as language use is concerned. What is used in such media is often regarded as the officially acceptable form. They can facilitate the spread of new expressions very effectively. Increasingly, however, less formal usage of language appears in the media, much to the annoyance of linguistic purists. Nowadays it is very common to hear broadcasters on the BBC with rather broad regional accents, and many of the reporters use colloquial expressions in their reporting, just as ordinary people would in their everyday social interaction. Moreover, new forms of social media have had a fundamental impact on language use. What was traditionally regarded as non-standard, incomplete, even ungrammatical language usage is commonplace in Internet-mediated communication (Crystal, 2006, 2008, 2011). While there is a great deal of interest in describing the features of language use in the media, there is relatively little research looking at the role of the media, especially new media, in language planning and language policy.

10.5.2   Instruments

The instruments or tools that institutions use to implement their language policies range from the specific, such as dictionaries, grammar books, school textbooks, examination papers and other assessments, to the general, such as the media, schools and public services.

We tend not to think of things such as textbooks and exam papers as instruments of language planning or policy, but they are. Even if they are based on empirical evidence of how people use language in real life, the fact that they are coded and printed in a formal way means that they have a prescriptive effect on language users, especially on learners, whether young learners of their first languages or learners of additional languages. They set the norm for language use. People think of them as representing the standard language, except for dictionaries of slangs or grammars of regional dialects. Compiling dictionaries, writing grammars and textbooks, and setting examination papers, have always been an integral part of corpus and acquisition planning. But they are also important instruments for status planning, both for standard languages and for minority languages, regional dialects or endangered languages that need protection.

Schools and the media are important institutions for language planning and language policy. They can also be regarded as key instruments in language planning and language policy as they can be effective promoters of certain languages. The language use in these specific domains is often dictated and protected by law; and they tend to follow legislation imposed upon them by the government or other regulatory bodies. They therefore act as advocates of official policies. Nevertheless, they have the capacity to devise their own policies regarding language use. Their policies have immediate impact on the people receiving their services.

Other public services such as banks and hospitals can also be used as instruments for language planning and language policy. Most of these institutions may not have specific language policies, but they implement language policies that are imposed by the government, by law and by other institutions. Their language use also has an immediate impact on the lives of the people who use their services. For example, health services in England are usually provided in English. Speakers of languages other than English will have to make a special request to receive the service in other languages. Similar situations can be found in most countries, and are not restricted to the English-speaking world.

In the age of global digital media, modern communication and information technologies have become important for language policy and language planning. One of the most interesting cases is the design and promotion of a romanization system for Cantonese after the transfer of sovereignty of Hong Kong from Britain to China. The Basic Law, which governs post-1997 Hong Kong affairs, grants Cantonese official status along with Putonghua, the standard national variety of Chinese, and English. But Cantonese has traditionally been regarded as a regional dialect, despite its large number of native speakers, and never had a standard dictionary or romanization system that would help its speakers to use a standard computer keyboard to input Chinese characters for online communication. In contrast, Putonghua does have an accompanying romanized system, called *pinyin*, which is widely taught in mainland China and to learners of standard Chinese. So people in Hong Kong who speak Cantonese as their first language are faced with a dilemma: learn *pinyin* and Putonghua and use them in online communication or learn a special, rather clumsy, input system which breaks each character into parts and then builds them together. A specially designed writing pad that recognizes Chinese characters is available, but it is still much slower than using a standard English keyboard. The Hong Kong Linguistics Society decided to design a romanization system for Cantonese, known as *jyutping*, which would hugely improve the input speed for Cantonese in online and mobile communications. This corpus planning effort had the effect of protecting the status of Cantonese as equal to Putonghua in Hong Kong.

10.5.3   Individuals

There are many different individuals who can exert influence on language use in everyday life. Some never intend to play such an influential role. For example, celebrities and people working in the media are often taken as role models by young people in their language practices. But their behaviour is often a presentation of their identities and not intended to promote a certain language norm. Writers also can be very influential on other people's use of language. Again, most of them are more concerned with constructing their own style rather than planning to change other people's linguistic behaviour.

But there are individuals who do play a crucial, and intentional, role in language planning and language policy. In history, the clergy and the royals occupied privileged positions of deciding which language was to be used in what social domain and even the specific way the languages should be used, in terms of pronunciation, spelling and grammar. Dictionaries and grammar books often had royal patronage, and religious texts were held as examples of standard language use. In contemporary society, politicians and law makers have significant influence on the language life of ordinary people. Many countries have specific legislation on which language should be used in schools, the media and in the court of law. In both historical times and contemporary society, academic linguists are often involved in language planning. Their academic research may be used as evidence by the law and policy makers in advocating particular legislation. Many linguists are also directly involved in constructing grammars and writing systems for endangered, 'unknown' and minority languages. Major efforts of 'linguist rescue' work are taking place in China, the Pacific islands, parts of Africa and the Amazon.

Academic linguists are also involved in management of usage of new words and expressions. Technological advances in modern society have prompted rapid lexical expansion of the world's major languages as well as in translation between languages. Linguists have played a key role in the standardization and spread of new terms through textbooks, dictionaries and professional publications, as well as frequent use among the specialists themselves.

Other individuals play important roles in language planning and language policy not as planners or policy makers but as implementers and managers. Key individuals in the institutions mentioned above play such roles. School teachers, for example, implement language policies consciously or subconsciously through their own use in the classroom as well as their policing via school tests and assessments. Professionals in health and social services sometimes play a similar role to school teachers, in implementing official language policies through their own language use with the people to whom they provide services.

It is important to realize that while the macro-societal-level institutions have significant influence in language planning and policy, it is down to individuals in their collective action to make any policy work. There is ample evidence across different communities in the world of how specific language policies have been contested, resisted or fought against. Without individuals' acceptance, language planning and language policy will not work.

STUDY ACTIVITY 10.3

Observe an institution for a day. This may be a workplace with which you are familiar, or a community organization, a university department or a family. Answer the following questions:

1. Is there an explicit language policy?
2. Do people talk about language or language use in their everyday conversation?
3. Can you see any examples of people's attitude towards specific use of language?
4. Is anyone policing language use in the institution? If yes, how is it done?

10.6 What are the Consequences of Language Policy and Language Planning?

You can see from the discussion in the previous sections that language policy and language planning affect a very wide range of contexts, organizations and people. The consequences are by no means restricted to the structures of language, nor to the everyday use of particular languages. Yes, language policy and language planning can influence the way a language is codified, taught and used. But a long-term and long-lasting consequence of language policy and language planning is the different social status assigned to different languages and, by implication, the different social status of the speakers of the languages.

At a macro level, specific languages may be designated as national languages or regional languages. The designation of a language as a national language enables it to be used in many public and official domains, whereas a regional language would not be permitted. Some countries adopt a language as their national language even though it was not a language of any of the indigenous communities. Singapore, for example, has English as one of the national languages, despite the fact that the population is predominantly Chinese-speaking, with smaller populations speaking Malay or Tamil as native languages. Consequently, English is used in all public domains and in education. People who do not know English cannot have full access to the public services and support, nor can they succeed in the education system. More interesting and intriguing perhaps is when a country adopts a foreign language for national communication. Kazakhstan, after independence from the Soviet Union, introduced a policy to promote English as a language for public communication. It is intended to raise the country's profile on the global stage. Substantial investment has been made in teaching English in schools and universities. In the capital city Astana, many public signs are in English. As a result, people, especially school children, feel that they must learn English in order to be successful in society.

In the education sphere, language planning and language policy can have a significant impact on access to knowledge. In some post-colonial countries in Africa, school text-books are only available in the former colonial languages of English or French or in the majority language, such as Swahili. Speakers of languages other than these would have to learn the language of the textbooks first before they could learn the contents. Before the return of sovereignty of Hong Kong from Britain to China in 1997, many secondary schools in the former British colony used English-only textbooks. Children moving from primary schools where they learned in Cantonese suddenly found themselves in a situa-tion where they could not follow the teacher's instructions in class, nor could they under-stand the textbooks. Since 1997, however, a new language has been introduced into the schools in Hong Kong, namely Putonghua. While the supply and quality of textbooks in Putonghua are of a high standard, the school children have to learn this new language in order to access certain information.

An important question in investigating the consequences of language planning and language policy is how should the effectiveness of language planning and language pol-icy be judged? Should it be purely in quantitative terms of the scale of the effect, that is, the more people accept or follow the policy the better, or should it be qualitative in terms of positive versus negative effect, that is, value judged? One can look at situations such as that in Hong Kong as a success story of language spread, in this case of Putonghua, the national standard language of China. Yet in the meantime, one can also see the result of the marginalization of other varieties of the Chinese language, such as Cantonese and Hakka, which are widely spoken in Hong Kong but increasingly regarded as regional or local sub-varieties.

Perhaps the most important consequence of language planning and language policy lies in the effects on language attitudes. It is often said that language attitude is not really about language but about the people who speak the language. Even a cursory look at the media representation of minority and disadvantaged groups in society will tell you how closely linked are our attitudes towards specific forms of language and our attitudes towards the people who speak them. Not sharing a common language often causes ten-sions and conflicts between groups. Prejudices against certain languages are often similar

---

STUDY ACTIVITY 10.4

Think of a public service that you may encounter – for example, a hospital, bank or school.

1. Does it have an explicit language policy?
2. What language(s) is(are) usually used in this context?
3. What happens if a person in need of the service does not know the language that is usually used in this context?
4. What are the consequences of a possible language 'mismatch' between the service provider and the service receiver, especially on the latter?

to the prejudices against certain people. Even among speakers of the same language, there are strong, often negative and biased, attitudes towards people who seemingly speak in a way that is 'non-standard' or 'posh'. Social psychologists have carried out studies using what they call the 'matched guise device' to elicit listeners' judgements on the speaker's education level, intelligence, occupation, and so on, using recordings by the same speaker speaking in different accents or different languages. Their findings suggest that people hold strong views on the 'personalities' of languages and language varieties.

10.7 Summary

Language planning and language policy affect all domains of our everyday social life. They are not something that only macro-level societal institutions are concerned with. Individual members of a community are involved in explicit and implicit language planning and policy making or implementation all the time. This chapter introduced some of the key issues in language planning and language policy.

Language planning and language policy can affect the structures of the language, its use by individual members of a speech community and the status of the language in society. The social status of the language has further implications for the way we view its users. If a language is viewed as of low status or of restricted practical value, its users may also be viewed in similar ways.

Study Questions

1. What roles can schools play in language policy and language planning?
2. What factors can affect a family's decision on language choice and language practice within the home context?
3. What are the common concerns expressed in the popular press regarding language standards?
4. How does an organization's language policy affect its members' everyday linguistic practice?
5. How does globalization affect language policy and language planning?

Recommended Reading

Ferguson, Gibson. 2006. *Language Planning and Education*. Edinburgh: Edinburgh University Press. This book discusses language policy in relation to migration, globalization, cultural diversity, nation-building, education and ethnic identity throughout several countries and continents. It focuses on issues related to education.

Garrett, Peter. 2010. *Attitudes to Language*. Cambridge: Cambridge University Press. Drawing on a range of examples including punctuation, words, grammar, pronunciation, accents, dialects and languages, the book discusses language attitudes and the implications they have for our use of language, for social advantage or discrimination and for social identity.

King, Kendall A., Lyn Fogle and Aubrey Logan-Terry. 2008. Family language policy. *Language and Linguistics Compass* 2 (5), 907–922. This introduces the newly emerging field of family language policy, defined as explicit and overt planning in relation to language use within the home among family members, and provides an integrated overview of research on how languages are managed, learned and negotiated within families.

Ricento, Thomas. 2006. *An Introduction to Language Policy: Theory and Method*. Oxford: Blackwell. This covers the major theories and methods currently employed in the field.

Spolsky, Bernard. 2004. *Language Policy*. Cambridge: Cambridge University Press. An overview of the key issues at the forefront of language policy: ideas of correctness and bad language; bilingualism and multilingualism; language death and efforts to preserve endangered languages; language choice as a human and civil right; and language education policy.

Spolsky, Bernard. 2009. *Language Management*. Cambridge: Cambridge University Press. This discusses conscious and explicit efforts by language managers to control language choices. It reviews research on the family, religion, the workplace, the media, schools, legal and health institutions, the military and government.

part IV

Language in Public Life

chapter 11

Language Assessment

Li Wei

Chapter Outline

Learning Outcomes

After reading this chapter, you should be

- aware of the large number of varieties of language assessment and the different contexts in which language assessment occurs;
- familiar with the key concepts of test design, such as validity and reliability, and criterion-referenced and norm-referenced assessments;
- aware of the impact of language testing;

Applied Linguistics, First Edition. Edited by Li Wei.
© 2014 John Wiley & Sons, Ltd. Published 2014 by John Wiley & Sons, Ltd.

- aware of the socio-political dimensions, including the socio-political uses and the consequences of language testing;
- aware of the ethical considerations of language testing.

Key Terms

- Criterion-referenced
- Democratic assessment
- Fairness framework
- Norm-referenced

- Reliability
- Validity
- Washback

11.1 Introduction

Vicky Mak is an Australian-trained educational psychologist from Hong Kong specializing in children's reading difficulties. She's from a Cantonese-speaking family and has worked in Singapore and mainland China. She is fluent in English, Cantonese and Mandarin. In 2007 she decided to take a job as a special educational needs advisor in Sichuan Province, China. Upon arrival at Chengdu, the capital city of Sichuan, she was told that as her position was part of the civil service of the provincial government, she needed to take a proficiency test in Putonghua, the standard national language of China, which is required of all government employees. Although she was confident that she would pass the test, she was worried that her pronunciation was not standard enough and that she might mix the simplified characters – another feature of the Chinese used in mainland China – with the so-called complex characters that are more commonly used in Hong Kong and Taiwan. Nevertheless, Vicky passed the test with flying colours.

Soon, however, she found out that most of her 'clients' were schools with a high concentration of ethnic minority children, mostly of Tibetan origin. Vicky tried very hard to look for standard tests of reading proficiency in Tibetan and sought advice from linguists and other professionals who had worked with Tibetan and the Tibetan-speaking children. But apart from standard reference books on Tibetan grammar and vocabulary, there was no standardized assessment. Moreover, there was little information about the variety of Tibetan spoken by the children in Sichuan, who were from different tribes from those in Tibet itself. All the children were also multilingual, in a Tibetan dialect, a Sichuan dialect and Putonghua. Vicky could not find any information about bi-scriptal reading in Tibetan and Chinese. She constructed informal reading tests based on the Tibetan and Chinese textbooks that were used in the schools. But it was very difficult to design any intervention programmes. In the meantime, Vicky was told that any child with reading difficulties in Tibetan should just be concentrating on learning Chinese and that the only way for the children to develop their reading skills was to memorize the written characters by copying them 100 times each.

While most of us tend to think that language tests no longer concern us once we finish school education, few realise the important implications of testing in our everyday life. As globalization opens new doors to employment, tourism and entertainment, the need to learn other languages and to have formal certification of the attainment level in the languages becomes more pressing. People's attitudes towards formal language assessment also change as their needs change, from a narrow, pragmatic focus on developing skills to pass a test to a broader, purposeful interest in using the test to consolidate learning and to identify areas for improvement.

In this chapter, we will look at the variety of language assessment first, moving on to the core concepts in test construction and evaluation. We will then look at some of the socio-political uses of language testing, before considering the consequences of testing and the ethics of language testing.

11.2   Varieties of Language Assessment

One can categorize language assessment in many different ways. In terms of social context, some are classroom-based and tied closely to the school curriculum, while others can be based in speech and language therapy clinics, hospitals (e.g. for patients with aphasia and other language-related disabilities), the workplace (e.g. as part of a job application or for a particular employment purpose) and formal test centres. Glen Fulcher, a leading researcher in the field of language assessment, maintains a useful resource website (http://languagetesting.info/) where he describes six scenarios of language testing in different social contexts:

1. *Testing for education*. This is a context that most people can immediately think of when talking about language assessment. The use of language tests for admission to educational institutions is widespread, particularly for higher-education institutions where English is the medium of teaching. The stakes are high for students who compete for places at the most prestigious universities and colleges.
2. *Legal language testing*. Language tests are provided for legal personnel who wish to practise in a second language and for court interpreters who make the legal system accessible to second language speakers. This is an area that has received a significant amount of attention from researchers in Applied Linguistics.
3. *Medical language testing*. There has long been evidence that a failure in communication between medical staff, emergency services personnel and patients can lead to the provision of inappropriate or even harmful treatments. There are two separate contexts of interest. First is the need to ensure that medical or emergency staff who do not speak the primary language of the country in which they are seeking to work have adequate command of that language to function safely. Second is the concern to provide interpretation facilities for those patients who do not speak the language used by the health services.
4. *Aviation English testing*. English is the international language of aviation, and the International Civil Aviation Organization (ICAO) requires all pilots and air traffic controllers to be competent in English, and in particular, to be familiar with a fixed set of words and phrases that is used to cover the operating procedures and eventualities. Aviation English tests have been developed to assess the knowledge of this very

distinctive 'domain-specific' English in candidates who wish to become pilots and air traffic controllers.

5. *Call centre assessment.* Call centres are becoming increasingly common in the globalized business world. Successful business depends on efficient communication with customers. So when call centre activities are outsourced it is essential that the staff be not only intelligible, but also able to use service encounter discourse effectively. The latter entails a different kind of service provider–customer interaction which focuses on personalization of relationships. Training and assessment are needed to ensure that the call centre staff are maximizing the key element of 'rapport' between the operator and the customer.

6. *Military language testing.* Language testing has been used in the military since the First World War, primarily to 'ensure safety and comfort'. Today personnel are tested for their ability to communicate with local people in peacekeeping contexts.

These scenarios are mainly for formal language testing. In fact, we often encounter informal assessment of our language abilities in everyday interactions, but we tend not to think of them as testing. For instance, in major retail outlets in New York, London or Sydney, an interpreting service is available in Mandarin Chinese and Japanese. It is usually offered after an informal assessment of the customers' ability to speak and understand English. If the sales executive feels that the customer has sufficient English for the transaction, no interpreting service will be offered. Sometimes, the initial impression of these informal assessments may be wrong. Further into the negotiation, the sales executive may find that the customer cannot actually understand her. Some researchers make a distinction between *testing* and *assessment*, the former being more formal and structured than the latter. But in most of the literature, these terms are used interchangeably.

A trend in the twentieth century was the globalization of standardized language tests, especially tests for education. The earliest large-scale international test was the *Test of English as a Foreign Language* (TOEFL), launched in 1961 by Educational Testing Service in Princeton, New Jersey, in the United States. The test was designed to assess the English

---

Case Study 11.1: The Rise of the Testing Culture

By Valerie Strauss

Washington Post Staff Writer

Pop quizzes, spelling bees and the three letters that strike dread into high school students across the country – SAT. We have become a Test Nation, and the results can determine the course of a student's life. Some are beginning to question: Is it all too much? Has our obsession with testing pushed students too hard? Just what do tests really tell us? The Washington Post published a series of articles examining the nature of testing and its effects.

                    http://www.washingtonpost.com/wp-dyn/content/article
                                        /2006/10/09/AR2006100900925.html

---

language ability of students applying for admission to US and Canadian colleges and universities and has been one of the most influential language tests around the world. Similarly, *International English Language Testing System*, or IELTS, was established in the 1980s by Cambridge University English for Speakers of Other Language (ESOL) Examinations, the British Council and IDP Education Pty. Ltd., and is accepted by most Australian, British, Canadian, Irish, New Zealand and South African academic institutions for admission purposes. It is also a requirement for immigration to Australia, New Zealand and Canada. Some countries have developed their own standardized English language tests, including, for example, *The General English Proficiency Test* (GEPT) in Taiwan, the *College English Test* in China, and the *STEP Eiken* in Japan. In the meantime, organizations such as Alliance Française of France, the Goethe-Institut of Germany, Instituto Cervantes of Spain, and Hanban of China have developed standardized tests for French, German, Spanish and Chinese, respectively, which are used globally.

In terms of their purpose, these globalized standard language tests are mainly used to assess the candidate's suitability for admission into academic institutions. Evidence of passing such tests may increase the candidate's chances of immigration or employment, but they are usually not the chief objectives of these tests. Some countries, such as the United Kingdom, have nationality tests for immigrants who wish to obtain citizenship. They are, of course, language-based, but the contents tend to focus on the history and culture of the country rather than the language itself.

Language tests, like all educational assessments, are often divided into *formative* and *summative* categories. Summative tests are generally carried out at the end of a learning course. They are typically used to evaluate the outcome of the learning by assigning the candidate a grade. Formative assessments, on the other hand, can be carried out throughout a course. They are used to aid learning, by providing feedback on a candidate's progress, and would not necessarily be used for grading purposes.

Test results can be compared against an established criterion, against the performance of other candidates or against the same candidate's previous performance. *Criterion-referenced tests* are used to measure the candidate's performance against some predefined criteria or standard, and aim to determine whether or not the candidate has demonstrated mastery of a certain skill or set of skills. These results are usually 'pass' or 'fail' and are used in making decisions about job entry, certification or licensure. For example, most professional interpreters and translators need to pass criterion-referenced language tests to gain a licence to practise.

Norm-referenced tests are used to measure a candidate's performance relative to the group undertaking the assessment. Standardized examinations such as the General Certificate of Secondary Education (GCSE) tests are norm-referenced tests. In effect, they compare the candidates with each other. Many entrance tests to schools or universities are norm-referenced, permitting a fixed proportion of students to pass, and passing in this context means being accepted into the school or university rather than showing an explicit level of ability. This means that standards may vary from year to year, depending on the quality of the cohort; criterion-referenced assessment does not vary from year to year unless the criteria change.

A third type of comparison is between the present performance and the prior performance of the same candidate being assessed. This is often known as *ipsative* assessment. Some school-based tests are ipsative assessments in that they compare the candidate's progress in learning at the beginning and the end of a school year. They are also used in professional contexts, such as speech and language therapy and educational psychology, to assess an individual's improvement in a particular skill after intervention.

Most standard language tests assess the candidate's skills in four modalities – listening, speaking, reading and writing – and some have components where integrated skills are assessed. Equal weight may be placed on *competence* – knowledge of how the language works theoretically, usually assessed through comprehension – and *proficiency* – the ability to use the language practically, assessed through production – in each of the individual skills, or greater weight may be given to one aspect or the other. New technologies have made an impact on test design. Computer-based TOEFL and IELTS are now widely used, with automated scoring. For some tests, the candidate does not even need to go to a testing centre and can use telephone technology to record the speaking and obtain automated scoring of their speaking tests. However, computer-assisted language tests may require greater organizational capacity and other additional skills compared with traditional pen-and-paper tests. This particular dimension of the test is not always reflected in the scoring criteria.

11.3   Key Concepts in Test Construction and Use

Designing or constructing a language assessment is a very complex process and requires professional training and experience. Over the years, the construction of new, large-scale language assessments has become highly professionalized and is usually done by a team of trained test writers, employed by large professional, often commercial, companies, and with several trials. Language teachers and other professional practitioners may be engaged in designing more or less informal tests for a specific use (e.g. an end-of-term classroom-based test). These tests are rarely used by others beyond the specific context that they were designed for in the first place. It is more likely that the language teachers and other professional practitioners need to choose a particular standard test for their immediate professional context, which requires evaluating available tests.

There are two key concepts with which language test designers and evaluators are often concerned: *validity* and *reliability*. It was once believed that 'by following established procedures, it is possible to design a format for administering and scoring a valid and reliable language performance test' (Jones, 1979: 50). Current inquiry into the issues of validity and reliability in language assessment includes multiple perspectives and much more sophisticated methodologies (Chapelle, 1999).

Validity concerns the extent to which meaningful inferences can be drawn from test scores. When a test measures what it is intended to measure and nothing else, it is valid. The most important kinds of validity in language tests, and indeed in most educational assessments, are *content validity*, *constructive validity* and *predictive validity*. Should the content of the test focus on specific aspects of the ability domain or should it cover all domains in suitable proportion? For instance, if the target of the test is oral language ability, is there any involvement of the written language in the test, for example, test instructions and answers? Should the content be based on what the instructor wants the learner to learn, or should it also consider the learner's needs and characteristics, and the instructional and learning context? Does the test accurately reflect the principles of a valid model of language description, language learning and language use? How are these principles operationalized in the construction of test items, that is, how are they turned into ways of eliciting the candidate's language knowledge and language use? Is there a balanced sample without bias towards test items that are easiest to write or towards test material that happens to be available? And how accurately can a prediction be made regarding the candidate's future performance in language use?

There are also more practical considerations in judging the validity of a language test. For example, does the test look like a reasonable way of assessing the learner? Do the instructors and the learners think that the test is too easy or too difficult? Some researchers call this *face validity*. More recently, language testing researchers have also raised the question of consequential validity, which concerns how the results of the language testing impact on the candidate's future in both a narrowly focused learning context and the broader social context. For example, will the result be used to exclude the candidate from taking part in any particular learning or social activities? And how will the candidate regard themselves once they know the test result?

Reliability concerns the extent to which the test provides consistent, replicable information about candidates' language performance. The reliability of a test is high when any difference in test results between two individuals represents the true difference between them irrespective of the context in which the test is taken (e.g. in the morning or afternoon, in a test centre or a more familiar location), which version of the test they have taken, and the way the test is marked. Test constructors are more concerned with intrinsic reliability, that is, whether two or more test items that aim to measure the same thing would yield the same result. Test users, on the other hand, are more concerned with extrinsic reliability, which is about the impact of either the variability of testing conditions or examiner variability on test results. Reliability can be seen as a prerequisite to validity in assessment in the sense that the test must provide consistent, replicable information about candidates' language performance.

Another kind of reliability refers to the consistency of the ratings by the examiners. There are essentially two issues of concern: (i) would a student receive a different grade (written or oral) if he or she took the test with a different examiner using the same marking scale (i.e. inter-rater reliability)? (ii) would a student's grade (written or oral) be the same if the test was taken at a different time/date with the same examiner (i.e. intra-rater reliability)? For most tests, a rating scale is required – for example, a holistic scale (general impressions) or an analytic scale (more detailed and specific). Examiners should understand the principles behind the particular rating scales they must work with and be able to interpret their descriptors consistently. Once the general principles are understood, inter-rater reliability can be improved through routine double marking where every piece of work that a student produces is marked by two different examiners and a mean grade is obtained, or sampling double marking by the central examiner where one examiner takes the lead in monitoring the marking process as it actually happens and double marks a sample of tests to check consistency in marking. It is also essential that the internal consistency of the examiner is checked. Intra-rater reliability can be achieved through the routine re-marking of scripts by the same examiner. Giving teachers or examiners too many examination scripts to mark may adversely affect intra-rater reliability.

Self-assessment is not an alien concept to human behaviour. All human beings are involved, either consciously or subconsciously, in an on-going process of self-evaluation. Until recently, however, the value of self-assessment in language learning was largely ignored. Learners were rarely asked to assess their performance. They have even less of a

---

STUDY ACTIVITY 11.1

1. Have you experienced any language test in the last 12 months?
2. Was the test standardized, informal or self-administered? Who constructed the test?
3. Was the test normative or criterion-referenced?
4. How do you measure the validity and reliability of the test you took?

---

say in the construction of language tests. In the last decade, with increased attention being given to learner-centred curricula, needs analysis and learner autonomy, the topic of self-assessment has become of particular interest in testing and evaluation (Blanche, 1988; Oscarson, 1997). It is now being recognized that learners do have the ability to provide meaningful input into the assessment of their performance, and that this assessment can be valid. In fact, with regard to second and foreign languages, research reveals an emerging pattern of consistent, overall high correlations between self-assessment results and ratings based on a variety of external criteria (Blanche, 1988; Oscarson, 1984, 1997).

11.4 Socio-political Uses of Language Testing

As we mentioned earlier, language testing can be used in a variety of social contexts. Nevertheless, the primary objective of testing in most contexts is to assess an individual's language ability with a view to improving it. However, there are other uses of language testing whose chief objective is not about improving one's language ability, but about social inclusion and exclusion.

In the United States, an immigrant can become a naturalized citizen if he or she fulfils certain requirements, including passing an English language test and the Civics Test. One is also required to answer questions during a formal interview. The English test has three components: reading, writing and speaking. The US Citizenship and Immigration Services website provides detailed information on how to prepare for the test (http://www.uscis.gov/portal/site/uscis under 'Citizenship'). Each applicant is given two opportunities to take the English and Civics tests and to answer all questions relating to the naturalization application in English. If an applicant fails any of the tests at the initial interview, he or she will be retested on the portion of the test that they failed (English or Civics) between 60 and 90 days from the date of the initial interview. Further failures will disqualify the applicant from the naturalization application. Language testing thus becomes an integral and crucial part of an important social process.

There are of course exemptions for some applicants. The following are the exemption rules:

- If you are age 50 or older and have been a permanent resident of the United States for 20 years you can take the test in your native language.
- If you are age 55 or older and have been a permanent resident of the United States for 15 years you can take the test in your native language.

- If you are age 65 or older and have been a permanent resident of the United States for 20 years you can take a simplified civics test in your native language.
- Applicants with a physical or developmental disability or a mental impairment so severe that it prevents acquiring or demonstrating the required knowledge of English and civics may be eligible for an exception to these requirements.

Similarly, in the United Kingdom, if an immigrant wants to apply for settlement or naturalization as a British citizen, they must show that they have a good knowledge of the English language and of life in the UK. According to the UK Border Agency (UKBA), who manage the process on behalf of the Home Office, there are two ways to demonstrate this knowledge:

- If you are an English speaker, you must pass the 'Life in the UK test'.
- If you are not an English speaker, you must pass a course in English for speakers of other languages (ESOL), which contains citizenship materials.

In England, Wales and Northern Ireland, the ESOL course is offered at three levels: Entry 1 (lowest), Entry 2, and Entry 3 (highest). In Scotland, the levels are: Access 2, Access 3, and Intermediate 1. The UKBA regulations specifically state that

> You qualify as an English speaker if your English skills are at or above ESOL Entry Level 3 or Scottish Intermediate 1.

Moreover, the ESOL courses can only be taken at UKBA accredited centres, which are also accredited by various other bodies such as Ofsted (Office for Standards in Education), Accreditation UK, the British Accreditation Council (BAC), the Accreditation Body for Language Services (ABLS) or the Accreditation Service for International Colleges (ASIC). Similar regimes are in place in Canada, Australia and other English-speaking countries for people who wish to become citizens of the country.

Sometimes, we can find language testing being used for specific employment. As the example at the beginning of this chapter shows, in China civil service jobs require proficiency tests in Putonghua, the standard national language. In fact, China was the first country in the world to implement a nationwide standardized test, in the Sui Dynasty in AD 605. The main purpose of this Imperial Examination, as it became known, was to select able candidates for specific governmental positions. A large proportion of the examination was devoted to the Confucian classics, which the candidates needed to memorize and understand, and to essay writing based on their understanding of the Confucian classics and how they might be applied to all spheres of social life. The examinations would last between 24 and 72 hours, and were conducted in cubicles. In order to obtain objectivity in evaluation, candidates were identified by number rather than name, and examination answers were recopied by a third person before being evaluated to prevent the candidate's handwriting from being recognized. The system was seen as a major social development to widen participation of the general population of non-aristocratic background in government affairs, and had a huge influence in neighbouring Asian countries such as Japan, Korea and Vietnam. England adopted a similar examination system in 1806 to select specific candidates for positions in Her Majesty's Civil Service. The Chinese Imperial Examination was abolished in 1905, but the modern examination system for selecting civil service staff, including the current tests of Putonghua proficiency for candidates wanting a government position, has many resemblances to aspects of the imperial one.

─────────── 11.5   The Consequences of Language Testing

Language testing can have many different consequences for the individuals involved in constructing and administering the test, individuals who take the test, and the institutions and communities to which these individuals belong (Messick, 1996). But of all stakeholders in language testing, test-takers have the highest stake of all. As we discussed in the last section, failing an English test may mean one cannot gain citizenship in the United States or the United Kingdom, and failing the Putonghua test may disqualify someone from taking up a government position in China.

In the sphere of education, a school-based language test result may lead the teacher to certain pedagogical decisions in the subsequent school term, including the choice of teaching material, the method of teaching, additional learning resources, and so on. It can affect the students, who may be grouped into different levels; some may receive enhanced support. The class of students, or even the whole school, may be affected as the test result may be used in the construction of league tables of attainment.

A prominent concept in Applied Linguistics is *washback*, which refers to the extent to which the introduction and use of a test influences language teachers and learners to do things they would not otherwise do that promote or inhibit language learning. Some proponents have even maintained that a test's validity should be appraised by the degree to which it manifests positive or negative washback, a notion very akin to the proposal of 'systemic validity' in the general educational assessment literature. In other words, washback can be seen as an example of the consequential aspect of construct validity of language assessment.

So-called positive washback refers to test effects that are expected and helpful. For example, a test may encourage students to study more or may promote a connection between standards and instruction. Negative washback, on the other hand, refers to the unexpected, harmful consequences of a test. For example, instruction may focus too heavily on test preparation at the expense of other activities. Washback from tests can impact on individual teachers and students as well as whole classes and programmes. Sometimes, the washback effect is partial, in the sense that a test might influence what is taught but not how it is taught, or it might influence the teacher's behaviour but not the learner's behaviour. While in general terms it is desirable to make an effort to increase the positive washback of tests, it may be more important to try to understand how testing affects different teachers and learners differentially and why some tests may have more positive effects than negative ones. For example, research shows that test properties are likely to have a strong washback effect. The authenticity and directness of the test can determine the level of positive washback. Authentic assessments include engaging tasks in realistic settings or close simulations so that the tasks, as well as available time and resources, parallel those in the real world. Direct assessments involve open-ended tasks in which the respondent can freely perform the complex skill at issue, unfettered by structured item forms or restrictive response formats. What it means is that test construction needs to reflect the real-life situations of the learners as far as possible and that the content of the tests should be made relevant to the learners' everyday lives.

Case Study 11.2

The website of the Center for Applied Linguistics, in Washington, DC gives the following example of positive washback of language testing:

Oakdale Middle School has a foreign language programme offering Spanish and French through level two. Members of the foreign language department were proud of their program but frustrated with students' lack of effort in their classes. The teachers felt many students did not take their foreign language classes seriously; since they weren't studying and practicing much, the teachers knew they were not working up to their potential. During the past year, the teachers began to implement authentic assessments of oral language, reading, and writing. These standards-based assessments, which were given every six weeks, involved the students in real-life tasks.

The department chair sent home parent surveys and found that students were spending more time working on their foreign language skills at home and that they were talking more about their foreign language classes with parents. Parents and students also liked the feedback that they got from the regular assessments. One student commented in an interview that knowing what was going to be on the assessments helped him to prepare effectively and that the results helped him know what to do to improve. At the end of the year, 75% of eighth grade language students were placed into level 2 for high school. Overall, the foreign language teachers felt that student performance was improving and they attributed this to the new assessment program. Moreover, the district's foreign language supervisor recognized the school's efforts and was able to find additional funding for curriculum and assessment development the next year.

http://www.cal.org/flad/tutorial/impact/5exwashback.html

The impact of language testing is by no means constrained to the teaching and learning process. In fact, far more significant may be the long-term social consequences of language testing. Elana Shohamy, a leading researcher and critic in language testing, has argued that language testing is a covert mechanism of language planning and a *de facto* language policy (e.g. 2001, 2007). At a micro level, language testing can privilege certain forms and levels of language knowledge, as language tests often set correct grammar and native-like accents as part of the criteria. At the macro level, the tested languages become the most important languages to acquire and master. Tests are often more powerful than written policy documents, as they can lead to 'the elimination and suppression of certain languages in societies' (Shohamy, 2007: 120). Language tests can also become barriers for keeping unwanted groups, such as immigrants and ethnic minority groups, from entering educational institutions or the workplace.

The socio-political consequence of language testing thus concerns both the status of languages and the status of speakers. The act of testing grants status to the language that gets tested. When those in authority decide to include a certain language as part of school or university examinations, it automatically grants it high status as it provides an indication that it is being valued highly by the authorities. By implication, the languages that are not tested are deemed marginal and irrelevant. In most nation states, tests of national and official languages are given priority in national testing so as to perpetuate the languages' high status within the hierarchy of languages. In Israel, as Shohamy shows, entrance tests to higher education are conducted in Hebrew even though all Arabic students conduct their schooling through Arabic; the act of testing further perpetuates the high status of Hebrew and low status of Arabic within Israeli society. Similarly, the status of English versus all other languages in the United States is reinforced with the No Child Left Behind (NCLB) tests. In the case of immersion programmes where the content is taught via other languages (e.g. Navajo in some schools in Arizona), the NCLB provides a direct message about that language, namely that Navajo has no meaningful worth or prestige (Evans and Hornberger, 2005; Menken, 2008).

Language testing also often perpetuates the myth that there is such a thing as native language proficiency and that proficiency is, quite literally, the birthright of the native speaker. The native language proficiency assumption is connected to the claim that human beings have an innate capacity to acquire abstract linguistic rules as well as the capacity to put their knowledge of the linguistic rules into practice. It is evidenced by the native speaker's ability to produce fluent spontaneous speech, be creative in their language use, manage their language use according to the context and make judgements on linguistic structures. Yet, there is ample evidence to show that second language users can develop high levels of linguistic proficiency in all these respects. The only true difference between a native speaker and a non-native speaker seems to be biography, in that the native speaker acquires the L1 of which s/he is a native speaker from birth, which is impossible for the non-native speaker by definition (Davies, 2003). The notion of the native speaker and the associated assumption of native language proficiency have no scientific grounding and are socially discriminatory.

The notions of the native speaker and native language proficiency also tend to assume one language only or one language at a time. Again, there is ample evidence that the vast majority of the world's population is multilingual. It is very common for young children to acquire multiple languages simultaneously. Furthermore, multilingual speakers mix and alternate between different languages and language varieties all the time. Multilingualism is the norm for most societies today. Yet language testing has not taken this fact to heart and rarely attempts to use multilingualism as the norm in test design and administration.

11.6   Ethical Issues in Language Testing

The social consequences of language testing bring forward the issue of ethics. Of the many millions of people who take language tests for various reasons, virtually none will have participated in the test's design, in writing test items, in critiquing the test methods, in setting cut scores or in writing or commenting on the performance descriptions that tie to their all-important scores. Such a situation cannot be considered fair.

Hamp-Lyons (1997) called for an expanded sense of the responsibility of language testers, giving more attention to the consequences of testing on language learning at the classroom as well as the educational, social and political levels. Similarly, Kunnan (2004) linked the issues of test validity and reliability with issues of access and justice in what he called 'a fairness framework' for language testing. Questions need to be asked as to the comparable validity and reliability of test scores in terms of subgroups such as gender, race and ethnicity, class, and so on, of the test-taker, absence of bias, including culturally opaque references, stereotyping of people, and so on, and issues such as opportunity to learn and testing accommodations. In addition, organizations that design and administer tests need to be challenged in terms of their practices with regard to justice and equality towards the test-taking communities and in terms of their duty and obligation towards their disadvantaged clients. An important issue here is that of accountability. This has to do with a sense of responsibility to the people most immediately affected by the test, principally the test-takers, but also those who will use the information it provides. The test, and hence the test developer, needs to be accountable to them.

Shohamy (2001) takes a more critical approach to language testing and has advocated what she calls 'democratic assessment' as an alternative. She bases her approach on the following principles:

* The need for citizens in democratic societies to play a participatory and active role and transfer and share power from elites to and with local bodies;
* The need for those who develop powerful tools to be responsible for their consequences;
* The need to consider voices of diverse and different groups in multicultural societies;
* The need to protect the rights of citizens from powerful institutions.

According to Shohamy, these needs should 'lead to assessment practices which are aimed at monitoring and limiting the uses of tests, especially those that have the potential to exclude and discriminate against groups and individuals' (2001: 373). Of the proposals Shohamy made, shared and collaborative assessment models, where different voices can be included in the assessment and the test-takers feel that they are protected from misuse of the test by people and institutions in authority, are crucial. In particular, Shohamy invites people to critically assess the impact of industrialized language testing – the existence of language assessment on a huge international scale. For example, there are approximately one million individual administrations of the TOEFL test in any year, in a large number of countries. What are we to make of this phenomenon in critical terms?

STUDY ACTIVITY 11.2

Choose a standard language test that you have taken or administered recently. Ask the following questions:

1. What is the target population of the test?
2. Who designed the test?
3. What is the purpose of the test?
4. How are the test scores used?
5. Could the test-takers be involved in any aspect of the design and administration of the test and the use of the test results?

What factors are influencing decisions regarding the administration of the test and the use of test results? What impact has the test made on the lives of the millions of test-takers, and on government policies?

11.7 Summary

Language assessment can vary from formal tests to informal judgement of a language user's abilities to understand or produce language. It has been a powerful tool not only in education and learning but also in increasingly diverse social and professional contexts. While the construction of a language test raises a wide range of technical issues regarding the validity and reliability of the test items and scoring systems, the social implications of language assessment invite critical reflection. There is a range of ethical issues that need to be considered, as well as the democratic principles in the management of language assessment. As a field of study, language assessment is linked to language teaching and learning, language policy and language planning, as well as learner identity, language attitudes and language ideology.

Study Questions

1. In what way can language testing facilitate language learning?
2. In what way can the concepts of validity and reliability in test construction be linked to fairness and democratic principles in language testing?
3. In what way can language testing impact on language policy?
4. What factors should be considered in language testing practices in order to avoid social discrimination?
5. In what way can the learner become an active participant in the design and implementation of a language test?

Recommended Reading

Chapelle, Carol. 1999. Validity in language assessment. *Annual Review of Applied Linguistics, vol.19.* 254–227. New York: Cambridge University Press. A review article focusing on the issue of validity in language assessment.

Davies, Alan. 2003. *The Native Speaker: Myth and Reality.* Clevedon: Multilingual Matters. A critique of the notion of the native speaker. It discusses implications for various areas of Applied Linguistics.

Hamp-Lyons, Liz. 1997. Washback, impact and validity: ethical concerns. *Language Testing* 14 (3), 295–303. This considers washback from an ethical perspective.

Kunnan, Antony J. 2004. Test fairness. In M. Milanovic and C. Weir (eds.), *European Language Testing in a Global Context*, 27–48. Cambridge: Cambridge University Press. This discusses fairness of language tests and related matters, such as test standards, test bias and equity and ethics for testing professionals.

McNamara, Tim. 2000. *Language Testing*. Oxford: Oxford University Press. An introduction to the basic concepts and theoretical models in language testing.

McNamara, Tim and Carsten Roever. 2006. *Language Testing: The Social Dimension*. Oxford: Blackwell. This book considers language assessment as a socially situated event and examines the societal consequences of language tests.

Menken, Kate. 2008. *English Learners Left Behind: Standardized Testing as Language Policy*. Clevedon: Multilingual Matters. This examines how high-stakes tests mandated by No Child Left Behind have become *de facto* language policy in US schools.

Messick, Samuel. 1996. Validity and washback in language testing. *Language Testing* 13 (3), 241–256. A classic reference on validity and washback.

Oscarson, Mats. 1997. Self-assessment of foreign and second language proficiency. In C. Clapham and D. Corson (eds.), *Language Testing and Assessment*. Vol. 7 of *The Encyclopaedia of Language and Education*. Dordrecht: Kluwer Academic, 175–187. A review of self-assessment.

Shohamy, Elana. 2001. *The Power of Tests: A Critical Perspective on the Uses of Language Tests*. Harlow: Longman. This book applies a critical perspective on language testing by examining its uses and consequences in education and in society.

List of language proficiency tests in different languages:

http://en.wikipedia.org/wiki/List_of_language_proficiency_tests

chapter 12

Language in Media, Health and Law

Malcolm Edwards

Chapter Outline

12.1 Introduction
12.2 How Does Language Construct Events in the Media?
12.3 How are Health and Illness Constructed through Language?
12.4 What is the Relationship between Language and the Law?
12.5 Summary

Learning Outcomes

After reading this chapter, you should be able to

- analyse the roles of language in the representation of events, groups and individuals;
- assess the role and functions of discourses as different ways of framing reality;
- identify relationships between language and power in different domains;
- identify and analyse the functions of metaphor in discourse;
- understand the relationship between language and disadvantage.

Applied Linguistics, First Edition. Edited by Li Wei.
© 2014 John Wiley & Sons, Ltd. Published 2014 by John Wiley & Sons, Ltd.

Key Terms

- Asymmetry
- Common-sense discourse
- Construction
- Discourse
- Metaphor

- Reification
- Representation
- Social power
- Transitivity

12.1 Introduction

Commenting on a successful appeal against deportation by Abu Qatada, a Jordanian citizen alleged to be involved with a terrorist organization, a popular British newspaper published a photograph of Abu Qatada, with this caption:

> FREED fanatic Abu Qatada smirks as he arrives home yesterday – after again dodging attempts to boot him out of Britain.

When we look closely at the caption, it becomes clear that the language is chosen to condense a complex situation into a short statement and to implicitly criticize the decision. The capitalization of 'FREED' conveys outrage, and obscures the reality that Abu Qatada will be subject to constraints on his movements and activities. The choice of the words 'smirks' and 'dodging' constructs Abu Qatada as devious and contemptuous of the law. 'Dodging' also identifies Abu Qatada himself as somehow responsible for the decision, rather than the actions of legal professionals.

In this chapter we explore the ways in which language is used to construct accounts of events and experiences in three areas: the media, medicine and the law. We will also see how language may function to exercise social power, and how complex processes and situations are translated into the professional and technical languages of medicine and the law.

Study of the language of the media, medicine and the law represents a fast expanding area of Applied Linguistics, with Discourse Analysis (DA) and Critical Discourse Analysis (CDA) providing the main theoretical and analytic frameworks. This area is also connected to issues of identity (see Chapter 9: 'Language, Identity and Power'), and Language and Intercultural Communication (Chapter 6). It is an area in which Applied Linguists have demonstrated the impact of their work on people's understanding of politics, public policies and institutional structures, ideologies, and practices. This chapter draws on the methods of DA and CDA, but will not be discussing them per se. A good introduction to Discourse Analysis is Johnstone (2007), in the same series as the present volume, covering discourse structures, participant roles and relations, discourse and the medium, intentions and interpretation, as well as the relationship between discourse, culture and ideology. It also considers a variety of approaches to discourse, including CDA, Conversation Analysis (CA), interactional and variationist sociolinguistics, ethnography, corpus linguistics and other qualitative and quantitative methods. Fairclough (2003) draws on a range of social theories and introduces the student to the practice of CDA. It is illustrated with a range of real texts, from written texts to TV debates and radio broadcasts.

———————————— 12.2   How Does Language Construct Events in the Media?

When we talk about the 'media' we are usually referring to the public mass media of news and information dissemination – the press, radio and television. Today, most of us are also familiar with new media, in the form of online, digital and communications technology. The rapid expansion of new media, in the form of email, blogs, and social media, has led to a situation in which ordinary citizens can become active media creators, offering alternatives to the established media. The role of citizen journalists and social media has been a particular feature of recent events such as the Arab Spring. While new media represents a challenge to the dominance of traditional media, most research into language and media has focused on broadcasting and the press. In this section, we will consider how language is used to represent events in the press, and how public participation programmes in broadcast media frame the voices of the public.

The media inform us about events in the world, but the process of 'translating' events into language is neither direct nor neutral. Reporting any event involves choices as to how processes, people and groups are represented, and this forms an aspect of how the media 'mediate' information, functioning as an intermediary between news events and the public, selecting and filtering information through a linguistic and ideological prism. The filtering process involves choices as to what is selected as newsworthy, what aspects of a situation or event to represent, and what form the representation will take. In doing so, the media both sustain and help to create social knowledge and social meaning in the form of discourses – ways of talking and thinking about the world that are systematic and naturalized.

Language is fundamental to this process, as different linguistic choices can create markedly different representations of the same event. Here are two newspaper extracts describing the same event (Fowler *et al.*, 1979).

(1)   Notting Hill's West Indian Carnival, plagued by muggings and sporadic street fighting throughout yesterday, erupted into an ugly all-out battle between the police and West Indians last night. In the Portobello Road we saw West Indian youths – even some white youths – ripping up paving stones and smashing them against walls to use as missiles against the police who were trying to defend themselves with riot shields.

(2)   The violence which had been predicted and feared at the Notting Hill carnival finally spilled over last night. Police moved in in force to the area around Acklam Road under the flyover after most of the revellers had left the Notting Hill streets. Bottles and bricks flew throughout the air and crashed against police coaches as they tried to force their way through. Lines of police with riot shields and dustbin lids drew up in hasty formation behind their shields as they tried to dodge missiles.

Before we examine the language of these extracts, consider your own immediate response. Is one version more alive than the other? Is one version easier to understand? What responses are these two texts likely to produce in the reader? The answers to these questions relate to the linguistic choices within the text.

The vocabulary of the first text is concrete, specific and dynamic, creating a narrative of spiralling violence. The carnival is described as *'plagued'* by muggings and *'sporadic street fighting'*. Although we are not told how common these incidents were in reality, *'plagued'* suggests that they were frequent. The reference to *'muggings'* and street fighting adds to the picture of anarchy and lawlessness, as does the use of semantically intense verbs such as *'erupted'*, *'ripping up'* and *'smashing'*.

We can also consider how processes involving people and other actors are represented. The opening sentence begins with a reference to the Carnival, depicted as the site of muggings and street fighting, aligning and identifying the Carnival itself with violence. In the second sentence, West Indian youths are foregrounded, and depicted as attacking the police. Within the story, particular events and participants are thus placed in the foreground, while others remain in the background, and yet others are not explicitly mentioned but assumed or implied. This latter feature is important, as when we read the text, we infer more than is actually said, 'reading in' information. Although 'muggings' and 'street fighting' do not specify who was involved, the climactic battle is between West Indian youths and the police. Casting the West Indians in the role of aggressors suggests that the violence was perpetrated by West Indian youths.

In the second account, the language choices create a more abstract, questioning account. The text begins with 'the *violence*'. Using a noun rather than a verb (verbs identify participants, and imply responsibility) foregrounds 'violence' as the problem. We are told that the police *'moved in in force'*, but not why they moved in, or against whom. Bottles and missiles *'are thrown'*, but we are not told who threw them. In this version, we are told that the police acted after most revellers had gone home, suggesting that the incident was limited and localized. In this version, then, the event is localized and perhaps an isolated incident, and the text is neutral with regard to attributing or implying responsibility.

The two texts present different perspectives on the event, and each is shaped by and aims to reproduce and argue for particular patterns of beliefs, attitudes and values. These patterns in the ways we talk about – and think about – the world are discourses. How the event is constructed is related to the ideological position of the intended audience. The first extract implicitly expresses an 'us' and 'them' perspective (van Dijk, 1998), where 'us' is represented by the police, and 'them' by the West Indian youths. The phrase *'even white youths'* is particularly telling in this respect. West Indian youth is seen as a problem, and this in turn relates to what Fairclough (1989) calls 'common-sense' discourses concerning race and multiculturalism.

We turn now to consider public participation in the media. The phone-in and the discussion programme are popular broadcast media genres, which ostensibly allow members of the public to express their views or participate in group discussions on social, political or personal issues. While such programmes appear to allow the public a voice unmediated by the voices of experts or institutional representatives, they can also depoliticize issues and present them in a managed and sometimes sensationalist form.

Case Study 12.1

The method of analysis used above derives from techniques developed in Critical Discourse Analysis (CDA). CDA assumes that language is not a neutral medium, but a form of social and ultimately ideological practice through which experience is constructed. 'Discourses' – the ways in which we talk about and represent the world, and thus construct experience – are constituted of choices which express ideological positions, and in particular power relations (Fairclough, 1989). Benwell and Stokoe (2006: 105) point out that 'critical' in this usage is associated with critique, and with the project of work within CDA to deconstruct and reveal the ways in which language and discourse mediate and reproduce ideologies. CDA takes an avowedly political stance, focusing on social and political phenomena such as marketization (Fairclough, 1993; Chouliaraki and Fairclough, 1999), racism (Van Dijk, 1991) and media (Fowler, 1991). CDA has evolved into an inter-disciplinary branch of linguistics, composed of a range of approaches which share the basic ideological assumptions and orientation that language is constitutive and expressive of social relations and ideology. CDA has been criticized on a number of grounds, including its reliance on categories that are assumed *a priori* and imposed in analysis, its deterministic assumption that readers are not free to read texts 'critically', and the claim that CD analyses are themselves selective interpretations. Some critics, such as Widdowson (1995), have questioned whether CDA can generate 'new' knowledge, given that its project is to demonstrate what the analyst assumes to be the case, thus leaving no room for unexpected findings. CDA has been responsive to these and other criticisms, and continues to evolve into a broad and diversified framework for analysing the role of ideology and power relations in public discourse.

(Chouliaraiaki and Fairclough, 1999)

STUDY ACTIVITY 12.1

How is the event constructed in this account from another paper? Compare this account with the two above.

Rampaging teenage gangs turned London's Notting Hill Carnival into a bloody riot last night. Running battles broke out throughout the carnival area as the wreckers pelted police with bricks, stones and bottles. Lines of officers, protected by riot shields, charged the mobs, while frightened revellers cowered behind walls, sheltering little children from missiles raining down.

The example of phone-ins is illustrative. While phone-ins seem to allow the Caller to present an agenda for discussion, Hutchby (1996) points out that the Caller can introduce an agenda but may not remain in control of it. Hutchby shows that by using utterances such as 'So?', the Host can challenge the Caller's agenda or argument, without offering a counter-argument, as in the extract below:

(3) CALLER: I have got three appeals letters here this week. All asking for donations.
                 Two from those that I always contribute to anyway
     HOST: Yes?
     CALLER: But I expect to get a lot more
     HOST: So?
     CALLER: Now the point is there is a limit to ....
     HOST: ... what's that got to do with telethons though?

The Host's 'So?' questions the relevance of the Caller's complaint about charity
appeals, which she regards as a form of blackmail, and also obliges her to take the
conversational floor again to attempt to explain the relevance of her argument. The
Host may also exercise the privilege of selectively formulating the Caller's argument,
as in the next example:

(4) CALLER: Charity does [increase the distance between donors and recipients] yes,
                 I mean
     HOST: You're going back to that original argument we shouldn't have charity
     CALLER: Well, no. I um. I wouldn't go that far.

Hutchby observes that the 'argumentative resources' are not equally shared between the
Caller and the Host, as the Caller has to nominate the agenda or topic, while the Host is
able to demand that the Caller account for their claim, without having to advance an
alternative view.

   Similar forms of asymmetrical privilege and hence power over the direction of talk
can be seen in discussion shows, where participants – usually members of the public –
are required to present a story concerning some aspect of their life. In such programmes the framing discourse is that of experts or the institutional structure in
which the story is told, so that the discourse of lay participants is constrained within
the institutional format. This can be seen in the extract from *Kilroy*, below. The Host is
asking a young woman about her experience of living in a household in which the
parental figures were two men.

(5) K: Tell me about this ( ) household
     PT: erm well both my parents are very loving very accepting of lots of things ( )
           and ( ) that rubs off on my sister and I –erm
     K: How old are you?
     PT: Nineteen
     K: mmm. ... how old were you when you lived with dad and X?
     PT: erm ( ) I was 17 when I moved
     K: Cause you problems?
     PT: no
     K: did you find it strange?
     PT: no
     K: find it difficult?
     PT: no it's just like any other parent and their lover
     K: it's just like living with any other parent and their partner
                                         (*Kilroy*: 'Adoption', 1994, in Thornborrow, 1997)

Here too the Host has unique privileges with regard to directing and managing the talk. The role of the Host is to ask questions and, in this example, to direct the talk to specific topics. The Host's questions are direct, are delivered rapidly and elicit information about private and potentially face-threatening topics. Given the format of the interaction, and the Host's questioning style, the Participant may find it hard to resist giving answers. Notice that the Host uses short questions which embody presuppositions, such as *'find it difficult?'*, which assumes the domestic situation described by the Participant might be seen as difficult, though the specific sense of 'difficult' in this context is not made clear.

The constraining effect of such questions becomes clear when compared with other questions, such as 'how did you find it?', which would allow the Participant to take the floor and relate their own experience. This questioning technique speeds the interview along, and allows the Participant little opportunity for detailed or qualified response. In effect, the Host's interventions appropriate, shape and evaluate the Participant's story. As Thornborrow (1997) notes, the format of such programmes raises the question of whether they are forums, which allow ordinary voices to be heard and which promote genuine public debate, or whether they remain institutions with powers to filter what is talked about and by whom.

In the discussion above we have seen that linguistic choices serve to frame events within discourses that lend the account a particular 'angle'. In the case of public participation programmes, we saw how such programmes may be constrained by their format and the privileged status of the host. The approach has been critical, focusing on examples of ideological construction and power asymmetries in the media. The relationship between the media and the public is, however, a complex and varied one. While the media undoubtedly has considerable influence, we should be careful not to overstate its power, or to assume that consumers of the media are uncritically accepting of its products. From a different direction, the advent of 'new' media in the form of social media, the Internet, blogs and citizen journalism, offers an alternative and,

STUDY ACTIVITY 12.2

1. Find two newspapers. One should be a paper aimed at the 'dominant group' in society, and the other a paper for a minority community, either in English or another language. What items feature most prominently in the two papers? What differences are there in the selection and organization of items?
2. Now find a story covered in both papers and compare how the event, the actors in the event and its significance are represented, and consider how the different representations relate to particular discourse positions.
3. Listen to or watch a programme in which members of the public are participating and consider the degree to which the format and conduct of the programme either enables or controls their contribution.

at times, a challenge to mainstream media, providing access to information that does not feature in, or is not available through, conventional media.

12.3   How are Health and Illness Constructed through Language?

In the previous section we saw that linguistic choices represent or 'construct' events, and how institutional and social power is exercised through language. In this section we consider how health and illness are constructed through language. The idea that health and illness are constructed through language may seem strange; after all, health and illness are conditions of the body or mind. However, we talk and think of health and illness as discrete and delimited qualities or entities, rather than as contingent states or processes, with the implication that health and illness are necessarily distinct, and one has either one or the other. The reality is, as Semino (2008: 176) explains, that illness and health are 'complex, subjective and poorly delineated'. Given the amorphous nature of illness (and health), these conditions lend themselves to being constructed through language. In what follows, we will consider how illness is constructed in both biomedical discourse and lay discourse, and examine an example of the interaction of the two frames of reference.

We start with an example of the technical language of medicine. The extract below is from a hospital admission summary (Fleischman, 2001: 477).

(6)   The patient is a 21-year-old Gravida III, Para I, Ab I black female at 32 weeks gestation, by her dates. She states that she has been having uterine contractions every thirty minutes, beginning two days prior to admission. The patient has history of vaginal bleeding on 10/23, at which time she reports she was seen in the Emergency Room and sent home. Additionally she does state that there is foetal movement. She denies any rupture of membranes. She states that she has a known history of sickle-cell trait.

For most of us, the most striking feature of this report is likely to be the use of technical terminology: the patient is a *Gravida III*, who has *'uterine contractions'*, reports *'foetal movement'* and denies *'rupture of membranes'*. The patient is unlikely to have used these expressions, and their meaning and medical significance is opaque to the non-specialist. The report foregrounds biomedical information, while the use of reportative verbs such as *'states …'*, *'reports …'* presents the patient's own account as subjective and potentially

---

STUDY ACTIVITY 12.3

Why do you think the language of medical reports has the form it does? How might this form of language impact on the treatment of the patient, positively or negatively?

---

unreliable. The language of the report has *medicalized* the patient, translating her experience into the biomedical discourse of the body and its functioning.

Lay discussions of health by individuals, or in the media, typically assume that 'good' health is the norm, and that it is the natural and rightful condition of the individual. Illness and disease are seen, and talked about, as intruders, which typically attack the healthy body from outside. Attacks take the form of a germ or virus, or an invading and occupying entity such as cancer. The idea that health is the norm, potentially under attack from outside, is reflected in the prominence given to the actual or supposed harmful effects of environmental pollutants, 'unhealthy' food or stress caused by factors such as the workplace. This binary depiction of health-versus-illness is a simplification of a complex reality, but it remains the central dichotomy in how we conceptualize and talk about health.

Linguistically, talk about illness among both health professionals and laypeople is characterized by both reification (talking about an abstraction as if it were a material entity) and metaphor (talking of one thing in terms of another). The construction of disease as an unwelcome and damaging intruder is an example of reification. When we talk about disease 'attacking' the healthy body we are using metaphor.

In western cultures health-talk makes use of two dominant and systematic metaphors. One is the metaphor of the body as a machine: we talk of providing the body with 'fuel' in the form of food or energy-giving supplements and drinks. The healthy or athletic body is spoken of as 'finely tuned'. Joints and organs, or whole bodies, *wear out*, as do machines, immune systems and minds *break down* and hearts and kidneys *fail*. Treatment, too, is described with mechanical metaphors: damaged organs are repaired, or replaced in *'spare part* surgery', and surgery is used to 'fix' the body. One effect of the body-as-machine metaphor is that it constructs the body as something distinct from the self, though it is the self that *experiences* illness or malfunction.

The other dominant metaphor is war. We talk of 'fighting' a cold, and *'the war against AIDS'*. Disease *attacks* the body, just as cancers and infections *invade* it. Medical science itself is said to be engaged in a war against disease. Sontag (1979) observes that cancer is seen as a form of invasion by mutant and virulent cells and is treated by bombardment with destructive rays or with toxic chemicals. The prominence of the war metaphor and its derivatives is seen in the frequency with which in everyday talk, as well as in interaction with medical professionals, patients are described as conducting a 'fight' or 'battle' with cancer, or other diseases.

As in science generally, metaphor is evident across the spectrum of medical discourse and plays a central role in describing the body and its processes. These processes and those of illness are modelled by experts in terms of metaphors. A scientific medicine would not be possible without metaphor (cf. Semino, 2008: 166).

Metaphor also features usefully in communication between doctors and patients, where it often overlaps with euphemism, as in expressions such as 'how are the waterworks?' or 'any trouble with the plumbing?' Such uses of metaphor are likely to be more accessible or familiar to patients than technical language, and help to reduce the distance between patient and doctor, and also help to mitigate potential embarrassment on the part of both patient and doctor.

While metaphors can be facilitative, some writers, notably Susan Sontag (1979), have argued that the war metaphor, with its emphasis on 'fighting disease', has the effect of obscuring the patient. While the illness is demonized as a malign aggressor, the sufferer is the metaphorical battleground, and these two metaphors may, according to Sontag, increase the sense of fear and helplessness experienced by the patient. Fleischman (2001) points out that war metaphors have both positive and negative aspects. The sense of 'fighting' a condition may mobilize (another martial metaphor!) a patient's resources, giving them purpose and motivation, and the recognition that others, including medical professionals, are also in the fight can provide a sense of support. However, the same metaphors may isolate the patient, making them feel that they are failing in the fight if their condition does not improve.

These martial and mechanical metaphors are ultimately connected to a 'scientific' and technological conception of medicine. The 'common-sense' and culture-bound character of such metaphors becomes apparent when we consider how illness is conceptualized in other cultures and traditions. In traditional Chinese medicine (Stibbe, 1996), for example, the body is a system in which energy flows, and illness is a blockage of energy, resulting from an imbalance, which is treated by redressing the balance. Although the central metaphorical structures of modern Western and Chinese traditional medicine are different, both illustrate the tendency to construct areas of experience around metaphors. In her study of medical metaphors, Van Rijn-Van Tongeren (1997) follows the view of Lakoff and Johnson (1980) that metaphors are not simply figurative stylistic devices, but are basic to the way in which we structure experience, thinking and understanding.

Given that most people have to consult medical professionals at some stage, and that encounters between laypeople and professionals are complicated by social and power relations, and by linguistic differences, medical encounters have been extensively studied. As Coupland, Robinson and Coupland (1994) observe, there is much research that shows that doctors assume a powerful role, placing the patient at a disadvantage. The doctor's power is manifested linguistically by unique privileges with regard to asking questions, controlling turn-taking, holding the floor and topic management. Coupland *et al.* are careful to point out that this power asymmetry is not necessarily an indication of a fault in medical care, as asymmetry is a feature of many forms of talk in a range of contexts, and some patients find the status and authority of medical professionals supportive or comforting.

A study by Mishler (1984) demonstrates how two distinct frames of reference come into contact in doctor–patient interaction. Mishler terms these 'the voice of medicine', which is based on a scientific, technical model of the body, health and disease, and the 'voice of the lifeworld', representing the 'natural attitude of the everyday world'. In the extracts from Mishler's study below we see how the two voices come from different frames of reference, and pursue different objectives.

Study Activity 12.4

Find examples of discussions of health issues in newspapers or magazines. What metaphors are used? Do you think the metaphors function to constrain or enhance the discussion?

(7a) D[OCTOR]:   Hm hm... now what do you mean by a sour stomach?
     P[ATIENT]:   ... what's a sour stomach? A heartburn like a heartburn or something
     D: does it burn over here?
     P: Yea:h

The Patient's reference to having a 'sour stomach' reflects the lifeworld of everyday experience, but is assimilated into the biomedical language of 'heartburn', and further extended by the question as to where it 'burns'. The Doctor later asks when the Patient gets the pain:

(7b) P: .... Wel:l when I eat something wrong
     D: how – how soon after you eat it?
     P: wel:l... probably an hour... maybe less
     D: about an hour
     P: maybe less... I've cheated and I've been drinking which I shouldn't have
           done
     D: does drinking make it worse?
     P: ( ) Ho ho uh ooh yes... especially the carbonation and the alcohol
     D: hm hm ... how much do you drink?
     P: I don't know.. enough to make me go to sleep at night..and that's quite a bit.

Here, the Patient talks of *'eating something wrong'*, but is vague (what does *'wrong'* mean in this context?). 'Wrong' also reflects a right/wrong opposition belonging to the domain of morality in the lifeworld. We can also wonder if the Patient here is 'confessing' her 'bad' behaviour to a powerful authority figure. The moral element appears later when the Patient says she has *'cheated'*. The Patient then uses two technical terms, *carbonation* and *alcohol*, contrasting with the personal confession *'I've cheated'*. Her response to the Doctor's question about how much she drinks is met with another lifeworld response *'enough to make me go to sleep'*.

Mishler suggests that what is going on here is that, for the Patient, the lifeworld of experience is represented symbolically, using ordinary language, while the Doctor is employing the purposive and rational discourse of the biomedical interview. The

---

STUDY ACTIVITY 12.5

1. Using a published personal account of physical or mental illness, consider the language the writer uses to construct their experience in light of the discussion above.
2. Susan Sontag (1979) argues that the 'war' and 'fight' metaphors used in relation to illness are dangerous because they simplify the reality of illness, and also imply that the patient is responsible for their own health. Do you think that such metaphors can be helpful to the patient or to medical staff?

Doctor's biomedical enquiry and the Patient's socio-relational talk are not compatible, as can be seen from the fact that the Doctor seeks to bring the interaction within the voice of medicine.

12.4   What is the Relationship between Language and the Law?

Language and the law are linked to a degree that leads Gibbons (1999: 156) to say that '*law is language*'. Law is a social institution which is both codified in and applied through language. While the law exists in part to protect citizens, legal language is specialized to a degree that excludes non-specialists. In addition, the law embodies social and institutional powers which are expressed through language. The complexity – and difficulty – of legal language is illustrated in this extract from a contract (Tiersma, 2008: 20).

(8)   I give, devise and bequeath all of said rest, residue and remainder of my property which I may own at the time of my death, real, personal and mixed, of whatsoever kind and nature, and wheresoever situate, including all property which I may acquire or to which I may become entitled after the execution of this will, in equal shares, absolutely and forever, to A and B.

One striking feature of this text is its 'written' character: it consists of a single sentence, which is itself composed of a series of subordinate clauses and apparently redundant repetitions. Readers unfamiliar with legal discourse are likely to find that the complex structure makes it impossible to recover the meaning of the text. In the first line, two key words are followed by synonyms – '*give, devise and bequeath*', and '*rest, residue and remainder*'. The term '*property*' is similarly qualified (after some intervening material) by the adjectives '*real, personal and mixed*'. Qualification is expressed in clauses such as 'which I *may acquire or to which I may become entitled…*'. In addition to this syntactic complexity, the vocabulary of the text includes familiar words used with specific technical meanings, such as '*devise*' and '*situate*' (here in adjectival function), and archaic usages such as '*wheresoever*'.

Tiersma points out that the passage is simply saying '*I give the rest of my estate to A and B*', leading us to ask why the language is so complex. Law, and hence legal language, must

---

STUDY ACTIVITY 12.6

Many consumer items and services come with a legal document: the agreement governing the use of a credit card, a warranty or the terms of an insurance policy. Find examples of such documents. How easy or difficult are they are to understand? What difficulties are lay consumers likely to have with such language, and to what problems might it give rise?

be precise, and avoid vagueness and ambiguity. The compression and apparent redundancy in the text ensure that all possible circumstances and interpretations are accounted for.

The complex, technical nature of legal language becomes problematic when laypeople come into contact with the law. Spoken forms of legal language can be similarly complex and arcane, and legal procedures from the police caution to court proceedings have a formal and ritualistic character, stemming from the fact that legal discourse must frequently address two audiences: the person or persons directly addressed, and a present or future legal audience. Most of us will be familiar with the caution (the '*Miranda*' in the USA) from film and television. The caution must be delivered in complete form and without interruption, because, in addition to serving as a warning to the suspect, it will be reported in court, confirming that due process has been observed. Legal language is not solely or even primarily transactional or propositional, but rather a form of institutional discourse designed to assert the power and authority of the law (Gibbons, 1999: 158).

These characteristics of legal language are evident in the exchange below (Hall, 2004: 75).

(9)   POLICE: Do you recall having a conversation with a middle-aged female, being
                   the driver of a vehicle stopped in front of you?
      SUSPECT: I would not call it a conversation
      POLICE: Can you tell me what it was?
      SUSPECT: I would, would more like say an exchange. A conversation's a rational
                   speech between two people.
      POLICE: Do you recall what type of vehicle the female was driving on the date
                   that you spoke to her?

The police interview is not primarily to do with facts, but with assembling legally relevant information regarding motives, intent, planning and knowledge. In this extract we see this information being elicited by the officer, who uses formal expressions such as '*recall*' and '*vehicle*', rather than the everyday '*remember*' and '*car*', as well as elaborate forms such as '*having a conversation*' and '*middle-aged female*'. Out of context, these forms appear stilted and artificial (and are often parodied for comic effect). They act as markers of the officer's status and authority, but also serve the ultimate objective of the interview, which is to produce a precise and detailed written document admissible as evidence in court. As this brief extract demonstrates, the language of the report is determined by the police officer, and is in effect a construction of the suspect's version of events.

This can be seen when we consider how the interview is driven and shaped by institutional objectives. When the Suspect contests the officer's use of '*conversation*', the officer asks the Suspect to provide a different term (the suspect's alternative version may contain material relevant to the case). The officer disregards the Suspect's argument, and switches immediately to another topic relevant to the objective of building acceptable evidence. The officer has unique privileges with regard to asking questions, and controlling the topics discussed. In this extract, the officer employs a standard technique of asking a series of questions using a 'frame' ('*do you recall…*') to establish the Suspect's state of knowledge in a series of steps.

The evidence-building objective of police interviews leads to forms of interaction that are unexpected in ordinary discourse. An article by Stokoe and Edwards (2008) examines the function of 'silly questions' in police interviews. 'Silly' questions are questions to which the answer is predictable, but which are necessary to establish the Suspect's state of knowledge or intention:

(10)   P[OLICE OFFICER]:   did you know whose window it is?
       S[USPECT]:   mm
       P: mm
       P: D'you have permission to smash it basically?
       S   No.

                                                          (Stokoe and Edwards, 2008: 93)

Where the interviewer's objective is to elicit a confession, questioning may be direct and coercive. In the next example (Hall, 2008: 69), the interviewer's questions embody the assumption that the suspect carried out the attack, although guilt has not been confirmed or admitted at this stage. The officer is ostensibly attempting to establish a motive for the attack mentioned, but repeats the question *'why did you do it?'* in different forms. The Suspect resists by responding to the *presupposition* that he committed the crime, rather than the issue of motivation.

(11)   POLICE: John it was a brutal attack on that girl
       SUSPECT: I know
       POLICE: … I want to know why you did it, I want to know what made you do it.
       SUSPECT: I didn't do it.
       POLICE: If we knew why you did it and what made you do it, well perhaps we
                  could understand…
       SUSPECT: …Yes
       POLICE: well, wouldn't you feel better if you told us what it was all about?
       SUSPECT: I didn't kill her

The language of courtrooms is also highly structured, controlled and ritualized. Linguistic power and privileges of communication in the courtroom are mainly controlled by the judge and the lawyers. Questioning is central to the legal process, functioning as in interviews to establish relevant facts and to ascertain intentions and states of mind, but also and more commonly to challenge witness testimony. In adversarial traditions, such as English law, questioning aims to make friendly witnesses appear credible, and hostile witnesses appear unreliable.

   Danet and Kermish (1978) ranked questions in court according to the degree of coerciveness they embody. Open questions such as *'Can (could, would) you tell us what happened?'*, which allow the witness to construct a narrative, are the least coercive. Such questions are sometimes referred to as 'requestions', which pose a question in the form of a polite request. Information questions such as 'what did you do then?' are more coercive, as they constrain the response to particular items of information. 'Yes/no' questions such as 'did you then remove the carpet?' are particularly constraining, as they embody, and hence insinuate, the possibility that the addressee did remove the carpet, and limit their response to either confirmation or denial. The most coercive form of question is in effect a speculative accusation, taking the form of a statement accompanied by a question tag, such as *'You then moved the stained carpet, didn't you?'*

Case Study 12.2

Diana Eades has researched the linguistic dimension of disadvantage before the law. Eades (2008) notes that speakers of non-standard or second dialects are frequently stigmatized, and regarded as uneducated, lazy or ignorant. In Australia, Aborigines are 20 times more likely to be subject to the criminal justice system than non-Aborigines, and the linguistic problems that arise in their interactions with the legal system demonstrate the complexity and sensitivity of language difference when minority speakers come into contact with the authorities. Differences of phonology, grammar and meaning between dialects commonly give rise to miscommunication and misunderstanding. Eades argues that while Aboriginal English varieties resemble General Australian English, there are significant pragmatic differences which are subtle and liable to give rise to misunderstandings as to meaning or attitude. Silence is one area of difference, and the importance attributed to silence in many legal systems means that cultural conventions governing the use of silence can be a significant source of misunderstanding. Among Aborigines it is normal to respond to a question by a period of silence, before providing an answer. Eades observes that in the legal system of Australia, and in white society generally, responding to a question with silence is typically interpreted negatively, perhaps as indicating that the person has something to withhold or hide (cf. Kurzon, 2008). In addition to such inferences, legal professionals tend to interpret silence as indicating that the suspect has nothing to say, or is refusing to speak, and move directly to the next question. The consequences of this misinterpretation of silence can be serious: Eades (1996) cites the case of an Aboriginal woman who appealed against her conviction for murder on the grounds that her lawyers had not waited for her to answer questions. They had concluded she had nothing to say, while she inferred that they had no interest in hearing what she had to say.

Another pragmatic feature of Aboriginal communicative style is 'gratuitous concurrence'. Aboriginal cultures place importance on preserving harmony and Aborigines often appear to agree to a 'yes/no' question, regardless of whether they have understood the question, or do in fact agree. In a police interview, appearing to agree to a proposition can have unfortunate consequences.

The implications of Eades's findings extend to other 'linguistically different' groups, including children, the deaf, intellectually disabled people and members of non-dominant cultures or sub-cultures, all of whom are potentially disadvantaged when interacting with the law and other institutions.

The formal and ritualistic conduct of proceedings, and the asymmetrical distribution of rights with regard to asking questions and initiating exchanges, serve legal ends in demonstrating that procedures are followed, but may be intimidating and constricting for witnesses. Conley, O'Barr and Lind (1979) investigated witness testimony, distinguishing between 'powerless' and powerful styles. Powerless style is characterized by the use of markers of tentativeness, including hedges, such as *'sort of'*, *'I guess'*, *'I think so'*, noticeably polite forms of expression, such as *'Could you please repeat that if you wouldn't mind'*, tags, as in *'it's obvious, isn't it?'*, and the use of exaggerated stress, as in *'he was SO upset'*. The use of powerless style may lead the jury to conclude that the witness is unsure of their ground, and hence unreliable. We can contrast this with a more powerful 'narrative' style, which is factual, confident and forthright, as in: *'Yes. I was late that day, and arrived at work about 8. Mr Smith was already in his office, and I remember that he waved as I passed his door.'* We can compare this style with the style Conley *et al.* call 'fragmented':

(12) W: I was late
      B: What time did you arrive at work?
      W.   8
      L: 8 am?
      W: Yes
      L: Did you see Mr Blueskies at that time?
      W: Yes. He was there....

Fragmented style allows the speaker to assert power, and can be used strategically, as the barrister has to work harder to elicit information. However, it may also produce a negative impression of the witness as appearing to withhold information, or having something to conceal.

12.5 Summary

In this chapter we have looked at the ways in which language choices can be used to construct representations of complex events within a framework of ideological assumptions. In the case of the media, language choices play a central role in the depiction of events, groups and processes and thus have a role in the reproduction and perpetuation of social and ideological structures. In our discussion of the language of health and illness, we have seen that issues and experiences of health and illness are constructed through language, and in particular through the use of metaphor. Finally, we considered how the language of the law, while necessarily elaborately codified, frequently gives rise to problems of communication, and ultimately may disadvantage individuals and groups. The fact that language plays a central, and arguably constitutive, role in all three areas affirms the need for continued and rigorous linguistic studies of them.

Study Questions

1. Using material from newspapers or broadcast media aimed at minority communities, conduct an analysis of a selection of newsworthy items, and the ways in which events and participants are represented.

2. Examine a selection of discussions of a topical issue (for example immigration, healthcare, education, the European Union) from the media. How do linguistic choices express positions in relation to the issue? What dominant discourse(s) emerge?

3. Find examples of public health problems in either a published form (e.g. a newspaper or magazine) or a debate on the radio or television.

4. Using a personal account of an individual's experience of illness,

consider how the experience is constructed through language.

5. We have seen that legal discourse is intimately linked to the exercise of social power, and that those who are not familiar with the law, or who are from a non-dominant or minority group, may be disadvantaged before the law. What types of research can provide evidence for the need to recognize linguistic disadvantage before the law?

Recommended Reading

Coulthard, Malcolm and Alison Johnson. 2007. *An Introduction to Forensic Linguistics: Language in Evidence*. Oxford: Routledge. This book provides a solid all-round general introduction to language and the law, written by two professional linguists. The first part of the book deals with language in the law, while the second looks in detail at the work of forensic linguistics. There are discussions on methodologies and data collection, as well as research tasks.

Durant, Alan and Marina Lambrou. 2009. *Language and Media: A Resource Book for Students*. Oxford: Routledge. This book does not assume any prior knowledge of linguistics or media, and presents a range of analytical frameworks for exploring the use of language across a range of media genres.

Fairclough, Norman. 2003. *Analysing Discourse: Textual Analysis for Social Research*. London: Routledge. This is an accessible introductory textbook on a form of language analysis with a consistently social perspective. Illustrated by and investigated through a range of real texts, from written texts to a television debate about the monarchy and a radio broadcast about the Lockerbie bombing.

Gwyn, Richard. 2001. *Communicating Health and Illness*. London: SAGE. Gwyn's book offers a systematic and theoretically informed approach to the language of medicine as discourse, and looks at how we talk and write about the body, illness, cure and treatment. As well as chapters dealing with metaphor in talk about health, and how health and disease are presented in the media, the book explores themes of power in health contexts, and the role of narrative.

Johnstone, Barbara. 2007. *Discourse Analysis*, 2nd edn. Oxford: Wiley-Blackwell. An introductory text for students taking their first course in linguistic approaches to discourse. It considers a variety of approaches to the subject, including Critical Discourse Analysis, Conversation Analysis, interactional and variationist sociolinguistics, ethnography, corpus linguistics and other qualitative and quantitative methods. It features detailed descriptions of the results of Discourse Analysts' work.

chapter 13

Translation and Interpreting

Malcolm Edwards

Chapter Outline

Learning Outcomes

After reading this chapter, you should be able to

- discuss the role and importance of translation in contemporary life;
- discuss problems in translation theory and practice;
- understand the role of linguistic, pragmatic and sociocultural aspects of translation;
- discuss the challenges posed by audio-visual translation;
- reflect on the role of the interpreter as translator and mediator.

Applied Linguistics, First Edition. Edited by Li Wei.
© 2014 John Wiley & Sons, Ltd. Published 2014 by John Wiley & Sons, Ltd.

Key Terms

- Audio-visual translation
- Discourse
- Equivalence
- Formal/dynamic
- Literal/free
- Pragmatics
- Source/target text
- Translation

13.1   Introduction

When J.K. Rowling's debut novel, *Harry Potter and the Philosopher's Stone*, was published in the United States a year after the British edition, the title was changed to *Harry Potter and the* Sorcerer's *Stone*. In the Arabic translation of the same book, 'Privet Close', where the Dursley family live, becomes 'Privet *Street*'. These two facts may appear to be unrelated: one reflects a decision by a publisher to substitute one English word with another, while in the second case, the Arabic translator has replaced an English word with an Arabic word with a similar but not identical meaning. In the first case, the change of 'philosopher' to 'sorcerer' is motivated by the need for a title that evokes wizardry and magic. In the second case, the use of the Arabic word for '*street*' is motivated by the lack of an equivalent for '*close*' in Arabic.

Our examples illustrate several important features of translation. Firstly, translation is a process of making decisions. Secondly, choices about how to translate are motivated, in the sense that they are determined by factors including the availability in the target language of a similar term, or the need to reach the audience who will read the translation. A related feature is that the lack of equivalence between languages means that translation is seldom exact. Finally, as our examples show, translation entails both loss and gain of meaning: 'street' is less specific than 'close', and a sorcerer is a magician, but a philosopher is not. In this chapter we explore these themes – motivated decision, equivalence, and loss and gain, and their wider implications for the theory and practice of translation.

13.2   What *is* Translation?

The idea of translation that most of us have is likely to involve the reproduction of a source text (ST) in a target text (TT) which faithfully represents the content, meaning, spirit and style of the original. In practice, this ideal is rarely, if ever, achievable, and moreover, the term 'translation' itself subsumes a diverse range of forms and practices. Consider this example from Hatim and Munday (2004: 15):

(1a)   Sample text
    ST: *Couvercle et cuves en polycarbonate. Matériau haute résistance utilisé pour les hublots d'avion. Résiste à de hautes températures et aux chocs*

[Lid and bowls in polycarbonate. High resistance material used for aircraft windows. Resists high temperatures and shocks]

Tableau de commandes simple et fonctionnel. 3 commandes suffisent à maîtriser Compact 3100.
[Simple and functional control panel. 3 controls suffice to master Compact 3100.]

(1b)   Target text

Workbowls and lid are made from polycarbonate, the same substance as the windows of Concorde. It's shatterproof and won't melt with boiling liquids or crack under pressure

Technically advanced, simple to use: just on, off or pulse.

Notice that the TT is not an exact or even close version of the ST: material has been added, omitted and changed, but it is undoubtedly a translation fit for its purpose. As this example shows, the ambit of 'translation' as either a set of products or a set of practices subsumes a diversity of forms, products and practices, including prototypical translations, interlinear glosses, such as the bracketed translation in Text 1, summaries of the type found in consecutive translation, and adaptations, such as Fitzgerald's translation of the Rubaiyyat of Omar Khayyam, which bears only a notional resemblance to its ST.

In considering what 'translation' is, we therefore need an approach that allows us to identify and explore the commonalities between the different forms and realizations of translation.

Here we can invoke the work of Roman Jakobson (1959), who distinguished three types of translation:

1.   Intralingual: '…interpretation of verbal signs by means of other signs of the same language';
2.   Interlingual: '…interpretation of verbal signs by means of some other language';
3.   Intersemiotic: '…interpretation of verbal signs by means of signs of non-verbal sign systems'.

Replacing '*philosopher*' with '*sorcerer*' is an instance of intralingual translation. Jakobson observes that intralingual translation does not guarantee complete equivalence between the original and the 'translated' term, because synonyms within a language are rarely exactly equivalent: '*abdomen*' and '*stomach*' are potential translations of each other, but each term is appropriate to particular contexts. '*Stomach*' can denote an area of the body or a specific internal organ.

Interlingual translation is the prototype form of translation, which Jakobson calls 'translation proper'. Jakobson notes that there is ordinarily no full equivalence between languages, and gives the example of the word '*cheese*', which is not an exact equivalent to its apparent Russian counterpart ('*syr*'), as the Russian word does not include cottage cheese.

Jakobson's third category covers the use of signs and symbols. An example of intersemiotic translation is a sign on a gate depicting a ferocious dog, with or without the accompanying words '*Beware of the Dog*'.

STUDY ACTIVITY 13.1

1. Where can we find examples of translation in everyday life?
2. You are at a railway ticket office and the person in front of you, a Greek speaker, is having difficulty making her/himself understood. You know some very basic Greek, and mediate between the ticket seller and the customer, using a mixture of English, Greek, gestures and goodwill, and the transaction is successfully accomplished. What features does this instance of communication share with 'real' translating? In what ways do you think it is different from 'real' translating?

The importance of Jakobson's threefold typology of translation is that it recognizes that all three forms share essential features, and that to privilege one form ignores these essential similarities. Taking this idea forward, it becomes clear that regarding 'translation' exclusively as a professionalized and specialized activity prevents us from understanding the relationships between what happens in translating and other forms of communicative activity.

Until the middle of the last century, writing on translation was primarily concerned with the translation of literature, regarded as the most difficult and 'highest' form of translation. Work in this tradition tended to be subjective and prescriptive, either justifying a particular translation or method, or critically comparing translations. With the emergence of linguistics as a discipline that offered systematic models of language and the promise of understanding problems of meaning, interest turned to the application of linguistic concepts and methods to problems of translation. In the past two decades, the study of translation has been influenced by developments in sociolinguistics and Discourse Analysis, as well as by neighbouring disciplines, such as cultural studies. Linguistics-based studies of translation have enabled the development of systematic and neutral approaches to translation as a linguistic and communicative phenomenon: a communicative act in which a new act of communication is created out of an existing one (Hatim and Mason, 1990: 1).

From another quarter, the so-called *cultural turn* (Munday, 2012, Chapter 8) has challenged the notion of translation as a predominantly linguistic exercise, and drawn attention to the need to recognize the variability of the concept of 'translation' at different periods, as well as the place of translations in cultural and literary systems.

In this brief discussion we have seen that the term 'translation' covers a multifarious set of activities and products, and that a restrictive or prescriptive approach to defining translation restricts the potential for understanding translation as a communicative process.

13.3 What Happens in Translation?

If translation is an act of communication, it is a singularly complex one. In translation a text in one language or code is converted into a text in a different language or code, with the translator acting as a mediator who interprets the source text and decides how the various aspects of that text are represented in the target text. This task would be straightforward if words and other linguistic expressions were simply equivalent labels for universal concepts. The reality, as Jakobson's *'cheese'* example shows, is that languages represent the world of objects and experience in different ways. The words *'uncle'* and *'aunt'* correspond to two pairs of unrelated words in Arabic, according to whether the relationship is on the paternal ('amm/'amma) or maternal (xa:l/xa:la) side of the family. In this case, we can find equivalents, but often, as Baker (1992, 17) shows, there may be no equivalent at all. English distinguishes lexically between *cool and cold*, but Arabic has only one word (*ba:rid*) for both *'cool'* and *'cold'*.

Non-equivalence between grammatical forms also presents problems. In Arabic, nouns have a dual form, denoting two objects, as well as singular and plural forms. The translation of *'she has children'* into Arabic must thus indicate whether there are two children (requiring the dual) or more than two. And translating the Arabic sentence *sa:far ila amri:ka wa tajawwaz* (literally, (he) *went to America and married*) requires the addition of the pronoun *'he'*. The translator has also to decide whether to translate the verbs as simple past forms or as present perfect, as Arabic lacks this distinction. Jakobson (1959) points out that what can be said in one language can be said, more or less, in another, but this is normally at the cost of both loss and gain of meaning.

Translation, however, is not solely or even primarily concerned with word- or grammar-level correspondence, but with language used in context. To translate the sentence *'You're leaving'*, we need to know who is being addressed, as many languages distinguish between familiar and polite forms of pronouns. We will also have to determine the significance of the use of the contracted form *'you're'*, which is associated with informal contexts, and may indicate something about the relationship between speaker and addressee. Beyond these structural features, we must assess intended function of the sentence within its context: is it simply an observation, an instruction or a command? Does it express sorrow, pleasure or anger? All of these factors will bear on the decision as to how to translate.

Outside of books on linguistics (and translation), translation is usually concerned with texts. Texts are made up of networks of grammatical, semantic and rhetorical relationships which determine the connections between various parts of the text, and give it unity and coherence. The connective elements in texts are frequently inferred in the process of interpretation, rather than being overt or explicit, as Example 2 illustrates.

(2)   The Minister urges caution, and rightly so. Threats, even veiled ones, are dangerous. A respectful approach, acknowledging the realities of nuclear weaponry in the Middle East, is likely to prove successful, though no perfect solution is possible.

To understand the text the reader must identify the function of each sentence. The first sentence expresses support for the Minister's position. The second sentence elaborates the reasons for caution, and warns against the use of threats. The third recommends an approach, while acknowledging that there is no perfect solution.

Understanding a text is therefore not simply a matter of reading linguistic clues, but an active process of engagement to recreate intended meaning, using both knowledge of the world and knowledge of how similar texts are constructed. Translating this text will require a consideration of how the target language expresses similar functions and textual relationships. Often it will be necessary to make the functions and links explicit, by adding material such as: 'in our opinion ... Mr Straw is right ...', ' because threats are dangerous ...'.

Blum-Kulka (2004) provides a rich illustration of how the linguistic levels of meaning, grammar, discourse and pragmatics interact within a text, using the example of a Hebrew translation of the opening lines of Harold Pinter's play *Old Times*.

(3)   1.   KATE: Dark (pause)   kehah (dark)
      2.   DEELEY: Fat or thin?   shmena or raza (fat or thin)
      3.   KATE: Fuller than me, I think   yoter mlea mimeni (more full than me)

Here the first word, '*dark*', in English is non-specific. We do not know whether the 'dark' Kate is talking about is a person or an object. The Hebrew word *kehah* is used of people, and the translation thus makes it clear that Kate is talking about a person. The Hebrew word is also marked for gender on adjectives, making it clear that the person is female. The deliberate use of non-specific isolated words to create curiosity in the hearer is thus disrupted in the translation, but the disambiguation of '*dark*' impacts on the following text, as the person/object ambiguity continues in English with the words '*fat or thin*', whose Hebrew translations again refer to people.

In this section we have seen that translation is not a straightforward process of exchanging meanings between languages on an item-for-item basis. This is because meaning is not restricted to individual words or sentences, but derives from the interaction between linguistic expressions, context and the reader. To answer the question at the start of this section, translation is possible, but is rarely, if ever, exact.

STUDY ACTIVITY 13.2

Translate this extract from *The Mill on the Floss* into contemporary English. What problems arise in relation to the vocabulary of the text, the form and style of the writing and the dialogue, and the cultural dimensions of the incident described? What decisions do you have to make, and what are the effects of those decisions in terms of loss and gain?

'Do you call this acting the part of a man and a gentleman, sir?' Tom said, in a voice of harsh scorn ...

'What do you mean?' answered Philip haughtily.

'Mean? Stand farther from me, lest I should lay hands on you ... I mean taking advantage of a young girl's foolishness and ignorance to get her to have secret meetings with you. I mean trifling with the reputation of a respectable family.'

13.4   Literal or Free?

Historically, the central debate regarding translation has revolved around whether translations should be 'literal' or 'free', and the literal/free dichotomy continues to be a feature of discussions of translation today. The debate is, in essence, to do with how translations should be done, and not how they are done. Strict literalism in translation in which there is close adherence to the structure and vocabulary of the ST will often result in a TT that is incomprehensible, as in this excerpt from a tourist brochure.

(4)   *What offer the civilisation beside the nature? The animals let see in the fresh morning. Out of the waves snap gasp for breath pikes and eels.*

Literalism is not only a problem of vocabulary and structure. Consider now this text, which advertises banking services in the Arabian Gulf (Hatim and Munday, 2004: 21).

(5)   X Bank offers banking services by telephone. The Telebanking System greets you with 'assalamu alaykum', deals with enquiries and transactions fast and says goodbye 'fi aman allah'.

This translation contains some literalisms, but the intended message is clear. The problem here is that the form of the message is not appropriate for the primary target audience, which is English-speaking and largely non-Muslim. 'Free' translation can also produce incongruous or unfortunate effects. The American linguist Nida proposed that the biblical *'greeted them with a holy kiss'* be translated as *'gave them a hearty handshake all round'*. Nida's aim was to acculturate the text to Anglo-Saxon cultural conventions, but the resulting translation is incongruous.

There are a number of problems with the literal/free dichotomy. One problem is that the terms 'literal' and 'free' have no precise or agreed definition: does 'literal' mean keeping to the ST meaning and forms, as in the first text above, with the result that the meaning is largely lost? Or does it mean translating closely, but preserving important aspects of the ST, resulting in a text that is unidiomatic and incongruous? And does 'free' mean that the translator has the freedom to translate as she or he sees fit? A further problem is that the question of literal or free translation has been discussed as if the two were in an 'either/or' relationship, whereas the reality is that translators employ more or less literal or more or less free strategies, often within a single text.

Nida (1964) proposed that the problem could be reformulated in terms of different forms of equivalence, which he called 'formal' and 'dynamic'. Formal equivalence aims to closely reflect the form and content of the ST, while dynamic equivalence aims to produce an equivalent effect on the reader to that experienced by the reader of the original text. Nida's formal/dynamic dichotomy is appealing, as it recognizes that 'literal' and 'free' are not all-or-nothing choices, and that sometimes it is important to capture or reflect specific features of the original text, and at others to alter the ST with the aim of reaching the audience.

'Formal' equivalence differs from literal equivalence, as the qualification 'as closely as possible' indicates. A formal translation aims to capture the meaning of the original, without compromising the target text or impeding understanding. In dynamic equivalence *'...the relationship between receptor and message should be substantially the same as that which*

Case Study 13.1

Nida's proposals were instrumental in causing a shift in thinking about translation towards a more nuanced view of translation strategies and the role of the receiver or reader of the translation. At the same time, the proposals raise further questions. Nida describes 'formal' and 'dynamic' sketchily, and does not explain how to 'do' a formal or dynamic translation. Another difficulty arises with texts where form and content are very closely linked, as in some types of literature, poetry, advertising and religious or ritual texts. More problematic is the question of 'effect' on the target audience. How can effects be assessed or predicted by the translator, and can we be sure of the 'effect' of a text in its original cultural context? Lawrence Venuti, for example, has argued that Anglo-American translations of creative works (literature, film, plays) display a strategy Venuti calls domestication (Venuti, 1995). Domesticating translations reduces or eliminates 'foreign' characteristics of translated texts to make the language and culture of the original text familiar to the readers of the translation. Venuti sees this process as producing a flattening and homogeneous style of translation which deprives the text of vital features. To counter domestication, Venuti calls for a foreignizing strategy, which consciously defamiliarizes the translation through the use of close representations or borrowings of aspects of the language of the original text. Venuti's 'foreignizing' approximates to literal translation, but involves deliberate manipulation of the target text to make the reader aware of its foreignness.

STUDY ACTIVITY 13.3

1. What types of text are most likely to need a literal translation, and why? Which types require a dynamic approach?
2. Example (6), 'Jabberwocky', given below, shows that 'meaning' embraces more than the semantics of words and sentences. Are there other forms of language use which have problems for translation because they rely on language-specific features?
3. Below are two translations of the opening of Genesis, the first book of the Bible. Which is 'formal', in Nida's terms, and which 'dynamic'? Which do you think works best and why?.
   a. King James Version (1611)
      1:1   *In the beginning God created the heaven and the earth.*
      1:2   *And the earth was without form, and void; and darkness was upon the face of the deep. And the spirit of God moved upon the face of the waters.*
      1:3   *And God said, 'Let there be light': And there was light*
   b. New English Bible (1970)
      1:1   *In the beginning God created the heavens and the earth.*
      1:2   *Now the earth was without shape, and empty, and darkness was moving over the surface of the watery deep, but the Spirit of God was moving over the surface of the water.*
      1:3   *And God said, 'Let there be light': And there was light.*

Case Study 13.2

In the 1990s a number of publications appeared that applied linguistic ideas and methods, in particular pragmatics and Discourse Analysis, to the analysis of translation. Hatim and Mason's *Discourse and the Translator* (1990) and *The Translator as Communicator* (1997b) developed a text-based, multi-level approach to understanding translation, founded on the principle that language in use (discourse) reflects socio-cultural action and social relations. Through close analysis of a range of real texts, Hatim and Mason identify the interactions between textual strategies, pragmatics, semiotics and register (variation in language according to domain, activity or social relations) and demonstrate how these elements impact, positively and negatively, on the translation process.

Baker's 1992 book *In Other Words* also takes a linguistics-based approach to translation, presenting principles of lexical semantics, cohesion, text organization and pragmatics in relation to textual structure, textual function and coherence, and demonstrates how these principles can be applied in the translation of a variety of text-types, including adverts, novels and technical texts.

Linguistics and discourse-based approaches to translation can provide insights into textual and communicative strategies, how these vary between languages and how they impact on translation. They also have the advantage of being based in independently established principles and theories, and thus allow a systematic and objective perspective on translation. However, the focus on linguistic features has been argued by cultural theorists such as Venuti (1995) to restrict the scope for consideration of significant factors which transcend the text, such as authorial intention, the function of the text within its sociocultural context and the effect of cultural, commercial and ideological factors on translations. Keith Harvey's analysis of 'camp' (Harvey, 2004) is a revealing demonstration of how linguistic and cultural perspectives can be combined to illuminate problems of language register, culture and the relationships between translations, their audiences and commercial pressures.

---

existed between the original receptors and the message' (Nida, 1964). Nida's proposals can be seen as moving from a polarizing and prescriptive approach to a more graded and realistic position, reflecting the reality of translation practice and, importantly, including the audience as a factor in the translation process.

The literal/free dichotomy is related to the problem of form versus content. What should a translator do when form and meaning are indissolubly linked, as in instances of wordplay, jokes and 'poetic' forms of expression? Language that creatively exploits sound patterns, rhythm, meaning or other properties of words is notoriously difficult to translate, and is found in many everyday contexts. The slogan '*Beanz Meanz Heinz*' achieves its effect through a combination of rhythm, assonance, rhyme and the graphic innovation of misspelling the first two words while preserving their phonetic form. The features of coincidence between phonetic and orthographic forms, and the assonance, are unlikely to have identical or close correspondents in another language.

An extreme example of form as content is found in the opening lines of Lewis Carroll's nonsense poem 'Jabberwocky'. The first verse is given below, followed by a translation into French.

(6) (1a) T'was brillig, and the slithy toves
           Did gyre and gimble in the wabe:
           All mimsy were the borogroves,
           And the mome raths outgrabe.

     (b)   Il brilgue: les tôves lubricilleux
           Se gyrent en vrillant dans le guave.
           Enmîmés sont les gougebosqueux,
           Et le mômerade horsgrave.

The English verse observes the rules of English syntax, but the content words are inventions, designed to resemble actual English words, and it is this reflexive invention of non-existent but recognizable words that gives the poem much of its meaning. The French translation succeeds in capturing the essential element of language play, and this is possible in large part because English and French share many cognate words, and both cultures have a tradition of heroic poetry. 'Jabberwocky' is an extreme example of the primacy of 'form' over 'meaning', but playful and creative use of linguistic features is not limited to literature, and can be found in genres ranging from casual conversation to political oratory.

──────────────────────────── 13.5 What Happens in Subtitling?

Subtitling involves translation of dialogue in visual media such as film into written text on the screen. Subtitling is a constrained form of translation, which places considerable demands on the translator. The transition from speech to writing means that significant features of spoken language, such as intonation, pitch and volume, are lost. Similarly, dialectal, varietal and idiolectal features, such as non-standard pronunciation or vocabulary and character-specific use of verbal mannerisms, pose problems for subtitles. Subtitles are usually limited to between 33 and 40 keyboard character spaces to one line, with a further restriction to two lines appearing on screen at a time. Subtitles must also track the dialogue, but must be visible for at least two seconds, which causes problems with fast-moving dialogue, or when multiple speakers are speaking in a scene.

These constraints of space and time result in a reduction of the dialogue, with consequences for the relaying of meaning and for coherence, as when, for example, links to preceding or overlapping speech identifiable in spoken dialogue may not be easily retrievable from the abbreviated content of the subtitles. The challenges for the translator are thus many: how to provide a coherent, readable and representative version of the dialogue within the time and space allowed.

Hatim and Mason (1997: 85) analyse a sequence from the 1992 film *Un Coeur en Hiver*, to show that the subtitles fail to represent significant features of the characters' speech and distort the nature of the interaction between them.

(7) **Source**   **Subtitle**

CAMILLE:	Ça vous convient	Like it?
	that you suits?	
STEPHANE:	Oui, m...	Yes, but...
	Yes b...	
CAMILLE:	Dites	Go on
	Say (it)	
STEPHANE:	Vous n'avez pas joué un	You took it a bit
	peu vite?	fast
	did you not play a bit fast?	

Hatim and Mason note that the question *'does that suit you?'*, is intended as a challenge, but the translation *'like it?'*, is casual and neutral. Stephane's reply, in the French dialogue, is incomplete, though the translation consists of the word 'but'. What is missed here is the fact that Stephane is characteristically reserved and non-committal, and this is reflected in his habit of not finishing sentences. The translation turns his non-committal *'m...'* into a more emphatic 'but'. Stephane's indirectness and evasiveness is seen in his next turn, which in French is a question, mitigated both by the use of the negative, and the phrase *'un peu'* [a little]. The subtitle is a blunt statement: *'you took it a bit fast'*. The interaction between Camille and Stephane is a struggle between provocation and refusal to be provoked, but as Hatim and Mason point out, if we go by the English subtitles it comes to resemble a violin lesson, with Camille as a surly pupil and Stephane as a diffident tutor. Hatim and Mason's point is that, to understand what is happening, we need to understand what is being expressed and revealed to us indirectly, rather than what is said. In this case, the subtitles convey a pattern of implied meaning and interactional dynamics that is significantly different to that in the original dialogue. Hatim and Mason emphasize that their intention is not to criticize the translator, but to show how important pragmatic features of dialogue may be changed or lost in subtitling.

Non-standard varieties of languages are also problematic. O'Sullivan (2011: 144) points out that subtitles place a burden on viewers, and subtitlers tend to avoid factors likely to decrease reading and comprehension, such as interruptions, inconsistencies and unusual forms of language. For these reasons, subtitles typically offer a regularized and standardized form of language. O'Sullivan cites the case of the film *La Haine* (1995), directed by Mathieu Kassovitz, in which the dialogue is composed of slang forms, *verlan* (a back-slang), Americanisms and Arabic expressions and is characterized by use of non-standard grammar. The original subtitles translated the dialogue into a variety of English with a heavy admixture of African-American English, which had the effect of eliminating the linguistic differences between the three main protagonists of the film.

Similarly, code-switching (the use of two or more languages within a speech event) may conflict with the need for regularized and easily processable dialogue. In this example from Istvan Szabo's film *Colonel Redl* (1984), four languages are used in a single scene, but only two (German and French) are subtitled.

(8)   Young Kubinyi (English):   Harry, come here [said to the dog].
      Grandmother Kubinyi   Sit down, Sit-DOWN!
      (in English, to the dog):
      Grandfather Kubinyi   Tell me Redl. The Kaiser's empire is so vast
      (German):   and there are so many peoples in it that I do
                                   not know from which part of his Majesty's
                                   peoples you come.
      Redl (German):   I was born in Galizia.
      Grandfather (German):   Polish? [unhesitatingly]
      Redl (German):   No. My father is Ruthenian, of German
                                   descent. As far as I know, my mother's
                                   grandfather was Hungarian.
                                   Yes. They were Hungarian(s).
      Grandfather (German):   Fine. Then you must have some Hungarian
                                   blood in you.
      Redl (German):   *Yes* [not subtitled]. My mother used to sing a
                                   Hungarian lullaby: A Csitari Hegyek Alatt.

(Redl sings the first verse of the song in Hungarian, which is not subtitled)

      Grandmother (French):   **Il est très gentil** ['he's very nice' (not
                                   subtitled)]
      Kubinyi (French):   He doesn't speak French, Grandmother.
      Grandmother (French):   **Il faut apprendre mon chéri** ['one should
                                   learn, my dear' (not subtitled)]

At the start of the scene, young Kubinyi and his grandmother speak to the dog in English,
which is left unsubtitled in the English-language subtitles. Grandfather Kubinyi addresses
Redl in German, which is the main language of the film, and Redl responds, also in
German. After Redl has sung a verse of a song in Hungarian (unsubtitled) the Kubinyis
switch to French. The mixing of languages in the film reflects the language practices of the
aristocracy at the time, but at the same time appears to hold up the themes of language
and nationality that are discussed in the scene to ironic scrutiny. The use of English and
French at either end of the scene is also significant in depicting Redl as an outsider, who
is excluded because he has no knowledge of either language. For viewers who have no
access to the languages used in the scene, the significance of their use will be lost.

Study Activity 13.4

1.   Study the subtitles of a film in a language that you know. What is omitted or changed,
     and with what consequences for the dialogue?
2.   Study the intralingual subtitles for television programmes. What changes occur in the
     translation? What effects are the changes likely to have?

———————————————— 13.6   What Happens in Interpreting?

'Interpreting' covers various forms of oral translation, usually of spoken discourse, but sometimes extending to oral translation of written texts. Interpreting as a profession and as an activity is distinct from translation. Interpreters must have highly developed listening skills, and be fluent and clear speakers. They must also be able to work very fast: unlike translators, who can usually carry out research while working on a translation, interpreters must be equipped with prior knowledge of the field or topic they are interpreting, and whereas translators are able to deliberate over translation decisions, interpreters must make decisions immediately. The interpreter's status and role are highly constrained. In courtroom work, impartiality dictates that interpreters maintain a distance from witnesses, and leads to them being excluded from pre-trial discussions and documents relevant to the case.

There are three main modes of interpreting. In simultaneous interpreting, the interpreter sits in a booth, listening to the source through headphones, and speaks into a microphone. In consecutive interpreting, the interpreter listens to a segment of speech, perhaps making notes, and interprets the segment, whereupon the process repeats itself. This mode is commonly found in courtroom interpreting, and community interpreting (interpreting in public service contexts, such as police stations, social service and welfare centres, hospitals and schools). The third mode is known as *chuchotage* or whispered interpreting. The interpreter sits next to the recipient of the interpretation and whispers a translation to them.

In this section we will look at examples of consecutive interpreting in two settings – courtrooms and healthcare – in which sociolinguistic, cultural and interpersonal dynamics may influence the role assumed by the interpreter and impact on the translation. 'Court interpreting' is used to refer to legal interpreting generally and is not confined to courtrooms but is found in police premises and customs and immigration offices. The functions of court interpreting are mainly to enable a client, typically a witness or defendant who does not speak the language of the court, to understand what is said, and to enable other participants in the process, such as legal professionals and a jury, to understand witness testimony delivered in a language other than that of the court. Technically, court interpreters are committed to translating faithfully and impartially. In practice, these requirements are often hard to meet, as the interpreter is working under pressures of time, understanding and the expectations of the court.

In addition, the interpreter must decide which elements of the testimony to translate, as witness testimony is sometimes confused, ambiguous, incomplete or incoherent. Witness speech frequently contains hesitations, qualifications or mitigations ('hedges'), mistakes and repairs.

The first major linguistic study of interpreting was by Berk-Seligson (1990). Berk-Seligson's study, published as a book, was based on recorded and transcribed data obtained in immigration courts in the USA, where the defendants or witnesses were Spanish-speakers. Berk-Seligson found evidence that interpreters tend to *regularize* testimony, omitting apparently irrelevant features, and rendering testimony in a grammatically correct and coherent form, as in the example below.

(9) P. Att: *Mr Gomez, when you were hit, what, what was taken from you?*
     Int: *Que cuando fue golpeado, qué es que le quitaron, qué es lo que tomaron?*
     Gloss: So when were hit what is that from you took what is it that they took?
     W: *Pues todo. Todo se llevaron con mi car- … El pasaporte, este, tarjetas que traiba*
              de importancia, mi – Una prueba, más prueba voy a darle, mire: acabo de sacar el
              permiso de, del, de la emigración u aquí está, mire. Ahí está, porque se llevaron
              todo.sss!
     Gloss: Well everything. Everything they took with my wall(et) … The passport,
              uh, important cards I was carrying, my –, a proof, more proof I'm going to
              give you, look: I've just got the permit from, from, from Immigration, and
              here it is, look. There it is. Because they took everything. God…
     Int: *Everything, my passport, important cards, important cards that I have. I've just,*
              uh, I've just applied for immigration and this is it, because they took everything
              from me.

The Interpreter omits most of what the Witness actually says, perhaps on the grounds that
his speech is fragmented. Arguably, however, the Witness's attempts to convey his
distress, and to establish his good faith, merit translation. Berk-Seligson cites this episode
as an example of reduction and omission, which can significantly alter testimony and
affect the court's view of the Witness.

Berk-Seligson also identifies systematic and recurrent patterns of interpreter modification of testimony in the form of additions which make testimony more explicit in the
translation. In the following example, the Witness's reply is unhesitating and clear. In the
translation, the Interpreter inserts *'probably'*, and adds *'uh'* at the start of her translation,
making the Witness appear more tentative and uncertain than was the case.

(10) Att: Approximately how many?
  1. Int: Aproximadamente cuántos?
  2. W: Un promedio de veintiuno

              An average of twenty-one

     Int: Uh, probably an average of twenty-one people

Berk-Seligson suggests that reductions and additions are motivated by the pressure to
reduce testimony to sense. She also found that interpreters may alter linguistic forms in
ways that do not conform to the formal linguistic procedures of the courtroom, and which
she attributes to efforts to reflect empathy with the witness or their situation on the part
of the interpreter. In the next example, the Attorney's questions are constructed within a
repeated frame, using the same wording, with the purpose of eliciting information one
item at a time. Each question contains the clause *'you were apprehended by the border patrol'*,
around which the Attorney builds his questions.

(11) a. Att: Sir, do you remember when you were apprehended by the border
                patrol?
     Int: do you remember, sir, when the border patrol apprehended you?
     b. Att: Where was it that you were apprehended by the border patrol?
     Int: in what place were you apprehended by the border patrol?

c. ATT: after you were app, apprehended by the border patrol, did you give a statement?

INT: after you were apprehended by the border patrol did you give a statement?

d. ATT: Do you remember being asked where and when you entered the US?

INT: Do you remember, sir, while the patrolman was asking you questions for your sworn statement…

The changes made by the Interpreter appear to be superficial, but Berk-Seligson argues that they are both significant and revealing. Firstly, as noted above, the wording of the translated questions does not consistently repeat the pattern established by the Attorney. The Attorney uses the passive construction 'you were apprehended', foregrounding (Berk-Seligson uses the term 'focusing') the Witness as the subject of 'apprehended'. The interpreter alternates between passive sentences and sentences with an agent ('… the border patrol apprehended you'; 'the patrolman was asking you questions'). When the Interpreter departs from the use of the passive, the focus of the question shifts, the patrolman now foregrounded. In the Attorney's questions the focus remains on the Witness throughout, with the patrol backgrounded. Berk-Seligson suggests that these shifts are motivated by the Interpreter's desire to make the Witness feel more at ease by departing from the formulaic and potentially intimidating structure of the attorney's questions. She attributes the switching between passive and active forms to the Interpreter's empathic identification with the Witness's experience. Berk-Seligson's study suggests that interpreters, even in formal contexts such as courtrooms, may assume a dual role as translators and as mediators.

Our next example (from Baraldi and Gavioli, 2007) illustrates a similar duality of roles within the less formal context of a healthcare setting.

(12)   D: ti volevo chiedere (.) come mai hai la faccia così sofferente?
I wanted to ask you (.) why you look so suffering?

INT: lesh uigihik hek tabaan bain aleki
why is your face so tired?

PT: ((Arabic untranscribable))
((Partly for this pain))

INT: fi hagia muaiana mdaiktk fi hagia uiani mdaiik blbit mushkila muaiana
Is there anything wrong, like something that worries you at home, a particular problem

---

STUDY ACTIVITY 13.5

1. What negative consequences might result from the alterations to testimony that Berk-Seligson describes? Could there be positive consequences?
2. What positive and negative consequences are likely to result if an interpreter attempts to interpret testimony fully and faithfully?

When the Doctor asks why the Patient looks as if she is in pain, the question is addressed to the Patient, and also conveys personal concern. It is relayed by the Interpreter, who uses a more direct, less personal question. When the Patient says that she is experiencing pain, the Interpreter asks if she has a particular problem, perhaps of a domestic nature, without prompting from the Doctor. The Interpreter has shifted role from that of translator of the Doctor's questions and interventions to a more active role of confidante. Baraldi and Gavioli's study demonstrates that in such healthcare settings, the Interpreter adopts the additional role of intercultural mediator and coordinator, establishing a direct relationship with the Patient as a member of the same cultural group, which excludes the Doctor.

13.7 Summary

In this chapter we have considered the nature of translation from a linguistic perspective. Running through the account of translation above is the assumption that many of the problems and challenges of translation can be interpreted and explored using those branches of linguistics that are especially concerned with language as communication: pragmatics, Discourse Analysis and text linguistics. The interest of translation, in all its forms, to linguistics and Applied Linguistics is, in the words of Hatim and Mason (1990: 1), that translation provides a test case for examining the role of language in social life. For linguistics, translation raises questions about the nature of meaning, and the role of context in determining and conveying meaning, as well as questions about the equivalences and differences between modes of expression and communicative strategies between languages. The field of translation studies, which began in the 1960s with a linguistic focus, now embraces a large number of independent disciplines, many of which have only partial or tenuous links with linguistics. Cultural and literary theory has drawn attention to the role and position of translation and translations within literary and cultural traditions. With the rise of globalization, interest is growing in technological and media-related translation, including audio-visual translation and 'localization', in which a product is made culturally and linguistically 'appropriate' to a country, region or language. Back within the domain of Applied Linguistics, two recent publications (Campbell, 2008; Cook, 2010) have renewed interest in the pedagogical and cognitive relevance of translation to language learning.

Study Questions

1. What factors might explain the persistence of the literal-versus-free debate in writing about translation?
2. This chapter has presented a linguistic perspective on translation. Writers such as Venuti (1986) argue that linguistic approaches are insufficient, as they are restricted to features of language and texts, and cannot explain the role of translations and translating within sociocultural contexts. What do you think are the advantages and limitations of a linguistic approach to translation?

3. Watch a film in both subtitled and dubbed versions. What differences are there in the types of information relayed in the two modes?
4. Conduct some research into 'localization', and how and why it is done. What are the differences between 'normal' translation and localization?

5. Contemporary writing on translation is critical of prescriptive approaches and the idea that there can be 'rules' of translation. Do you agree with this position? What problems arise in attempting to formulate rules for translating?

Recommended Reading

Baker, Mona. 1992. *In Other Words*. London: Routledge. Baker's book is written for students interested in translation who have little or no knowledge of linguistics, and demonstrates how linguistic concepts and methods of analysing meaning and language use are relevant to translation. Among the book's strengths are its use of well-chosen examples from a range of sources and languages, and the exercises, which enable the reader to develop their understanding of concepts and of translation processes in relation to real textual examples.

Munday, Jeremy. 2012. *Introducing Translation Studies: Theories and Applications*, 3rd edn. London: Routledge. This is the best all-round introduction to translation studies. It assumes no prior knowledge of translation theory (though, as ever, some experience of translating is useful), and builds on an introductory discussion of themes and problems in translation studies to consider the advantages and limitations of linguistic, cultural and philosophical approaches to translation. The latest edition has sections on translation and new technologies, and a chapter on writing translation commentaries and research projects.

Pöchhacker, Franz. 2006. *Introducing Interpreting Studies*. London: Routledge. This book is the first of its type, designed to introduce students, researchers and practitioners to the discipline of interpreting studies. It covers international conference, court and hospital interpreting in both spoken and signed languages.

Venuti, Lawrence. 2012. *The Translation Studies Reader*, 3rd edn. Abingdon: Routledge. The Reader brings together 32 significant writings on translation from the middle ages up to the late twentieth century, arranged chronologically into sections, each with a helpful introduction by the editor. Major readings on translation by translation theorists and linguists are included, together with works by literary and cultural theorists. The linguistic contributions are all important in relation to the development of translation studies. The texts in the book vary in level of difficulty, and the book is best used as a follow-up to the introductory works listed above.

Glossary

Accent phonological features of a speaker's pronunciation, often associated with regional or social factors.

Acquisition planning a process whereby a national, state or local institution aims to influence the learning of a language by specific groups within a community, usually through educational means.

Adjacency pairs pairs of utterances in adjacent position where the production of the first part sequentially implicates the production of a second part.

Affordances perceived opportunities for action that are latent in the environment.

Agrammatism the speech of Broca's aphasics, which is characterized by simple sentence structure predominantly consisting of nouns and verbs with limited use of grammatical inflections for person, number, tense or gender and little use of complex syntactic forms.

Agraphia an acquired impairment in the ability to write due to neurological illness in a previously literate person.

Alexia an acquired impairment in the ability to read due to neurological illness in a previously literate person.

Anomia a form of aphasic impairment characterized by word-finding difficulty particularly affecting nouns in speech and by the inability to name objects.

Aphasia the medical term for any language disorder that is the result of brain damage.

Automaticity speech production or reception where no conscious intervention is needed.

Bilingual and multilingual first language acquisition (abbreviated as BAMFLA) the language development in children who are exposed to two or more languages from birth.

Biliteracy ability to read in two languages, sometimes involving different scripts.

Bi/multimodal pertaining to the use of two or more language modalities.

Broca's aphasia a type of aphasia characterized by effortful hesitant speech that is typically limited to short simple phrases comprised mainly of nouns and verbs but lacking grammatical complexity with relatively preserved comprehension, caused by a lesion to the left frontal cortex involving Broca's area.

Child-directed speech (abbreviated as CDS) speech directed to young children by caregivers such as mothers, fathers, and so on, also known as motherese or baby talk. It differs from normal speech on a variety of dimensions, with adults making socioculturally appropriate adjustments according to children's age and linguistic ability.

Code-switching process in which bilinguals combine several language varieties within the same conversation or speech event. It is often difficult to draw a clear line between this and *borrowing*, whereby a language adopts words, structures or sounds from another and integrates them to the point where they are no longer felt as foreign elements.

Common-sense (or dominant) discourse   the accepted way a culture or group talks about and represents an aspect of the world.

Community of Practice   term propagated by Penelope Eckert to designate common linguistic practices associated with a particular group of people/sphere of activity.

Competence   term proposed by Chomsky to refer to a native speaker's implicit knowledge of what is permissible or not in a language. It allows a native speaker to create new utterances that may not have been heard previously and to differentiate those new but permissible utterances from those not permissible in a language (cf. performance).

Congenital deafness   deafness from birth.

Continua of biliteracy   model developed by Nancy Hornberger to depict the multiple and complex interrelationships between bilingualism and literacy and the importance of the contexts, media and content through which biliteracy develops. Specifically, it depicts the development of biliteracy along intersecting first language–second language, receptive–productive and oral–written language skills continua; through the medium of two (or more) languages and literacies whose linguistic structures vary from similar to dissimilar, whose scripts range from convergent to divergent, and to which the developing biliterate individual's exposure varies from simultaneous to successive; in contexts that encompass micro to macrolevels and are characterized by varying mixes along the monolingual–bilingual and oral–literate continua; and with content that ranges from majority to minority perspectives and experiences, literary to vernacular styles and genres, and decontextualized to contextualized language texts.

Conversational implicature   the additional meaning conveyed and derived from what a speaker said on the basis of the assumption that the speaker is adhering to the Cooperative Principle.

Cooperative Principle   introduced by Paul Grice, it describes how effective communication in conversation is achieved in common social situations. It consists of four maxims of quality, quantity, relation and manner.

Corpus planning   the design of the structure of a particular language. It often involves three interrelated processes: codification, standardization and modernization.

Criterion-referenced test   test used to measure the candidate's performance against some predefined criterion or standard, and aiming to determine whether or not the candidate has demonstrated mastery of a certain skill or set of skills. These results are usually 'pass' or 'fail'.

Critical period hypothesis   hypothesis that when language learning starts past a certain age it becomes much more difficult to reach the level of native speakers of that language.

Crossing   a term coined by Ben Rampton (1995) to describe the way in which London teenagers from different ethnic groupings appropriate ('cross into') the speech style of Caribbean Creole speakers.

Cultural ideologies   shared sets of ideas which construct representations of issues/ groupings, and so on. This in turn may motivate social action.

Cultural key words   words that describe the main characteristics of a culture.

Cultural subjectivities   shared sets of ideas about particular classes of people (e.g. male/ female) or individuals.

Democratic assessment an alternative approach to language testing advocated by Elana Shohamy based on the principles that citizens in democratic societies should play a participatory and active role and transfer and share power from elites to and with local bodies, that those who develop powerful tools need to be responsible for their consequences, and that the voices of diverse and different groups in multicultural societies need to be considered and the rights of citizens need to be protected.

Developmental stages/milestones language perception or production skills shown by a majority of children in an age band. They are broad measures of language development and are often used as reference points in clinical diagnosis.

Developmental universals a term used in cross-linguistic studies of language development to refer to patterns that are common across languages (cf. Language-specific patterns).

Direct speech act a speech act where there is correspondence between the surface form of the utterance and its intended meaning.

Discourse (i) a coherent stretch of language larger than a single sentence; (ii) ways of talking about the world that are imbued with and reproduce values and ideological beliefs.

Discursive identity an inter-subjective enactment of identity brought about through interaction.

Domesticating Venuti's term for translation that assimilates a text to its target language and culture, resulting in flattened and homogeneous translation.

Double-discontinuity hypothesis hypothesis which suggests that there is no relationship between sign language and written language skills.

Dynamic translation one of Nida's forms of translation equivalence. A dynamic translation aims to produce an effect on the audience of the target text (TT) equivalent to that of the source text (ST) on its original audience.

Dyslexia a neurologically based learning difficulty specifically related to literacy.

Early second language learning language development of monolingual children who are exposed to a second language after they have already started learning.

Emic analysis analysis based on participants' perspectives and interpretations of behaviour, events and situations using their descriptive language.

Essentialism a belief that things have a set of fixed characteristics that make them what they are.

Etic analysis analysis based on the use of carefully defined and relatively stable concepts from the analytic language of the social sciences.

Explicit–implicit learning conscious and controlled versus unconscious or incidental learning.

Face the public self-image that a person wants to claim for him-or herself in interaction.

Fairness framework a framework developed by Antony Kunnan which links issues of test validity and reliability with issues of access and justice in language testing.

Family language policy a field of study focusing on explicit and overt planning in relation to language use within the home among family members, and how languages are managed, learned and negotiated within families.

Foreign language anxiety communicative anxiety when having to use a foreign language.

Foreignizing Venuti's term for an approach to translating that deliberately draws attention to the fact that the target text (TT) is a translation by incorporating literalisms, foreignisms and invented forms.

Formal translation   the complementary term to 'dynamic translation' in Nida's dichotomy of forms of equivalence. A formal translation closely reflects properties of the source text (ST) without endangering comprehensibility.

Grapheme   the smallest significant unit used to represent the written form of a language.

High context   a communication style in which speakers rely on factors other than explicit speech (such as setting, shared knowledge) to convey their messages (cf. Low context).

Implicature   a contextually derived proposition or meaning intended but not literally expressed by a speaker: *'it's hot in here'* may lead to the implicature 'open a window'.

Indirect speech act   a speech act where there is a mismatch between the literal meaning of the utterance and the speaker's intended meaning.

Indirectness   the performance of one speech act by means of another one.

Intercultural Communicative Competence (ICC)   an ability to communicate effectively and appropriately in intercultural encounters (also known as intercultural competence).

Interculturality   a situation where people from different cultures interact with each other; or a research paradigm in which cultural differences are studied as a social phenomenon and discursive practice rather than something given.

Interference hypothesis   hypothesis which proposes that sign language competence has a negative impact on the acquisition/learning of written forms.

Interlanguage   the independent linguistic system of an L2 learner/user. It contains elements from all languages known to the L2 learner/user as well as unique, new forms.

L2 socialization   the process of acquiring a new set of norms, customs and ideologies allowing an L2 learner/user to participate in the L2 society.

L2 user   an individual who has been using an L2 for real-life purposes for some time at various levels of proficiency.

Language   ambiguous term which may designate the most widespread form of communication between humans, as a general phenomenon; *or* a psycholinguistic capacity ('the language faculty'); *or* particular varieties (e.g. English; Japanese) usually associated with nation states, and often standardized.

Language Acquisition Device (LAD)   a term proposed in Chomsky's early works to describe the form in which the so-called language faculty exists. LAD presupposes that children are born with a list of predefined grammars and language acquisition is essentially about testing which grammar is the best fit on the basis of input data (cf. Universal Grammar).

Language attitude   feelings people have about their own language variety or the languages or language varieties of others. It can also refer to attitudes towards language use.

Language faculty   a term proposed by Chomsky to refer to a specific faculty of the mind/brain that is responsible for the use and acquisition of language. Chomsky believes that the language faculty is *innate* and biologically determined.

Language ideology   the perceptions held by people about a specific language or language in general, what language can do, and how language should be used.

Language shift   social process whereby one variety replaces or comes to dominate over another, sometimes to the point of rendering it extinct, in which case we talk of *language death* (e.g. Cornish was rendered extinct by the spread of English).

Language socialization   the process by which children, adolescents or newer members of communities learn to speak the language in a way appropriate to the community and adapt to the beliefs and norms associated with speaking that language.

Language-specific patterns   also known as 'particulars', a term used in cross-linguistic studies of language development to refer to patterns that only occur in a particular language or language group (cf. developmental universals).

Language transfer   the phenomenon in bilingual language acquisition that one feature of one language occurs in the other and results in an atypical error pattern.

Lesion   the medical term for damage to a particular part of the brain due to disease or trauma.

Lifeworld   Mishler's term for the lived experience of the individual.

Linguistic community   variously defined as a group of people who have at least one language variety in common, or as a group which may include diverse competencies but where there is a shared set of norms (e.g. about what is correct).

Linguistic determinism   a (strong) version of the Sapir–Whorf hypothesis of the relation between language, culture and thought, which asserts that language controls thought and culture.

Linguistic landscape   a field of study that focuses on the presence, representation, meanings and interpretation of language displayed in public places, often in multimodalities.

Linguistic relativity   a (weak) version and a moderate claim of the Sapir–Whorf hypothesis of the relation between language, culture and thought, which argues that language influences thought and worldviews and that, therefore, differences between languages cause differences in the thought of their speakers.

Literal/free translation   problematic but time-honoured dichotomy of translation strategies.

Low context   a communication style in which speakers rely on explicit speech rather than setting, shared knowledge, and so on, to convey their messages (cf. high context).

Metalinguistic skill   the ability to understand the rules used to govern language.

Metaphor   an expression from one semantic field used to refer to something in another semantic field.

Multicompetence   knowledge of two or more languages.

Multiliteracy   ability to read in two or more languages, sometimes involving different scripts. The term is also used by some researchers to mean the ability to read different kinds of scripts and signs, linguistic as well as non-linguistic.

Multimodality   multiple semiotic modes and channels through which messages are communicated. Examples include print articles that use words and pictures, websites that contain audio clips alongside the words, or film that uses words, music, sound effects and moving images. The study of multimodality involves looking at the different components of multimodal communication and the ways they communicate meaning, both separately and in combination.

National language   a language variety that has some connection, *de facto* or *de jure*, with a people and perhaps, by extension, the territory they occupy. It may represent a nation or country, or be a designation given to one or more languages spoken as first languages in the territory of a country.

Naturalistic acquisition   unguided language acquisition.

Negative face   people's wish to preserve their territory and be free from imposition.

Neurolinguistics   the study of how language is organized in the brain.

Norm-referenced tests   tests used to measure a candidate's performance relative to the group undertaking the assessment. They compare the candidates with each other.

Orthography   the system of writing used to represent a spoken language.

Paraphasia   impaired word production that may be phonologically or semantically related to the intended lexical form.

Performance   the production of actual sentences (cf. competence). A term used by Chomsky.

Performativity   a theory which conceives of identity as a discursive production and accomplishment.

Phonological awareness   awareness of the sound structure of spoken words at the level of syllables and phonemes.

Pidgin/creole   pidgins are varieties that develop between speakers who do not have a common language or *lingua franca*. They have simplified grammars and reduced lexicons. Where they are used over long periods – for example, by a whole generation – they can become as complex as any other natural language, both in form and in function.

Positive face   people's desire to be liked and accepted as members of a group.

Pragmatic competence   the ability to understand and produce intended meaning in context.

Pragmatics   the branch of linguistics that studies language use and the generation of meaning within contexts.

Pre-discursive identity   predetermined individual or social categorizations of identity.

Presupposition   an assumption that is not explicitly stated, and assumed to be valid: '*The King of France is bald*' presupposes that there is a King of France.

Register   a systematic variation in language according to situation or what is being talked about: hence, 'technical', 'legal', 'medical' register.

Reification   talking about an abstract or inchoate thing as if it were a physical entity.

Reliability   the extent to which a test provides consistent, replicable information about candidates' language performance.

Sapir–Whorf hypothesis   the observations by Edward Sapir and Benjamin Whorf on the interrelationship of language, culture and thought. There are different versions of the hypothesis. The most well-known are linguistic determinism and linguistic relativity.

Schema   a collection of knowledge of past experience that is stored in memory and retrieved when prompted to guide behaviour and sense-making.

Semiotics   the study of signs and sign systems, including language.

Social construction   a perspective that views 'identity' as a product of social interaction.

Social literacy   social skills in a social setting that help people to communicate in an appropriate manner, as well as become involved in a community as an active participant. It may begin with an ability to read and use various linguistic and communication signs but goes beyond linguistic abilities.

Sociolinguistic competence   the ability to recognize, understand and produce speech belonging to various registers or speech styles.

Source text (ST)/target text (TT)   ST is the text that is subject to translation, resulting in the TT.

Specific Language Impairment   the medical term for a difficulty acquiring language from birth for which no known neurological, psychological or social reason exists in a child without any other learning or perceptual problems.

Speech act   a linguistic act through which an action is performed.

Standard language   a language variety that has undergone a process of standardization, during which it is organized for description in grammars and dictionaries and encoded in such reference works. Typically, varieties that become standardized are the local dialects spoken in the centres of commerce and government, where a need arises for a variety that will serve more than local needs.

Standardization   process of selection of grammatical and lexical forms for official purposes and often recommended for use in the media and in education.

Status planning   planning the status, or standing, of a language vis-à-vis other languages within a community. It often refers to the official or juridical status of a language.

Stroke   the common term for impaired blood flow in an artery or vessel that leads to damage to a part of the surrounding brain.

Synchronic/diachronic   adjectives referring to different methods of studying language: a synchronic study takes place within a given time frame, normally the present, whereas a diachronic one considers the development of the language over a given historical period or at different times.

Synthetic personalization   a term first used by Fairclough (1989) to describe a simulated solidarity between writer and reader through the use of specific linguistic devices (e.g. inclusive personal pronouns).

The logical or projection problem of language acquisition   an essential learning problem in language acquisition that is the gap between what is to be acquired and what is available. While children are expected to develop adult-like performance and competence, the input to which they are exposed does not offer optimal opportunities.

Transitivity   (i) a grammatical property of verbs; (ii) the ways in which languages and users can depict a process or event in terms of how participants are represented, as in the active/passive distinction.

Ultimate attainment   the furthest and highest point in the development of an interlanguage.

Universal Grammar (UG)   a term proposed by Chomsky to replace Language Acquisition Device. Compared with LAD, UG is a form that is more general and abstract than a list of predefined grammars. It contains a set of universal principles that underlie the structure of all languages as well as a finite set of parameters to allow for cross-linguistic variations (cf. Language Acquisition Device).

Utterance   a unit of speech, not in the abstract but as employed on a particular occasion. An utterance can be made up of a word, a phrase or a sentence.

Validity   the extent to which meaningful inferences can be drawn from test scores. When a test measures what it is intended to measure and nothing else, it is valid. The most important kinds of validity in language tests are *content validity* (the degree to which the test content is representative of whatever objectives or specifications the test is designed to measure), *construct validity* (the experimental demonstration that a test is measuring the construct (e.g. attribute, proficiency, ability or skill) it claims to be measuring) and *predictive validity* (the degree of correlation between the scores on a test and some other measure that the test is designed to predict).

Variationist sociolinguistics   a field of sociolinguistics devoted to identifying and explaining variable language use by different social actors or groupings.

Variety   a catch-all term used in linguistics to include (standard) languages, *dialects* (regional or social), *registers* (forms of speech determined by their association with a particular context (e.g. 'the legal register') or level of formality), *idiolects* (individual ways of speaking), and so on.

Washback the extent to which the introduction and use of a test influence language teachers and learners to do things they would not otherwise do that promote or inhibit language learning. Washback effect can be positive or negative.

Wernicke's aphasia a type of aphasia affecting speech comprehension with fluent but grammatically ill-formed speech production caused by a lesion to the left temporal cortex involving Wernicke's area.

Resources List

Li Wei and Zhu Hua

The section contains lists of key references, handbooks, book series, journals, corpora, professional associations and websites in Applied Linguistics.

1. Key References

Because of the vast number of articles published in Applied Linguistics, the following lists contain predominantly books and collections of articles, especially those published since 2000. Relevant handbooks are listed in Section 2, book series in Section 3 and journals in Section 4.

Language Teaching (General)

Brown, H.D. 2006. *Principles of Language Teaching and Learning*, 5th edn. Harlow: Pearson.
Carter, R. and D. Nunan (eds.). 2001. *The Cambridge Guide to Teaching English to Speakers of Other Languages*. Cambridge: Cambridge University Press.
Celce-Marcia, M. (ed.). 2001. *Teaching English as a Second or Foreign Language*, 3rd edn. Boston: Heinle & Heinle.
Widdowson, H.G. 2003. *Defining Issues in English Language Teaching*. Oxford: Oxford University Press.

Language Teaching (Approaches)

Cook, V. 2008. *Second Language Learning and Language Teaching*. London: Arnold.
Doughty, C. and J. Williams (eds.). 1998. *Focus on Form in Classroom Second Language Acquisition*. Cambridge: Cambridge University Press.
Edbert, J.E. and E. Hanson-Smith (eds.). 1999. *CALL Environments: Research, Practice and Critical Issues*. Alexandria, VA: TESOL.
Ellis, R. 2003. *Task-Based Language Teaching and Learning*. Oxford: Oxford University Press.
Kramsch, C. (ed.). 2002. *Language Acquisition and Language Socialization: Ecological Perspectives*. London: Continuum.
Larsen-Freeman, D. and L. Cameron. 2008. *Complex Systems and Applied Linguistics*. Oxford: Oxford University Press.
Norton, B. and K. Toohey (eds.). 2004. *Critical Pedagogies and Language Learning*. Cambridge: Cambridge University Press.
Nunan, D. 2004. *Task-Based Language Teaching*. Cambridge: Cambridge University Press.

Applied Linguistics, First Edition. Edited by Li Wei.
© 2014 John Wiley & Sons, Ltd. Published 2014 by John Wiley & Sons, Ltd.

O'Keefe, A., M. McCarthy and R. Carter. 2007. *From Corpus to Classroom: Language Use and Language Teaching*. Cambridge: Cambridge University Press.

Richards, J. and W. Renandya (eds.). 2002. *Methodology in Language Teaching: An Anthology of Current Practice*. Cambridge: Cambridge University Press.

Richards, J. and T. Rodgers. 2001. *Approaches and Methods in Language Teaching*. Cambridge: Cambridge University Press.

Young, R. 2009. *Discursive Practice in Language Learning and Teaching*. Oxford: Wiley-Blackwell.

van den Branden, K. 2006. *Task-Based Language Education*. Cambridge: Cambridge University Press.

Language Teaching (Skills and Structures)

Anderson, N. 2008. *Reading*. New York: McGraw-Hill.

Blachowicz, C. and D. Ogle. 2008. *Reading Comprehension: Strategies for Independent Learners*, 2nd edn. New York: Guilford Press.

Block, C. and S. Parris. 2008. *Comprehension Instruction: Research-Based Best Practices*, 2nd edn. New York: Guilford Press.

Carter, R., R. Hughes and M.J. McCarthy. 2001. *Exploring Grammar in Context*. Cambridge: Cambridge University Press.

Celce-Marcia, M. and E. Olshtain. 2000. *Discourse and Context in Language Teaching*. Cambridge: Cambridge University Press.

Cook, V. and B. Bassetti (eds.). 2005. *Second Language Writing Systems*. Clevedon: Multilingual Matters.

Day, R.R. and J. Bamford. 1998. *Extensive Reading in the Second Language Classroom*. Cambridge: Cambridge University Press.

Ferris, D. and J. Hedgcock. 2005. *Teaching ESL Composition: Purpose, Process, and Practice*, 2nd edn. Mahwah, NJ: Lawrence Erlbaum.

Flowerdew, J. (ed.). 2005. *Academic Discourse*. Harlow: Longman.

Flowerdew, J. and L. Miller. 2005. *Second Language Listening: Theory and Practice*. Cambridge: Cambridge University Press.

Grabe, W. 2009. *Reading in a Second Language: Moving from Theory to Practice*. Cambridge: Cambridge University Press.

Grabe, W. and F. Stoller. 2002. *Teaching and Research Reading*. Harlow: Longman.

Han, Z.-H. and N. Anderson (eds.). 2009. *Second Language Reading: Research and Instruction*. Mahwah, NJ: Lawrence Erlbaum.

Hinkel, E. and S. Fotos (eds.). 2002. *New Perspectives on Grammar Teaching in Second Language Classrooms*. Mahwah, NJ: Lawrence Erlbaum.

Hudson, T. 2007. *Teaching Second Language Reading*. Oxford: Oxford University Press.

Hyland, K. 2004. *Disciplinary Discourses: Social Interactions in Academic Writing*. Ann Arbor: University of Michigan Press.

Koda, K. 2005. *Insights into Second Language Reading*. Cambridge: Cambridge University Press.

Krashen, S. 2004. *The Power of Reading*, 2nd edn. Portsmouth, NH: Heinemann.

Kroll, B. (ed.). 2003. *Exploring the Dynamics of Second Language Writing*. Cambridge: Cambridge University Press.

Larsen-Freeman, D. 2003. *Teaching Language: From Grammar to Grammaring*. Boston: Heinle & Heinle.

Lynch, T. 2009. *Teaching Second Language Listening*. Oxford: Oxford University Press.

Nation, I.S.P. 2001. *Learning Vocabulary in Another Language*. Cambridge: Cambridge University Press.

Nation, I.S.P. 2009. *Teaching ESL/EFL Reading and Writing*. Abingdon: Routledge.

Pressley, M. 2006. *Reading Instruction that Works*, 3rd edn. New York: Guilford Press.

Schmitt, N. 2000. *Vocabulary in Language Teaching*. Cambridge: Cambridge University Press.

Schmitt, N. (ed.). 2004. *Formulaic Sequences*. Amsterdam: John Benjamins.

Silva, T. and P.K. Matsuda (eds.). 2001. *On Second Language Writing*. Mahwah, NJ: Lawrence Erlbaum.

Swales, J. 2004. *Research Genres: Explorations and Applications*. Cambridge: Cambridge University Press.

Language Teaching (Learner-Related Issues)

Benson, P. 2001. *Teaching and Researching: Autonomy in Language Learning*. Harlow: Pearson.
Cohen, A.D. and E. Macaro (eds.). 2007. *Language Learning Strategies*. Oxford: Oxford University Press.
Dornyei, Z. 2001. *Teaching and Researching Motivation*. Harlow: Longman.
Griffiths, C. (ed.). 2009. *Lessons from Good Language Learners*. Cambridge: Cambridge University Press.
Macaro, E. 2001. *Learning Strategies in Foreign and Second Language Classrooms*. London: Continuum.
O'Malley, J.M. and A.U. Chamot. 1990. *Learning Strategies in Second Language Acquisition*. Cambridge: Cambridge University Press.
Oxford, R.L. 1990. *Language Learning Strategies: What Every Teacher Should Know*. Boston: Newbury House.

Language Teaching (Classroom)

Cole, K.M. and J. Zuengler. 2007. *The Research Process in Classroom Discourse Analysis: Current Perspectives*. Abingdon: Routledge.
Gibbons, P. 2006. *Bridging Discourses in the ESL Classroom: Teachers, Students and Researchers*. London: Continuum.
Hall, J.K. and L.S. Verplaetse (eds.). 2000. *Second and Foreign Language Learning Through Classroom Interaction*. Abingdon: Routledge.
Luk, J.C.M. and A.M.Y. Lin. 2006. *Classroom Interactions as Cross-cultural Encounters: Native Speakers in EFL Lessons*. Abingdon: Routledge.
Mackay, S.L. 2006. *Researching Second Language Classrooms*. Mahwah, NJ: Lawrence Erlbaum.
Rex, L.A. and L. Schiller. 2009. *Using Discourse Analysis to Improve Classroom Interaction*. Abingdon, Oxon Routledge.
Runesson, U. 2009. *Classroom Discourse and the Space of Learning*. Mahwah, NJ: Lawrence Erlbaum.
Seedhouse, P. 2005. *The Interactional Architecture of the Language Classroom*. Oxford: Blackwell.
Walsh, S. 2006. *Investigating Classroom Discourse*. Abingdon: Routledge.

Language Teaching (Teacher-Related Issues)

Burns, A. and J. Richards. 2009. *Cambridge Guide to Second Language Teacher Education*. Cambridge: Cambridge University Press.
Cohen, A.D. and S.J. Weaver. 2006. *Styles- and Strategies-Based Instruction: A Teachers' Guide*. Minneapolis: Center for Advanced Research on Language Acquisition, University of Minnesota.
Dornyei, Z. 2001. *Motivational Strategies in the Language Classroom*. Cambridge: Cambridge University Press.
Ellis, R. 2001. *Form-Focused Instruction and Second Language Learning*. Oxford: Blackwell.
James, P. 2001. *Teachers in Action: Tasks for In-Service Language Teacher Education and Development*. Cambridge: Cambridge University Press.
Johnson, K.E. 2009. *Second Language Teacher Education: A Sociocultural Perspective*. Abingdon: Routledge.
Tomlinson, B. (ed.). 2003. *Developing Materials for Language Teaching*. London: Continuum.

Language Teaching (Assessments)

Alderson, J.C. 2000. *Assessing Reading*. Cambridge: Cambridge University Press.
Alderson, J.C. 2005. *Diagnosing Foreign Language Proficiency: The Interface between Learning and Assessment*. London: Continuum.
Brown, H.D. 2004. *Language Assessment: Principles and Classroom Practice*. White Plains, NY: Pearson.
Buck, G. 2001. *Assessing Listening*. Cambridge: Cambridge University Press.

Chapelle, C.A. and D. Douglas. 2006. *Assessing Language through Computer Technology*. Cambridge: Cambridge University Press.
Douglas, D. 2000. *Testing Language for Specific Purposes: Theory and Practice*. Cambridge: Cambridge University Press.
Ekbatani, G. and H. Pierson (eds.). *Learner-Directed Assessment in ESL*. Mahwah, NJ: Lawrence Erlbaum.
Gottlieb, M. and D. Nguyen. 2007. *Assessment and Accountability in Language Education Programs*. Philadelphia, PA: Caslon.
Hughes, A. 2003. *Testing for Language Teachers*. Cambridge: Cambridge University Press.
Luoma, S. 2004. *Assessing Speaking*. Cambridge: Cambridge University Press.
McKay, P. 2006. *Assessing Young Language Learners*. Cambridge: Cambridge University Press.
McNamara, T. and C. Roever. 2006. *Language Testing: The Social Dimension*. Oxford: Blackwell.
Purpura, J. 2004. *Assessing Grammar*. Cambridge: Cambridge University Press.
Read, J. 2000. *Assessing Vocabulary*. Cambridge: Cambridge University Press.
Shohamy, E. 2001. *The Power of Tests*. Harlow: Longman.
Weigle, S.C. 2002. *Assessing Writing*. Cambridge: Cambridge University Press.

Culture and Politics in Language Teaching and Learning

Alderson, C. 2009. *The Politics of Language Education: Individuals and Institutions*. Bristol: Multilingual Matters.
Corbett, J. 2003. *An Intercultural Approach to English Language Teaching*. Clevedon: Multilingual Matters.
Guilherme, M. 2002. *Critical Citizens for an Intercultural World: Foreign Language Education as Cultural Politics*. Clevedon: Multilingual Matters.
Hellermann, J. 2003. *Social Actions for Classroom Language Learning*. Clevedon: Multilingual Matters.
Holliday, A. 2005. *The Struggle to Teach English as an International Language*. Oxford: Oxford University Press.
Kramsch, C. 2002. *Language Acquisition and Language Socialization*. London: Continuum.
Lantolf, J. and S. Thorne. 2006. *Sociocultural Theory and the Genesis of Second Language Development*. Oxford: Oxford University Press.
Norton, B. 2000. *Identity and Language Learning: Gender, Ethnicity and Educational Change*. Harlow: Longman.
Zhu Hua, P. Seedhouse, Li Wei and V. Cook (eds.). 2007. *Language Learning and Teaching as Social Inter-Action*. Basingstoke: Palgrave.

Identity in Language Learning

Block, D. 2007. *Second Language Identities*. London: Continuum.
Breen, M. (ed.). 2001. *Learner Contributions to Language Learning*. Harlow: Longman.
Lin, A.M.Y. (ed.). 2006. *Problematizing Identity: Everyday Struggles in Language, Culture and Education*. Mahwah, NJ: Lawrence Erlbaum.
Mantero, M. 2006. *Identity and Second Language Learning: Culture, Inquiry, and Dialogic Activity in Educational Contexts*. Norwood, NJ: Information Age Publishing.
Menard-Warwick, J. 2009. *Gendered Identities and Immigrant Language Learning*. Bristol: Multilingual Matters.
Norton, B. and A. Pavlenko (eds.). 2004. *Gender and English Language Learners*. Alexandria, VA: TESOL.
Pavlenko, A., A. Blackledge, I. Piller and M. Teutsch-Dwyer. 2001. *Multilingualism, Second Language Learning and Gender*. Berlin: Mouton de Gruyter.

Minority Learners

Block, D. 2006. *Multilingual Identities in a Global City: London Stories*. Basingstoke: Palgrave Macmillan.
Canagarajah, S. 2002. *Critical Academic Writing and Multilingual Students*. Ann Arbor: University of Michigan Press.

Edwards, J. 2009. *Language Diversity in the Classroom*. Bristol: Multilingual Matters.
Leung, C. and A. Creese (eds.). 2010. *English as an Additional Language: Approaches to Teaching Linguistic Minority Students*. London: Naldic/SAGE.
Menard-Warwick, J. 2009. *Gendered Identities and Immigrant Language Learning*. Bristol: Multilingual Matters.
Ramirez, D., T.G. Wiley, G. de Klerk, E. Lee and W.E. Wright. 2005. *Ebonics: The Urban Education Debate*, 2nd edn. Clevedon: Multilingual Matters.
Wiley, T.G., J.S. Lee and R.W. Rumberger. 2009. *The Education of Language Minority Immigrants in the United States*. Bristol: Multilingual Matters.

Language-in-Education Policy

Canagarajah, S. (ed.). 2005. *Reclaiming the Local in Language Policies and Practices*. Mahwah, NJ: Lawrence Erlbaum.
Crawford, James. 2000. *At War with Diversity: U.S. Language Policy in an Age of Anxiety*. Clevedon: Multilingual Matters.
Lin, A.M.Y. and P. Martin (eds.). 2005. *Decolonisation, Globalisation: Language-in-Education Policy and Practice*. Clevedon: Multilingual Matters.
Tollefson, J.W. 2001. *Language Policies in Education: Critical Issues*. Abingdon: Routledge.

Second Language Acquisition

Block, David. 2003. *The Social Turn in Second Language Acquisition*. Edinburgh: Edinburgh University Press.
de Bot, K., W. Lowie and M. Verspoor. 2005. *Second Language Acquisition: An Advanced Resource Book*. Abingdon: Routledge.
DeKeyser, R. (ed.). 2007. *Practice in a Second Language*. Cambridge: Cambridge University Press.
Dornyei, Z. 2005. *The Psychology of the Language Learner: Individual Differences in Second Language Acquisition*. Mahwah, NJ: Lawrence Erlbaum.
Dornyei, Z. 2009. *The Psychology of Second Language Acquisition*. Oxford: Oxford University Press.
Ellis, N.C. and D. Larsen-Freeman (eds.). 2006. *Language Emergence: Implications for Applied Linguistics*. Special issue, *Applied Linguistics* 27(4).
Ellis, R. 2008. *The Study of Second Language Acquisition*, 2nd edn. Oxford: Oxford University Press.
Gass, S. and L. Selinker. 2008. *Second Language Acquisition: An Introductory Course*, 3rd edn. Mahwah, NJ: Lawrence Erlbaum.
Han, Z.-H. 2004. *Fossilization in Adult Second Language Acquisition*. Clevedon: Multilingual Matters.
Han, Z.-H. (ed.). 2008. *Understanding Second Language Process*. Clevedon: Multilingual Matters.
Han, Z.-H. and T. Odlin. 2006. *Studies in Fossilization in Second Language Acquisition*. Clevedon: Multilingual Matters.
Housen, A. and M. Pierrard (eds.). 2005. *Current Issues in Instructed Second Language Acquisition*. Berlin: Mouton de Gruyter.
Lantolf, J.P. 2000. *Sociocultural Theory and Second Language Learning*. Oxford: Oxford University Press.
Lightbown, P.M. and N. Spada. 2006. *How Languages Are Learned*, 3rd edn. Oxford: Oxford University Press.
Macaro, E. (ed.). 2010. *The Continuum Companion to Second Language Acquisition*. London: Continuum.
Mackey, A. (ed.). 2007. *Conversational Interaction in Second Language Acquisition*. Oxford: Oxford University Press.
Mitchell, R. and F. Myles. 2004. *Second Language Learning Theories*, 2nd edn. London: Arnold.
Ortega, L. 2007. *Second Language Acquisition*. London: Hodder Education.
Paradis, M. 2009. *Declarative and Procedural Determinants of Second Languages*. Amsterdam: John Benjamins.

Piennemann, M. 1998. *Language Processing and Second Language Development: Processability Theory*. Amsterdam: John Benjamins.

Ritchie, W. and T. Bhatia (eds.). 2009. *The New Handbook of Second Language Acquisition*. Bingley: Emerald.

Schumann, J.H., S.E. Crowell, N.E. Jones *et al.* 2004. *The Neurobiology of Learning: Perspectives from Second Language Acquisition*. Mahwah, NJ: Lawrence Erlbaum.

VanPatten, B. 1996. *Input Processing and Grammar Instruction in Second Language Acquisition*. Norwood, NJ: Ablex.

VanPatten, B. and J. Williams. 2006. *Theories in Second Language Acquisition: An Introduction*. Abingdon: Routledge.

White, L. 2003. *Second Language Acquisition and Universal Grammar*. Cambridge: Cambridge University Press.

New Approaches to Language Relevant to Language Learning

Goldberg, A. 2006. *Constructions at Work: The Nature of Generalization in Language*. Oxford: Oxford University Press.

Leeuwen, T. van. 2005. *Introducing Social Semiotics*. Abingdon: Routledge.

Tomasello, M. 2003. *Constructing a Language: A Usage-Based Theory of Language Acquisition*. Cambridge, MA: Harvard University Press.

Wodak, R. and M. Meyer (eds.). 2002. *Methods of Critical Discourse Analysis*. London: SAGE.

Wray, A. 2002. *Formulaic Language and the Lexicon*. Cambridge: Cambridge University Press.

General References

Biber, D., S. Johansson, G. Leech, S. Conrad and E. Finega (eds.). 1999. *Longman Grammar of Spoken and Written English*. Harlow: Longman.

Crystal, D. 2003. *The Cambridge Encyclopedia of the English Language*, 2nd edn. Cambridge: Cambridge University Press.

Davies, A. 2005. *A Glossary of Applied Linguistics*. Edinburgh: Edinburgh University Press.

Johnson, K. and H. Johnson (eds.). 1999. *The Encyclopedic Dictionary of Applied Linguistics*. Oxford: Blackwell.

Richards, J. and R. Schmidt (eds.). 2010. *Longman Dictionary of Language Teaching and Applied Linguistics*, 4th edn. Harlow: Longman.

2. Handbooks

Wiley-Blackwell publishes *The Encyclopedia of Applied Linguistics*, available online or as a 10-volume print set, under the general editorship of Carol A. Chapelle. It comprises over 1,100 original essays, covering the diverse field of applied linguistics. Web address:

http://onlinelibrary.wiley.com/book/10.1002/9781405198431

The Handbooks of Applied Linguistics series, published by Mouton de Gruyter under the general editorship of Karlfried Knapp and Gerd Antos, contains nine volumes so far:

Vol. 1: *Handbook of Communication Competence*. 2010. Rickheit, Gert and Hans Strohner (eds.).

Vol. 2: *Handbook of Interpersonal Communication*. 2008. Antos, Gerd and Eija Ventola (eds.).

Vol. 3: *Handbook of Communication in Organisations and Professions*. 2011. Candlin, Christopher N. and Srikant Sarangi (eds.).

Vol. 4: *Handbook of Communication in the Public Sphere*. 2008. Wodak, Ruth and Veronika Koller (eds.).

Vol. 5: *Handbook of Multilingualism and Multilingual Communication*. 2007. Auer, Peter and Li Wei (eds.).

Vol. 6: *Handbook of Foreign Language Communication and Learning*. 2009. Knapp, Karlfried and Barbara Seidlhofer (eds.).

Vol. 7: *Handbook of Intercultural Communication*. 2007. Kotthoff, Helga and Helen Spencer-Oatey (eds.).

Vol. 8: *Handbook of Technical Communication*. 2012. Mehler, Alexander and Laurent Romary (eds.).
Vol. 9: *Handbook of Language and Communication: Diversity and Change*. 2007. Hellinger, Marlis and
    Anne Pauwels (eds.).

The *Routledge Handbooks in Applied Linguistics* series provides comprehensive overviews of the key
topics in Applied Linguistics.

Coulthard, Malcolm and Alison Johnson (eds.). 2013. *The Routledge Handbook of Forensic Linguistics*.
    London: Routledge.
Fulcher, Glenn and Fred Davidson (eds.). 2012. *The Routledge Handbook of Language Testing*. London:
    Routledge.
Gass, Susan M. and Alison Mackey (eds.). 2011. *The Routledge Handbook of Second Language Acquisition*.
    London: Routledge.
Gee, James and Michael Handford (eds.). 2011. *The Routledge Handbook of Discourse Analysis*. London:
    Routledge.
Jackson, Jane (ed.). 2012. *The Routledge Handbook of Language and Intercultural Communication*. London:
    Routledge.
Kirkpatrick, Andy (ed.). 2012. *The Routledge Handbook of World Englishes*. London: Routledge.
Martin-Jones, Marilyn, Adrian Blackledge and Angela Creese (eds.). 2012. *The Routledge Handbook of
    Multilingualism*. London: Routledge.
Millán, Carmen and Francesca Bartrina (eds.). 2012. *The Routledge Handbook of Translation Studies*.
    London: Routledge.
O'Keeffe, Anne and Michael McCarthy (eds.). 2012. *The Routledge Handbook of Corpus Linguistics*.
    London: Routledge.
Simpson, James (ed.) 2011. *The Routledge Handbook of Applied Linguistics*. London: Routledge.

Encyclopedia of Language and Education, published by Springer in 2008 under the general editorship
of Nancy Hornberger, comprises 10 volumes:

Vol. 1: *Language Policy and Political Issues in Education*. May, Stephen (ed.).
Vol. 2: *Literacy*. Street, Brian (ed.).
Vol. 3: *Discourse and Education*. Martin-Jones, Marilyn and Anne-Marie de Mejía (eds.).
Vol. 4: *Second and Foreign Language Education*. Van Deusen-Scholl, Nelleke (ed.).
Vol. 5: *Bilingual Education*. Cummins, Jim (ed.).
Vol. 6: *Knowledge about Language*. Cenoz, Jasone (ed.).
Vol. 7: *Language Testing and Assessment*. Shohamy, Elana (ed.).
Vol. 8: *Language Socialization*. Duff, Patricia (ed.).
Vol. 9: *Ecology of Language*. Creese, Angela and Peter Martin (eds.).
Vol. 10: *Research Methods in Language and Education*. King, Kendall (ed.).

The following single-volume handbooks provide comprehensive and in-depth surveys of the field:

Davies, A. and C. Elder (eds.). 2004. *Handbook of Applied Linguistics*. Oxford: Blackwell.
Kaplan, R. 2005. *The Oxford Handbook of Applied Linguistics*. Oxford: Oxford University Press.
Spolsky, Bernard and Francis M. Hult (eds.). 2007. *Handbook of Educational Linguistics*. Oxford:
    Wiley-Blackwell.

Other relevant handbooks include

Aarts, B. and A. McMahon (eds.). 2006. *The Handbook of English Linguistics*. Oxford: Blackwell.
Bhatia, T.K. and W.C. Ritchie (eds.). 2013. *The Handbook of Bilingualism and Multilingualism*. Oxford:
    Wiley-Blackwell.

Coulmas, F. (ed.). 1998. *The Handbook of Sociolinguistics*. Oxford: Blackwell.

Coupland, N. (ed.). 2010. *The Handbook of Language and Globalization*. Oxford: Wiley-Blackwell.

Doughty, C.J. and M. Long (eds.). 2003. *The Handbook of Second Language Acquisition*. Oxford: Blackwell.

Fitch, K. and R.E. Sanders (eds.). 2005. *Handbook of Language and Social Interaction*. Mahwah, NJ: Lawrence Erlbaum.

Fletcher, P. and B. MacWhinney (eds.). 1996. *The Handbook of Child Language*. Oxford: Blackwell.

Hickey, R. (ed.). 2010. *The Handbook of Language Contact*. Oxford: Wiley-Blackwell.

Hinkel, E. (ed.). 2005. *The Handbook of Research in Second Language Teaching and Learning*. Mahwah, NJ: Lawrence Erlbaum.

Holmes, J. and M. Meyerhoff. 2003. *The Handbook of Language and Gender*. Oxford: Blackwell.

Horn, L. and G. Ward (eds.). 2005. *The Handbook of Pragmatics*. Oxford: Blackwell.

Joshi, R. and P. Aaron (eds.). 2006. *Handbook of Orthography and Literacy*. Mahwah, NJ: Lawrence Erlbaum.

Kachru, B., Y. Kachru and C. Nelson (eds.). 2006. *The Handbook of World Englishes*. Oxford: Blackwell.

Kroll, J.F. and A.M.B. de Groot (eds.). 2005. *Handbook of Bilingualism: Psycholinguistic Approaches*. Oxford: Oxford University Press.

Long, M. and C. Doughty (eds.). 2009. *The Handbook of Language Teaching*. Oxford: Wiley-Blackwell.

Robinson, P. and N. Ellis (eds.). 2008. *Handbook of Cognitive Linguistics and Second Language Acquisition*. Abingdon: Routledge.

Schiffrin, D., D. Tannen and H.E. Hamilton (eds.). 2001. *The Handbook of Discourse Analysis*. Oxford: Blackwell.

3. Research Methods Guides

Wiley-Blackwell publishes a series of guides to research methods in language and linguistics under the general editorship of Li Wei. So far the volumes include

Hoff, Erika (ed.). 2011. *Research Methods in Child Language: A Practical Guide*. Oxford: Wiley-Blackwell.

Holmes, Janet and Kirk Hazen (eds.). 2013. *Research Methods in Sociolinguistics: A Practical Guide*. Oxford: Wiley-Blackwell.

Mackey, Alison and Susan Gass (eds.). 2011. *Research Methods in Second Language Acquisition: A Practical Guide*. Oxford: Wiley-Blackwell.

Müller, Nicole and Martin Ball (eds.). 2012. *Research Methods in Clinical Linguistics and Phonetics: A Practical Guide*. Oxford: Wiley-Blackwell.

Other guides to research methods include

Baayen, R. Harald. 2008. *Analyzing Linguistic Data: A Practical Introduction to Statistics using R*. Cambridge: Cambridge University Press.

Brown, James Dean and Rodgers, Theodore. 2003. *Doing Second Language Research*. Oxford: Oxford University Press.

Burns, Anne. 2009. *Doing Action Research in English Language Teaching*. Abingdon: Routledge.

Dörnyei, Zoltán. 2002. *Questionnaires in Second Language Research: Construction, Administration and Processing*. Hove: Psychology Press.

Dörnyei, Zoltán. 2007. *Research Methods in Applied Linguistics: Quantitative, Qualitative, and Mixed Methodologies*. Oxford: Oxford University Press.

Duff, Patricia. 2008. *Case Study Research in Applied Linguistics*. Mahwah, NJ: Lawrence Erlbaum Associates.

Hatch, Evelyn and Anne Lazaraton. 1991. *The Research Manual: Design and Statistics for Applied Linguistics*. Boston: Heinle & Heinle.

Larson-Hall, Jenifer. 2009. *A Guide to Doing Statistics in Second Language Research Using SPSS*. Abingdon: Routledge.

Li Wei and Melissa Moyer (eds.). 2008. *The Blackwell Guide to Research Methods in Bilingualism and Multilingualism*. Oxford: Wiley-Blackwell.

Mackey, Alison and Susan Gass. 2005. *Second Language Research: Methodology and Design*. Abingdon: Routledge.

Nunan, David. 1992. *Research Methods in Language Learning*. Cambridge: Cambridge University Press.

Paltridge, Brian and Aek Phakiti. 2010. *Continuum Companion to Research Methods in Applied Linguistics*. London: Continuum.

Perry, Fred Lehman. 2005. *Research in Applied Linguistics: Becoming a Discerning Consumer*. Abingdon: Routledge.

Wray, Alison and Aileen Bloomer. 2006. *Projects in Linguistics: A Practical Guide to Researching Language*, 2nd edn. London: Hodder Arnold.

4. Book series

Cambridge Applied Linguistics contains the following titles:

Second Language Instruction
Computer Applications in Second Language Acquisition
Corpora in Applied Linguistics
Criterion-Referenced Language Testing
Critical Pedagogies and Language Learning
Culture in Second Language Teaching and Learning
Evaluating Second Language Education
Exploring the Dynamics of Second Language Writing
Exploring the Second Language Mental Lexicon
Feedback in Second Language Writing
Focus on Form in Classroom Second Language Acquisition
Immersion Education
Interactive Approaches to Second Language Reading
Interfaces between Second Language Acquisition and Language Testing Research
Language Program Evaluation
Language Transfer
Learning Strategies in Second Language Acquisition
Learning Vocabulary in Another Language
Modelling and Assessing Vocabulary Knowledge
Network-Based Language Teaching: Concepts and Practice
Practice in a Second Language
Pragmatics in Language Teaching
Reading in a Second Language
Researching and Applying Metaphor
Research Perspectives on English for Academic Purposes
Second Language Needs Analysis
Second Language Vocabulary Acquisition
Second Language Writing
Task-Based Language Education
The Learner-Centred Curriculum
Understanding Expertise in Teaching

Cambridge Handbooks for Language Teachers contains the following titles:

Communicative Activities for EAP
Dialogue Activities
Dictation
Dictionary Activities
Extensive Reading Activities for Teaching Language
Games for Language Learning
Intercultural Language Activities
Keep Talking
Language Activities for Teenagers
Laughing Matters
Learner Autonomy
Learner English
Learning One-to-One
Lessons from Nothing
Literature in the Language Classroom
Personalizing Language Learning
Pictures for Language Learning
Planning Lessons and Courses
Pronunciation Practice Activities
Stories
Teach Business English
Teaching Adult Second Language Learners
Teaching English Spelling
Teaching Large Multilevel Classes
Teaching Listening Comprehension
Testing Spoken Language
The Internet and the Language Classroom
Using Authentic Video in the Language Classroom
Using Folktales
Using Newspapers in the Classroom
Using the Board in the Language Classroom
Working with Images
Working with Words

Other series published by Cambridge University Press include *Cambridge Language Assessment,* *Cambridge Language Education* and *Cambridge Teacher Training and Development.*

Oxford Applied Linguistics contains the following titles:

A Cognitive Approach to Language Learning
Analysing Learner Language
Complex Systems and Applied Linguistics
Context and Culture in Language Teaching
Conversational Interaction in a Second Language
English as a Lingua Franca: Attitude and Identity
Formulaic Language: Pushing the Boundaries
Individual Freedom in Language Teaching
Language Learner Strategies
Language Play, Language Learning

Language Testing in Practice
Lexical Phrases in Language Teaching
Linguistics Imperialism
Literacy and Second Language Oracy
Research Methods in Applied Linguistics
Resisting Linguistic Imperialism in English Teaching
Sociocultural Theory and Second Language Learning
Sociocultural Theory and the Genesis of Second Language Development
Task-Based Language Learning and Teaching
The Phonology of English as an International Language
The Psychology of Second Language Acquisition
The Struggle to Teach English as an International Language

Oxford Handbooks for Language Teachers contain the following titles:

Communication in the Language Classroom
Doing Second Language Research
Doing Task-Based Teaching
ESOL: A Critical Guide
Exploring Learner Language
From Experience to Knowledge in ELT
How Languages Are Learned
Intercultural Business Communication
Teaching American English Pronunciation
Teaching Business English
Teaching English as an International Language
Teaching English Overseas
Teaching Second Language Listening
Teaching Second Language Reading
Teaching the Pronunciation of English as a Lingua Franca
Teaching Young Language Learners

Oxford University Press also publishes a series, *Oxford Introductions to Language Study*, and other series on teacher education and professional development.

Routledge Introductions to Applied Linguistics is a series of textbooks covering the core topics in Applied Linguistics, primarily designed for those beginning postgraduate studies, or language professionals returning to academic studies, under the general editorship of Ronald Carter and Guy Cook. Published titles include

Cheng, Winnie. 2011. *Exploring Corpus Linguistics: Language in Action*. London: Routledge.
Ellis, Rod and Natsuko Shintani. 2013. *Exploring Language Pedagogy through Second Language Acquisition Research*. London: Routledge.
Gardner, Dee. 2013. *Exploring Vocabulary: Language in Action*. London: Routledge.
Green, Anthony. 2013. *Exploring Language Assessment and Testing: Language in Action*. London: Routledge.
Hall, Graham. 2011. *Exploring English Language Teaching: Language in Action*. London: Routledge.
Harvey, Kevin and Nelya Koteyko. 2012. *Exploring Health Communication: Language in Action*. London: Routledge.
Schnurr, Stephanie. 2012. *Exploring Professional Communication: Language in Action*. London: Routledge.

Seargeant, Philip. 2012. *Exploring World Englishes: Language in Action*. London: Routledge.
Walsh, Steve. 2011. *Exploring Classroom Discourse: Language in Action*. London: Routledge.
Zhu Hua. 2014. *Exploring Intercultural Communication: Language in Action*. London: Routledge.

Other book series include

ESL & Applied Linguistics Professional Series, formerly by Lawrence Erlbaum, now Routledge, Taylor
    & Francis.
Education Linguistics, Springer.
Research and Practice in Applied Linguistics, Palgrave Macmillan.
AILA Applied Linguistics Series, John Benjamins.
Penguin English Applied Linguistics Series, Penguin.
Studies in Applied Linguistics, Equinox.

5. Journals

There are many high-quality journals that are published in and for specific regions. The following
are international journals:

AILA Review
Annual Review of Applied Linguistics
Applied Linguistics
Applied Linguistics Review
Computer-Assisted Language Learning
ELT Journal
English for Specific Purposes
European Journal of Applied Linguistics
International Journal of Applied Linguistics
International Journal of Bilingual Education and Bilingualism
International Journal of Corpus Linguistics
International Review of Applied Linguistics in Language Teaching
Journal of Applied Linguistics
Journal of English for Academic Purposes
Journal of Second Language Writing
Language Acquisition
Language and Education
Language Awareness
Language, Culture and Curriculum
Language, Identity and Education
Language Learning
Language Teaching
Language Teaching Research
Language Testing
Linguistics and Education
Modern Language Journal
Second Language Research
Studies in Second Language Acquisition
System
TESOL Quarterly

6. Corpora

Bank of English

http://www.titania.bham.ac.uk/docs/svenguide.html#Getting%20Connected
A corpus collected at the University of Birmingham, currently containing a 450-million-word corpus of present-day English and a subcorpus aimed at teaching consisting of 56 million words. The COBUILD series of dictionaries and grammars are built on this corpus.

British National Corpus

http://corpus.byu.edu/bnc/
A corpus collected by Oxford University Press, Longman, Chambers, the British Library and the Universities of Oxford and Lancaster. It contains both spoken and written British English.

The Corpus of Contemporary American English (COCA)

http://www.americancorpus.org/
The largest corpus of American English. It contains over 400 million words.

Cambridge Learner Corpus (CLC)

http://www.cambridge.org/gb/elt/catalogue/subject/custom/item3646603/Cambridge-English-Corpus-Cambridge-Learner-Corpus/?site_locale=en_GB
As part of the Cambridge International Corpus, CLC has been compiled by Cambridge University Press and Cambridge ESOL. It contains a large collection of examples of English writing from anonymized exam scripts written by students taking Cambridge ESOL exams around the world. It currently contains over 30 million words from over 95,000 students speaking 130 different first languages.

Longman Corpus Network

http://www.pearsonlongman.com/dictionaries/corpus/index.html
A database of 330 million words from a wide range of real-life sources such as books, newspapers and magazines. Longman dictionaries are compiled using the database.

International Corpus of Learner English

http://cecl.fltr.ucl.ac.be/Cecl-Projects/Icle/icle.htm
One of the first learners' English corpora, currently containing over 3 million words of writing by learners of English from 21 different language backgrounds.

French Learner Language Oral Corpora

http://www.flloc.soton.ac.uk/
A comprehensive list of French learner corpora including Linguistic Development Corpus, Progression Corpus, Salford Corpus, Brussels Corpus, Reading Corpus, Newcastle Corpus, UEA Corpus.

English as a Lingua Franca in Academic Settings (ELFA)

http://www.uta.fi/ltl/en/english/research/projects/elfa.html
A joint research project between the University of Tampere and the University of Helsinki in Finland. The project has compiled a corpus of spoken academic English in intercultural contexts.

Vienna–Oxford International Corpus of English (VOICE)

http://www.univie.ac.at/voice/page/index.php
A database containing 1 million words of spoken ELF interactions among speakers from 50 different first languages (mainly, though not exclusively, European languages).

Michigan Corpus of Academic Spoken English (MICASE)

http://micase.elicorpora.info/
A collection of nearly 1.8 million words of transcribed speech (almost 200 hours of recordings) at the University of Michigan in Ann Arbor. It contains data from a wide range of speech events, such as lectures, classroom discussions, lab sections, seminars and advisory sessions, and locations across the university.

TalkBank

http://talkbank.org/
An interdisciplinary project, containing a number of sample databases within each of the subfields of communication, such as AphasiaBank, CHILDES, BilingBank, CABank, DementiaBank, and PhonBank. Its primary aim is to set up a system for sharing and studying conversational interactions.

CHILDES

http://childes.psy.cmu.edu/
The child language component of the TalkBank system. It contains transcript and media data collected from conversations between young children and their playmates and carers in different languages.

7. Professional Associations

International

International Association of Applied Linguistics (http://www.aila.info/)

America

American Association for Applied Linguistics (http://www.aaal.org/)
Center for Applied Linguistics (http://www.cal.org/)
Canadian Association of Applied Linguistics (http://www.aclacaal.org/)
Asociación Mexicana de Lingüística Aplicada (http://www.cele.unam.mx/amla/)
Asociación de Lingüística y Filología de América Latina/Associação de Linguística e Filologia da América Latina (http://www.mundoalfal.org/)

Europe

Association Belge de Linguistique Appliquée (http://centres.fusl.ac.be/ABLA/document/Abla/ABLA-FR/Bienvenue.html)
Asociación Española de Lingüística Aplicada (http://www.aesla.uji.es/)
Association Finlandaise de Linguistique Appliquée
Association Française de Linguistique Appliquée (http://www.afla-asso.org/)
Associazione Italiana di Linguistica Applicata (http://www.aitla.unimo.it/)
Association Néerlandaise de Linguistique Appliquée (http://www.anela.nl/)
Association Norvégienne de Linguistique Appliquée
Association Suédoise de Linguistique Appliquée (http://www.asla.se/)
Association Suisse de Linguistique Appliquée (http://www.vals-asla.ch/cms/)

British Association for Applied Linguistics (http://www.baal.org.uk/)
Estonian Association of Applied Linguistics
Gesellschaft für Angewandte Linguistik (http://www.gal-ev.de/)
Greek Applied Linguistics Association (http://www.enl.auth.gr/gala/)
Irish Association for Applied Linguistics (http://www.iraal.ie/)
Polish Association of Applied Linguistics (http://www.ptls.uw.edu.pl/en_GB/)

Oceania

Applied Linguistics Association of New Zealand (http://www.alanz.ac.nz/)
Applied Linguistics Association of Australia (http://www.alaa.org.au/)

Asia

Asian Association of TEFL (Asia TEFL) (http://www.asiatefl.org/)
Applied Linguistics Association of Korea (http://www.alak.or.kr/)
China English Language Education Association (http://www.celea.org.cn/)
Hong Kong Association for Applied Linguistics (http://www.haal.hk/)
Japan Association of College English Teachers (http://www.jacet.org/index.html)
Linguistic Society of the Philippines (http://www.dlsu.edu.ph/inside/organizations/lsp/default.asp)
Singapore Association for Applied Linguistics (http://www.saal.org.sg/)

Middle East and Africa

Israel Association of Applied Linguistics (http://www.tau.ac.il/~ilash/)
Southern African Applied Linguistics Association (http://www.saala.org.za/)

8. Websites

All the professional associations have their websites, which contain useful information. In addition, Center for Applied Linguistics at Washington, DC has a useful website: www.cal.org.

The Linguist List, http://linguistlist.org, provides up-to-date information about conferences, publications and exchanges of views among linguists of all interests.

Ethnologue, http://ethnologue.com, is a searchable database of language resources.

Vivian Cook, one of the leading scholars in the field of Applied Linguistics, runs a website, http://homepage.ntlworld.com/vivian.c/Vivian%20Cook.htm, which contains very useful information and a bibliography on various topics in Applied Linguistics.

Applied Linguistics.Org provides useful information on Applied Linguistics, language acquisition and language teaching: http://www.appliedlinguistics.org/.

References

Abrahamsson, Niclas and Kenneth Hyltenstam. 2008. The robustness of aptitude effects in near-native second language acquisition. *Studies in Second Language Acquisition* 30 (4), 481–509.

Abrahamsson, Niclas and Kenneth Hyltenstam. 2009. Age of onset and nativelikeness in a second language: Listener perception versus linguistic scrutiny. *Language Learning* 59 (2), 249–306.

AIE. 2009. *Autobiography of Intercultural Encounters. Context, Concepts and Theories.* Council of Europe. http://www.coe.int/t/dg4/autobiography/source/aie_en/aie_context_concepts_and_theories_en.pdf (last accessed 28 May, 2013).

Albert, Martin L. and Loraine K. Obler. 1978. *The Bilingual Brain.* New York: Academic Press.

Allport, Gordon. W. 1954. *The Nature of Prejudice.* Cambridge, MA: Perseus Books.

Andrewes, David. 2002. *Neuropsychology: From Theory to Practice.* Hove: Psychology Press.

Androutsopoulos, Jannis. 2006. Multilingualism, diaspora, and the Internet: Codes and identities on German-based diaspora websites. *Journal of Sociolinguistics* 10 (4), 524–551.

Anonymous. Aphasia: Frequently asked questions. http://www.aphasia.org/Aphasia%20Facts/aphasia_faq.html (last accessed 28 May, 2013).

Antaki, Charles and Susan Widdicombe (eds.). 1998. *Identities in Talk.* London: SAGE.

Anthony, Jason L. and David J. Francis. 2005. Development of phonological awareness. *Current Directions in Psychological Science* 14 (5), 255–259.

Ardito, Barbara, Maria Cristina Caselli, Angela Vecchietti and Virginia Volterra. 2008. Deaf and hearing children: Reading together in preschool. In Carolina Plaza-Pust and Esperanza Morales-López (eds.), *Sign Bilingualism: Language Development, Interaction, and Maintenance in Sign Language Contact Situations*, 137–164. Amsterdam: John Benjamins.

Arminen, Ilkka. 2005. *Institutional Interaction: Studies of Talk at Work.* Aldershot: Ashgate.

Arnold, Jane. 2011. Attention to affect in language learning. *Anglistik: International Journal of English Studies* 22 (1), 11–22.

Austin, John L. 1962. *How to Do Things with Words: The William James Lectures Delivered at Harvard University in 1955.* Oxford: Clarendon Press.

Avrutin, Sergey. 2001. Linguistics and agrammatism. *GLOT International* 5, 3–11.

Axelson, Elizabeth. 2007. Vocatives: A double-edged strategy in intercultural discourse among graduate students. *Pragmatics* 17 (1), 95–122.

Bailey, Benjamin. 2001. The language of multiple identities among Dominican Americans. *Journal of Linguistic Anthropology* 10 (2), 190–223.

Bailey, Benjamin. 2007. Heteroglossia and boundaries. In M. Heller (ed.), *Bilingualism: A Social Approach*, 257–274. Basingstoke: Palgrave.

Baker, Charlotte. 1977. Regulators and turn-taking in American Sign Language discourse. In Lynn A. Friedman (ed.), *On the Other Hand: New Perspectives on American Sign Language*, 215–236. New York: Academic Press.

Baker, Mona. 1992. *In Other Words.* London: Routledge.

Ballaster, R., M. Beetham, E. Frazer and S. Hebron. 1996. A critical analysis of women's magazines. In H. Baehr and A. Gray (eds.), *Turning It On: A Reader in Women and Media.* London: Arnold.

Baquedano-López, Patricia and Shlomy Kattan. 2007. Growing up in a multilingual community: Insights from language socialization. In P. Auer and Li Wei (eds.), *Handbook of Multilingualism and Multilingual Communication*, 69–100. Berlin: Mouton de Gruyter.

Baraldi, Claudio and Laura Gavioli. 2007. Dialogue interpreting as intercultural mediation. In M. Grein and E. Weigand (eds.), *Dialogue and Culture*, 155–176. Amsterdam: John Benjamins.

Barcelos, Ana Maria Ferreira, Paula Kalaja and Vera Menezes. 2008. *EFL Narrativized: Learning and Teaching Experiences*. Basingstoke: Palgrave Macmillan.

Bell, Allan. 2009. Language style as audience design. In N. Coupland and A. Jaworski (eds.), *The New Sociolinguistics Reader*, 265–276. Basingstoke: Palgrave Macmillan.

Benwell, Bethan and Elizabeth Stokoe. 2006. *Discourse and Identity*. Edinburgh: Edinburgh University Press.

Berk-Seligson, Susan. 1990. *The Bilingual Courtroom: Court Interpreters in the Judicial Process*. Chicago: Chicago University Press.

Berk-Seligson, Susan. 2002. *The Bilingual Courtroom: Court Interpreters in the Judicial Process*, 2nd edn. Chicago: University of Chicago Press.

Berthele, Raphael and Amelia Lambelet. 2009. Approche empirique de l'intercompréhension: répertoire, processus et résultats. *Revue de linguistique et de didactique des langues (LIDIL)* 39, 151–162.

Bezemer, Jeff and Gunther Kress. 2008. Writing in multimodal texts: A social semiotic account of designs for learning. *Written Communication* 25 (2), 166–195.

Bialystok, Ellen, Fergus I.M. Craik and Gigi Luk. 2012. Bilingualism: Consequences for mind and brain. *Trends in Cognitive Sciences* 16, 240–250.

Biber, Douglas and Susan Conrad. 2009. *Register, Genre and Style*. Cambridge: Cambridge University Press.

Biedron, Adriana and Anna Szczepniak. 2012. Working memory and short-term memory abilities in accomplished multilinguals. *Modern Language Journal* 96 (2), 290–306.

Birdsong, David. 2009. Age and the end-state of second language acquisition. In William C. Ritchie and Tej K. Bhatia (eds.), *The New Handbook of Second Language Acquisition*, 401–424. Bingley: Emerald.

Bishop, Dorothy V.M. and Catherine Adams. 1989. Conversational characteristics of children with semantic-pragmatic disorder. II: What features lead to a judgement of inappropriacy? *British Journal of Disorders of Communication* 24, 241–263.

Bjelic, Dusan. 1987. On hanging up in telephone conversations. *Semiotica* 67, 195–210.

Blanche, Patrick. 1988. Self-assessment of foreign language skills: Implications for teachers and researchers. *RELC Journal* 19 (1), 75–93.

Block, David. 2009. Identity in applied linguistics: The need for conceptual exploration. In V. Cook and Li Wei (eds.), *Contemporary Applied Linguistics, vol. 1: Language Teaching and Learning*, 215–232. London: Continuum.

Blum-Kulka, Shoshana. 1997. *Dinner Talk: Cultural Patterns of Sociability and Socialization in Family Discourse*. London: Lawrence Erlbaum.

Blum-Kulka, Shoshana. 2004. Shifts of cohesion and coherence in translation. In Lawrence Venuti (ed.), *The Translation Studies Reader*, 290–305. London: Routledge.

Blum-Kulka, Shoshana and Juliane House. 1989. Cross-cultural and situational variation in requesting behavior. In Shoshana Blum-Kulka, Juliane House and Gabriele Kasper (eds.), *Cross-cultural Pragmatics: Requests and Apologies*, 123–154. Norwood, NJ: Ablex.

Blum-Kulka, Shoshana, Juliane House and Gabriele Kasper. 1989. The CCSARP coding manual. In Shoshana Blum-Kulka, Juliane House and Gabriele Kasper (eds.), *Cross-cultural Pragmatics: Requests and Apologies*, 273–294. Norwood, NJ: Ablex.

Breuer, Anja and Ronald Geluykens. 2007. Requests in American and British English. In Bettina Kraft and Ronald Geluykens (eds.), *Cross-cultural Pragmatics and Interlanguage English*, 107–125. Munich: Lincom.

Brown, Penelope and Stephen C. Levinson. 1987 [1978]. *Politeness: Some Universals in Language Usage*. Cambridge: Cambridge University Press.

Brown, Roger and Albert Gilman. 1972. The pronouns of power and solidarity. In Pier Paolo Giglioli (ed.), *Language and Social Context: Selected Readings*, 252–282. Harmondsworth: Penguin.

Bucholtz, Mary and Kira Hall. 2006. Language and identity. In A. Duranti (ed.), *A Companion to Linguistic Anthropology*, 369–394. Oxford: Blackwell.

Buhrig, Kristin and Jan D. ten Thije (eds.). 2006. *Beyond Misunderstanding*. Amsterdam: John Benjamins.

Burman, Diana. 2008. Researching Deaf Children's Literacy. Presentation at ESRC Research Methods Festival, St Catherine's College, Oxford (3 July 2008).

Burrell, Ian. 2009. Why 5 Live thinks Murray is the man for the new season. *Media, The Independent*, 44 (3 August).

Butler, Judith. 1990. *Gender Trouble: Feminism and the Subversion of Identity*. London: Routledge.

Byram, Michael. 1997. *Teaching and Assessing Intercultural Communicative Competence in Practice*. Clevedon: Multilingual Matters.

Byram, Michael and Carol Morgan. 1994. *Teaching-and-Learning Language-and-Culture*. Clevedon: Multilingual Matters.

Cameron, Deborah and Dan Kulick (eds.). 2006. *The Language and Sexuality Reader*. London: Routledge.

Campbell, Steven. 2008. *Translation into the Second Language*. London: Longman.

Carroll, John and Stanley Sapon. 1959. *Modern Language Aptitude Test (MLAT): Manual*. San Antonio, TX: Psychological Corp.

Cenoz, Jasone. 2003. The additive effect of bilingualism in third language acquisition: A review. *International Journal of Bilingualism* 7 (1), 71–87.

Chapelle, Carol. 1999. Validity in language assessment. *Annual Review of Applied Linguistics* 19, 254–272. New York: Cambridge University Press.

Chen, Guo Ming and William J. Starosta. 1996. Intercultural communication competence: A synthesis. *Communication Yearbook* 19, 353–383.

Chen, Guo Ming and William J. Starosta. 1998. *Foundations of Intercultural Communication*. Needham Heights, MA: Allyn & Bacon.

Chen, Rong. 1993. Responding to compliments: A contrastive study of politeness strategies between American English and Chinese speakers. *Journal of Pragmatics* 20, 49–75.

Cheshire, Jenny. 2009. Syntactic variation and beyond. In Nikolas Coupland and Adam Jaworski (eds.), *The New Sociolinguistics Reader*, 119–135. Basingstoke: Palgrave Macmillan.

Chomsky, Noam. 1965. *Aspects of the Theory of Syntax*. Cambridge, MA: MIT Press.

Chouliaraki, Lillie and Norman Fairclough. 1999. *Discourse in Late Modernity*. Edinburgh: Edinburgh University Press.

Clahsen, Harold, Sonia Eisenbeiß and Martina Penke. 1996. Lexical learning in early syntactic development. In H. Clahsen (ed.), *Generative Perspectives on Language Acquisition*, 129–159. Amsterdam: John Benjamins.

Clyne, Michael, Catrin Norrby and Jane Warren. 2009. *Language and Human Relations: Styles of Address in Contemporary Language*. Cambridge: Cambridge University Press.

Coates, Jennifer (ed.). 1998. *Language and Gender: A Reader*. Oxford: Blackwell.

Coates, Jennifer. 1998. Gossip revisited. In J. Coates (ed.), *Language and Gender: A Reader*, 226–254. Oxford: Blackwell.

Coates, Jennifer. 1996. *Women Talk: Conversation between Women Friends*. Oxford: Blackwell.

Coates, Jennifer. 2003. *Men Talk*. Oxford: Blackwell.

Coates, Jennifer. 2004. *Women, Men and Language: A Sociolinguistic Account of Gender Differences in Language*. London: Longman.

Coates, Jennifer and Pia Pichler (eds.). 2011. *Language and Gender: A Reader*. Oxford: Wiley-Blackwell.

Conley, John M., William O'Barr and E. Allan Lind. 1979. The power of language: Presentational style in the courtroom. *Duke Law Journal* 6.

Cook, Guy. 2010. *Translation in Language Teaching*. Oxford: Oxford University Press.

Cook, Vivian J. (ed.). 2002. *Portraits of the L2 User*. Clevedon: Multilingual Matters.

Cook, Vivian J. and Benedetta Bassetti. 2010. *Language and Bilingual Cognition*. New York and Hove: Psychology Press.

Cook, Vivian J. and Li Wei (eds.). 2009. *Contemporary Applied Linguistics, vol. 1: Language Teaching and Learning; vol. 2: Linguistics for the Real World*. London: Continuum.

Cooper, Robert L. 1989. *Language Planning and Social Change*. New York: Cambridge University Press.

Coupland, Justine, Jeffrey D. Robinson and Nicolas Coupland. 1994. Frame negotiation in doctor–elderly patient consultations. *Discourse and Society* 5 (1), 89–124.

Creswell, John. 2003. *Research Design: Qualitative, Quantitative, and Mixed Methods Approaches*. London: SAGE.

Cromdal, Jakob. 2009. Childhood and social interaction in everyday life: Introduction to the special issue. *Journal of Pragmatics* 41 (8), 1473–1476.

Crystal, David. 2006. *Language and the Internet*, 2nd edn. Cambridge: Cambridge University Press.

Crystal, David. 2008. *Txtng: The Gr8 Db8*. Oxford: Oxford University Press.

Crystal, David. 2011. *Internet Linguistics: A Student Guide*. London: Routledge.

Culpeper, Jeremy and Dawn Archer. 2008. Requests and directness in Early Modern English trial proceedings and play texts, 1640–1760. In Andreas H. Jucker and Irma Taavitsainen (eds.), *Speech Acts in the History of English*, 45–84. Amsterdam: John Benjamins.

Cummins, Jim. 1979. Linguistic interdependence and the educational development of bilingual children. *Review of Educational Research* 49 (2), 222–251.

Cummins, Jim. 1991. Interdependence of first- and second-language proficiency in bilingual children. In Ellen Bialystok (ed.), *Language Processing in Bilingual Children*, 70–90. Cambridge: Cambridge University Press.

Cummins, Jim. 2000. *Language, Power and Pedagogy: Bilingual Children in the Crossfire*. Clevedon: Multilingual Matters.

Dagenais, Diane, Daniele Moore, Cecile Sabatier *et al.* 2009. Linguistic landscape and language awareness. In Elana Shohamy and Durk Gorter (eds.), *Linguistic Landscape: Expanding the Scenery*, 253–269. London: Routledge.

Danet, Brenda and Nicole Kermish. 1978. Courtroom questioning: A sociolinguistic perspective. In Louis N. Massery (ed.), *Psychology and Persuasion in Advocacy*, 412–441 Washington, DC: Association of Trial Lawyers of America.

Dascal, Marcelo. 1983. *Pragmatics and the Philosophy of Mind*. Amsterdam: John Benjamins.

Davies, Alan. 2003. *The Native Speaker: Myth and Reality*. Clevedon: Multilingual Matters.

De Angelis, Gessica. 2007. *Third or Additional Language Acquisition*. Clevedon: Multilingual Matters.

De Angelis, Gessica and Jean-Marc Dewaele. 2011. *New Trends in Crosslinguistic Influence and Multilingualism Research*. Bristol: Multilingual Matters.

De Graaff, Rick and Alex Housen. 2009. Investigating the effects and effectiveness of L2 instruction. In Michael Long and Catherine Doughty (eds.), *The Handbook of Language Teaching*, 726–755. Oxford: Wiley-Blackwell.

De Houwer, Annick. 2009a. *An Introduction to Bilingual Development*. Bristol: Multilingual Matters.

De Houwer, Annick. 2009b. *Bilingual First Language Acquisition*. Bristol: Multilingual Matters.

de Vaus, David. 2001. *Research Design in Social Research*. London: SAGE.

Debelle, Speech. 2009. You'll be hearing a lot more from her. *Culture, The Sunday Times*, 26–27 (26 July).

DeKeyser, Robert M. 1995. Learning second language grammar rules: An experiment with a miniature linguistic system. *Studies in Second Language Acquisition* 17, 379–410.

DeKeyser, Robert M. 1997. Beyond explicit rule learning: Automatizing second language morphosyntax. *Studies in Second Language Acquisition* 19, 195–221.

DeKeyser, Robert M. 2000. The robustness of critical period effects in second language acquisition. *Studies in Second Language Acquisition*, 22 (4), 499–533.

DeKeyser, Robert M. and Jennifer Larson-Hall. 2005. What does the critical period really mean? In Judith F. Kroll and Annette de Groot (eds.), *Handbook of Bilingualism: Psycholinguistic Approaches*, 88–108. Oxford: Oxford University Press.

Dewaele, Jean-Marc. 2007. Diachronic and/or synchronic variation? The acquisition of sociolinguistic competence in L2 French. In Dalila Ayoun (ed.), *Handbook of French Applied Linguistics*, 208–236. Amsterdam: John Benjamins.

Dewaele, Jean-Marc. 2008. Appropriateness in foreign language acquisition and use: Some theoretical, methodological and ethical considerations. *International Review of Applied Linguistics* 46, 235–255.

Dewaele, Jean-Marc. 2009. Individual differences in second language acquisition. In William C. Ritchie and Tej K. Bhatia (eds.), *The New Handbook of Second Language Acquisition*, 623–646. Bingley: Emerald.

Dewaele, Jean-Marc. 2010. Multilingualism and affordances: Variation in self-perceived communicative competence and communicative anxiety in French L1, L2, L3 and L4. *International Review of Applied Linguistics* 48, 105–129.

Dewaele, Jean-Marc. 2012. Learner-internal psychological factors. In Julia Herschensohn and Martha Young-Scholten (eds.), *The Cambridge Handbook of Second Language Acquisition*, 159–179. Cambridge: Cambridge University Press.

Dewaele, Jean-Marc and Li Wei. 2012. Is multilingualism linked to a higher tolerance of ambiguity? *Bilingualism: Language and Cognition*. DOI: 10.1017/S1366728912000570.

Dewaele, Jean-Marc and Li Wei. 2013. Is multilingualism linked to a higher tolerance of ambiguity? *Bilingualism: Language and Cognition* 16 (1), 231–240.

Dewaele, Jean-Marc and Anat Stavans. 2012. The effect of immigration, acculturation and multicompetence on personality profiles of Israeli multilinguals. *International Journal of Bilingualism*. DOI: 10.1177/1367006912439941.

Dewaele, Jean-Marc and Helen Thirtle. 2009. Why do some young learners drop foreign languages? A focus on learner-internal variables. *International Journal of Bilingual Education and Bilingualism* 12 (6), 635–649.

Dewaele, Jean-Marc and Jan Pieter Van Oudenhoven. 2009. The effect of multilingualism/multiculturalism on personality: No gain without pain for Third Culture Kids? *International Journal of Multilingualism* 6 (4), 443–459.

Dewaele, Jean-Marc, Konstantinos V. Petrides and Adrian Furnham. 2008. The effects of trait emotional intelligence and sociobiographical variables on communicative anxiety and foreign language anxiety among adult multilinguals: A review and empirical investigation. *Language Learning* 58 (4), 911–960.

Dimitropoulou, Maria, Jon Duñabeitia and Manuel Carreiras. 2011. Transliteration and transcription effects in bi-scriptal readers: the case of Greeklish. *Psychonomic Bulletin & Review* 18 (4), 729–735.

Dorian, Nancy. 1981. *The Life Cycle of a Scottish Gaelic Dialect*. Philadelphia: University of Pennsylvania Press.

Dorian, Nancy. 2010. *Investigating Variation: The Effects of Social Organization and Social Setting*. New York: Oxford University Press.

Dörnyei, Zoltán. 2005. *The Psychology of the Language Learner: Individual Differences in Second Language Acquisition*. Mahwah, NJ: Lawrence Erlbaum.

Dörnyei, Zoltán. 2006. Individual differences in second language acquisition. *AILA Review* 19, 42–68.

Dörnyei, Zoltán. 2007. *Research Methods in Applied Linguistics*. Oxford: Oxford University Press.

Dörnyei, Zoltán and Ema Ushioda (eds.). 2009. *Motivation, Language Identity and the L2 Self*. Bristol: Multilingual Matters.

Du Plessis, T. 2010. Bloemfontein/Mangaung, a city on the move. In Elana Shohamy, Elizier Ben Rafael and Monica Barni (eds.), *Linguistic Landscape in the City*, 74–95. Bristol: Multilingual Matters.

Duranti, Alessandro, Elinor Ochs and Bambi B. Schieffelin (eds.). 2012. *The Handbook of Language Socialization*. Oxford: Wiley-Blackwell.

Eades, Diana. 1996. Legal recognition of cultural differences in communication: The case of Robyn Kina. *Language and Communication* 16 (3), 215–227.

Eades, Diana. 2008. *Courtroom Talk and Neocolonial Control*. Berlin: Mouton de Gruyter.

Eckert, Penelope. 2000. *Language Variation as Social Practice: The Linguistic Construction of Identity in Belten High*. Oxford: Blackwell.

Eckert, Penelope. 2012. Three waves of variation study: The emergence of meaning in the study of sociolinguistic variation. *Annual Review of Anthropology* 41, 87–100.

Edwards, Susan. 2005. *Fluent Aphasia*. Cambridge: Cambridge University Press.

Eelen, Gino. 2001. *A Critique of Politeness Theories*. Manchester: St. Jerome.

Eisenbeiß, Sonja. 2009. Generative approaches to language learning. *Linguistics* 47 (2), 273–310.

Ellis, Nick. 2005. Measuring implicit and explicit knowledge of a second language: A psychometric study. *Studies in Second Language Acquisition* 27, 141–172.

Ellis, Rod. 2004. *The Study of Second Language Acquisition*. Oxford: Oxford University Press.

Ely, Richard and Jean Berko Gleason. 1995. Socialisation across contexts. In Paul Fletcher and Brian MacWhinney (eds.), *The Handbook of Child Language*, 251–270. Oxford: Blackwell.

Evans, Bruce A. and Nancy H. Hornberger. 2005. No Child Left Behind: Repealing and unpeeling federal language education policy in the United States. *Language Policy* 4 (1), 87–106.

Fairclough, Norman. 1989. *Language and Power*. London: Longman.

Fairclough, Norman. 1993. Critical discourse analysis and the marketization of public discourse. *Discourse and Society* 4 (2), 133–159.

Fairclough, Norman. 1995. *Media Discourse*. London: Arnold.

Fairclough, Norman. 2000. *New Labour, New Language*. London: Routledge.

Fairclough, Norman. 2003. *Analysing Discourse: Textual Analysis for Social Research*. London: Routledge.

Fant, Lars. 1992. Scandinavians and Spaniards in negotiation. In Annick Sjögren and Lena Janson (eds.), *Culture and Management in the Field of Ethnology and Business Administration*, 125–153. Stockholm: Stockholm School of Economics; Swedish Immigration Institute and Museum.

Fantini, Alvino E. 2000. A central concern: Developing intercultural competence. In Alvino E. Fantini (ed.), *About our Institution* (SIT Occasional Paper Series), 25–42. Brattleboro, VT: School for International Training.

Ferdman, Bernardo M., Rose-Marie Weber and Arnulfo G. Ramírez (eds.). 1994. *Literacy Across Languages and Literatures*. Albany, NY: State University of New York Press.

Ferguson, Charles. 1959. Diglossia. *Word* 15, 325–337. Reprinted in Li Wei (ed.). 2000. *The Bilingualism Reader*, 65–80. London: Routledge.

Fishman, Joshua (ed.). 2001. *Can Threatened Languages be Saved? Reversing Language Shift Revisited: A 21st Century Perspective*. Clevedon: Multilingual Matters.

Fitch, Kristine L. 1998. *Speaking Relationally: Culture, Communication, and Interpersonal Connection*. New York: Guilford Press.

Fleischmann, Suzanne. 2001. Language and medicine. In Deborah Schiffrin, Deborah Tannen and Heidi Hamilton (eds.), *The Handbook of Discourse Analysis* (Blackwell Handbooks in Linguistics), 470–502, 470–502. Oxford: Blackwell.

Fletcher, Paul and Brian MacWhinney (eds.). 1995. *The Handbook of Child Language*. Oxford: Blackwell.

Flynn, Nancy and Tom Flynn. 2003. *Writing Effective Email*, rev. edn. Menlo Park, CA: Crisp Publications.

Fowler, Roger. 1991. *Language in the News: Discourse and Ideology in the British Press*. London: Routledge.

Fowler, Roger, Bob Hodge, Gunther Kress and Tony Trew. 1979. *Language and Control*. London: Routledge and Kegan Paul.

Gafaranga, Joseph and Nicky Britten. 2003. 'Fire away': the opening sequence in general practice consultations. *Family Practice* 20, 242–247.

Gal, Susan. 1978. Peasant men can't get wives: Language change and sex roles in a bilingual community. *Language in Society* 7 (1), 1–16.

Gal, Susan. 1979. *Language Shift: Social Determinants of Linguistic Change in Bilingual Austria*. New York: Academic Press.

García, Ofelia, Lesley Bartlett and JoAnne Kleifgen. 2008. From biliteracy to pluriliteracies. In Peter Auer and Li Wei (eds.), *Handbook of Multilingualism and Multilingual Communication*, 207–228. New York: De Gruyter.

Gardner, Robert C. 1985. *Social Psychology and Second Language Learning: The Role of Attitudes and Motivation*. London: Edward Arnold.

Gardner, Robert C. 2006. The socio-educational model of second language acquisition: A research paradigm. *EUROSLA Yearbook* 6, 237–260.

Gardner-Chloros, Penelope. 2009. *Code-switching*. Cambridge: Cambridge University Press.

Gee, James P. 2008. *What Video Games Have to Teach Us About Learning and Literacy*, 2nd edn. Basingstoke: Palgrave Macmillan.

Gee, James P. 2011. *Social Linguistics and Literacies: Ideology in Discourses*, 4th edn. London: Routledge.

Georgakopoulou, Alexandra. 1997. Self-presentation and interactional alliances in e-mail discourse: The style- and code-switches of Greek messages. *International Journal of Applied Linguistics* 7 (2), 141–164.

Geschwind, Norman and Albert M. Galaburda. 1985. Cerebral lateralization: Biological mechanisms, associations, and pathology. *Archives of Neurology* 42, 428–459.

Gibbons, John. 1999. Language and the law. *Annual Review of Applied Linguistics* 19, 156–173.

Gibbons, John. 2003. *Forensic Linguistics*. Oxford: Blackwell.

Gibbons, John and Maria T. Turell. 2008. *Dimensions of Forensic Linguistics*. Amsterdam: John Benjamins.

Goffman, Erving. 1972 [1955]. *Interaction Ritual: Essays on Face-to-Face Behaviour*. Harmondsworth: Penguin.

Goodglass, Harold. 1993. *Understanding Aphasia*. New York: Academic Press.

Goodglass, Harold and Sheila Blumstein (eds.). 1973. *Psycholinguistics and Aphasia*. Baltimore: Johns Hopkins University Press.

Goodglass, Harold and Norman Geschwind. 1976. Language disorders (aphasia). In Edward C. Carterette and Morton P. Friedman (eds.), *Handbook of Perception, vol. 7: Language and Speech*, 389–428. New York: Academic Press.

Goodglass, Harold and Edith Kaplan. 1983. *The Assessment of Aphasia and Related Disorders*. Philadelphia, PA: Lea & Febiger.

Goodglass, Harold and Arthur Wingfield. 1997. *Anomia*. New York: Academic Press.

Goodman, Kenneth, Yetta Goodman and Barbara Flores. 1979. *Reading in the Bilingual Classroom: Literacy and Biliteracy*. Rosslyn, VA: National Clearinghouse for Bilingual Education.

Greenstreet, Rosanna. 2009. Q&A: Jane Horrocks. *Guardian Weekend*, 10 (31 October).

Grice, P. 1975 [1967]. Logic in conversation. In Peter Cole and Jerry L. Morgan (eds.), *Speech Acts* (Syntax and Semantics 3), 41–58. New York: Academic Press.

Griessler, Marion. 2001. The effects of third language learning on L2 proficiency: An Austrian example. *International Journal of Bilingual Education and Bilingualism* 4 (1), 50–60.

Griffiths, Carol (ed.). 2008. *Lessons from Good Language Learners*. Cambridge: Cambridge University Press.

Grodzinsky, Yosef. 1990. *Theoretical Perspectives on Language Deficits*. Cambridge, MA: MIT Press.

Gudykunst, William. 1994. *Bridging Differences: Effective Intergroup Communication*. Thousand Oaks, CA: SAGE.

Gudykunst, William (ed.). 2005. *Theorizing About Intercultural Communication*. Thousand Oaks, CA: SAGE.

Gudykunst, William B. and Young Yun Kim. 2003. *Communicating with Strangers: An Approach to Intercultural Communication*, 4th edn. New York: McGraw-Hill.

Gudykunst, William B. and Stella Ting-Toomey. 1988. Verbal communication styles. In William B. Gudykunst and Stella Ting-Toomey (eds.), *Culture and Interpersonal Communication*, 99–115. Newbury Park, CA: SAGE.

Gumperz, John. 1978. The conversational analysis of interethnic communication. In E. Lamar Ross (ed.), *Interethnic Communication*, 13–31. Proceedings of the Southern Anthropological Society. Athens, GA: University of Georgia Press.

Gumperz, John. 1982. *Discourse Strategies*. Cambridge: Cambridge University Press.

Gumperz, John and Deborah Tannen. 1979. Individual and social differences in language use. In C. Fillmore, D. Kempler and W. Wang (eds.), *Individual Differences in Language Ability and Language Behaviour*, 305–325. London: Academic Press.

Gumperz, John, Tom Jupp and Celia Roberts. 1979. *Crosstalk*. Southall: National Centre for Industrial Language Training.

Hall, Edward T. 1966. *The Hidden Dimension*. Garden City, NY: Doubleday.

Hall, Edward T. 1976. *Beyond Culture*. Garden City, NY: Doubleday.

Hall, Philip. 2004. Prone to distortion? Undue reliance on unreliable records in the NSW Police Service's formal interview model. In John Gibbons (ed.), *Language and Justice*, 44–81. Bombay: Longman Orient.

Hall, Phil. 2008. Policespeak. In J. Gibbons and M.T. Turell (eds.), *Dimensions of Forensic Linguistics*, 67–94. Amsterdam: John Benjamins.

Halliday, Michael A.K. 1978. *Language as Social Semiotic: The Social Interpretation of Language and Meaning*. Baltimore: University Park Press.

Hammer, Mitchell, Milton Bennett and Richard Wiseman. 2003. Measuring intercultural sensitivity: The intercultural development inventory. *International Journal of Intercultural Relations* 27, 421–443.

Hamp-Lyons, Liz. 1997. Washback, impact and validity: Ethical concerns. *Language Testing* 14 (3), 295–303.

Han, Zhao Hong. 2009. Interlanguage and fossilization: Towards an analytic model. In Vivian J. Cook and Li Wei (eds.), *Language Teaching and Learning*, 137–162. London: Continuum.

Hanauer, D. 2009. Science and the linguistic landscape: A genre analysis of representational wall space in a micro-biology laboratory. In E. Shohamy and D. Gorter (eds.), *Linguistic Landscape: Expanding the Scenery*, 287–301. London: Routledge.

Harrington, Jonathan, Sallyanne Palethorpe and Catherine Watson. 2000. Monophthongal vowel changes in Received Pronunciation: An acoustic analysis of the Queen's Christmas broadcasts. *Journal of the International Phonetic Association* 30 (1), 63–78, (2) 1–4.

Harris, George. 2009. I woke up with a Russian accent. *The Guardian* (9 May).

Harvey, Keith. 2004. Translating camp talk. In Lawrence Venuti (ed.), *The Translation Studies Reader*, 2nd edn, 402–422. London: Routledge.

Hatim, Basil and Ian Mason. 1990. *Discourse and the Translator*. London: Longman.

Hatim, Basil and Ian Mason. 1997a. Politeness in screen translating. In Basil Hatim and Ian Mason, *The Translator as Communicator*, 65–80. London: Routledge.

Hatim, Basil and Ian Mason. 1997b. *The Translator as Communicator*. London: Routledge.

Hatim, Basil and Jeremy Munday. 2004. *Translation: An Advanced Resource Book*. London: Routledge.

Haugen, Einar. 1966. Linguistics and language planning. In William Bright (ed.), *Sociolinguistics: Proceedings of the UCLA Sociolinguistics Conference 1964*, 50–71. The Hague: Mouton.

Heath, Shirley Brice. 1986. Sociocultural contexts of language development. In *Beyond Language: Social and Cultural Factors in Schooling Language Minority Students*, 145–186. Los Angeles: California State University, Evaluation, Dissemination and Assessment Center.

Heft, Harry. 2001. *Ecological Psychology in Context: James Gibson, Roger Barker, and the Legacy of William James's Radical Empiricism*. Mahwah, NJ: Lawrence Erlbaum.

Hickok, Gregory, Ursula Bellugi and Edward Klima. 1998. The neural organization of language: Evidence from sign language aphasia. *Trends in Cognitive Sciences* 2 (4), 129–136.

Hines, Nico and Philip Webster. Jacqui Janes accepts Gordon Brown's apology. 2009. *The Times* online (10 November). http://www.thetimes.co.uk/tto/news/politics/article2030134.ece (last accessed 28 May 2013).

Hinnenkamp, Volker. 2008. Deutsch, Doyc or Doitsch? Chatters as languagers – the case of a German-Turkish chat room. *International Journal of Multilingualism* 5 (3), 253–275.

Hinrichs, Lars. 2006. *Codeswitching on the Web*. Amsterdam and Philadelphia, PA: John Benjamins.

Hofstede, Geert. 2001. *Culture's Consequences: International Differences in Work-related Values*, 2nd edn. Beverly Hills, CA: SAGE.

Höhle, Barbara. 2009. Bootstrapping mechanisms in first language acquisition. *Linguistics* 47 (2), 359–382.

Hornberger, Nancy H. 1989. Continua of biliteracy. *Review of Educational Research* 59, 271–296.

Hornberger, Nancy H. 1990. Creating successful learning contexts for bilingual literacy. *Teachers College Record* 92 (2), 212–229.

Hornberger, Nancy H. 2000. Multilingual literacies, literacy practices, and the continua of biliteracy. In Marilyn Martin-Jones and Kathryn Jones (eds.), *Multilingual Literacies*, 353–368. Amsterdam: John Benjamins.

Hornberger, Nancy H. 2003. *Continua of Biliteracy: An Ecological Framework for Educational Policy, Research and Practice in Multilingual Settings*. Clevedon: Multilingual Matters.

Hornberger, Nancy H. and Ellen Skilton-Sylvester. 2000. Revisiting the continua of biliteracy: International and critical perspectives. *Language and Education: An International Journal* 14 (2), 96–122.

Housen, Alex and Michel Pierrard (eds.). 2005. *Investigations in Instructed Second Language Acquisition*. Berlin: Mouton de Gruyter.

Housen, Alex, Michel Pierrard and Siska Van Daele. 2005. Rule complexity and the efficacy of explicit grammar instruction. In Alex Housen and Michel Pierrard (eds.), *Investigations in Instructed Second Language Acquisition*, 235–270. Berlin: Mouton de Gruyter.

Housen, Alex, Els Schoonjans, Sonia Janssens *et al.* 2011. Conceptualizing and measuring the impact of contextual factors in instructed SLA – the role of language prominence. *International Review of Applied Linguistics* 49, 83–112.

Howard, Martin, Raymond Mougeon and Jean-Marc Dewaele. 2013. Sociolinguistics and second language acquisition. In Robert Bayley, Richard Cameron and Ceil Lucas (eds.), *The Oxford Handbook of Sociolinguistics*, 340–359. New York: Oxford University Press.

Hutchby, Ian. 1996. Power in discourse: The case of arguments on a British talk radio show. *Discourse and Society* 7 (4), 481–497.

Hutchby, Ian and Simone Barnett. 2005. Aspects of the sequential organization of mobile phone conversation. *Discourse Studies* 7, 147–171.

Hyams, Nina. 1996. The underspecification of functional categories in early grammar. In H. Clahsen (ed.), *Generative Perspectives on Language Acquisition*, 91–127. Amsterdam: John Benjamins.

Ide, Sachiko. 2005. How and why honorifics can signify dignity and elegance: The indexicality and reflexivity of linguistic rituals. In Robin T. Lakoff and Sachiko Ide (eds.), *Broadening the Horizon of Linguistic Politeness*, 45–64. Amsterdam: John Benjamins. Reprinted in Zhu Hua (ed.), 2011. *The Language and Intercultural Communication Reader*. London: Routledge.

Ijalba, Elizabeth, Loraine Obler and Shyamala Chengappa. 2004. Bilingual aphasia. In Tej K. Bhatia and William C. Ritchie (eds.), *The Handbook of Bilingualism*, 71–89. Oxford: Blackwell.

Irvine, J. 1989. When talk isn't cheap: Language and political economy. *American Ethnologist* 16 (2), 248–267.

Jaffe, Alexandra. 2012. *Stance: Sociolinguistic Perspectives*. New York: Oxford University Press.

Jakobson, Roman. 1959. On linguistic aspects of translation. In Lawrence Venuti (ed.), 2004. *The Translation Studies Reader*, 138–143. London: Routledge.

Jakobson, Roman. 1968[1941]. *Child Language, Aphasia and Phonological Universals*. The Hague: Mouton.

Jarvis, Scott and Aneta Pavlenko. 2008. *Crosslinguistic Influence in Language and Cognition*. New York: Routledge.

Jaworski, Adam and Simone Yeung. 2010. Life in the Garden of Eden: Naming in Hong Kong. In Elana Shohamy, Eliezer Ben Rafael and Monica Barni (eds.), *Linguistic Landscape in the City*, 153–181. Bristol: Multilingual Matters.

Jenkins, Lyle. 2000. *Biolinguistics*. Cambridge: Cambridge University Press.

Jeon, Eun Hee and Tadayoshi Kaya. 2006. Effects of L2 instruction on interlanguage pragmatic development. In John M. Norris and Lourdes Ortega (eds.), *Synthesizing Research on Language Learning and Teaching*, 165–211. Amsterdam and Philadelphia, PA: John Benjamins.

Jessner, Ulrike. 2006. *Linguistic Awareness in Multilinguals*. Edinburgh: Edinburgh University Press.

Johnson, Jacqueline S. and Elissa L. Newport. 1989. Critical period effects in second language learning: The influence of maturational state on the acquisition of ESL. *Cognitive Psychology* 21, 60–99.

Johnstone, Barbara. 2007. *Discourse Analysis*, 2nd edn. Oxford: Wiley-Blackwell.

Jones, R. 1979. Performance testing of second language proficiency. In E. Briere and F. Hinofotis (eds.), *Concepts in Language Testing*, 50–57. Washington, DC: TESOL.

Jurgensen, John. 2009. Cormac McCarthy on *The Road*. *The Times Saturday Review*, 1 (14 November).

Kasper, Gabrielle. 2009. L2 pragmatic development. In William C. Ritchie and Tej K. Bhatia (eds.), *The New Handbook of Second Language Acquisition*, 259–293. Bingley: Emerald.

Kauschke, Christina and Christoph Hofmeister. 2002. Early lexical development in German: A study on vocabulary growth and vocabulary acquisition during the second and third year of life. *Journal of Child Language* 29, 735–757.

Kean, Mary Louise (ed.). 1985. *Agrammatism*. New York: Academic Press.

Kemp, Charlotte. 2007. Strategic processing in grammar learning: Do multilinguals use more strategies? *International Journal of Multilingualism* 4, 241–261.

Kenner, C. 2004. *Becoming Biliterate: Young Children Learning Different Writing Systems*. Stoke-on-Trent: Trentham.

Kerbrat-Orecchioni, Catherine. 1997. A multilevel approach in the study of talk-in-interaction. *Pragmatics* 7, 1–20.

Kern, Richard. 2011. Technology and language learning. In James Simpson (ed.), *The Routledge Handbook of Applied Linguistics*, 200–214. London: Routledge.

Kerswill, Paul. 2001. Koineization and accommodation. In J.K. Chambers, Peter Trudgill and Natalie Schilling-Estes, *The Handbook of Language Variation and Change*, 669–702. Oxford: Blackwell.

Kinginger, Celeste. 2004. Alice doesn't live here anymore: Foreign language learning and renegotiated identity. In Aneta Pavlenko and Adrian Blackledge (eds.), *Negotiation of Identities in Multilingual Contexts*, 219–242. Clevedon: Multilingual Matters.

Kinginger, Celeste. 2008. *Language Learning in Study Abroad: Case Studies of Americans in France*. Oxford: Wiley-Blackwell.

Kinginger, Celeste and Géraldine Blattner. 2008. Histories of engagement and sociolinguistic awareness in study abroad: Colloquial French. In Lourdes Ortega and Heidi Byrnes (eds.), *The Longitudinal Study of Advanced L2 Capacities*, 223–246. Mahwah, NJ: Lawrence Erlbaum.

Kloss, H. 1969. Research Possibilities on Group Bilingualism: A Report. Quebec: International Centre for Research on Bilingualism.

Kluckhohn, Florence and Fred Strodtbeck. 1961. *Variations in Value Orientations*. New York: Row, Petersen.

Kolb, David A. 1984. *Experiential Learning: Experience as the Source of Learning and Development*. Englewood Cliffs, NJ: Prentice-Hall.

Kramsch, Claire. 1991. Culture in language learning: A view from the States. In Kees de Bot, Ralph B. Ginsberg and Claire Kramsch (eds.), *Foreign Language Research in Cross-cultural Perspective*, 217–240. Amsterdam: John Benjamins.

Kramsch, Claire J. 2001. Intercultural communication. In R. Carter and D. Nunan (eds.), *The Cambridge Guide to Teaching English to Speakers of Other Languages*, 201–206. Cambridge: Cambridge University Press.

Kramsch, Claire J. 2006. From communicative competence to symbolic competence. *Modern Language Journal* 90 (2), 249–252.

Krashen, Stephen D. 1981. *Second Language Acquisition and Second Language Learning*. Oxford: Pergamon.

Krashen, Stephen D. 1982. *Principles and Practice in Second Language Acquisition*. Hemel Hempstead: Prentice Hall International.

Kress, Gunther, Carey Jewitt, Jill Bourne *et al*. 2005. *English in Urban Classrooms: Multimodal Perspectives on Teaching and Learning*. London: Routledge/Falmer.

Kroskrity, Paul V. 1998. Arizona Tewa Kwa speech as a manifestation of linguistic ideology. *Pragmatics* 3, 297–309.

Kunnan, Antony J. 2004. Test fairness. In M. Milanovic, C. Weir and S. Bolton (eds.), *Europe Language Testing in a Global Context: Selected Papers from the ALTE Conference in Barcelona*, 27–48. Cambridge: Cambridge University Press.

Kurzon, Daniel. 2008. The silent witness: Pragmatic and literal interpretations. In John Gibbons and Maria T. Turell (eds.), *Dimensions of Forensic Linguistics*, 161–178. Amsterdam: John Benjamins.

Labov, William. 1963. The social motivation of a sound change. *Word* 19, 273–309.

Labov, William. 1972. *Sociolinguistic Patterns*. Philadelphia: University of Pennsylvania Press.

Labov, William. 1982. Objectivity and commitment in linguistic science: The case of the Black English trial in Ann Arbor. *Language in Society* 11 (2), 165–201.

Labov, William. 1997. How I Got Into Linguistics, and What I Got Out Of It. http://linguistlist.org/fund-drive/2008/linguist-of-the-day/Labov.cfm (last accessed 28 May 2013).

Ladd, Paddy. 2003. *Understanding Deaf Culture*. Clevedon: Multilingual Matters.

Lado, Robert. 1957. *Linguistics Across Cultures*. Ann Arbor: University of Michigan Press.

Lakoff, George and Mark Johnson. 1980. *Metaphors We Live By*. Chicago: University of Chicago Press.

Lantolf, Jim P. and Aneta Pavlenko. 2001. (S)econd (L)anguage (A)ctivity Theory: Understanding second language learners as people. In M. Breen (ed.), *Learner Contributions to Language Learning: New Directions in Research*, 141–158. London: Longman.

Lanza, Elizabeth. 2007. Multilingualism and the family. In Peter Auer and Li Wei (eds.), *Handbook of Multilingualism and Multilingual Communication*, 45–66. Berlin: Mouton de Gruyter.

LaPointe, Leonard L. 2097. *Aphasia and Related Neurogenic Language Disorders*, 2nd edn. New York: Thieme.

Lasagabaster, David. 1998. The threshold hypothesis applied to three languages in contact at school. *International Journal of Bilingual Education and Bilingualism* 4 (5), 310–328.

Le Page, Robert B. and Andrée Tabouret-Keller. 1985. *Acts of Identity*. Cambridge: Cambridge University Press.

Le Pichon Vorstman, Emmanuelle, Henriette de Swart, Viktorija Ceginskas and Huub van den Bergh. 2009. Language learning experience in school context and metacognitive awareness of multilingual children. *International Journal of Multilingualism* 6 (3), 258–280.

Leech, Geoffrey N. 1983. *Principles of Pragmatics*. London: Longman.

Leeman, J. and G. Modan. 2010. Selling the city: Language, ethnicity and commodified space. In Elana Shohamy, Eliezer Ben Rafael and Monica Barni (eds.), *Linguistic Landscape in the City*, 184–200. Bristol: Multilingual Matters.

Lehtonen, Jaakko and Kari Sajaavara. 1985. The silent Finn. In Deborah Tannen and Muriel Saville-Troike (eds.), *Perspectives on Silence*, 193–201. Norwood, NJ: Ablex.

Lenneberg, Eric H. 1967. *Biological Foundations of Language*. New York: John Wiley & Sons.

Leonard, Lawrence B. 1998. *Children with Specific Language Impairment*. Cambridge, MA: MIT Press.

Lewin, Kurt. 1946. Action research and minority problems. *Journal of Social Issues* 2 (4), 34–46.

Lexander, Kristin Vold. 2010. Vœux électroniques plurilingues: nouvelles pratiques, nouvelles fonctions pour les langues africaines? *Journal of Language Contact, THEMA* 3, 228–246.

Li Wei. 1994. *Three Generations, Two Languages, One Family: Language Choice and Language Shift in a Chinese Community in Britain*. Clevedon: Multilingual Matters.

Li Wei. 1998. Banana split? Variations in language choice and code-switching patterns of two groups of British-born Chinese in Tyneside. In Rodolfo Jacobson (ed.), *Codeswitching Worldwide*, 153–176. Berlin: Mouton de Gruyter.

Li Wei (ed.). 2000. *The Bilingualism Reader*. London: Routledge.

Li Wei (ed.). 2011. *The Routledge Applied Linguistics Reader*. London: Routledge.

Liddicoat, Anthony. 2011. *An Introduction to Conversation Analysis*, 2nd edn. London: Continuum.

Lightbown, Patricia M. and Nina Spada. 1994. An innovative program for primary ESL in Quebec. *TESOL Quarterly* 28 (3), 563–579.

Lindlof, Thomas and Bryan Taylor. 2002. *Qualitative Communication Research Methods*, 2nd edn. London: SAGE.

Lippi-Green, R. 1997. *English with an Accent: Language, Ideology, and Discrimination in the United States*. London: Routledge.

Litosseliti, Lia. 2006. *Gender and Language: Theory and Practice*. London: Hodder Arnold.

Littlewood, Dominic. 2009. How to drive a hard bargain. *The Daily Telegraph*, Money, Y4 (4 July).

Locher, Miriam A. and Richard J. Watts. 2005. Politeness theory and relational work. *Journal of Politeness Research* 1, 9–33.

Lou, J.J. 2010. Chinese on the side: The marginalization of Chinese on the linguistic landscape of Chinatown in Washington, DC. In E. Shohamy, E. Ben Rafael and C. Barni (eds.), *Linguistic Landscape in the City*, 96–114. Bristol: Multilingual Matters.

Lust, Barbara. 2006. *Child Language: Acquisition and Growth*. Cambridge: Cambridge University Press.

Lustig, Myron and Jolene Koester. 2003. *Intercultural Competence: Interpersonal Communication Across Cultures*. Boston: Allyn & Bacon.

Lytra, Vally. 2012. Multilingualism and multimodality. In Marilyn Martin-Jones, Angela Creese and Adrian Blackledge (eds.), *Routledge Handbook of Multilingualism*. London: Routledge.

Macaulay, Ronald K.S. 2011. *Seven Ways of Looking at Language*. Basingstoke: Palgrave.

MacIntyre, Peter D., Richard Clément, Zoltán Dörnyei and Kimberly A. Noels. 1998. Conceptualizing willingness to communicate in a L2: A situated model of confidence and affiliation. *Modern Language Journal* 82, 545–562.

Matsumoto, Yoshiko. 1988. Reexamination of the universality of face: Politeness phenomena in Japanese. *Journal of Pragmatics* 12, 403–426.

Matychuk, Paul. 2005. The role of child-directed speech in language acquisition: A case study. *Language Sciences* 27, 301–379.

Maybin, J. 2007. Literacy under and over the desk: Oppositions and heterogeneity. *Language and Education*, 21 (6), 515–530.

Mayer, Connie and C. Tane Akamatsu. 1999. Bilingual-bicultural models of literacy education for deaf students: Considering the claims. *Journal of Deaf Studies and Deaf Education* 4, 1–8.

Mayer, Connie and C. Tane Akamatsu. 2000. Deaf children creating written texts: Contributions of American Sign Language and signed forms of English. *American Annals of the Deaf* 145 (5), 394–403.

McCarthy, John. 2001. *A Thematic Guide to Optimality Theory*. Cambridge: Cambridge University Press.

McCarthy, Michael. 2001. *Issues in Applied Linguistics*. Cambridge: Cambridge University Press.

McSweeney, Brendan. 2002. Hofstede's model of national cultural differences and their consequences: A triumph of faith – a failure of analysis. *Human Relations* 55 (1), 89–118.

Meeke, Kieran. 2009. 60 second interview: Dylan Lewis. *Metro*, 10 (12 August).

Menken, Kate. 2008. *English Learners Left Behind: Standardized Testing as Language Policy*. Clevedon: Multilingual Matters.

Menn, Lise and Loraine Obler (eds.). 1990. *Agrammatic Aphasia: A Cross-language Narrative Sourcebook*. Amsterdam: John Benjamins.

Messick, Samuel. 1996. Validity and washback in language testing. *Language Testing* 13 (3), 241–256.

Meyer, Bernd and Apfelbaum, Birgit (eds.). 2010. *Multilingualism at Work: From Policies to Practices in Public, Medical and Business Settings*. Amsterdam: John Benjamins.

Meyerhoff, Miriam. 2001. Communities of practice. In J.K. Chambers, Peter Trudgill and Natalie Schilling-Estes (eds.), *The Handbook of Language Variation and Change*, 526–549. Oxford: Blackwell.

Milroy, Lesley. 1987. *Language and Social Networks*, 2nd edn. Oxford: Blackwell.

Mishler, Elliot. 1984. *The Discourse of Medicine: The Dialectics of Medical Interviewing*. Norwood, NJ: Ablex.

Moore, Emma. 2006. 'You tell all the stories': Using narrative to explore hierarchy within a Community of Practice. *Journal of Sociolinguistics* 10 (5), 611–640.

Mori, Junko. 2003. The construction of interculturality: A study of initial encounters between Japanese and American students. *Research on Language and Social Interaction* 36 (2), 143–184.

Mundaym, Jeremy. 2012. *Introducing Translation Studies: Theories and Applications*. London: Routledge.

Muñoz, Carmen (ed.). 2006. *Age and the Rate of Foreign Language Learning*. Clevedon: Multilingual Matters.

Muñoz, Carmen. 2008. Symmetries and asymmetries of age effects in naturalistic and instructed L2 learning. *Applied Linguistics* 29 (4), 578–596.

Myers, Penelope S. 1997. Right hemisphere syndrome. In Leonard L. LaPointe (ed.), *Aphasia and Related Neurogenic Language Disorders*, 2nd edn, 201–247. New York: Thieme.

Naeser, Margaret A. and Robert W. Hayward. 1978. Lesion localization in aphasia with cranial computed tomography and the Boston Diagnostic Aphasia Exam. *Neurology* 28, 545–551.

Naeser, Margaret A. and Carol L. Palumbo. 1995. How to analyze CT/MRI scan lesion sites to predict potential for long-term recovery in aphasia. *Neurological Disease and Therapy* 33, 91–148.

Naiman, Neil, Maria Fröhlich, Hans H. Stern and Angie Todesco. 1978. *The Good Language Learner*. Toronto: Ontario Institute for Studies in Education.

Nardo, Davide and Susanne M. Reiterer. 2009. Musicality and phonetic language aptitude. In Grzegorz Dogil and Susanne M. Reiterer (eds.), *Language Talent and Brain Activity*, 213–256. Berlin: Mouton de Gruyter.

Neuman, Susan B. and David K. Dickinson (eds.). 2011. *Handbook of Early Literacy Research*, vol. 3. New York: Guilford Press.

Newman, Stanley. 1955. Vocabulary levels: Zuni sacred and slang usage. *Southwestern Journal of Anthropology* 11, 345–354.

Nida, Eugene. 1964. *Toward a Science of Translating*. Leiden: E.J. Brill.

Niederberger, Nathalie. 2008. Does the knowledge of a natural sign language facilitate deaf children's learning to read and write? Insights from French Sign Language and written French data. In Carolina Plaza-Pust and Esperanza Morales-López (eds.), *Sign Bilingualism: Language Development, Interaction, and Maintenance in Sign Language Contact Situations*, 29–50. Amsterdam: John Benjamins.

Nishizaka, Aug. 1995. The interactive constitution of interculturality: How to be a Japanese with words. *Human Studies* 18, 301–326.

Norris, John and Lourdes Ortega. 2001. Does type of instruction make a difference? Substantive findings from a meta-analytic review. *Language Learning* 51, 157–213.

Norton, Bonny. 2001. Non-participation, imagined communities and the language classroom. In Michael P. Breen (ed.), *Learner Contributions to Language Learning: New Directions in Research*, 159–171. Harlow: Longman.

Nunan, David. 2013. *What is This Thing Called Language?*, 2nd edn. Basingstoke: Palgrave.

O'Barr, William M. and Bowman K. Atkins. 1998. 'Women's language' or 'Powerless language'? In Jennifer Coates (ed.), *Language and Gender: A Reader*, 377–388. Oxford: Blackwell.

Ochs, Elinor, 1979. Transcription as theory. In Elinor Ochs and Bambi Schieffelin (eds.), *Developmental Pragmatics*, 43–72. New York: Academic Press.

Ochs, Elinor. 1986. Introduction. In Bambi Schieffelin and Elinor Ochs (eds.), *Language Socialization Across Cultures*, 1–13. New York: Cambridge University Press.

Ochs, Elinor and Bambi Schieffelin. 1995. The impact of language socialization on grammatical development. In Paul Fletcher and Brian MacWhinney (eds.), *The Handbook of Child Language*, 73–94. Oxford: Blackwell.

Oscarson, M. 1984. *Self-assessment of Foreign Language Skills: A Survey of Research and Development Work.* Strasbourg: Council of Europe.

Oscarson, Mats. 1997. Self-assessment of foreign and second language proficiency. In *Encyclopedia of Language and Education, vol. 7: Language Testing and Assessment*, 175–187. Dordrecht: Kluwer Academic.

O'Sullivan, Josephine. 2011. *Translating Popular Film.* London: Palgrave Macmillan.

Ożańska-Ponikwia, Katarzyna and Jean-Marc Dewaele. 2012. Personality and L2 use: The advantage of being openminded and self-confident in an immigration context. *EUROSLA Yearbook* 12, 112–134.

Pahl, Kate and Jennifer Rowsell. 2006. Introduction. In Kate Pahl and Jennifer Rowsell (eds.), *Travel Notes from the New Literacy Studies: Instances of Practice*, 1–15. Clevedon: Multilingual Matters.

Paradis, Michel. 1977. Bilingualism and aphasia. In Haiganoosh Whitaker and Harry A. Whitaker (eds.), *Studies in Neurolinguistics*, vol. 3, 65–121. New York: Academic Press.

Paradis, Michel. 2001. Bilingual and polyglot aphasia. In R.S. Berndt (ed.), *Handbook of Neuropsychology*, 2nd edn, *vol. 3: Language and Aphasia*, 69–91. Amsterdam: Elsevier Science.

Paradis, Michel. 2004. *A Neurolinguistic Theory of Bilingualism.* Amsterdam: John Benjamins.

Paradis, Michel. 2009. *Declarative and Procedural Determinants of Second Languages.* Philadelphia, PA: John Benjamins.

Paradis, Michel, Hiroko Hagiwara and Nancy Hildebrandt. 1985. *Neurolinguistic Aspects of the Japanese Writing System.* New York: Academic Press.

Pavlenko, Aneta. 2005. *Emotions and Multilingualism.* Cambridge: Cambridge University Press.

Pavlenko, Aneta. 2008. Non-native speakers of English and the Miranda warnings. *TESOL Quarterly* 42 (1), 1–30.

Pavlenko, Aneta. 2010. Linguistic landscape of Kyiv, Ukraine: A diachronic study. In Elana Shohamy, Eliezer Ben Rafael and Monica Barni (eds.), *Linguistic Landscape in the City*, 133–154. Bristol: Multilingual Matters.

Pavlidou, Theodossia-Soula. 2000. Telephone conversations in Greek and German: Attending to the relationship aspect of communication. In Helen Spencer-Oatey (ed.), *Culturally Speaking: Managing Rapport Through Talk Across Cultures*, 121–140. London: Continuum.

Pennycook, Alastair. 2001. *Critical Applied Linguistics: A Critical Introduction.* London: Lawrence Erlbaum Associates.

Pennycook, Alastair. 2009. Linguistic landscapes and the transgressive semiotics of graffiti. In Elana Shohamy and Durk Gorter (eds.), *Linguistic Landscape: Expanding the Scenery*, 302–312. London: Routledge.

Perkins, Michael. 2007. *Pragmatic Impairment.* Cambridge: Cambridge University Press.

Pica, Teresa. 2009. Second language acquisition in the instructional environment. In William C. Ritchie and Tej K. Bhatia (eds.), *The New Handbook of Second Language Acquisition*, 473–501. Bingley: Emerald.

Piller, Ingrid. 2011. *Intercultural Communication: A Critical Introduction.* Edinburgh: Edinburgh University Press.

Pinker, Steven. 1984. *Language Learnability and Language Development.* Cambridge, MA: Harvard University Press.

Pinker, Steven. 1987. The bootstrapping problem in language acquisition. In Brian MacWhinney (ed.), *Mechanisms of Language Acquisition*, 399–441. Hillsdale, NJ: Lawrence Erlbaum.

Placencia, María Elena. 2001. Inequality in address behavior at public institutions in La Paz, Bolivia. *Anthropological Linguistics* 43, 198–217.

Placencia, María Elena. 2011. Regional pragmatic variation. In Gisle Andersen and Karin Aijmer (eds.), *Pragmatics of Society*, 79–113. Berlin: De Gruyter.

Placencia, María Elena and Amanda Lower. Forthcoming. Doing Sociability on Facebook. The Case of Complimenting Behaviour. *Intercultural Pragmatics.*

Placencia, María Elena and Ana Mancera Rueda. 2011a. Dame un cortado de máquina, cuando puedas: Estrategias de cortesía en la realización de la transacción central en bares de Sevilla. In Catalina Fuentes Rodríguez, Esperanza Alcaide Lara and Ester Brenes Peña (eds.), *Aproximaciones a la (des)cortesía verbal en español*, 491–508. Bern: Peter Lang.

Placencia, María Elena and Ana Mancera Rueda. 2011b. Vaya, ¡qué chungo! Rapport-building talk in service encounters: The case of bars in Seville at breakfast time. In Nuria Lorenzo-Dus (ed.), *Spanish at Work: Analysing Institutional Discourse Across the Spanish-speaking World*, 192–207. Basingstoke: Palgrave Macmillan.

Plaza-Pust, Carolina. 2008. Why variation matters: On language contact in the development of L2 written German. In Carolina Plaza-Pust and Esperanza Morales-López (eds.), *Sign Bilingualism: Language Development, Interaction, and Maintenance in Sign Language Contact Situations*, 73–135. Amsterdam: John Benjamins.

Poarch, Gregory J. and Janet G. Van Hell. 2012. Cross-language activation in children's speech production: Evidence from second language learners, bilinguals, and trilinguals. *Journal of Experimental Child Psychology* 111 (3), 419–438.

Poizner, Howard, Edward Klima and Ursula Bellugi. 1990. *What the Hands Reveal About the Brain*. Cambridge, MA: MIT Press.

Poplack, Shana. 1980. Sometimes I'll start a sentence in Spanish Y TERMINO EN ESPAÑOL: Toward a typology of code-switching. *Linguistics* 18, 581–618. Reprinted in Li Wei (ed.), 2000. *The Bilingualism Reader*, 241–256. London: Routledge.

Poplack, S. 1988. Contrasting patterns of code-switching in two communities. In Heller, Monica (ed.), *Codeswitching: Anthropological and Sociolinguistic Perspectives*, 215–245. Berlin: Mouton de Gruyter.

Preston, Dennis R. and Robert Bayley. 2009. Variationist linguistics and second language acquisition. In William C. Ritchie and Tej K. Bhatia (eds.), *The New Handbook of Second Language Acquisition*, 89–113. Bingley: Emerald.

Radford, Andrew. 1996. Towards a structure-building model of acquisition. In H. Clahsen (ed.), *Generative Perspectives on Language Acquisition*, 43–90. Amsterdam: John Benjamins.

Raga Gimeno, Francisco. 2005. Médicos, *marabouts* y mediadores: problemas de comunicación intercultural en la atención sanitaria a los inmigrantes de origen senegalés. In Carmen Valero Garcés (ed.), *Traducción como mediación entre lenguas y culturas*, 123–133. Alcalá de Henares: Universidad de Alcalá de Henares.

Rampton, Ben. 1995. *Crossing: Language and Ethnicity Among Adolescents*. London: Longman.

Rampton, Ben. 1997. Retuning in applied linguistics? *International Journal of Applied Linguistics* 7 (1), 3–25.

Rampton, Ben. 2006. *Language in Late Modernity: Interaction in an Urban School*. Cambridge: Cambridge University Press.

Regan, Vera, Martin Howard and Isabelle Lemée. 2009. *Acquisition of Sociolinguistic Competence in a Study Abroad Context*. Irish Learners of French. Bristol: Multilingual Matters.

Reyes, María de la Luz. 2001. Unleashing possibilities: Biliteracy in the primary grades. In María de la Luz Reyes and John J. Halcón (eds.), *The Best for Our Children: Critical Perspectives on Literacy for Latino Students*, 96–121. New York and London: Teachers College Press.

Rindler-Schjerve, Rosita. 1998. Code-switching as an indicator for language shift? Evidence from Sardinian-Italian bilingualism. In R. Jacobson (ed.), *Codeswitching Worldwide*, 221–248. Berlin and New York: Mouton de Gruyter.

Ringbom, Håkan. 2007. *Cross-linguistic Similarity in Foreign Language Learning*. Clevedon: Multilingual Matters.

Rivers, William P. and Ewa M. Golonka. 2009. Third language acquisition theory and practice. In Michael Long and Catherine Doughty (eds.), *The Handbook of Second and Foreign Language Teaching*, 250–266. Oxford: Wiley-Blackwell.

Rizzi, Luigi. 1993/1994. Some notes on linguistic theory and language development: The case of root infinitives. *Language Acquisition* 3, 371–393.

Roberts, Celia. 2011. Institutional discourse. In James Simpson (ed.), *The Routledge Handbook of Applied Linguistics*, 81–95. London: Routledge.

Sacks, Harvey, Emanuel A. Schegloff and Gail Jefferson. 1974. A simplest systematics for the organization of turn-taking for conversation. *Language* 50 (4), 696–735.

Sarangi, Srikant. 1994. Intercultural or not? Beyond celebration of cultural differences in miscommunication analysis. *Pragmatics* 4, 409–427.

Sayer, Peter. 2009. Using the linguistic landscape as a pedagogical resource. *ELT Journal Advance Access* 15, 2–12.

Schegloff, Emanuel A. 1979. Identification and recognition in telephone conversation openings. In George Psathas (ed.), *Everyday Language: Studies in Ethnomethodology*, 23–78. New York: Irvington.

Schieffelin, Bambi and Elinor Ochs (eds.). 1986. *Language Socialisation Across Cultures*. Cambridge: Cambridge University Press.

Schiffrin, Deborah, Deborah Tannen and Heidi E. Hamilton (eds.). 2001. *The Handbook of Discourse Analysis* (Blackwell Handbooks in Linguistics). Oxford: Blackwell.

Schwartz, Shalom H. 1992. Universals in the content and structure of values: Theory and empirical tests in 20 countries. In M. Zanna (ed.), *Advances in Experimental Social Psychology*, vol. 25, 1–65. New York: Academic Press.

Schwartz, Shalom H. 1994. Are there universal aspects in the structure and contents of human values? *Journal of Social Issues* 50 (4), 19–45.

Scollon, Ronald and Suzanne B.K. Scollon. 1981. *Narrative, Literacy, and Face in Interethnic Communication*. Norwood, NJ: Ablex.

Scollon, Ronald and Suzanne Wong Scollon. 2001. *Intercultural Communication: A Discourse Approach*, 2nd edn. Oxford: Blackwell.

Sealey, Alison and Bob Carter. 2004. *Applied Linguistics as Social Science*. London: Continuum.

Searle, John R. 1969. *Speech Acts: An Essay in the Philosophy of Language*. Cambridge: Cambridge University Press.

Searle, John R. 1975. Indirect speech acts. In Peter Cole and Jerry L. Morgan (eds.), *Speech Acts* (Syntax and Semantics 3), 59–82. New York: Academic Press.

Sebba, Mark. 1993. *London Jamaican: Language Systems in Interaction*. London and New York: Longman.

Sebba, Mark. 1997. *Contact Languages: Pidgins and Creoles*. Basingstoke and New York: Palgrave.

Sebba, Mark, Shahrzad Mahootian and Carla Jonsson. 2012. *Language Mixing and Code-switching in Writing*. New York and Abingdon: Routledge.

Segalowitz, Norman. 2003. Automaticity and second languages. In Michael Long and Catherine Doughty (eds.), *The Handbook of Second Language Acquisition*, 382–408. Oxford: Blackwell.

Semino, Elena. 2008. *Metaphor and Discourse*. Cambridge: Cambridge University Press.

Sharwood Smith, Michael. 1994. *Second Language Learning: Theoretical Foundations*. London: Longman.

Sheen, Ron. 2005. Focus on forms as a means of improving accurate oral production. In Alex Housen and Michel Pierrard (eds.), *Investigations in Instructed Second Language Acquisition*, 271–310. Berlin: Mouton de Gruyter.

Shohamy, Elana. 2001. *The Power of Tests: A Critical Perspective on the Uses of Language Tests*. London: Pearson.

Shohamy, Elana. 2007. Language tests as language policy tools. *Assessment in Education* 14 (1), 117–130.

Shohamy, Elana. 2012. Linguistic landscapes and multilingualism. In Marilyn Martin-Jones, Angela Creese and Adrian Blackledge (eds.), *Routledge Handbook of Multilingualism*, 538–551. London: Routledge.

Shohamy, Elana, Eliezer Ben Rafael and Monica Barni (eds.). 2010. *Linguistic Landscape in the City*. Bristol: Multilingual Matters.

Shuy, Roger. 1993. *Language Crimes*. Oxford: Blackwell.

Shuy, Roger. 1998. *The Language of Confession, Interrogation and Deception*. Thousand Oaks, CA: SAGE.

Sifianou, Maria. 1992. *Politeness Phenomena in England and Greece: A Cross-cultural Perspective*. Oxford: Clarendon Press.

Singleton, David and Larissa Aronin. 2007. Multiple language learning in the light of the theory of affordances. *Innovation in Language Learning and Teaching* 1, 83–96.

Skinner, Burrhus F. 1957. *Verbal Behavior*. New York: Appleton-Century-Crofts.

Smith, Neil. 1973. *The Acquisition of Phonology*. Cambridge: Cambridge University Press.

Snow, Catherine. 1995. Issues in the study of input: Finetuning, universality, individual and developmental differences, and necessary causes. In Paul Fletcher and Brian MacWhinney (eds.), *The Handbook of Child Language*, 180–193. Oxford: Blackwell.

Sontag, Susan. 1979. *Illness as Metaphor*. London: Penguin.

Spencer-Oatey, Helen. 2008 [2000]. Face, (im)politeness and rapport. In Helen Spencer-Oatey (ed.), *Culturally Speaking: Culture, Communication and Politeness Theory*, 2nd edn, 11–47. London: Continuum.

Sperber, Dan and Deirdre Wilson. 1986. *Relevance: Communication and Cognition*. Oxford: Blackwell.

Spitzberg, Brian H. and William R. Cupach. 1984. *Interpersonal Communication Competence*. Newsbury Park, CA: SAGE.

Spolsky, Bernard. 2004. *Language Policy*. Cambridge: Cambridge University Press.

Spolsky, Bernard. 2009. *Language Management*. Cambridge: Cambridge University Press.

Stewart, William A. 1968. A sociolinguistic typology for describing national multilingualism. In Joshua Fishman (ed.), *Readings in the Sociology of Language*, 531–545. The Hague: Mouton.

Stibbe, Arran. 1996. The metaphorical construction of illness in Chinese culture. *Journal of Asian Pacific Communication* 7 (3/4), 177–188.

Stokoe, Elizabeth and Derek Edwards. 2008. 'Did you have permission to smash your neighbour's door?' Silly questions and their answers in police-suspect interviews. *Discourse Studies* 10 (1), 8.

Stubbs, Michael. 1983. *Discourse Analysis: The Sociolinguistic Analysis of Natural Language*. Oxford: Blackwell.

Swain, Merrill, Sharon Lapkin, Norman Rowen and Doug Hart. 1990. The role of mother tongue literacy in third language learning. *Language, Culture and Curriculum* 3 (1), 65–81.

Tajfel, Henri and John Turner. 1979. An integrative theory of intergroup conflict. In W.G. Austin and S. Worchel (eds.), *The Social Psychology of Intergroup Relations*, 94–109. Monterey, CA: Brooks-Cole.

Talbot, M. 1995. A synthetic sisterhood: false friends in a teenage magazine. In K. Hall and M. Bucholtz (eds.), *Gender Articulated: Language and the Socially Constructed Self*, 143–165. New York: Routledge.

Tannen, Deborah. 1979. Ethnicity as conversation style. *Sociolinguistics Working Paper 55*. Austin, TX: Southwest Educational Development Laboratory.

Thatcher, Barry. 2004. Rhetorics and communication media across cultures. *Journal of English for Academic Purposes* 3 (4), 305–320.

Thiessen, E. 2009. Statistical learning. In E.L. Bavin (ed.), *The Cambridge Handbook of Child Language*, 35–50. Cambridge: Cambridge University Press.

Thomas, Jenny. 1995. *Meaning in Interaction: An Introduction to Pragmatics*. London: Longman.

Thomason, Sarah G. 2001. *Language Contact: An Introduction*. Edinburgh: Edinburgh University Press.

Thornborrow, Joanna. 1997. 'Having their say': The function of stories in talk show discourse. *Text* 17(2), 241–262.

Tiersma, Paul. 2008. The nature of legal language. In John Gibbons and Maria T. Turell (eds.), *Dimensions of Forensic Linguistics*, 7–25. Amsterdam: John Benjamins.

Ting-Toomey, Stella. 1999. *Communicating Across Cultures*. New York: Guilford Press.

Tomasello, Michael. 2009. The usage-based theory of language acquisition. In E.L. Bavin (ed.), *The Cambridge Handbook of Child Language*, 69–88. Cambridge: Cambridge University Press.

Tracy, Karen. 2002. *Everyday Talk: Building and Reflecting Identities*. London: Guilford Press.

Trompenaars, Fons and Charles Hampden-Turner. 1998. *Riding the Waves of Culture: Understanding Diversity in Global Business*, 2nd edn. New York: McGraw-Hill.

UNESCO Education Sector. 2004. The plurality of literacy and its implications for policies and programmes: Position Paper. 13. Citing an international expert meeting in June 2003 at UNESCO. Paris: United National Educational, Scientific and Cultural Organization. http://unesdoc.unesco.org/images/0013/001362/136246e.pdf (last accessed 28 May 2013).

Ushioda, Ema and Zoltán Dörnyei. 2012. Motivation. In Susan Gass and Alison Mackey (eds.), *The Routledge Handbook of Second Language Acquisition*, 396–409. London: Routledge.

Van Dijk, Teun. 1989. Mediating racism: The role of the media in the reproduction of racism. In Ruth Wodak (ed.), *Language, Power and Ideology*, 199–226. Amsterdam: John Benjamins.

Van Dijk, Teun. 1991. *Racism and the Press*. London: Routledge.

Van Dijk, Teun. 1998. *Ideology: A Multidisciplinary Approach*. London: SAGE.

Van Rijn-Van Tongeren, Geraldine. 1997. *Metaphors in Medical Texts* (Utrecht Studies in Language and Communication). Amsterdam and Atlanta, GA: Rodopi.

Venuti, Lawrence. 1986. *The Translator's Invisibility: A History of Translation*. London: Routledge.

Venuti, Lawrence. 1995. *The Translator's Invisibility: A History of Translation*. London: Routledge.

Venuti, Lawrence. 2004. *The Translation Studies Reader*. London: Routledge.

Waksman, Shoshi and Elana Shohamy. 2010. The competing narratives of Tel Aviv-Jaffa's approaching its centennial: complementary narratives via linguistic landscape. In Elana Shohamy, Eliezer Ben Rafael and Monica Barni (eds.), *Linguistic Landscape in the City*, 57–73. Bristol: Multilingual Matters.

Wei Zhang. 2005. Code-choice in bidialectal interaction: The choice between Putonghua and Cantonese in a radio phone-in program in Shenzhen. *Journal of Pragmatics* 37 (3), 355–375.

Weinreich, Uriel. 1953. *Languages in Contact: Problems and Findings*. Amsterdam: John Benjamins.

Weizman, Elda. 1989. Requestive hints. In Shoshana Blum-Kulka, Juliane House and Gabriele Kasper (eds.), *Cross-cultural Pragmatics: Requests and Apologies*, 71–95. Norwood, NJ: Ablex.

West, Candace. 1998. When the doctor is a 'lady': Power, status and gender in physician–patient encounters. In Jennifer Coates (ed.), *Language and Gender: A Reader*, 396–413. Oxford: Blackwell.

Westermann, Gert, Nicolas Ruh and Kim Plunkett. 2009. Connectionist approaches to language learning. *Linguistics* 47(2), 413–452.

Wetzel, Patricia J. 1998. Are 'powerless' communication strategies the Japanese norm? In Jennifer Coates (ed.), *Language and Gender: A Reader*, 388–396. Oxford: Blackwell.

Wexler, Ken. 1994. Optional infinitives, head movement and the economy of derivations. In D. Lightfoot and N. Hornstein (eds.), *Verb Movement*, 305–350. Cambridge: Cambridge University Press.

White, Lesley. 2009. A perfectionist climbing to the top, Elliot Cowan is moving on from Mr Darcy to A Streetcar Named Desire – carefully avoiding Brando. He talks to Lesley White. *Culture, The Sunday Times*, 18–19 (26 July).

Widdowson, Henry. 1995. Discourse analysis: a critical view. *Language and Literature* 4 (3), 157–172.

Williams, James and Grace Capizzi Snipper. 1990. *Literacy and Bilingualism*. New York: Longman.

Williams, John N. 2009. Implicit learning in second language acquisition. In William C. Ritchie and Tej K. Bhatia (eds.), *The New Handbook of Second Language Acquisition*, 319–353. Bingley: Emerald.

Wolfram, Walt and Natalie Schilling-Estes. 2006. *American English: Dialects and Variation*, 2nd edn. Oxford: Blackwell.

Wray, Alison and Aileen Bloomer. 2006. *Projects in Linguistics: A Practical Guide to Researching Language*, 2nd edn. London: Hodder Arnold.

Xiaochen Hu and Susanne M. Reiterer. 2009. Personality and pronunciation talent. In Grzegorz Dogil and Susanne M. Reiterer (eds.), *Language Talent and Brain Activity*, 97–130. Berlin: Mouton de Gruyter.

Yahoo!Answers UK and Ireland, http://uk.answers.yahoo.com (last accessed 28 May 2013).

Yang Hsueh-yin and Zhu Hua. 2010. The phonological development of a trilingual child: Facts and factors. *International Journal of Bilingualism* 14 (1), 105–126.

Zhu Hua. 2010. Language socialisation and interculturality: Address terms in intergenerational talk in Chinese diasporic families. *Language and Intercultural Communication* 10 (3), 189–205.

Zhu Hua (ed.) 2011. *The Language and Intercultural Communication Reader*. London: Routledge.

Zhu Hua and Barbara Dodd. 2006. Towards developmental universals. In Zhu Hua and Barbara Dodd (eds.), *Phonological Development and Disorders in Children: A Multilingual Perspective*, 431–449. Clevedon: Multilingual Matters.

Zhu Hua and Li Wei. 2005. Bi- and multilingual language acquisition. In Martin Ball (ed.), *Clinical Sociolinguistics*, 165–179. Oxford: Blackwell.

Ziegler, Johannes and Usha Goswami. 2005. Reading acquisition, developmental dyslexia, and skilled reading across languages: A psycholinguistic grain size theory. *Psychological Bulletin* 131 (1), 3–29.

Index
